SAN RAFAEL PUBLIC LIBRARY
1100 E STREET
SAN RAFAEL, CA 94901
415-485-3323

D0374492

═══►◉◄═══

N
& THE

DATE DUE

Demco

J(

NAPLES & THE AMALFI COAST

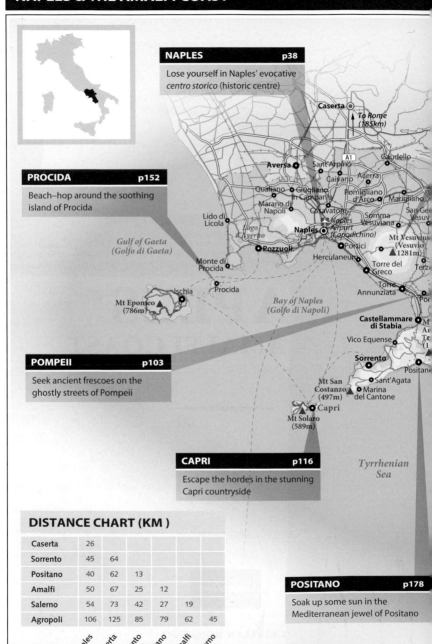

NAPLES p38

Lose yourself in Naples' evocative *centro storico* (historic centre)

PROCIDA p152

Beach–hop around the soothing island of Procida

POMPEII p103

Seek ancient frescoes on the ghostly streets of Pompeii

CAPRI p116

Escape the hordes in the stunning Capri countryside

POSITANO p178

Soak up some sun in the Mediterranean jewel of Positano

DISTANCE CHART (KM)

	Naples	Caserta	Sorrento	Positano	Amalfi	Salerno
Caserta	26					
Sorrento	45	64				
Positano	40	62	13			
Amalfi	50	67	25	12		
Salerno	54	73	42	27	19	
Agropoli	106	125	85	79	62	45

Note: Distances between destinations are approximate

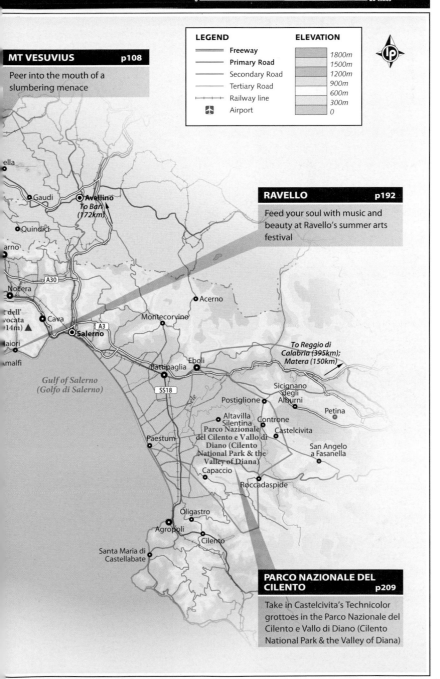

MT VESUVIUS p108

Peer into the mouth of a slumbering menace

LEGEND
- Freeway
- Primary Road
- Secondary Road
- Tertiary Road
- Railway line
- Airport

ELEVATION
- 1800m
- 1500m
- 1200m
- 900m
- 600m
- 300m
- 0

RAVELLO p192

Feed your soul with music and beauty at Ravello's summer arts festival

ella

Gaudi   Avellino
         *To Bari
         (172km)*

Quindici

arno

Nocera

dell'
vocata
14m) ▲   Cava   A30

Maiori   A3   Salerno

Amalfi

Acerno

Montecorvino

*To Reggio di
Calabria (395km);
Matera (150km)*

*Gulf of Salerno
(Golfo di Salerno)*

Eboli

Battipaglia

SS18

Sicignano
degli
Alburni

Petina

Postiglione

Altavilla
Silentina   Controne
Parco Nazionale   Castelcivita
*del Cilento e Vallo di
Diano (Cilento
National Park &
the Valley of Diana)*

San Angelo
a Fasanella

Paestum

Capaccio

Roccadaspide

Oligastro

Agropoli
         Cilento

Santa Maria di
Castellabate

**PARCO NAZIONALE DEL
CILENTO** p209

Take in Castelcivita's Technicolor grottoes in the Parco Nazionale del Cilento e Vallo di Diano (Cilento National Park & the Valley of Diana)

0   40 km
0   20 miles

INTRODUCING NAPLES & THE AMALFI COAST

INTENSELY BEAUTIFUL AND BEAUTIFULLY INTENSE, NAPLES AND THE AMALFI COAST IS THE ITALY OF YOUR WILDEST AND MOST LINGERING DREAMS.

Volcanic, voluptuous and irrepressibly vivacious, few regions cast a spell like this one. From the hissing Campi Flegrei and the ruins of Pompeii to the cliff-gripping chic of Positano, drama defines the details.

It's a land of legends, miracles and scandals; one of ancient Greek temples in flower-speckled fields, of decadent Roman frescoes in Bourbon palaces, of Hollywood divas on dazzling VIP islands and of liquefying blood in jewel-box cathedrals.

At its heart is thumping, bombastic Naples, a heady maze of crumbling baroque *palazzi*, mighty museums, Arabesque streetlife and a Unesco-lauded historical core. Not bad for a city more renowned for bling-clad Mafiosi.

Naples' fabled bay is a treasure chest of island gems, from bewitching Capri, with its electric blue grotto, to steamy Ischia and artistic, windswept Procida. Beyond the bay awaits the dreamy Amalfi Coast, with its creamy seas, enchanting trails and tumbling towns, and beyond it still, the wild, rugged beauty of the Parco Nazionale del Cilento.

To it all, add a pinch of gastronomic brilliance, a splash of Mediterranean passion, and you have Italy at its red-blooded best.

POSITANO

RAVELLO

TOP The dramatic cliffs of Positano (p178) **BOTTOM LEFT** Views of the ocean from Ravello (p192) **BOTTOM RIGHT** The smouldering Mt Vesuvius (p108) at dusk

MT VESUVIUS

CAPRI

NAPLES

PROCIDA

PARCO NAZIONALE DEL CILENTO E VALLO DI DIANO

TOP LEFT Sweeping views of Capri (p116) from Belvedere di Tragara **TOP RIGHT** The bustling Marina Corricella (p153), Procida **BOTTOM LEFT** The impressive Piazza del Plebiscito (p60), Naples **BOTTOM CENTRE** The extraordinary Grotta di Castelcivita (p212), Parco Nazionale del Cilento e Vallo di Diano **BOTTOM RIGHT** The eerie streets of Pompeii (p103)

POMPEII

GETTING STARTED

WHAT'S NEW?

★ An art museum inside the Chiesa Santa Maria Donnaregina Nuova (p51)

★ Controversial culture at the new Museo Nitsch (p57)

★ A freshly restored Teatro San Carlo (p61)

★ An international theatre festival in Naples (p10)

★ A cacti-garden-cum-cultural-centre on Ischia (p145)

★ A stylish new fine-art gallery in Positano (p181)

CLIMATE: NAPLES

Average Max/Min

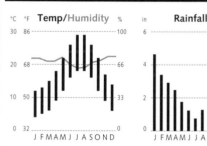

Temp/Humidity — Rainfall charts (J F M A M J J A S O N D)

PRICE GUIDE

	BUDGET	MIDRANGE	TOP END
SLEEPING	<€100	€100-200	>€200
MEALS	<€20	€20-45	>€45
PARKING	€1.10	€7.20	€20

DALLAS STRIBLEY

TOP LEFT Life at Marina Grande (p152), Procida **LEFT** Waterfront shopping at Marina Grande (p152), Procida **BOTTOM RIGHT** Night at the opera, Teatro San Carlo (p61), Naples **FAR RIGHT** Sorrento (p159) at dusk

ACCOMMODATION

From frescoed *palazzi* to converted convents, accommodation in Naples spans all predilections and prices. Top-end hotels are classically styled, with a new design hotel to shake things up. Midrange spans personable hotels to chic B&Bs, while budget includes some fab hostels. On the islands and Amalfi Coast, hotels steer towards luxe, although budget options and B&Bs are emerging. *Agriturismi* (farm-stay accommodation) await in the Parco Nazionale del Cilento, while on the coast here, accommodation is mainly three star. For more, see p263.

MAIN POINTS OF ENTRY

STAZIONE CENTRALE (Map pp42-3; ☎ 081 554 31 88) In Naples; serves regional, national and international routes.

STAZIONE CIRCUMVESUVIANA (☎ 081 772 24 44; wwww.vesuviana.it; Corso Giuseppe Garibaldi, Naples) Has trains to Ercolano, Pompeii and Sorrento.

CAPODICHINO AIRPORT (NAP; ☎ 081 789 62 59; www.gesac.it) Naples' airport is the main airport for the region, serving major airlines and budget carriers.

STAZIONE MARITTIMA Naples' main port terminal.

THINGS TO TAKE

GREG ELMS

* Comfortable shoes to combat cobbles

* A jacket or large scarf to cover shoulders in churches

* A healthy appetite to tackle Campania's culinary brilliance

* A sense of humour and a healthy dose of patience

* Swimwear, towel and flip-flops (thongs) for spa treatments and summertime beachside lounging

WEBLINKS

NAPLES (www.inaples.it) Naples' tourist board website.

CAMPANIA TRASPORTI (www.campaniatrasporti.it) Comprehensive transport website with route planner.

PORTANAPOLI (www.portanapoli.com) Regional culture, cuisine, listings and inspiration.

CAPRI (www.capri.net) Information-rich website dedicated to Capri.

TRENITALIA (www.trenitalia.com) Italy's national railways website.

FEBRUARY

CARNEVALE

During the period before Ash Wednesday, kids don fancy costumes and throw *coriandoli* (coloured confetti), while everyone indulges one last time before Lent.

FESTA DI SANT'ANTONINO

SORRENTO
Sorrento's patron saint is celebrated on 14 February with fireworks and musical processions through the historic centre.

MARCH/APRIL

SETTIMANA SANTA

Processions and Passion plays mark Easter Holy Week in Naples. Most famous are the processions of Procida and Sorrento.

SETTIMANA PER LA CULTURA

A week-long initiative celebrating Italy's heritage, where publicly owned galleries and museums are free. (www.beneculturali.it)

MAY

FESTA DI SAN GENNARO

DUOMO, NAPLES
Thousands gather in the Duomo on the Saturday before the first Sunday of the month to see the saint's blood liquefy.

MAGGIO DEI MONUMENTI

NAPLES
A mammoth month-long program of exhibitions, concerts, performances and tours. (☎ 081 247 11 23)

JUNE

NAPOLI TEATRO FESTIVAL ITALIA

NAPLES
Over three weeks of international theatre in the city. (www.teatrofestivalitalia.it)

RAVELLO FESTIVAL

RAVELLO
The Amalfi Coast's top cultural event features world-class musicians from June to September in the gardens of Villa Rufolo. (www.ravellofestival.com)

JULY/AUGUST

FESTA DI SANT'ANNA

ISCHIA
St Anne's feast day on 26 July sees the allegorical 'burning of the Castello Aragonese', a boat procession and fireworks.

TOP Settimana Santa, Sorrento **RIGHT** Festa di San Gennaro, Naples

MADONNA DEL CARMINE

PIAZZA DEL CARMINE, NAPLES
Held in Piazza del Carmine on 16 July, the celebration of the Madonna del Carmine culminates in spectacular fireworks.

SAGRA DEL TONNO

CETARA
Held over four days at the end of July, Cetara's tuna festival has free tastings, as well as traditional music and dance. (☎ 089 26 14 74; www.prolococetara.it)

NEAPOLIS FESTIVAL

NAPLES
Southern Italy's largest contemporary music fest is held in July. Past acts include Prodigy and Juliette Lewis. (www.neapolis.it)

FERRAGOSTO

The busiest day of the beach year, the feast of the Assumption heralds concerts and local events on 15 August.

SEPTEMBER

FESTA DI SAN GENNARO

DUOMO, NAPLES
Repeat performance of San Gennaro's powder-to-blood miracle on 19 September.

PIZZAFEST

NAPLES
Pizza makers from all over Italy head to various pizza-based events. (www.pizzafest.info)

DECEMBER

FESTA DI SAN GENNARO

DUOMO, NAPLES
Third running of San Gennaro's miracle on 16 December.

NATALE

Church concerts, exhibitions and a shopping frenzy for *presepi* (nativity scenes) in Naples' Via San Gregorio Armeno.

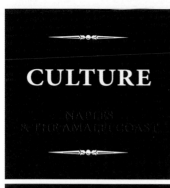

CULTURE

NAPLES
& THE AMALFI COAST

BOOKS

CAPRI AND NO LONGER CAPRI (Raffaele La Capria) La Capria goes beyond the island's decadent reputation to present his slightly melancholic vision of modern Capri.

FALLING PALACE: A ROMANCE OF NAPLES (Dan Hofstadler) Naples' electric streets are brought to life in this evocative love story.

NAPLES'44: AN INTELLIGENCE OFFICER IN THE ITALIAN LABYRINTH (Norman Lewis) An engrossing account of postwar Naples.

THE ANCIENT SHORE: DISPATCHES FROM NAPLES (Shirley Hazzard & Francis Steegmuller) Eloquent musings on Neapolitan life and history.

THE BOURBONS OF NAPLES (Harold Acton) All the politics, intrigue and idiosyncrasies of Naples' former royal rulers.

MUSICAL SCORE

Ask for a stereotypical Italian tune and chances are you'll get Giovanni Capurro's 1898 hit 'O Sole Mio'. This Neapolitan classic is just one of the many that early-20th-century Italian immigrants took to the corners of the world. The defining moment for *la canzone napoletana* (Neapolitan song) was in 1839 with 'Te Voglio Bene Assaje' (I Love You Loads). Written by Raffaele Sacco and composed by Donizetti, it became a sensation, selling over 180,000 copies of the song's lyrics and causing pandemonium. The genre's success was based on a combo of catchy melodies, Neapolitan lyrics, and themes of love, passion and longing. Kept alive by the likes of Roberto Murolo (1912–2003) and Sergio Bruni (1921–), it has since been given a pop makeover by, among others, Nino D'Angelo (1957–) and Gigi Alessio (1967–). For more on Neapolitan music, see p233.

TOP LEFT Shopping, Via Toledo (p95), Naples LEFT Palazzo Reale di Capodimonte (p71), Naples CENTRE RIGHT Chiesa del Gesù Nuovo (p44), Naples FAR RIGHT Art, Museo Nazionale di San Martino (p67), Naple

TOP EXTRAVAGENT INTERIORS

CERTOSA DI SAN MARTINO A who's who of baroque superstars decorated this monastery's jaw-dropping church (p67).

CHIESA DEL GESÙ NUOVO A Jesuit jewel with Fanzago-chiselled sculptures (p44).

CHIESA E CHIOSTRO DI SAN GREGORIO ARMENO A glorious coffered ceiling and obscenely lavish chancels (p47).

PALAZZO DELLO SPAGNUOLO A tucked-away staircase with diva appeal (p74).

PALAZZO REALE Caserta's look-at-me palace outdoes Versailles (p60).

JULIA CATT PHOTOGRAPHY / ALAMY

DON'T MISS EXPERIENCES

★ Piazza posing – Make certain you join the *bella gente* (beautiful people) for a predinner drop (p120)

★ Subterranean snooping – Head below Naples' streets for an out-of-the-ordinary history lesson (p49)

★ Alfresco concerts – Tap your feet under the stars (p193)

★ Shopping for fashion bargains – Completely revamp your image with plenty of change to spare (p96)

★ Buying artisan crafts – Purchase hand-crafted cameos, *presepi* and inlaid wooden treasures (p94, p170)

★ Ancient wonders – Travel back in time in the shadow of Vesuvius (p103)

DANIELE'S PLAYLIST

'A67 lead vocalist Daniele Sanzone's top recommendations:

MARCELLO COLASURDO (www.marcellocolasurdo.it) Folk music legend with an intense voice.

ENZO AVITABILE (www.enzo avitabile.it) Funk/world artist capturing 'real' Neapolitan culture.

JAMES SENESE (www.last. fm/music/James+Senese) Jazz legend whose sax is Naples.

99 POSSE (www.novenove.it) Rap-dub-trip-hop band and an Italian alt-scene great.

LETTI SFATTI (www.myspace. com/lettisfatti) Raw, popular rock meets singer-songwriter.

CULTURE

FILMS

GOMORRA (Matteo Garrone) Award-winning Camorra exposé.

LE MANI SULLA CITTÀ (Francesco Rosi) A condemnation of postwar corruption.

L'ORO DI NAPOLI (Vittorio de Sica) A Neapolitan classic.

NO GRAZIE, IL CAFFÈ MI RENDE NERVOSO (Ludovico Gasparini) Retro-schlock murder mystery.

LA LUNA ROSSA (Antonio Capuano) Camorra meets Greek tragedy.

LOCAL LORE

Nnapulitano (Neapolitan dialect) proverbs:

'A LÉNGUA NUN TÈNE ÒSSO MA RÒMPE LL'ÒSSA' (The tongue has no bone but it breaks bones)

'A MUGHIÈRA 'E LL'ÀTE É SÈMPE CCHIÙ BBÒNA' (Other people's wives are always more beautiful)

'ÒGNE SCARRAFÓNE È BBÈLLO 'A MÀMMA SÓIA' (Even a beetle is beautiful to its mother)

'E PARIÉNTE SO CÒMME 'E SCÀRPE: CCHIÙ SO STRÌTTE E CCHIÙ TE FÀNNO MÀLE' (Relatives are like shoes: the tighter they are the more they hurt)

'L'AMICO È COME L'OMBRELLO, QUANDO PIOVE NON LO TROVI MAI' (The friend is like the umbrella: when it's raining, you never find it)

THE NEAPOLITAN MINDSET

Consummate performers and as *furbo* (cunning) as they come, Neapolitans are famous for their ingenuity. Only in Naples will you hear of vendors flogging T-shirts printed with seat-belt designs to fool short-sighted cops. Tough times have forced Neapolitans to become who they are today. For much of its history, the city was fought over, occupied and invaded by foreign powers that saw the locals as little more than taxable plebs. Consequently the Neapolitans learned early to fend for themselves and to get by on what they had – a situation still all too common. For more on the Neapolitan psyche, see p233.

TOP Shopping in Sorrento (p170) **RIGHT** Amalfi's busy Piazza del Duomo, with Cattedrale di Sant'Andrea (p187) in the background

A BAROQUE METROPOLIS

The baroque burst onto the Neapolitan scene in the mid-17th century. An emotional style (matched to the locals' sensibilities), it provided the architectural and decorative vehicle for the city's Spanish-inspired facelift, begun under the 17th-century viceroys and continued in the 18th century under the Bourbon monarchs. But more than the Spanish authorities it was the Catholic Church that set Naples' baroque bandwagon in motion. Determined to reaffirm authority in the wake of the Protestant Reformation, it employed baroque art and architecture to conquer the hearts of the masses. The result was an ecclesiastical building boom – up to 900 churches were built between 1585 and 1650 – and the revamp of some of Naples' showcase churches. For more, see p249.

DOS & DON'TS

★ Learn a few Neapolitan words. It's the quickest way to win the locals' hearts.

★ Cover up when visiting churches and religious sites. Singlets and shorts are forbidden.

★ Steer clear of chrysanthemums when buying flowers for a local. In Italy they're only used to decorate graves.

★ Focus on the positives. Although Neapolitans regularly lament their city's short-comings, a foreigner's jibes can cause offence.

★ Never admit supporting the Lega Nord (Northern League), a northern Italian separatist party loathed in the south.

FOOD & DRINK

BOOKS

DAVID RUGGERIO'S ITALIAN KITCHEN: FAMILY RECIPES FROM THE OLD COUNTRY (David Ruggerio) Filled with the secrets of a Neapolitan kitchen.

GUILIANO BUGIALLI'S FOOD OF NAPLES AND CAMPANIA (Guiliano Bugialli) A culinary journey through the region led by a prolific Italian-cookery writer.

LA PIZZA: THE TRUE STORY FROM NAPLES (Nikko Amandonico and Natalia Borri) Sumptuously illustrated history of pizza, set in Naples' kaleidoscopic streets.

NAPLES AT TABLE: COOKING IN CAMPANIA (Arthur Schwartz) Local food trivia and 250 recipes.

THE FOOD LOVER'S COMPANION TO NAPLES AND THE CAMPANIA (Carla Capalbo) An encyclopedic guide to Campania's food producers and nosh spots.

THE CULT OF CAFFÈ

Neapolitans will proudly tell you that their coffee is the country's best. They may have a point. While bars and cafes use the same machines deployed across Italy, the espresso that drips out of the Neapolitan models seems darker and richer. It's because of the water, they'll tell you, or the air. *Caffè* (coffee) is the city's great social lubricant, cutting through all social barriers. Camorra bosses drink it, just as do judges and police officers. Elsewhere you might be asked out for a beer or for lunch; in Naples you're invited to meet for coffee. And your host will know just where to take you. Every verified coffee aficionado, and there are about a million in Naples, has a favourite bar where '*fanno un buon caffè*' (they make a good coffee). Curious about the caffeine scene? Turn to p255.

TOP LEFT Vegetable stall at a busy market **LEFT** *Limoncello* **CENTRE RIGHT** Pizza maker hard at work **FAR RIGHT** Fresh anchovies for sale

TOP PLACES TO SPOIL YOUR APPETITE

ATTANASIO Greet and eat a sublime *sfogliatella* (p84).

DOLCERÍA DELL' ANTÍCO PORTICO Sumptuous *sfogliatelle* in the form of a traditional *trullo* (p189).

FANTASIA GELATI Crème de la crème of Naples' gelato vendors (p87).

GAY-ODIN Lustfully good chocolate treats in a variety of combos (p85).

RAFFAELE BUONACORE Succumb to the feather-light *caprilu al limone* (p128).

ALAN BENSON

DON'T MISS EXPERIENCES

★ Building up an appetite at a Neapolitan street market (p57)

★ A boisterous, salt-of-the-earth slap up in the electric Quartieri Spagnoli (p87)

★ Languid, romantic dining by the Tyrrhenian Sea (p91)

★ Vino sipping and grazing on the stylish streets of Chiaia (p92)

★ Hearty feasting at an ecofriendly *agriturismo* in the Parco Nazionale del Cilento (p288)

★ A cappuccino session on Amalfi's Piazza del Duomo within confessional distance of the stunning cathedral (p187)

★ Digging into a giant, bubbling pizza at Pizzeria Gino Sorbillo (p86)

CAMPANIAN STAPLES

★ Pizza, both wood-fired and *fritta* (fried)

★ *Pane casareccio* (a rustic, thick-crusted bread)

★ *Spaghetti alle vongole* (spaghetti with clams)

★ Vegetables like tomatoes, *friarielli* (a local broccoli), eggplants, artichokes and zucchinis

★ *Limoncello*, the Bay of Naples' trademark lemon liqueur, served in an icy glass

★ Espresso, served scalding hot and wham-bam strong

FOOD & DRINK

ONLINE RESOURCES

ITINERARIO GUSTO (www. itinerariogusto.it) Create your own foodie-centric road trip.

GAMBERO ROSSO (www. gamberorosso.it, in Italian) Reviews and news from Italy's gastronomic guru.

MOZZARELLA ONLINE (www.mozzarellaonline.eu) The low-down on Campania's best-loved cheese.

TASTE OF SORRENTO (www.tasteofsorrento.sorrentoinfo.com) Recipes and local products.

CHOWHOUND (www.chow hound.com) Tips and reviews from global food fanatics.

TOP FESTIVE TREATS

CASATIELLO Savoury Easter bread made with lard, salami, *pecorino* cheese and eggs.

PASTIERA An Easter latticed tart, filled with ricotta, cream, candied fruit and cereals flavoured with orange-blossom water.

ROCOCÒ Crunchy, spicy, almondy Yuletide *biscotti* (biscuits).

TORRONE DEI MORTI A hard nougat loaf made with cocoa, hazelnuts, candied fruits and coffee and baked for All Souls' Day in November.

ZEPPOLE Custard-filled, cherry-topped doughnuts for the feast of San Giuseppe in March.

PASTE REALI Dainty fruit and vegetable miniatures, these sweets are made from almond paste and sugar (marzipan) and gobbled up at Christmas.

REGIONAL FLAVOURS

One of the greatest pleasures of travelling through Campania is taste testing its gastronomic diversity. Each corner of the region boasts its own traditions and specialities, from Ischia's *coniglio all'ischitana* (Ischian-style rabbit) to neighbouring Procida's *insalata al limone* (lemon salad). Campania's legendary *mozzarella di bufula* (buffalo mozzarella) is produced north of Naples in the Caserta region, as well as south in the Salerno area. Further south, the rugged Cilento area is also famed for its cheeses, among them the intense goat's milk *cacioricotta di capra* and the sweet cow's milk *caciocavallo podolico*. For more on Campania's local treats, turn to p255.

TOP Alfresco dining in trendy Capri (p126) **RIGHT** Tuck into a plate of *spaghetti alle vongole*

FAST FOOD, NAPLES STYLE

Few cities cater to peckish grazers like Naples. It's a buffet of cheap fast-food treats begging to be devoured. And we're not talking the Western glut of burgers and hot dogs. We're talking about tried-and-tested morsels that any self-respecting *nonna* (grandmother) would approve of – deep-fried eggplant and zucchini flowers, golden *arancini* (rice balls stuffed with meat sauce), *crocchè* (fried mashed-potato balls filled with mozzarella), *pizza fritta* (deep-fried pizza stuffed with ham, mozzarella or seaweed) and *frittatine di pasta* (deep-fried pasta balls stuffed with minced pork, béchamel sauce and peas). The best place to sample it all is at the old-school *frigittorie* – marble-clad takeaway outlets specialised in the art of frying. Still hungry? See p255.

DOS & DON'TS

⋆ Do make eye contact when toasting and never clink using plastic cups; it's bad luck!

⋆ Pasta is eaten with a fork only

⋆ Bread is not eaten with pasta – unless you're cleaning up the sauce afterwards

⋆ It's fine to eat pizza with your hands

⋆ If in doubt, dress smart

⋆ If invited to someone's home, take a tray of *dolci* (sweets) from a *pasticceria* (pastry shop)

THE OUTDOORS

SWIMMING SPOTS

BAIA DE LERANTO
A spectacular beach at the tip of the Punta Penna peninsula (p176).

GROTTA AZZURRA Dive into startling blue sea beside Capri's glittering Blue Grotto (p125).

SPIAGGIA MARMELLI
Retreat to a lush, soothing cove (p220).

MARINA DI PRAIA
An enticing inlet boasting crystal-clear water (p185).

SANTA MARIA DI CASTELLABATE Luxuriate in velvet-soft sand and powder-blue sea at this picturesque resort (p217).

SPIAGGIA DEL CASTELLO
Catch a boat to a petite beach set beneath a looming castle (see the boxed text, p82).

BAGNI REGINA GIOVANNA
Take a dip where ancient ruins meet the sea (p167).

WORLD HERITAGE SITES

A Unesco World Heritage Site and Italy's second-largest national park, Parco Nazionale del Cilento e Valle di Diano (National Park of the Cilento and the Valley of Diana) is one of Italy's natural marvels – think pristine Mediterranean waters, spectacular grottoes, silent mountains and veteran stone villages. In the days of the grand tour, the rugged, bandit-laced landscape thrilled adventure-seeking scribes like 19th-century Craufurd Tait Ramage, who documented his southern Italian sojourn in *The Nooks and By-ways of Italy: Wanderings in Search of its Ancient Remains and Modern Superstitions.* The bandits have long since gone, but the ruins remain, among them the mesmerising Greek temples at Paestum. Equally glorious are the gastronomic perks, from artichokes and olive oil to luscious white figs. For more on the Cilento's bounty, see p209.

TOP LEFT La Mortella gardens (p145), Ischia **LEFT** Grotta Azzurra (p125), Capri **CENTRE RIGHT** Castello Aragonese (p143), Ischia **FAR RIGHT** Spooky underground Naples (p244)

TOP KNOCKOUT VIEWS

MONTE ALBURNO Scale this mighty mountain for a rugged panorama (p214).

MONTE SOLARO Yachts, aquamarine seas and circling gulls from Capri's highest peak (p119).

MT VESUVIUS Crater-side views of city, bay and mountains (p108).

PARCO VIRGILIANO Two bays for the price of none (p76).

SENTIERO DEGLI DEI Hit the 'Walk of the Gods' for amazing Amalfi Coast landscapes (p180).

JEAN-BERNARD CARILLET

DON'T MISS EXPERIENCES

★ Solfatara Crater – Hissing, sulphurous spewings and an otherworldly vibe (p80)

★ Island-hopping – Celebrities, spas and low-key local hideaways (p116)

★ Glittering coastal grottoes – Glide into Campania's magical, watery caves (p125)

★ A bubbling beach – Catch a water taxi for a dip at steamy Il Sorgeto (p146)

★ Hiring a boat – Seek your own secluded piece of paradise (p188)

★ Santa Maria di Castellabate – Snorkel or scuba dive in crystal-clear waters (p217)

★ Grotta di Castelcivita – Dramatic geology and fabulous hues in Europe's oldest settlement (p212)

PARKS & GARDENS

PALAZZO REALE
Grand royal pathways, classic cascades and a gorgeous English Garden (p46).

VILLA FLORIDIANA
A Neapolitan nook with middle-class manners and romantic sea views (p66).

LA MORTELLA Moorish inspiration, exotic residents and a tranquil island setting (p145).

VILLA RUFOLO Fall for the gardens that once wowed Wagner (p192).

GIARDINA RAVINO
A fascinating 6000 sq metres of cacti and succulents (p145).

THE OUTDOORS

LOCAL FLORA

STONE PINE The 'umbrella pine' frames many a postcard vista.

RED VALERIAN Known for a purplish-red, late-spring flower.

HOLY OAK An evergreen tree with leathery leaves and a blackish bark.

BROOM Its sweetly perfumed yellow flower blooms in June.

ORCHID Some 70 varieties bloom in spring in the Cilento's Valley of the Orchids.

STRAWBERRY TREE Gorgeous bright-red drupes but, ironically, no strawberries.

RESOURCES

Many useful websites and publications on Campania's fauna, flora and hiking options are in Italian only. Helpful resources (some in English) include the following:

NATIONAL PARKS (www.parks.it) Italy's national parks website, including Parco Nazionale del Cilento.

VESUVIUS NATIONAL PARK (www.vesuviopark. it, mostly in Italian) Facts about, and walks around, Naples' volcano.

CAMPI FLEGREI (www.parcodeicampiflegrei.it, in Italian) Walking trails in the Campi Flegrei.

WALKING IN ITALY (www.lonelyplanet.com) A dedicated guidebook, with trails throughout Campania.

THERMAL TREATS

Unsurprisingly, in a region dominated by the volcanic presence of Mt Vesuvius, the Bay of Naples has been famed for its thermal waters for thousands of years. The island of Ischia (p139) bubbles with some 56 natural springs and 150 spa operators, while Capri's (p116) more modest number of steamy options tends towards luxe self-pampering. Closer to Naples, the Campi Flegrei (p76) is home to both ancient and modern thermal retreats.

TOP LEFT Warning sign at Solfatara Crater (p80), Pozzuoli **RIGHT** Relaxing at Parco Virgiliano (p76), Naples

TAKE A HIKE

Away from Naples' big city clamour, this region is great for stretching the calf muscles. Whether you fancy a gentle amble surrounded by vine groves or a more-serious workout trudging up mountains, there's plenty of scope. The Parco Nazionale del Cilento offers some challenging hikes with well-marked trails, reliable guides and excellent maps (p214). More surprisingly, the high-profile, high-octane island of Capri (p118) offers some of the best hiking in the Bay of Naples, while the Amalfi Coast's lyrically named Walk of the Gods (p180) is suitably divine, with a meandering trail passing through a sumptuous landscape of ancient vineyards, craggy cliff faces and verdant valleys, plus some of the most spectacular views this side of heaven.

DOS & DON'TS

* Invest in comfortable lace-up walking shoes or sturdy boots
* Pack a small daypack with an extra layer of clothing should temperatures drop
* Depending on the season, don't forget sunscreen, sunglasses and a hat
* Pack a compass that works!
* Take plenty of water, as well as some energy-stoking snacks
* Invest in a good map with trails marked, particularly in the Parco Nazionale del Cilento

FAMILY TRAVEL

TOP RESOURCES

BODIES FROM THE ASH: LIFE AND DEATH IN ANCIENT POMPEII (James M Deem) Fascinating facts and illustrations for kids visiting Pompeii.

PIZZA FOR THE QUEEN (Nancy F Castaldo) A charming picture book about the history of Naples' legendary margherita.

TRAVEL WITH CHILDREN (Brigitte Barta et al) A comprehensive, in-the-know guide to hitting the road with kids.

DON'T MISS EXPERIENCES

NAPOLI SOTTERRANEA Snoop around below the streets of Naples (p49).

SOLFATARA CRATER Sidle up to a geological freak show (p80).

MAV Take a virtual step into ancient times (p103).

AMALFI COAST BEACHES Splash and swim on Italy's most fabled coast (p163).

MT VESUVIUS Peer into the crater of a sleeping monster (p108).

ANFITEATRO FLAVIO Imagine gory battles in Pozzuoli's ancient arena (p78).

EDENLANDIA Enough fun-park rides to thrill the kids and the kid within (p84).

TRAVEL WITH CHILDREN

Children are adored in Campania and welcomed almost anywhere. Encounters with hissing fissures, a dormant volcano or ancient skeletons should pique the interest of most young minds, though it's worth investing in a few children's history books to help their imagination along. On the downside, Naples' breathless pace, Pompeii's stroller-challenging cobblestones and the Amalfi Coast's twisting coastal road can be challenging. Always ask tourist-office staff about any family activities and child-friendly hotels. Most car-hire firms offer children's safety seats at a nominal cost, but should be booked ahead. The same goes for high chairs and cots (cribs): they're available in most restaurants and hotels, but numbers are limited. Click onto www.travelwithyourkids.com and www.familytravelnetwork.com for useful family holiday tips.

TOP Time for some serious beach fun at Positano (p178)

CONTENTS

THE AUTHORS

CRISTIAN BONETTO

Coordinating Author, Naples

Much to the chagrin of his northern Italian relatives, Cristian's loyalties lie with Naples. Such affection seems only natural for a writer of farce and soap with a penchant for running red lights. Based in Melbourne, Australia, Cristian makes regular trips to Italy, and his musings on its food, people and culture appear in print from Sydney to London. His Naples-based play *Il Cortile* toured Italy in 2003, and he is also the author of Lonely Planet's *Rome Encounter* guide.

JOSEPHINE QUINTERO

The Islands, the Amalfi Coast, Salerno & the Cilento

Born in England, Josephine started travelling with a backpack and guitar in the late '60s, stopping off in a kibbutz in Israel for a year. Further travels took her to Kuwait, where she was editor of the *Kuwaiti Digest* and was held hostage during the Iraqi invasion. Shortly thereafter she moved to the relaxed shores of Andalucía, Spain, from where she makes frequent trips to Italy to visit family and deepen her appreciation of the finer things in life.

LONELY PLANET AUTHORS

Why is our travel information the best in the world? It's simple: our authors are passionate, dedicated travellers. They don't take freebies in exchange for positive coverage so you can be sure the advice you're given is impartial. They travel widely to all the popular spots, and off the beaten track. They don't research using just the internet or phone. They discover new places not included in any other guidebook. They personally visit thousands of hotels, restaurants, palaces, trails, galleries, temples and more. They speak with dozens of locals every day to make sure you get the kind of insider knowledge only a local could tell you. They take pride in getting all the details right, and in telling it how it is. Think you can do it? Find out how at lonelyplanet.com.

ITINERARIES

NAPLES CITY BREAK

ONE WEEK // NAPLES ROUND TRIP

Spend a couple of days at the **centro storico** (historical centre; p41) wandering frescoed churches and munching at **Mangia e Bevi** (p86). Spend a morning at **Mercato di Porta Nolana** (p52) and another tackling the **Museo Archeologico Nazionale** (p54). Clear

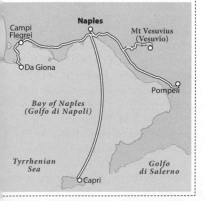

the mind with an evening saunter on **Via Chiaia** (p65) or the **Lungomare** (p65), followed by harbourside noshing at **La Scialuppa** (p89). Next day, head up to the **Certosa di San Martino** (p67), then underground with **Napoli Sotterranea** (p49). Dedicate a day to **Pompeii** (p103) and **Mt Vesuvius** (p108), and another celebrity-spotting on **Capri** (p116). For less-trampled ruins, explore **Campi Flegrei** (p76), lunching at **Da Giona** (p91). Cap your Neapolitan sojourn at the lavish **Parco e Palazzo Reale di Capodimonte** (p71).

ISLAND HOP THE BAY

4 DAYS // CAPRI TO ISCHIA TO PROCIDA // 40KM

Each Bay of Naples' island has a distinctive feel and appeal. From **Sorrento** (p159) hop on a ferry to glamorous **Capri Town** (p119) and visit the spectacular **Grotta Az-**

zurra (p115). Walk to sumptuous **Villa Jovis** (p122) and hop on a bus to **Anacapr** (p123), for delicious pizza at **Il Solitario** (p128) before soaring up the **Monte Solar** (p123) chairlift for heady coastal views. Next stop is **Ischia** (p139), and the exotic **La Mortella** gardens (p145). Lunch at **La Brocca** (p148), then collapse at the beach across the way. Stay overnight (p270) and take it easy with a self-pampering spa day (p144). Next day, take a ferry to **Procida** (p152), explore the *centro storico*, have lunch in picturesque **Marina Corricella** (p153) and hire a boat for an afternoon of leisurely beach-hopping (p154).

THE COASTAL AFFAIR

10 DAYS // NAPLES TO SALERNO // 110KM

Start with two electrifying days in **Naples** (p33) before heading to **Pompeii** (p103). You'll need the best part of a morning to investigate the ancient streets, fossilised by

ash from nearby **Mt Vesuvius** (p108). Stay overnight in buzzing **Sorrento** (p159), before pushing on to picture-perfect **Positano** (p178), where you can hire your own boat (p181) or a trek along the heavenly **Sentiero degli Dei** (p180). Follow the coastal road to **Amalfi** (p186). Dive into its historic streets and Museo della Carta, then spend a night in lofty **Ravello** (p192) to soak up its aristocratic air and superlative coastal views. Fall in love with the gardens of **Villa Rufolo** (p192) and **Villa Cimbrone** (p192) before heading o to busy **Salerno** (p199) and its appealing medieval core.

THE CILENTO COASTAL TRAIL

FOUR TO FIVE DAYS // AGROPOLI TO PALINURO // 43KM

Explore the historic quarter of **Agropoli** (p215). Lunch at panoramic **U'Sghiz** (p217) then walk off the carbs on the promenade. Drive to **Santa Maria di Castellabate** (p203) for a

beachfront dinner at **Arlecchino** (p219). On day two, head up to medieval **Castellabate** (p203). Continue the scenic coastal strip until **Acciaroli** (p218) with its biscuit-coloured houses and cafe-huddling harbour. After lunch continue to ancient **Pioppi** (p218) for gelato in Piazza de Millenario. Beach bums will love **Marina de Casal Velino's** (p203) blissfully long sandy stretch. Stay one night (or two) at **Agriturismo i Moresani** (p288) and go horse riding or hiking. Continue to the **Velia** (p218) excavations and hit the brakes at delightful **Palinuro** (p220), famous for its blue grotto, beautiful beaches and bustling holiday atmosphere.

HOLLYWOOD ON THE MED

ONE WEEK // RAVELLO TO CASERTA // 120KM

Start posing in **Ravello** (p192) and **Atrani** (p186), setting for John Huston's 1953 crime caper *Beat The Devil*. While **Amalfi** (p186) provides a backdrop to Mike Barker's 2004 *A*

Good Woman, featuring Scarlett Johansson, **Positano** (p178) was a deceptive location for the 2003 *Under the Tuscan Sun.* Relive 1999's *The Talented Mr Ripley* at Teatro San Carlo in **Naples** (p37), Ischia Ponte on **Ischia** (p139) and Marina Grande on **Procida** (p152). Still on Procida, Michael Radford's 1994 hit, *Il Postino* (The Postman) showcased Marina Corricella and Pozzo Vecchio beach. *Star Wars* fans shouldn't miss Palazzo Reale (aka Reggia) in **Caserta** (p46), whose interiors featured as Queen Amidala's residence in *Star Wars Episode 1: The Phantom Menace* (1999) and *Star Wars Episode 2: Attack of the Clones* (2002).

ITINERARIES

SOUTHERN LARDER

SEVEN DAYS // NAPLES TO CILENTO // 145KM

In Naples, pamper the pantry at **La Pignasecca** (p57) and chow down pizza at **Da Michele** (p85). Offshore on Ischia, sample local rabbit at **Il Focolare** (p148), then try

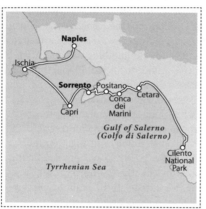

torta caprese (chocolate and almond cake) on **Capri** (p116). A short sail away, it's *limoncello* in **Sorrento** (p159) before a detour for pizza-by-the-metre at its birthplace, **Pizzeria da Gigino** (p177). It was in **Conca dei Marini** (p188) that the ricotta-filled *sfogliatella* was invented in the 18th century, while another sweet treat, *zeppole* (fried doughnuts with custard cream) is a famously irresistible Positano speciality. Further east, pick up some *colatura di alic* (anchovy seasoning) in **Cetara** (p196), then push south to the **Cilento** (p215) region, home to heavenly mozzarella and moreish ricotta and pear tart.

ANCIENT ODYSSEY

EIGHT DAYS // NAPLES TO ASCEA // 96KM

Begin your time travel in Naples, delving into ancient booty at the **Museo Archeo-logico Nazionale** (p54) and spending a day in the **Campi Flegrei** (p76) to eye-up the

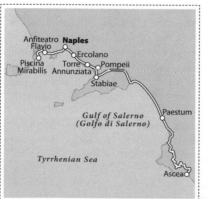

Anfiteatro Flavio (p78) and **Piscina Mirabilis** (p83). Next, take the train to Ercolano for virtual time travel at **MAV** (p103) and a wander through the evocative **Ruins of Herculaneum** (p100). Next stop is Torre Annunziata for fabulous ancient frescoes at **Oplontis** (p107). Just down the road, Europe's most evocative ruins await at **Pompeii** (p103), while further south, the two villas at Castellammare di Stabia are the only visible remains of ancient **Stabiae** (p107). Continue down the coast for remarkable Greek temples at **Paestum** (p207) and the Hellenic ruins of Velia at **Ascea** (p219).

NAPLES

3 PERFECT DAYS

3 DAY 1 // CLOISTERS, ANCIENT BOOTY AND COOL CAMPARIS

First stop is the Basilica di Santa Chiara (p44) and its colourful cloister. Continue down Via Benedetto Croce and Via San Biagio dei Librai, taking time to explore the densely packed *palazzi* and churches. Pray for a miracle at the Duomo (p49), before turning back into Via dei Tribunali for perfect pizza (see p85). Eye up the incredible Cappella Sansevero (p45), then make for the mighty Museo Archeologico Nazionale (p54). Take a late-afternoon stroll down Via Toledo to Piazza Trieste e Trento (p60) before rounding off the day in one of the many trattorias or bars in Chiaia (p88).

3 DAY 2 // MARKET DELICACIES, CULTURAL MASTERPIECES AND LANGUID SEASIDE SUPPING

Fill the picnic hamper at La Pignasecca (p57) for a perfect lunch in the Parco di Capodimonte (p71). Steps away is the fabulous art collection inside the Palazzo Reale di Capodimonte (p71). Alternatively, give Capodimonte a miss altogether and head up to Vomero for lunch in the grounds of Villa Floridiana (p66) and an afternoon of artistic highs at the Certosa di San Martino (p67). Finish up at bayside Borgo Marinaro (p64) for a lively drink or a languid seafood dinner.

3 DAY 3 // VOLCANIC VIEWS AND VICTIMS

Head into the suburbs and up Mt Vesuvius (p108) for dizzying views and a face-to-face with its deceptively peaceful crater. Back down the slope, walk the ghostly streets of Pompeii (p103) before heading back to town for a nightcap on buzzing Piazza Bellini (p44).

NAPLES

NAPLES

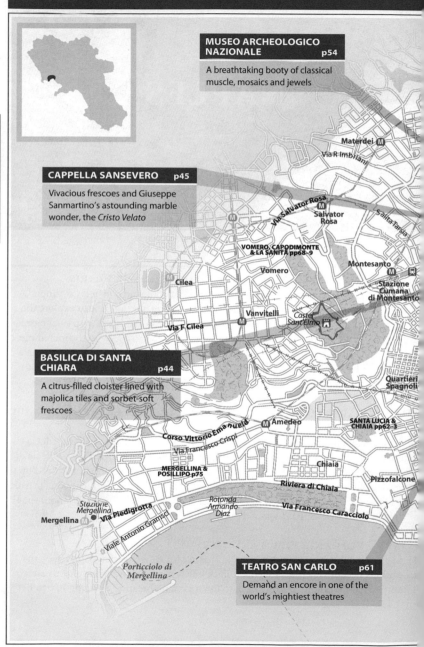

MUSEO ARCHEOLOGICO NAZIONALE p54

A breathtaking booty of classical muscle, mosaics and jewels

CAPPELLA SANSEVERO p45

Vivacious frescoes and Giuseppe Sanmartino's astounding marble wonder, the *Cristo Velato*

BASILICA DI SANTA CHIARA p44

A citrus-filled cloister lined with majolica tiles and sorbet-soft frescoes

TEATRO SAN CARLO p61

Demand an encore in one of the world's mightiest theatres

Map labels: Materdei, Via R Imbriani, Via Salvator Rosa, Salvator Rosa, Salita Tarsia, VOMERO, CAPODIMONTE & LA SANITA pp68–9, Vomero, Montesanto, Stazione Cumana di Montesanto, Cilea, Vanvitelli, Castel Sant'Elmo, Via F Cilea, Quartieri Spagnoli, Corso Vittorio Emanuele, Amedeo, SANTA LUCIA & CHIAIA pp62–3, Via Francesco Crispi, Chiaia, MERGELLINA & POSILLIPO p75, Pizzofalcone, Riviera di Chiaia, Stazione Mergellina, Via Piedigrotta, Rotonda Armando Diaz, Via Francesco Caracciolo, Mergellina, Viale Antonio Gramsci, Porticciolo di Mergellina

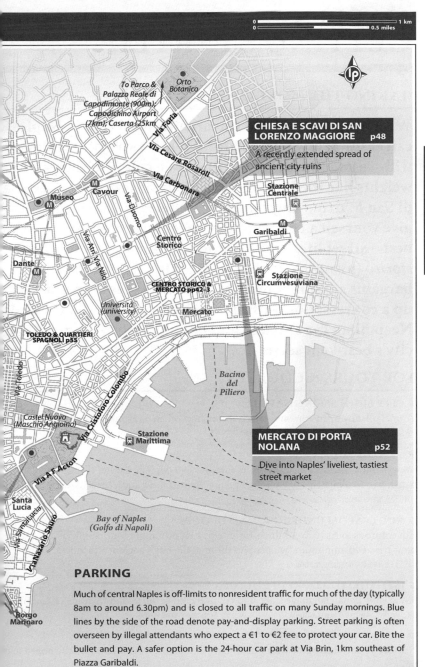

CHIESA E SCAVI DI SAN LORENZO MAGGIORE p48

A recently extended spread of ancient city ruins

MERCATO DI PORTA NOLANA p52

Dive into Naples' liveliest, tastiest street market

PARKING

Much of central Naples is off-limits to nonresident traffic for much of the day (typically 8am to around 6.30pm) and is closed to all traffic on many Sunday mornings. Blue lines by the side of the road denote pay-and-display parking. Street parking is often overseen by illegal attendants who expect a €1 to €2 fee to protect your car. Bite the bullet and pay. A safer option is the 24-hour car park at Via Brin, 1km southeast of Piazza Garibaldi.

NAPLES
=======

NAPLES
GETTING STARTED

MAKING THE MOST OF YOUR TIME

With its glut of artistic and architectural riches, Naples can easily overwhelm visitors. While two or three days will see you (busily) cover must-see cultural heavyweights like the Museo Archeologico Nazionale, Certosa di San Martino and the Palazzo Reale di Capodimonte, give yourself a couple of days to enjoy what Naples does best – street life. Wander down a laundry-strung *centro storico* (historic city centre) side street, hunt for bootleg bargains at a street market, or swill espresso and strike up a conversation with the barista – they're all essential Neapolitan experiences and bound to reveal some of the city's best-kept secrets.

TOP TOURS & COURSES

♣ CITY SIGHTSEEING NAPOLI
Tour Naples by open-top bus, with hop-on, hop-off stops around the city. (Map pp62-3; ☎ 081 551 72 79; www.napoli.city-sightseeing.it)

♣ YELLOW SUDMARINE
Idiosyncratic made-to-measure tours (around €90 per half-day) of Naples and Campania, from sailing trips to cooking and art-themed itineraries. (☎ 081 362 52 28, 329 1010328; www.yellowsudmarine.it)

♣ NUG (NAPOLI UNDERGROUND GROUP)
Adventurous tours (two- to three-hour trips €15, minimum four people; five- to six-hour trips €40, minimum two people) through the city's ancient aqueducts. (☎ 347 6455332; info@napoliunderground.org)

♣ ISTITUTO ITALIANO DI CULTURA
Hone your Italian language skills and cultural cred at the Italian Institute of Culture. (IIC; ☎ 081 546 16 62; www.istitalianodicultura.org; Via Bernardo Cavallino 89)

♣ ART WORKSHOPS WITH RICCARDO DALISI
Nurture your creative side with one of Italy's most inspiring artists (see the boxed text p67).

GETTING AWAY FROM IT ALL

While Naples' trademark intensity is exhilarating, it can also lead to sensory overload. When you hanker for harmony, consider the following:

★ **Chiesa e Pinacoteca dei Girolamini** Upstaged by its more famous porticoed rivals, this monastic complex harbours a beautiful citrus-filled cloister that's central, tranquil and free (p50)

★ **Find peace in Posillipo** High above the city, shady refuge comes with breathtaking views, bourgeois chic and a much-loved Thursday market at the Parco Virgiliano (p74)

★ **Seek out the sibyl** Ponder ancient myths, enter the Cumaean sibyl's cave and gaze out at the Tyrrhenian blue in one of Italy's least-trampled archaeological sites, the Acropoli di Cuma (p83)

RESOURCES

★ **Naples Tourist Board** (www.inaples.it) Sights, events and practical information

★ **Turismo Regione Campania** (www.turismoregionecampania.it) Up-to-date events listings, as well as audio clips and itineraries

★ **Pompeii Sites** (www.pompeiisites.org) Background and practicalities for Pompeii, Herculaneum and other archaeological must-sees

★ **Vesuvius National Park** (www.vesuviopark.it, mostly in Italian) Nature, walks and facts concerning Naples' infamous volcano

ADVANCE PLANNING

There are numerous top experiences that you would do well to book in advance.

★ **NUg (Napoli Underground Group)** (☎ 347 6455332; info@napoliunderground.org) Book tours at least a week in advance.

★ **Dora** (☎ 081 68 05 19) Naples' top seafood restaurant is a gastronomic event and justifiably popular, so make reservations.

★ **Teatro San Carlo** (☎ 081 797 23 31) A seat at this lavish theatre is a prized possession, so check upcoming events and book ahead as early as possible.

★ **Campania Artecard** (☎ 800 60 06 01; www.campaniaartecard.it) It's worth getting the Campania Artecard, which offers free transport and discounts to museums and sights (see the boxed text, p294).

TOP CHEAP EATS

❦ **TRATTORIA MANGIA E BEVI** Communal tables, convivial regulars and glorious home cooking (p86)

❦ **GINO SORBILLO** Perfect pizzas and to-die-for *semifreddi* (p86)

❦ **LA TAVERNA DEL BUONGUSTAIO** Tiles, postcards and lip-smacking *casareccio* (home-style) classics (p87)

❦ **NENNELLA** A Neapolitan classic, where wise-cracking waiters meet a €10 feed (p88)

❦ **FRIGGITORIA FIORENZANO** Stand-up snack joint peddling delicious Neapolitan-style tempura (p87)

NAPLES

NAPLES

INTRODUCING NAPLES

pop 3,100,000
**Sandwiched between a sleeping vol-
cano and the steaming Campi Flegrei,
Naples is a rumbling mass of con-
tradictions. Grimy streets hit palm-
fringed boulevards, crumbling facades
mask baroque ballrooms and cultish
shrines flank cutting-edge clubs. One
minute you're in dusty Tangiers, the
next you're thinking of Paris. Few
European cities intrigue and intoxi-
cate so intensely, and few are so easily misunderstood. Look behind the
grime and unearth an elegant, erudite
and deeply soulful metropolis.**

After founding nearby Cuma in the
8th century BC, the ancient Greeks settled the city in around 680 BC, calling it
Parthenope. Under the Romans, the area
became an ancient Miami of sorts: a sun-
soaked spa region that drew the likes of
Virgil. Dampening the bonhomie was Mt
Vesuvius' unexpected eruption in AD 79.

Naples fell into Norman hands in 1139
before the French Angevins took control
a century later, boosting the city's cred
with the mighty Castel Nuovo. By the
16th century, Naples was under Spanish
rule and riding high on Spain's colonial
riches. By 1600, it was Europe's largest
city and a burgeoning baroque beauty
adorned by artists like Luca Giordano,
Giuseppe de Ribera and Caravaggio.

Despite a devastating plague in 1656,
Naples' ego soared under the Bourbons
(1734–1860), with epic constructions
such as the Teatro San Carlo and the
Royal Palace in Caserta sealing the city's
showcase reputation.

An ill-fated attempt at republican rule
in 1799 was followed by a short stint
under the French and a final period of
Bourbon governance before nationalist
rebel Giuseppe Garibaldi inspired the

city to snip off the puppet strings and
join a united Italy in 1860.

ESSENTIAL INFORMATION

EMERGENCIES // Ambulance (☎ 118)
Farmacia Alma Salus (Map p55; ☎ 081 549 93
36; Piazza Dante 71) Open 24 hours. **Loreto-Mare
Hospital** (Ospedale Loreto-Mare; Map pp42-3;
☎ 081 20 10 33; Via Amerigo Vespucci 26) **Police**
(☎ 112, 113) **Police Station** (Questura; Map
p55; ☎ 081 794 11 11; Via Medina 75) Has an office for
foreigners.
TOURIST INFORMATION // Tourist Information Hotline (☎ 081 007 90 20, 800 223366;
🕑 8.30am-7.30pm) Offers information on everything
from museum opening times to train and ferry schedules. **Tourist Information Office** Piazza del
Gesù Nuovo (Map pp42-3; ☎ 081 552 33 28; Piazza
del Gesù Nuovo; 🕑 9am-7pm Mon-Sat, to 2pm Sun);
Stazione Centrale (Map pp42-3; ☎ 081 26 87 79; Piazza
Garibaldi; 🕑 9am-7pm Mon-Sat); Via San Carlo (Map
pp62-3; ☎ 081 40 23 94; Via San Carlo 7; 🕑 9.30am-
1.30pm & 2.30-6pm Mon-Sat, 9am-1.30pm Sun);
Stazione Mergellina (Map p75; ☎ 081 761 21 02; Piazza
Piedigrotta; 🕑 varies)

ORIENTATION

Stazione Centrale (Central Station) is
Naples' tatty doormat. At the eastern
end of anarchic Piazza Garibaldi, its surrounding streets are a multicultural en-
clave of budget hotels and shabby street
stalls. Directly southwest is the equally
raffish Mercato district, famed for its
street market. A few blocks west of Piazza Garibaldi sits the *centro storico*, home
to many of the city's finest churches and
sights.

At its western edge, shop-heavy Via
Toledo stretches from Piazza Trieste e
Trento in the south to Parco di Capodimonte in the north (changing its
name along the way); its chicer southern

NAPLES ACCOMMODATION

While the garbage-disposal crisis of 2008 inflicted a blow to Naples' tourist trade, the upside is that accommodation rates have changed little since. This is even sweeter news considering the city's plethora of slumber gems, from chic *palazzi* with sweeping views to art-filled B&Bs. Less inspiring are the options in Pompeii and Herculaneum, though their proximity to central Naples means there's no need to stay overnight.

★ A stunning spa retreat and Jap-Med aesthetics... **Romeo Hotel** (p267) is the choice for high-flying urbanistas

★ Chic lounging, a lofty pool and stylish monk's cell conversions await at **Hotel San Francesco al Monte** (p269)

★ Elegant, soothing and homely, **Chiaja Hotel de Charme** (p268) is a chic retreat right on shopaholic Via Chiaia

★ The independently minded will love **Sui Tetti di Napoli** (p268), where self-contained mini-apartments meet an atmospheric central address

★ Snooze in the restored *palazzo* of a Bourbon bishop at **Decumani Hotel de Charme** (p265), complete with in-house baroque hall

end is a favourite haunt for shopaholics munching *sfogliatella* (cinnamon-infused ricotta in a puff-pastry shell). Immediately to the west lie the gritty, washing-strung streets of the Quartieri Spagnoli.

South of Via Toledo, regal Santa Lucia boasts the mighty Piazza del Plebiscito, Palazzo Reale and world opera great Teatro San Carlo. Close at hand, Castel Nuovo (Maschio Angioino) looms over Piazza del Municipio like a giant toy castle.

Looking down on it all is middle-class Vomero, a leafy residential neighbourhood and home to the impressive Certosa di San Martino.

West of Piazza del Plebiscito, upmarket Chiaia is Naples' heart of cool, its sleek shops and bars stretching west towards the bobbing-boat port of Mergellina. From here, posh Posillipo climbs the promontory separating the Bay of Naples from the Bay of Pozzuoli, and Naples from the sulphurous Campi Flegrei.

WALKING TOUR

Distance: 3km
Duration: four hours
Starting from Piazza Garibaldi, head a short way down Corso Umberto I before turning right into Via Ranieri and then left into Via dell'Annunziata. A little way down on your left you'll see the **Santissima Annunziata** (1; p51), famous for its orphanage and *ruota*, the wooden wheel where babies were once abandoned. Continue down the street and turn right down Via Forcella. After crossing Via Pietro Colletta, follow the street as it veers left and merges into Via Vicaria Vecchia. Where it meets the busy cross street, Via Duomo, stands the **Basilica di San Giorgio Maggiore** (2; ☎ 081 28 79 32; Via Duomo 237; ☉ 8.15am-noon & 5-7.30pm Mon-Sat, 8.30am-1.30pm Sun) on your left and, two blocks northwest up Via Duomo, the **Duomo** (3; p49). Thousands gather at the majestic Duomo in May, September and December to witness San Gennaro's dried blood miraculously liquefy. Over

NAPLES WALKING TOUR

the road from the cathedral is the entrance to the **Chiesa e Pinacoteca dei Girolamini** (4; p50).

Double back down Via Duomo until you meet Via dei Tribunali. Known to the Romans as the *decumanus maior*, this street runs parallel to the *decumanus inferior*, aka Spaccanapoli, aka Via San Biagio dei Librai. Before heading right into the heart of the *centro storico*, quickly nip left to admire Caravaggio's masterpiece *Le Sette Opere di Misericordia* (The Seven Acts of Mercy) in the **Pio Monte della Misericordia** (5; p45). Before you retrace your steps to Via Duomo, have a quick look at the baroque **Guglia di San Gennaro** (6) in the small square opposite the church.

After you've crossed Via Duomo make for Piazza San Gaetano, about 150m down on the right. The tiny square where the Roman forum once stood is now dominated by the imposing **Chiesa di San Paolo Maggiore** (7; p49). Tucked away to the side is **Napoli Sotterranea** (8; p49). It is here that you enter Naples' extensive underworld. Some 30m to 40m under the surface, the ancient network of tunnels was originally cut out by the

Greeks to extract the tufa stone, but the tunnels were used in WWII as air-raid shelters. Back on the surface, opposite the piazza, is the **Chiesa di San Lorenzo Maggiore** (9; p48). A stark but beautiful Gothic church, it stands atop yet more Roman *scavi* (excavations) and is one of the highlights of the *centro storico*.

It's at this point that you leave Via dei Tribunali and head down **Via San Gregorio Armeno** (10; p47). In December people come from all over Italy to visit the shops that line this street. They specialise in the *presepi* (nativity scenes) that no traditional Italian house is without at Christmas. Along this street you'll also find the **Chiesa e Chiostro di San Gregorio Armeno** (11; p47), famous for its extravagant baroque decor and weekly miracle – the blood of Santa Patrizia is said to liquefy here every Tuesday.

At the end of the road you hit Via San Biagio dei Librai. Turn right and after about 250m you'll be on **Piazzetta Nilo** (12; p48), home to the legendary Statua del Nilo. Less imposing is the altar to footballer Maradona on the wall opposite the statue. Further down on the left, the **Chiesa di Sant'Angelo a Nilo** (13; p49) is home to an exquisite Renaissance tomb.

Cafe-fringed **Piazza San Domenico Maggiore** (14; p47) is home to the imposing **Chiesa di San Domenico Maggiore** (15; p47) and the soaring **Guglia di San Domenico** (16; p47). The not-to-be-missed **Cappella Sansevero** (17; p45) is just off this square in a lane east of the church. A jewel of a chapel, it's home to the mesmerising *Cristo Velato* (Veiled Christ) sculpture.

Back on Via San Biagio dei Librai, the road becomes Via Benedetto Croce and continues west to **Piazza del Gesù Nuovo** (18), the scene of much nightly revelry. The lively piazza is flanked by the **Basilica di Santa Chiara** (19; p44) and the **Chiesa del Gesù Nuovo** (20; p44), while in the centre the **Guglia dell'Immacolata** (21) is a study in baroque excess. The majolica-tiled cloisters of Santa Chiara provide one of the few peaceful spots in the *centro storico*, while the adjoining church stands as testament to the skill of Naples' restoration experts after it was almost completely destroyed by WWII bombs.

Backtrack from the square to the first intersection and turn left along Via San Sebastiano. At the next intersection on your left a short street leads down to book-lined **Port'Alba** (22; right), a city gate built in 1625, then to **Piazza Dante** (23; p56).

Double back the way you came, and ahead of you is Piazza Luigi Miraglia, flanked by Naples' conservatory and the **Chiesa San Pietro a Maiella** (24; p44). Turn back again, and a block to your right is **Piazza Bellini** (25; p44). A great place to rest your weary feet is in one of the piazza's cafes – just don't forget to inspect the remains of the ancient Greek city walls under the square.

EXPLORING NAPLES

CENTRO STORICO & MERCATO

Secret cloisters, cultish shrines and bellowing *pizzaioli* (pizza makers): the *centro storico* is a bewitching urban blend. Its three east–west *decumani* (main streets) follow the original street plan of ancient Neapolis. Most of the major sights are grouped around the busiest two of these classical thoroughfares; 'Spaccanapoli' (consisting of Via Benedetto Croce, Via San Biagio dei Librai and Via Vicaria Vecchia) and Via dei Tribunali. North of Via dei Tribunali, Via della Sapienza, Via Anticaglia and Via Santissimi Apostoli make up the quieter third *decumanus*.

Southeast of the *centro storico* await the shabby, frenetic streets of the Mercato district, a fast and filthy mix of cheap hotels, Chinese spice shops and rough-and-ready markets, including the lip-smacking Mercato di Porta Nolana.

♣ PORT'ALBA // SEEK OUT A LITERARY GEM

A Mediterranean Diagon Alley, **Port'Alba** (Map pp42–3; Via Port'Alba; Ⓜ Dante) is an atmospheric porthole into the *centro storico*, best experienced on weekday afternoons. Crammed with vintage bookshops and stalls, it's the place for leather-bound classics, a dog-eared Manzoni or kitsch Neapolitan postcards. The gate, which leads through to Piazza Dante, was opened in 1625 by Antonio Alvárez, the Spanish viceroy of Naples.

At the eastern end of Via Port'Alba, southbound **Via San Sebastiano** (Map pp42–3) boasts the world's greatest concentration of musical-instrument shops, alongside 49th St in New York.

NAPLES

NAPLES

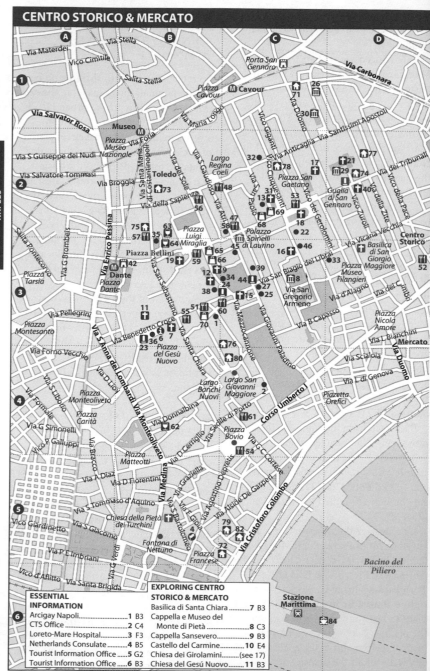

CENTRO STORICO & MERCATO

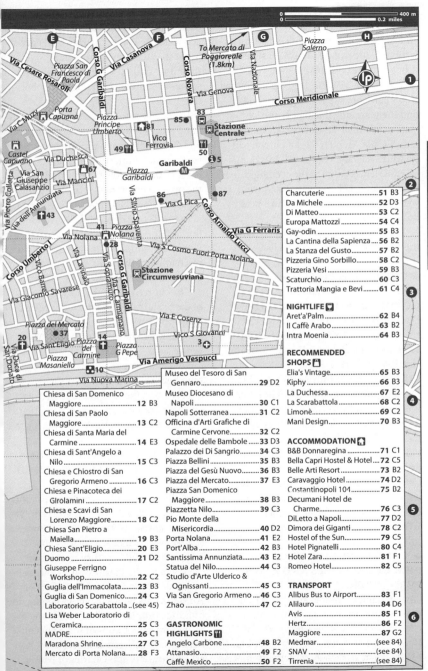

♥ PIAZZA BELLINI // KICK BACK WITH THE BOHEMIANS

One of the best spots to chill with a spritz is this eclectic **square** (Map pp42-3; Ⓜ Dante). A hot spot for bohemians, it's also home to the roguish Mastiffs, the Napoli football club's hardcore supporter group. You'll find them arguing the finer points of football outside their headquarters, between raffish Caffè Arabo (p93) and literary Intra Moenia (p93). For the full Piazza Bellini experience, come in the evening, when its string of bars hums with jazz-loving writers, left-leaning crowds and a healthy dose of flirtatious glances.

The ruins in the centre formed part of the 4th-century Greek city walls.

♥ CHIESA SAN PIETRO A MAIELLA // WITNESS A GOTHIC-BAROQUE STAND-OFF

Dedicated to hermit Pietro del Morrone, upgraded to Pope Celestine V in 1294, this **church** (Map pp42-3; ☎ 081 45 90 08; Piazza Luigi Miraglia 25; ☺ 8am-noon; Ⓜ Dante) is a striking combo of 14th-century Gothic restraint and blingy baroque. The latter is exemplified by its rich wooden ceiling, featuring 10 superlative paintings by Mattia Preti. Further baroque touches are provided by Cosimo Fanzago and Massimo Stanzione, whose *Madonna Appearing to Celestine V* hangs in one of the side chapels on the right. Naples Conservatory – one of Italy's finest music schools – is housed in the adjoining convent.

♥ CHIESA DEL GESÙ NUOVO // PICK UP BAD VIBES AND A HOLY PRESCRIPTION

One of Naples' finest examples of Renaissance architecture, the 16th-century **Chiesa del Gesù Nuovo** (Map pp42-3; ☎ 081 551 86 13; Piazza del Gesù Nuovo; ☺ 7am-1pm & 4-7.30pm; ☒ R4 to Via Monteoliveto) actually sports the 15th-century, Giuseppe Valeriani–designed facade of Palazzo Sanseverino, converted to create the church. Legend has it that the carved markings on its diamond-shaped *piperno* (volcanic rock) stones are subversive esoteric symbols (see p242).

Inside, it's a baroque affair, with greats like Francesco Solimena, Luca Giordano and Cosimo Fanzago transforming the barrel-vaulted interior into the frescoed wonder that you see today. Countering the opulence is a small chapel dedicated to the much-loved local saint Giuseppe Moscati (1880–1927), a good doc who served the city's poor. Here walls heave with *ex votos* (including golden syringes) and a re-creation of the great man's study, complete with the armchair in which he died.

The church lies on the northern side of the beautiful **Piazza del Gesù Nuovo** (Map pp42–3), a favourite late-night hang-out for students and lefties. At its centre soars Giuseppe Genuino's lavish **Guglia dell'Immacolata** (Map pp42–3), built between 1747 and 1750. On 8 December, the feast of the Immacolata, firemen scramble up to the top to place a wreath of flowers at the Virgin Mary's feet.

♥ BASILICA DI SANTA CHIARA // RETREAT TO A MAJOLICA-TILED MARVEL

Vast, Gothic and cleverly deceptive, this mighty **basilica** (Map pp42-3; ☎ 081 1957 5915; Via Benedetto Croce; ☺ 9am-1pm & 4.30-7.30pm Mon-Sat, 8am-1pm & 5.30-7.30pm Sun; Ⓜ Dante) is actually a 20th-century re-creation of Gagliardo Primario's 14th-century original. Commissioned by Robert of Anjou for his wife Sancia di Maiorca, the hulking complex was built to house 200 monks and the tombs of the Angevin royal family. Dissed as a 'stable' by Robert's ungrateful son Charles of Anjou, it received a luscious baroque makeover by Domenico Antonio Vaccaro, Gaetano Buonocore and Giovanni Del Gaizo four centuries later, before taking a direct hit during an Allied air raid on 4 August 1943. Features that survived the fire include part of a 14th-century fresco to the left of the main door and a chapel containing the tombs of the Bourbon kings from Ferdinand I to Francesco II.

To the left of the church are the glorious tiled **cloisters** (adult/concession €5/3.50; 9.30am-5.30pm Mon-Sat, to 1.30pm Sun). While the Angevin porticoes date back to the 14th century, the cloisters took on their current look in the 18th century thanks to the landscaping work of Domenico Antonio Vaccaro. The walkways that divide the central garden of lavender and citrus trees are lined with 72 ceramic-tiled octagonal columns connected by benches. Painted by Donato e Giuseppe Massa, the colourful tiles depict various rural scenes, from hunting to vignettes of peasant life. The four internal walls are covered with softly coloured 17th-century frescoes of Franciscan tales.

Adjacent to the cloisters, a small and elegant museum of mostly ecclesiastical props also features the excavated ruins of a 1st-century spa complex, including a remarkably well-preserved *laconicum* (sauna).

❧ PIO MONTE DELLA MISERICORDIA // MEDITATE ON CARAVAGGIO'S MASTERPIECE

Caravaggio's masterpiece *Le Sette Opere di Misericordia* (The Seven Acts of Mercy) is considered by many to be the single most important painting in Naples. And it's here that you'll see it, hung above the main altar of this small octagonal **church** (Map pp42-3; ☎ 081 44 69 44; www.piomontedella misericordia.it; Via dei Tribunali 253; admission free;

church 9am-2pm Thu-Tue; ☐ CS to Via Duomo). Magnificently demonstrating Caravaggio's chiaroscuro style, which had a revolutionary impact in Naples (see p249), the composition was considered unique in its ability to illustrate the various acts in one seamlessly choreographed scene.

On the 1st floor of the 17th-century church, a small **art gallery** (9am-2pm Thu-Tue; admission €5) boasts a fine collection of Renaissance and baroque paintings by the likes of Francesco de Mura, Giuseppe de Ribera and Paul van Somer.

❧ CAPPELLA E MUSEO DEL MONTE DI PIETÀ // ENJOY THE FRUITS OF INTEREST RATES

An imposing 16th-century complex, the **Cappella e Museo del Monte di Pietà** (Map pp42-3; ☎ 081 580 71 11; Via San Biagio dei Librai 114; admission free; 9am-7pm Sat, to 2pm Sun; ☐ CS to Via Duomo) was originally home to the Pio Monte di Pietà, an organisation set up to issue interest-free loans to impoverished debtors. Ironically, it now houses sumptuous paintings, embroidery and silverware belonging to the Banco di Napoli (Bank of Naples).

Most impressive, however, is the perfectly preserved mannerist chapel and its four richly decorated side rooms. Flanking the entrance to the single-barrel chapel are two sculptures by Pietro Bernini, while above sits Michelangelo Naccherino's *Pietà*. Inside, it's the striking 17th-century frescoes by Belisario Corenzio that take the breath away.

❧ CAPPELLA SANSEVERO // PONDER MAGIC IN AN ALCHEMIST'S BOLT-HOLE

For sheer how-the-hell-did-he-do-it impact, the *Cristo Velato* (Veiled Christ) sculpture at this Masonic-inspired **chapel** (Map pp42-3; ☎ 081 551 84 70; Via de Sanctis 19;

adult/10-25yr €6/4; ⊗ 10am-5.40pm Mon & Wed-Sat, to 1.10pm Sun, closed Tue; Ⓜ Dante) takes some beating. Giuseppe Sanmartino's incredible depiction of Jesus lying covered by a thin sheet is so realistic that it's tempting to try to lift the veil and look at Christ underneath.

The magnificent centrepiece of this opulent building is one of three works that defy belief. Similarly life-like, Francesco Queirolo's *Disinganno* (Disillusion) shows a man trying to untangle himself from a net, while *Pudicizia* (Modesty) by Antonio Corradini is a deliciously salacious veiled nude. Above them all you'll find riotously colourful frescoes by Francesco Maria Russo.

Originally built around the end of the 16th century to house the tombs of the di Sangro family, the chapel was given its current baroque fitout by the bizarre Prince Raimondo di Sangro (see p242). Between 1749 and 1766 he commissioned the top artists of the day to decorate the interior, while he quietly got on with the task of embalming his dead servants. Determined to crack the art of human preservation, Raimondo was regarded with considerable fear by the local population. You can judge for yourself whether they were right by going down the stairs and checking out the two meticulously preserved human arterial systems.

～ WORTH A TRIP ～

An easy 25km north of Naples, the modest town of Caserta is home to the colossal **Palazzo Reale** (Royal Palace; ☎ 0823 44 80 84; Via Douhet 22, Caserta; palace & grounds adult/EU 18-25yr/EU under 18yr & over 65yr €10/5/free, palace only €8/4/free; ⊗ 8.30am-7pm Wed-Mon). Commonly known as the Reggia di Caserta, this Unesco-listed palace is not only bigger than Versailles, it's one of the greatest – and last – achievements of Italian baroque architecture. It was also a shooting location for *Mission: Impossible 3*, *Star Wars Episode 1: The Phantom Menace* and *Star Wars Episode 2: Attack of the Clones*.

Commissioned by Charles VII of Bourbon and designed by Neapolitan Luigi Vanvitelli, work on 'la Reggia' commenced in 1752. The lavish royal apartments are richly decorated with tapestries, furniture and crystal. Beyond the library is a room containing a vast collection of hand-carved *presepi* (nativity scenes).

The **landscaped grounds** (⊗ 8.30am-7pm Wed-Mon Jun-Aug, to 5.30pm May & Sep, to 6pm Apr, to 4.30pm Oct, to 4pm Mar, to 3.30pm Nov-Feb, last entry 1hr before closing) stretch out for some 3km to a waterfall and fountain of Diana and the exquisite **Giardino Inglese** (English Garden; ⊗ 9am-5pm Wed-Mon Jun-Aug, 8.30am-3.30pm May & Sep, 8.30am-4pm Apr, 8.30am-2.30pm Oct, 8.30am-2pm Mar, 8.30am-1.30pm Nov-Feb, tours 9.30am-1pm). The weary can cover the same ground in a pony and trap (from €5) or for €1 you can hire a bike. Within the palace, the **Mostra Terrea Motus** (admission free with palace ticket; ⊗ 9am-6pm Wed-Mon) documents the 1980 earthquake that devastated the region.

CTP buses connect Caserta with Naples' Piazza Garibaldi (daily ticket €5.70) about every 35 minutes between 6am and 9pm, with hourly services on Sunday. Some Benevento services also stop in Caserta. Trains from Naples also reach the town (daily ticket €5.70). Both bus and train stations are near the palace entrance, signposted from each. Drivers should follow the signs for 'Reggia'.

NAPLES

❧ PIAZZA SAN DOMENICO MAGGIORE // BAROQUE GRATITUDE, A MURDEROUS TALE AND SLUMBERING ANGEVINS

A particular hit with lounging dread-locked students, this gracious **square** (Map pp42–3; Ⓜ Dante) has its fair share of icons. Taking centre stage is the flouncy **Guglia di San Domenico** (Map pp42–3). Decorated by baroque superstar Cosimo Fanzago and completed in 1737 by Domenico Antonio Vaccaro, it was a *grazie* (thanks) to San Domenico for ending the plague epidemic of 1656.

To the east at No 9, **Palazzo dei Di Sangrio** is best known for a gruesome crime of passion in which 16th-century Neapolitan musician Carlo Gesualdo murdered his wife, Maria d'Avalos, and her hunky bit on the side, Don Fabrizio (see p242) in 1590.

More upbeat is the Gothic **Chiesa di San Domenico Maggiore** (Map pp42–3; ☎ 081 45 91 88; Piazza San Domenico Maggiore 8a; ⏱ 8.30am–noon & 4.30-7pm), whose curious nave flanks the piazza's northern edge. See a face in the facade? You're not going crazy: it was an intentional add-on, created to 'shush' the church's derrière once the piazza was created.

Built onto the medieval church of San Michele Arcangelo, this was the royal church of the Angevins, completed in 1324 on the orders of Charles I of Anjou. Of the few 14th-century remnants surviving the countless makeovers, the frescoes by Pietro Cavallini in the Cappella Brancaccio take the cake. In the Cappellone del Crocifisso, the 13th-century *Crocifisso tra La Vergine e San Giovanni* is said to have spoken to St Thomas Aquinas, asking him: *'Bene scripsisti di me, Thoma; quam recipies a me pro tu labore mercedem?'* ('You've written good things about me, Thomas, what will you get in return?') – *'Domine, non aliam nisi te'* ('Nothing if not you, O Lord'), Thomas replied diplomatically.

The **sacristy** features a beautiful ceiling fresco by Francesco Solimena and 45 coffins of Aragon princes and other nobles. Curiously enough, the first bishop of New York, Richard Luke Concanen (1747–1810), is also buried here.

❧ VIA SAN GREGORIO ARMENO // STOCK UP FOR A NEAPOLITAN CHRISTMAS

Naples is famous for its traditional *presepi* (nativity scenes) and this atmospheric street of **artisans' studios** (Map pp42–3; 🚌 CS to Via Duomo) is where Italians come to buy theirs. Running off Spaccanapoli, the strip heaves with brush-clutching crib-makers who craft an eclectic range of figurines and nativity-scene pieces, from hand-carved baby saviours to kitsch celebrity caricatures. At No 8 you'll find the workshop of **Giuseppe Ferrigno**, whose terracotta figurines are sought by collectors worldwide.

❧ CHIESA E CHIOSTRO DI SAN GREGORIO ARMENO // OD ON OUTRAGEOUS BAROQUE

Overstatement knows no bounds at this excessively baroque 16th-century **church** (Map pp42–3; ☎ 081 420 63 85; Via San Gregorio Armeno 44; ⏱ church 9.30am–noon Mon-Sat, to 1pm Sun; 🚌 CS to Via Duomo). Lap up the lavish wood and papier-mâché choir stalls, Dionisio Lazzarn's 17th-century marble and Luca Giordano's masterpiece *The Embarkation, Journey and Arrival of the Armenia Nuns with the Relics of St Gregory*, which recounts the 13th-century exile of nuns fleeing persecution in Constantinople. Once in Naples, the holy escapees set up this church, naming it after the Bishop of Armenia, San Gregorio, whose earthly remains they were carrying with them. More famously, though, they also kept the relics and dried blood of Santa Patrizia (St Patricia), who, having escaped from Constantinople, died in Naples sometime between the 4th and 8th centuries. Patricia's powdered blood is said to liquefy every Tuesday, unlike that of Naples' patron saint, San Gennaro, who can only manage it three times a year.

Accessible by a gate on nearby Vicolo Giuseppe Maffei, the superb, citrus-filled **cloisters** (⏱ 9.30am-noon Mon-Sat, to 1pm Sun) feature a whimsical baroque fountain embellished with masks, dolphins and sea horses, and two exquisite statues portraying Christ and the Samaritan by Matteo Bottigliero.

♥ PIAZZETTA NILO // PAY HOMAGE TO THE GODS

Don't let the dusty appearance fool you. This little **square** (Map pp42-3; Piazzetta Nilo, Via Nilo; Ⓜ Dante) is a hang-out for local deities. First up is the **Statua del Nilo** (Map pp42–3), a rather grim statue of the ancient Egyptian river god Nilo. Erected by the city's Alexandrian merchants, who lived in the area during Roman times, it disappeared when the expats moved out, eventually turning up headless in the 15th century. Renamed *Il Corpo di Napoli* (The Body of Naples), its great bearded bonce was added in the 18th century.

Opposite the statue, on the wall outside Bar Nilo, Argentine football player and ex-Napoli superstar Diego Armando Maradona is worshipped with his own small **shrine** (Map pp42–3). Stuck to an epic poem written in his honour is a small, wiry black hair – 'Kapel Original of Maradona' reads the English label, a direct translation of the Italian *Capello originale di Maradona*. The small con-

tainer is full of genuine Maradona tears…and shame on anyone who suggests it's only water. Less charitable is Bar Nilo's request that people buy a coffee before taking a snap.

♥ OSPEDALE DELLE BAMBOLE // CHEER UP A DOWNTRODDEN DOLL

It's a case of Geppetto meets David Lynch at this fairy-lit **dolls' hospital** (Map pp42-3; ☎ 339 5872274; Via San Biagio dei Librai 81; 🚌 CS to Via Duomo), a pocket-sized workshop where dismembered dolls with vacant stares console injured saints and flower-sprouting mannequins. Dusty, vintage and oh-so-slightly macabre, it's the very essence of this city.

♥ CHIESA E SCAVI DI SAN LORENZO MAGGIORE // TIME TRAVEL BENEATH A GOTHIC CHURCH

Ancient ruins beneath a French Gothic marvel, the **Chiesa e Scavi di San Lorenzo** (Map pp42-3; ☎ 081 211 08 60; www .sanlorenzomaggiorenapoli.it; Via dei Tribunali 316; excavations & museum adult/under 18yr and over 65yr €5/3; ⏱ 9.30am-5.30pm Mon-Sat, to 1.30pm Sun; 🚌 CS to Via Duomo) is unmissable, especially since the 2009 expansion of the extraordinary subterranean **scavi** (excavations). Here you can conjure up the Graeco-Roman city as you walk past ancient bakeries, wineries and communal laundries. At the far end of the *cardo* (road) there's a *cryptoporticus* (covered market) with seven barrel-vaulted rooms. (It's worth buying the glossy leaflet explaining the excavations in Italian or English for €1.50.)

Back at current street level, the **church** itself was commenced in 1270 by French architects, who built the apse. Local architects took over the following century, recycling ancient columns in the nave.

A later baroque makeover was stripped back in the mid-20th century, although a concession was made for Ferdinando Sanfelice's petite baroque facade. Catherine of Austria, who died in 1323, is buried here in a beautiful mosaicked tomb. Legend has it that this was where Boccaccio first fell for Mary of Anjou, the inspiration for his character Fiammetta, while the poet Petrarch called the adjoining convent home in 1345.

The religious complex is also home to the **Museo dell'Opera di San Lorenzo Maggiore** and its intriguing booty of local archaeological finds, including Graeco-Roman sarcophagi, ceramics and crockery from the digs below. Other treasures include vivid 9th-century ceramics, Angevin frescoes, paintings by Giuseppe Marullo and Luigi Velpi, and camp ecclesiastical drag for 16th-century bishops.

🍴 NAPOLI SOTTERRANEA // TAKE A WALK ON THE DARK SIDE

From ancient caves and aqueducts to air-raid hideouts, Naples' subterranean otherworld is a mysterious, magical place. For an easy, crash-course tour, join the queue at **Napoli Sotterranea** (Underground Naples; Map pp42-3; ☎ 081 29 69 44; www.napolisotterranea.org; Piazza San Gaetano 68; tours €9.30; 🕑 90min tours noon, 2pm & 4pm Mon-Fri, extra tours 10am & 6pm Sat & Sun, 9pm Thu; 🚌 CS to Via Duomo), where guides take you 40m below the streets to explore the city's eerie labyrinth. For more on the city's subterranean secrets, see p244.

🍴 CHIESA DI SAN PAOLO MAGGIORE // PERFECT PAINTINGS AND A JEWEL-BOX SACRISTY

Baroque splendour awaits at the top of Francesco Grimaldi's 1603 diva double staircase. Here, the entrance to the **Chiesa di San Paolo Maggiore** (Map pp42-3; ☎ 081 45 40 48; Piazza San Gaetano 76; 🕑 9am-1pm & 3-6pm Mon-Fri, 9am-1pm Sat, to 12.30pm Sun; 🚌 CS to Via Duomo) is flanked by two columns hailing from the Roman temple to Castor and Pollux that stood on the site. The church itself dates to the 8th century but was almost entirely rebuilt at the end of the 16th century, its huge, gold-stuccoed interior featuring paintings by Massimo Stanzione and Paolo De Matteis and a striking geometric floor by Nicola Tammaro. Best of all is the sumptuous **sacristy**. Tucked away to the right of the altar, its crowning glory is luminous frescoes by baroque meister Francesco Solimena.

🍴 CHIESA DI SANT'ANGELO A NILO // REVERE A RENAISSANCE MASTERPIECE

Benignly presided over by a quartet of tubby gilt cherubs, this modest 14th-century **church** (Map pp42-3; ☎ 081 420 12 22; entrance at Vico Donnaromita 15; 🕑 9am-1pm & 4-6pm Mon-Sat, 9am-1pm Sun; 🚌 R4 to Via Monteoliveto) contains one of the first great art works to grace the Neapolitan Renaissance – the majestic tomb of Cardinal Brancaccio, the church's founder. Although considered a part of Naples' artistic heritage, the sarcophagus was actually sculpted by artists in Pisa. Donatello, Michelozzo and Pagno di Lapo Partigiani spent a year chipping away at it before shipping it down to Naples in 1427.

🍴 DUOMO // MIRACLES, MASTERPIECES AND EUROPE'S OLDEST BAPTISTRY

Home to the thrice-annual miracle of San Gennaro (see p240), Naples' **cathedral** (Map pp42-3; ☎ 081 44 90 97; www.duomo dinapoli.com; Via Duomo 147; 🕑 8am-12.30pm & 4.30-7pm Mon-Sat, 8.30am-1pm & 5-7pm Sun; 🚌 CS to Via Duomo) is the city's spiritual centrepiece.

Sitting on the site of earlier churches, themselves preceded by a pagan temple to Neptune, its construction was initiated by Charles I of Anjou in 1272. Consecrated in 1315, it was largely destroyed in a 1456 earthquake, while copious nips and tucks over the centuries, including the addition of a late-19th-century neo-Gothic facade, have created today's intriguing soup of styles.

Topping the central nave is a gilded coffered ceiling studded with late-mannerist art. The high sections of the nave and the transept were decorated by Luca Giordano.

The 17th-century **Cappella di San Gennaro** (Chapel of St Januarius, also known as the Chapel of the Treasury) was designed by Giovanni Cola di Franco and completed in 1637. The most celebrated artists of the period worked on the chapel, creating one of the city's finest baroque legacies. Highlights here include Giuseppe de Ribera's gripping canvas *St Gennaro Escaping the Furnace Unscathed* and Giovanni Lanfranco's dizzying dome fresco. Hidden away in a strongbox behind the altar is a 14th-century silver bust in which sits the skull of San Gennaro and the two phials that hold his miraculously liquefying blood.

The next chapel eastwards contains an urn with the saint's bones and a cupboard full of femurs, tibias and fibulas. Below the high altar is the **Cappella Carafa**, a Renaissance chapel built to house yet more of the saint's remains.

On the north aisle sits one of Naples' oldest basilicas, dating to the 4th century. Incorporated into the main cathedral, the **Basilica di Santa Restituta** was subject to an almost complete makeover after the earthquake of 1688. Beyond this lurks the Duomo's **archaeological zone** (admission €3; ⏱ 9am-noon & 4.30-7pm Mon-Sat,

9am-noon Sun), which showcases fascinating remains of Greek and Roman buildings and roads. Here, too, is the baptistry, the oldest in Western Europe, with its glittering 4th-century mosaics.

If you're intrigued by Naples' cultish love affair with San Gennaro, consider popping into the Duomo's adjacent **Museo del Tesoro di San Gennaro** (Map pp42-3; ☎ 081 29 49 80; Via Duomo 149; incl entry to Pio Monte della Misericordia adult/EU under 18yr & over 65yr €6/4.50; ⏱ 9.30am-5pm Tue-Sat, to 2.30pm Sun), whose glittering collection of precious *ex voto* gifts includes bronze busts, silver ampullae, sumptuous paintings and a gilded 18th-century sedan chair used to shelter the saint's bust on rainy procession days.

🌹 CHIESA E PINACOTECA DEI GIROLAMINI // SEEK ART AND LEMON-SCENTED SOLACE
Also called San Filippo Neri, the richly baroque **Chiesa dei Girolamini** (Map pp42-3; ☎ 081 44 91 39; Via Duomo 142; ⏱ vary; 🚌 CS to Via Duomo) features two facades; the more imposing 18th-century option can be admired from Piazza dei Girolamini on Via dei Tribunali. The real highlights, however, are next door in the 17th-century convent. The first is the beautiful main **cloister** (⏱ 9.30am-12.30pm Mon-Sat), complete with rambling citrus trees, faded majolica tiles and twittering birdsong. The second awaits upstairs, where a peaceful **art gallery** (admission free; ⏱ 9.30am-12.30pm Mon-Sat) boasts some superb local art from greats like Luca Giordano, Battista Caracciolo and Giuseppe de Ribera.

🌹 MADRE (MUSEO D'ARTE CONTEMPORANEA DONNAREGINA) // TAKE A BREAK FROM THE CLASSICS
Ditch old-school masters at Naples' slick **contemporary art museum** (Map

pp42-3; ☎ 081 193 130 16; www.museomadre.it; Via Settembrini 79; adult/concession €7/3.50, Mon free; ⏲ 10am-9pm Mon & Wed-Fri, to midnight Sat & Sun, closed Tue; Ⓜ Cavour), designed by Portuguese architect Alvaro Siza y Vieira and housed in the historic Palazzo Donnaregina. While the ground and 3rd floors host temporary exhibitions, the 1st floor is home to specially commissioned installations from top guns such as Francesco Clemente, Anish Kapoor and Rebecca Horn. Head up another floor for the main chunk of MADRE's collection, where a mix of painting, photography, sculpture and installations spans global stars including Mario Merz, Damien Hirst and current 'It kid' Olafur Eliasson. Check the website for special events, which sometimes include jazz soirées.

❤ MUSEO DIOCESANO DI NAPOLI // GLORIOUS ART IN AN EQUALLY GLORIOUS CHURCH-TURNED-GALLERY

The Chiesa di Santa Maria Donnaregina Nuova is back as the newly opened Diocesan Museum of Naples (Map pp42-3; ☎ 081 557 13 65; www.museodiocesanonapoli.it; Chiesa di Santa Maria Donnaregina Nuova, Largo Donnaregina; adult/concession €5/4; ⏲ 9.30am-4.30pm Mon & Wed-Sat, to 2pm Sun, closed Tue; Ⓜ Cavour). Here, splendid baroque architecture meets a stylishly curated collection of religiously themed art, from Renaissance triptychs and 19th-century wooden sculptures, to works from baroque masters including Fabrizio Santafede, Andrea Vaccaro and the mighty Luca Giordano, whose final canvases hang on either side of the church's main altar. Housed on two floors, the collection also boasts treasures like Paolo De Matteis's *San Sebastiano Curato dalle Pie Donne* (St Sebastian Attended to by the Pious Women) and a young Francesco Solimena's fresco

Il Miracolo delle Rose di San Francesco (The Miracle of the Roses of St Francis), above the church's presbytery.

❤ SANTISSIMA ANNUNZIATA // PONDER A WHEEL OF FATE, THEN SNEAK INTO VANVITELLI'S BEST-KEPT SECRET

Artistic highs meet historical lows at this intriguing, 14th-century religious complex, whose **basilica** (Map pp42-3; ☎ 081 254 26 08; Via dell'Annunziata 34; ⏲ 8am-noon & 5.30-7.30pm Mon-Sat, 7.30am-1pm Sun; 🚌 R2 to Corso Umberto I) was significantly restructured by Luigi Vanvitelli and his son Carlo after a devastating fire in 1757 (the soaring 67m-high cupola is one of their additions). Luckily, the 1580 **sacristy** (to the right of the impressive nave) survived the blaze. Here, exquisitely carved wooden armoires by Girolamo D'Auria and Salvatore Caccavello depict New Testament scenes, while vault frescoes by Belisario Corenzio take care of Old Testament tales. If the sacristy is closed, seek out sacristan Costantino Esposito, who can open it for you.

Another flame survivor is the wooden *mamma chiatta* (chubby mother), a sculpture of the Virgin Mary in the third chapel to the left of the nave. Its image was once reproduced on the leaden medals worn by the children left at the **former orphanage** (☎ 081 28 90 32; ⏲ 9am-6pm Mon-Sat), to the left of the basilica. Here you can still see the infamous **ruota** (wheel) set in the orphanage wall, in use up until the 1980s. Desperate parents would place the baby in a hollow in the wheel and turn it. On the other side of the wall sat a nun ready to take the baby, wash it in the adjacent basin and record its time and date of entry.

Continue through into the building's main courtyard, where the first door on

SECRET ARTISAN STUDIOS

Down dark streets, behind unmarked doors, in unsuspecting courtyards, artisan studios litter the *centro storico*. In these secret bolt holes, some of Naples' most intriguing artists celebrate, reinterpret and sometimes subvert Neapolitan traditions – think meticulously crafted nativity statues to pop portraits of a scooter-riding Holy Family. Dive into the city's idiosyncratic arts scene at the following locations:

Studio d'Arte Ulderico e Ognissanti (Map pp42-3; ☎ 320 0609909, 339 5830537; ulderico mare@libero.it; Studio 4, Via Nilo 34; ☯ 10am-7pm Mon-Fri; Ⓜ Dante) Hailing from Naples' underground art movement of the 1980s, this eclectic duo paint, sculpt and film their way through Neapolitan stereotypes, creating anything from tongue-in-cheek 'Pulcinella is dead' sculptures to playful portraits of local saints.

Laboratorio Scarabattola (Map pp42-3; ☎ 081 29 17 35; ☯ 11am-2pm & 4-6pm Mon-Fri, 11am-2pm Sat) On the opposite side of the same courtyard, this two-level workshop is where a charming team of siblings (and relatives) fire, paint and sew exquisite *presepe*-style sculptures for their shop La Scarabattola (p95). Melding 18th-century techniques with a modern sensibility, their attention to detail has won them worldwide acclaim.

Lisa Weber Laboratorio di Ceramica (Map pp42-3; ☎ 334 8410039; Via Giovanni Paladino 4; ☯ 11am-1.30pm & 5-7pm Tue-Fri, 11am-1.30pm Sat, 5-7pm Mon, closed Sun & Aug; Ⓜ Dante) This is

the right-hand wall leads into a small art-gallery space. Sneak through the red curtains on your left and feast your eyes on Carlo Vanvitelli's round, vaulted **crypt** (☯ 8am-noon & 5.30-7.30pm Mon-Sat, 7.30am-1pm Sun), complete with six altars. The main altar features a statue of *Madonna and Child* by Domenico Gagini, set against stucco work by Giuseppe Sanmartino, creator of the incredible *Cristo Velato* inside the Cappella Sansevero (p45).

♥ MERCATO DI PORTA NOLANA // WHET YOUR APPETITE AND BAG A BARGAIN

Naples at its vociferous, gut-rumbling best, the **Porta Nolana street market** (Map pp42-3; ☯ 8am-6pm Mon-Sat, to 2pm Sun; ☐ R2 to Corso Umberto I) is a must! Here, bellowing fishmongers and *frutti vendoli* (greengrocers) collide with fragrant delis and bakeries, industrious Chinese traders and contraband cigarette stalls. It's

a mesmering place where you can pick up anything from buxom tomatoes and mozzarella to golden-fried street snacks, cheap luggage or that bootleg '80s compilation CD you've been pining for.

The market's namesake is medieval city gate **Porta Nolana** (Map pp42–3), which stands at the head of Via Sopramuro. Its two cylindrical towers, optimistically named Faith and Hope, support an arch decorated with a bas-relief of Ferdinand I of Aragon on horseback.

♥ CHIESA DI SANTA MARIA DEL CARMINE // VISIT A HOTBED OF MIRACLES AND MURDERS

Doting mothers, political drama and the odd miracle: it's little wonder that this veteran **church** (Map pp42-3; ☎ 081 20 11 96; Piazza del Carmine; ☯ 7am-noon & 4.45-7.30pm Mon-Sat, 7am-1pm & 4.30-7.30pm Sun; ☐ C55 to Corso Giuseppe Garibaldi) plays a starring role in Neapolitan folklore. According to

the earthy workshop of Swiss-expat ceramicist Lisa Weber, whose creations span playfully translucent candle holders and Pompeii-esque terracotta vases and jugs, to whimsical teasets and lamps.

Zhao (Map pp42–3; ☎ 329 3469011; www.zhao.it, in Italian; Via Atri 31; ⏰ vary; Ⓜ Dante) In a tiny studio opened with a giant 18th-century key, sculptor and painter Salvatore Vitagliano takes fragments of ancient terracotta figurines and completes them, creating simple yet striking works that literally fuse old and new. This theme of 'temporal collision' extends to his Neapolitan playing cards, handpainted onto metro tickets. Call ahead to visit, though it's worth noting that Salvatore doesn't speak English.

Officina D'Arti Grafiche di Carmine Cervone (Map pp42–3; ☎ 081 29 54 83; carmine. cervone@libero.it; Via Anticaglia 12; ⏰ 9.30am-2pm & 3-6.30pm Mon-Sat; Ⓜ Cavour) Lovers of print and typography shouldn't miss Carmine's one-of-a-kind printing workshop, crammed with rare vintage machinery, including a late-19th-century linotype machine. That Carmine speaks little English never detracts from the young gun's passion for his craft and his love of showing it off. Indeed, he often collaborates with artists, producing limited-edition prints, lithographs and books. Best of all, he can even design and print you a one-of-a-kind business card or invitations (allow two days) if you fancy your own take-home memento.

NAPLES

legend, when Conrad (Corradino) of Swabia was charged for attempting to depose Charles I of Anjou in 1268, his mother, Elisabetta di Baviera, desperately tried to collect the money required to free her son. Alas, the money arrived too late, Conrad lost his head and his grief-stricken mamma handed the cash to the church (on the condition that the Carmelite brothers prayed for him every day). They agreed, the church went up and a monument to Conrad still remains in the transept. Yet Christ's own mother is the real protagonist here. Represented by a 13th-century Byzantine icon behind the main altar, the *Madonna della Bruna* has miraculous powers attributed to it. It's celebrated every year on 16 July when crowds flock here to watch fireworks leap from the 17th-century campanile, the city's tallest.

As for the wooden crucifix hanging in tabernacle beneath the church's main arch, it apparently dodged a cannonball fired at the church in 1439 during the war between Alfonso of Aragon and Robert of Anjou.

Just northwest of the church and Piazza del Carmine, the **Piazza del Mercato** (Map pp42–3) has a less fortunate past. The starting point for the deadly plague of 1656, it was here that over 200 supporters of the ill-fated Parthenopean Republic of 1799 were systematically executed.

At the southern end of the square, on the opposite side of busy Via Nuova Marina, stand remnants of the city's 14th-century medieval fortress, **Castello del Carmine** (Map pp42–3).

One block west along Via Sant'Eligio, the **Chiesa Sant'Eligio** (Map pp42–3; ☎ 081 553 84 29; Via Sant'Eligio; ⏰ 9am-1pm Mon-Sun) was the first Angevin church in Naples. Built in 1270 by Charles I of Anjou, it features a beautiful external arch adorned with a 15th-century clock.

TOLEDO & QUARTIERI SPAGNOLI

Constructed by Spanish viceroy Don Pedro de Toledo in the 16th century, *palazzo*-flanked Via Toledo (also known as Via Roma) is Naples' veritable high street and a popular strip for an evening *passeggiata* (stroll). Capped by buzzing Piazza Trento e Trieste at its southern end, it becomes Via Enrico Pessina further north, skimming past Piazza Dante and the Museo Archeologico Nazionale on its way towards Capodimonte.

Directly west of Via Toledo lie the razor-thin streets of the Quartieri Spagnoli (Spanish Quarter), originally built to house Don Pedro's Spanish troops. Low on sights per se, its washing-strung streets harbour hidden delights, from raucous trattorias and progressive cultural hang-outs, to the unmissable Pignasecca market. With an eye on your bag, dive in for a serve of pure *Napoli popolana* (working-class Naples).

♥ MUSEO ARCHEOLOGICO NAZIONALE // FEAST ON WORLD-CLASS ANCIENT BOOTY

Boasting many of the best finds from Pompeii and Herculaneum, priceless classical sculptures and a trove of ancient Roman porn, the **National Archaeological Museum** (Map p55; ☎ 081 44 01 66; www.marketplacc.it/museo.nazionale; Piazza Museo Nazionale 19; adult/EU 18-25yr/EU under 18yr & over 65yr €6.50/3.25/free; ☺ 9am-7.30pm Wed-Mon; Ⓜ Museo) is unmissable. Originally a cavalry barracks, the museum was established by the Bourbon king Charles VII in the late 18th century to house the rich collection of antiquities he had inherited from his mother, Elisabetta Farnese. Before tackling the four floors of galleries – numbered in Roman numerals – it's worth investing €7.50 in the green quick-guide *National Archaeological Museum of Naples* or, to concentrate on the highlights, €4 for an audioguide in English. It's also worth calling ahead to ensure the galleries you want to see are open, as staff shortages often mean that sections of the museum close for part of the day.

While the basement houses the Borgia collection of Egyptian relics and epigraphs, the ground-floor Farnese collection of colossal Greek and Roman sculptures includes the mighty *Toro Farnese* (Farnese Bull) in Room XVI and the muscle-bound *Ercole* (Hercules) in Room XI. Sculpted in the early 3rd century AD and noted in the writings of Pliny, the *Toro Farnese*, probably a Roman copy of a Greek original, depicts the death of Dirce, Queen of Thebes. According to Greek mythology she was tied to a wild bull by Zeto and Amphion as punishment for her treatment of their mother Antiope, the first wife of King Lykos of Thebes. Carved from a single colossal block of marble, the sculpture was discovered in 1545 near the Baths of Caracalla in Rome and was restored by Michelangelo, before eventually being shipped to Naples in 1787.

Ercole was discovered in the same Roman dig and like the *Toro Farnese* remained in Rome until 1787. Originally without legs, *Ercole* had a new pair made for him by Guglielmo della Porta. In fact the story goes that the Farnese were so impressed with della Porta's work that they refused to reinstate the original legs when they were subsequently found. The Bourbons, however, had no such qualms and later attached the originals in their rightful place. You can see the della Porta legs displayed on the wall behind *Ercole*.

TOLEDO & QUARTIERI SPAGNOLI

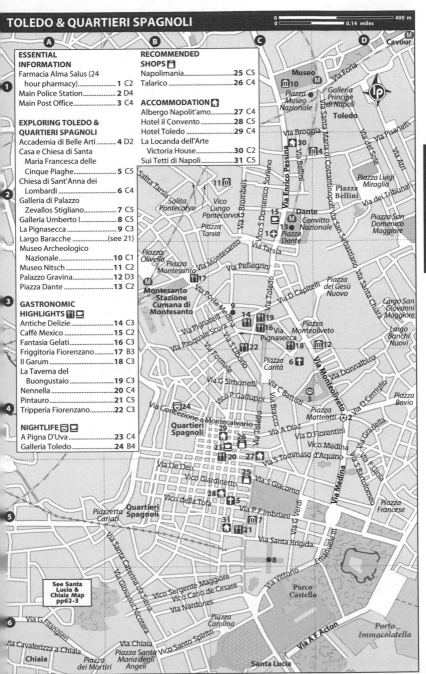

ESSENTIAL INFORMATION
Farmacia Alma Salus (24 hour pharmacy)................. **1** C2
Main Police Station........................ **2** D4
Main Post Office............................. **3** C4

EXPLORING TOLEDO & QUARTIERI SPAGNOLI
Accademia di Belle Arti **4** D2
Casa e Chiesa di Santa Maria Francesca delle Cinque Piaghe..................... **5** C5
Chiesa di Sant'Anna dei Lombardi........................ **6** C4
Galleria di Palazzo Zevallos Stigliano............. **7** C5
Galleria Umberto I.................. **8** C5
La Pignasecca......................... **9** C3
Largo Baracche.................(see 21)
Museo Archeologico Nazionale......................**10** C1
Museo Nitsch **11** C2
Palazzo Gravina......................**12** D3
Piazza Dante..........................**13** C2

GASTRONOMIC HIGHLIGHTS
Antiche Delizie.......................**14** C3
Caffè Mexico **15** C2
Fantasia Gelati.......................**16** C3
Friggitoria Fiorenzano...........**17** B3
Il Garum **18** C3
La Taverna del Buongustaio **19** C3
Nennella.................................**20** C4
Pintauro.................................**21** C5
Tripperia Fiorenzano..............**22** C3

NIGHTLIFE
A Pigna D'Uva........................**23** C4
Galleria Toledo **24** B4

RECOMMENDED SHOPS
Napolimania............................**25** C5
Talarico **26** C4

ACCOMMODATION
Albergo Napolit'amo..............**27** C4
Hotel il Convento **28** C5
Hotel Toledo **29** C4
La Locanda dell'Arte Victoria House....................**30** C2
Sui Tetti di Napoli..................**31** C5

NAPLES

The mezzanine floor houses exquisite mosaics from Pompeii. Of the series taken from the Casa del Fauno, it is *La Battaglia di Alessandro Contro Dario* (The Battle of Alexander against Darius) in Room LXI that stands out. The best-known depiction of Alexander the Great, the 20-sq-metre mosaic was probably made by Alexandrian craftsmen working in Italy around the end of the 2nd century BC. Other intriguing mosaics include that of a feline killing a duck in Room LX and a study of Nile animals in Room LXIII.

Beyond the mosaics, the **Gabinetto Segreto** (Secret Chamber) contains a small but much-studied collection of ancient erotica. Guarding the entrance is a marble statue of a lascivious-looking Pan draped over a very coy Daphne. Pan is then caught in the act, this time with a nanny goat, in the collection's most famous piece – a small and surprisingly sophisticated statue taken from the Villa dei Papiri in Herculaneum. There is also a series of nine paintings depicting erotic positions – a menu of sorts for brothel clients.

Originally the royal library, the enormous **Sala Meridiana** (Great Hall of the Sundial) on the 1st floor is home to the *Farnese Atlante*, a statue of Atlas carrying a globe on his shoulders, as well as various paintings from the Farnese collection. Look up and you'll find Pietro Bardellino's riotously colourful 1781 fresco depicting the Triumph of Ferdinand IV of Bourbon and Marie Caroline of Austria. The rest of the 1st floor is largely devoted to fascinating discoveries from Pompeii, Herculaneum, Stabiae and Cuma, from huge murals and frescoes to a pair of gladiator's helmets, ceramics and glassware – even eggcups. Rooms LXXXVI and LXXXVII house

an extraordinary collection of vases of mixed origins, many carefully reassembled from fragments. Also on this floor are various engraved coppers and Greek funerary vases, as well as temporary, classically themed exhibitions.

❧ ACCADEMIA DI BELLE ARTI // BRUSH UP ON YOUR LOCAL ART KNOWLEDGE

Buzzing with brush-clutching art students, the **Academy of Fine Arts Gallery** (Map p55; ☎ 081 44 18 87; Via Santa Maria di Costantinopoli 107; adult/under 18yr & over 65yr €5/3; ☉ 10am-2pm Tue-Thu & Sat, 2-6pm Fri; Ⓜ Dante) was once the convent of San Giovanni Battista delle Monache. Built in the 17th century, it was given a thorough makeover in 1864 by architect Enrico Alvino, who gave the building a neoclassical facade, a grand staircase and two noble lions to guard the main entrance. The 1st-floor **gallery** houses an important collection of mainly 19th-century Neapolitan work, many by former academy alumni, including watercolourist Giacinti Gigante and sculptor Vincenzo Gemito. That so many of Gemito's busts were created in 1874 is not a coincidence – he frantically chipped away to pay his way out of military service.

❧ PIAZZA DANTE // ABOVEGROUND THEATRICS AND UNDERGROUND CREATIVITY

On hot summer evenings, **Piazza Dante** (Map p55; Ⓜ Dante) turns into a communal living room, packed with entire families who stroll, eat, smoke, play cards, chase balloons, whinge about the in-laws or simply sit and stare.

Dominating the eastern flank of the square is the enormous facade of the **Convitto Nazionale** (Map p55). Now home to a boarding school, it was the pièce de résistance of Luigi Vanvitelli's spectacular 18th-century square. Dedicated to the Bourbon king Charles VII, its central protagonist is now a sandblasted marble Dante looking out over anarchic Via Toledo.

Below it all, the **Dante metro station** (Map p55) doubles as a cutting-edge art space, with installations from some art-world heavyweights. As you head down on the escalator, look up and catch Joseph Kosuth's *Queste Cose Visibili* (These Visible Things) above you. Eye-squintingly huge and neon, it's an epic quotation from Dante's *Il Convivio*. Along the wall at the bottom of the escalator you'll find artist Jannis Kounellis's renegade train tracks running over abandoned shoes. Right behind you, above the second set of escalators, sits *Intermediterraneo*, Michelangelo Pistoletto's giant mirror map of the Mediterranean Sea.

MUSEO NITSCH // PUSH YOUR ARTISTIC LIMITS

In 1974, experimental Austrian artist Hermann Nitsch was invited to perform one of his 'actions' (a bloody, ritualistic art performance) in Naples, leading to his immediate arrest and deportation from Italy. Not one for the squeamish or easily offended, this stylish new **museum and cultural centre** (Map p55; ☎ 081 564 16 55; www.museonitsch.org; Vico Lungo Pontecorvo 29d; admission €10; 10am-7pm Wed-Mon; M Dante) documents the now revered artist's intriguing, symbolic, confronting works through photographs, video, painting and props. Set in a converted power station with killer views from its rooftop, the centre also hosts regular cultural events, such as avant-garde film screenings.

CHIESA DI SANT'ANNA DEI LOMBARDI // REVEL IN RENAISSANCE GLORIES

Dubbed a veritable museum of Renaissance art, this magnificent **church** (Map p55; ☎ 081 551 33 33; Piazza Monteoliveto; 9am-noon Tue-Sun; R4 to Via Monteoliveto) is testament to the close links that once existed between the Neapolitan Aragonese and the Florentine Medici dynasty. One particular highlight is Guido Mazzoni's spectacular *Pietà*. Dating to 1492, the terracotta ensemble is made up of eight life-size terracotta figures surrounding the lifeless body of Christ. Originally the figures were painted, but even without colour they still make quite an impression. The **sacristy** is a work of art in itself. The walls are lined with gloriously inlaid wood panels by Giovanni da Verona, while the ceiling is covered by Giorgio Vasari's 16th-century frescoes that depict the Allegories and Symbols of Faith.

Across Via Monteoliveto from the church is the 16th-century **Palazzo Gravina** (Map p55), the seat of Naples University's architecture faculty.

LA PIGNASECCA // KINDLE YOUR HUNGER AT A FOODIE WONDERLAND

Naples' oldest **street market** (Map p55; Via Pignasecca; 8am-1pm; M Montesanto) is a multisensory escapade into a world of wriggling seafood, drool-worthy delis and clued-up *casalinghe* (housewives) on the hunt for filthy-fresh produce. Shop for local cheeses and vino at Antiche Delizie (p87), scoff down fabulous street food at Friggitoria Fiorenzano (p87), then scour the streetside stalls for everything from discounted perfume and linen to Neapolitan hip-hop CDs and fake designer bags and threads.

🌳 LARGO BARACCHE // FRESH ART IN A SECRET BUNKER

From ancient ruin to WWII air-raid shelter to subterranean **art gallery** (Map p55; ☎ 393 3641664; www.largobaracche.org; Largo Baracche; admission free; ☺ by appointment; 🚍 R2 to Piazza Trieste e Trento), underground Largo Baracche hosts some kicking temporary exhibitions, from up-and-coming local artists to international guests like Brazilian painter Carlos Vergara and Warhol Factory superstar Ultraviolet. Ask the guys to turn off the lights – it's the only way you'll catch the glow-in-the-dark murals by local street artists **cyop&kaf** (www.cyopekaf.org, in Italian). For more on the gallery's history, turn to above).

🌳 CASA E CHIESA DI SANTA MARIA FRANCESCA DELLE CINQUE PIAGHE // MAKE A WISH IN A MIRACULOUS CHAIR

The very essence of Naples' cultish brand of Catholicism, this **holy sanctuary** (Map p55; ☎ 081 42 50 11; Vico Tre Re a Toledo 13; ☺ church 7am-noon, apartment 9am-noon, also 4.30-7.30pm on the 6th of every month; 🚍 R2 to Piazza Trieste e Trento) was once the stomping ground of stigmatic and mystic Santa Maria Francesca delle Cinque Piaghe, the city's only canonised woman. It is also home to her miraculous wooden chair, a particular hit with infertile believers, who sit down on it in the hope of falling pregnant. (Those after a blessing can request one from the Daughters of Santa Maria Francesca, who run the place.)

The holy furniture piece inhabits the saint's meticulously preserved 18th-century **apartment**. Here, the walls heave with modern baby trinkets and vivid 18th- and 19th-century paintings depicting fantastical holy healings – *ex voti* offered by those whose prayers have

been answered. Other household objects include the stigmatic's blood-stained clothes, her bed and pillow, her self-flagellation cords and a rare, hand painted *spinetta* (spinet) from 1682.

The apartment is positioned above a tiny **chapel** famed for its beautiful 18th-century Neapolitan liturgical art, including glass-eyed holy statues. Particularly rare is the statue of the *Divina Pastora* (Divine Shepherdess) on the left side of the nave. The only sculpture of its kind in Naples, it features an unusual depiction of the Virgin Mary reclined and wearing a shepherdess' hat that has its roots in 18th-century Spain. To the left of the nave, a statue of Santa Maria Francesca contains the holy local's bones.

🌳 GALLERIA DI PALAZZO ZEVALLOS STIGLIANO // PAY TRIBUTE TO CARAVAGGIO'S FINAL CANVAS

Banking group Intesa Sanpaolo has put its profits to good use, restoring the exquisite 17th-century Palazzo Zevallos Stigliano it occupies and opening a small **art gallery** (Map p55; ☎ 800 16052007; www.palazzozevallos.com; Via Toledo 185; adult/concession €3/2; ☺ 10am-6pm Mon-Sat; 🚍 R2 to Piazza Trieste e Trento) on its *piano nobile* (main floor). While the 19th-century stucco detailing and frescoes are delightful, the gallery's pièce de résistance is Caravaggio's final masterpiece, *The Martyrdom of St Ursula* (1610). Completed a few weeks before the artist's lonely death, it depicts the brutal scene of a vengeful king of the Huns piercing the heart of his unwilling virgin bride-to-be, Ursula. Positioned behind the dying martyr is a haunted Caravaggio, an eerie premonition of his own impending death. The tumultuous history of both the artist and the painting is documented in

INTERVIEW: MARIO SPADA

What are your favourite corners of the city? There are several. One is Parco Virgiliano (p76), a place I go to connect with the city. I also like walking up the Salita Morarielli (Map pp68–9) in the Miracoli district. From here, Vesuvius forms the backdrop to the Centro Direzionale's skyscrapers. To me, it's a more realistic view of contemporary Naples than those traditional postcard panoramas.

Places you would take a novice to Naples? After breakfast at a *pasticceria*, we'd go straight to Pio Monte della Misericordia (p45) to see Caravaggio's incredible *Le Sette Opere di Misericordia* (The Seven Acts of Mercy), followed by a trip to see the *Cristo Velato* (Veiled Christ) at the Cappella Sansevero (p45). We'd probably go for a walk in Mergellina, stopping at Chalet Ciro Mergellina (p91) for a chocolate gelato brioche, or head to the Terme Stufe di Nerone (p81) to relax. Then we'd cap the night off in a *centro storico* bar.

What distinguishes Neapolitans from other Italians? In Morocco, I often find myself in situations that remind me of home. To me, Neapolitans are half *magrebini* (Maghrebis). Our temperament has a similar intensity – in both good and bad ways. Our faces and gestures recall Caravaggio's chiaroscuro. Speaking of which, visitors shouldn't miss Caravaggio's *The Martyrdom of St Ursula* at the Galleria di Palazzo Zevallos Stigliano (opposite).

A record 100,000 people attended an anti-Mafia memorial march in 2009. Does this give you hope for the future? No, because while people are hungry for change, the fundamental steps required aren't taken. Here, too many politicians prefer to let problems fester until they become *emergenze* (emergencies). This way they can step in with token gestures and exploit the crisis for their own political gain. The 'emergency' inevitably passes and the root of the problem remains.

So what changes do need to be made? The culture itself needs to change. We need passionate teachers who inspire underprivileged kids to learn, to challenge the way they think. We need spaces and programs that allow them to actively experience alternatives, to collaborate with others, and make a difference. Only like this can they develop the sense of social responsibility and civic pride that's missing in Naples.

What do you miss most when you're out of town? The food, the coffee and Naples' one-of-a-kind energy.

Mario Spada is an award-winning documentary photographer, a stills photographer for the film Gomorra *and a tried and-tested Neapolitan.*

the free audioguide, as well as in two documentaries (with English subtitles) shown in the Sala Pompeiana. Other works of note include a fascinating pictorial map of 17th-century Naples by Alessandro Baratta and 18th- and 19th-century landscape paintings by Anton Smink Pitloo and Gaspar van Wittel; the latter is the father of architect Luigi Vanvitelli.

🍃 GALLERIA UMBERTO I // STROLL A MALL WITH SOUL

Paging Milan's Galleria Vittorio Emanuele, Naples' most famous 19th-century **arcade** (Map p55; Galleria Umberto I, Via San Carlo; 🚇 R2 to Via San Carlo) is a breath-taking pairing of richly adorned neo-Renaissance fronts and a delicate glass ceiling capped by a lofty, 56m dome. The mysterious stars of David imbedded in the glasswork reputedly attest to local Jewish investment in the structure. Complete with a sumptuous marble floor, the *galleria* is at its most spectacular at night, when it becomes a surreal setting for impromptu soccer games.

SANTA LUCIA & CHIAIA

At its southern end, Via Toledo spills into lavish Santa Lucia, whose grandiose residents include the sweeping Piazza del Plebiscito, art-lined Palazzo Reale, the velvety Teatro San Carlo and, further east, one-time Angevin stronghold Castel Nuovo (Maschio Angioino). Directly south of Castel Nuovo, ferries dock at Stazione Marittima, while further southwest diners seated at candlelit tables tuck into seafood at harbourside Borgo Marinaro.

Soaring above Via Santa Lucia is Monte Echia and the Pizzofalcone district, inhabited since the 7th century BC and a little-known warren of dark streets, macabre votive shrines and knockout views.

Further west, Chiaia is Naples' epicentre of 'posh', home to fashion-obsessed Via Calabritto, former Rothschild address Villa Pignatelli and the city's chicest bars.

♥ PIAZZA DEL PLEBISCITO // INDULGE IN A LITTLE PEOPLE WATCHING

For old-fashioned Continental grandeur, it's hard to beat **Piazza del Plebiscito** (Map pp62-3; 🚌 R2 to Piazza Trieste e Trento). Whichever way you look, the view is impressive. To the northwest, vine-covered slopes lead up to Castel Sant'Elmo (p71) and the Certosa di San Martino (p67); to the east, the pink-hued Palazzo Reale (right) shows off its oldest facade. And to the west stands Pietro Banchini's neoclassical facsimile of

Rome's Pantheon, the colossal **Chiesa di San Francesco di Paola** (Map pp62-3; 🕿 081 74 51 33, ☺8am-noon & 3.30-6pm Mon-Sat, 8am-1pm Sun). A later addition to the columned colonnade of Joachim Murat's original 1809 piazza design, the church was commissioned by Ferdinand I in 1817 to celebrate the restoration of his kingdom after the Napoleonic interlude. Standing guard outside are Antonio Canova's statue of a galloping King Charles VII of the Bourbons and Antonio Calì's rendering of Charles' son Ferdinand I.

At its northern end, Piazza Plebiscito spills onto **Piazza Trieste e Trento** (Map pp62-3), the city's buzzing heart and home to its most glamorous cafe, Caffé Gambrinus (p88) – a fabulous spot to slip on those shades, join the poseurs and eye up the passing parade.

♥ PALAZZO REALE // SNOOP AROUND A DOWNTOWN ROYAL PALACE

Envisaged as a 16th-century monument to Spanish glory (Naples was under Spanish rule at the time), the magnificent **Palazzo Reale** (Map pp62-3; Royal Palace; 🕿 081 40 04 54; entrance on Piazza Trieste e Trento; adult/EU 18-25yr/EU under18yr & over 65yr €4/2/free, audioguide €4; ☺9am-7pm Thu-Tue; 🚌 R2 to Piazza Trieste e Trento) is home to the **Museo del Palazzo Reale**, a rich and eclectic collection of baroque and neoclassical furnishings, porcelain, tapestries, statues and paintings, spread across the palace's royal apartments. Among the many highlights is the 1768 Teatrino di Corte (closed indefinitely for restoration in 2009), a lavish private theatre created by Ferdinando Fuga to celebrate the marriage of Ferdinand IV and Marie Caroline of Austria. Incredibly, Angelo Viva's statues of Apollo and the Muses et along the walls are made of papier mâché.

Snigger smugly in Sala (Room) XII, where the 16th-century canvas *Gli Esatori delle Imposte* (The Tax Collectors) by Dutch artist Marinus Claesz Van Roymerswaele confirms that attitudes to tax collectors have changed little in 500 years.

The next room, Sala XIII, used to be Joachim Murat's study in the 19th century but was used as a snack bar by Allied troops in WWII. Meanwhile, what looks like a waterwheel in Sala XXIII is actually a nifty rotating reading desk made for Marie Caroline by Giovanni Uldrich in the 18th century.

The Cappella Reale (Royal Chapel) houses a colossal 18th-century *presepe*. Impressively detailed, its cast of wise men, busty peasants and munching mules was crafted by a series of celebrated Neapolitan artists including Giuseppe Sanmartino, creator of the incredible *Cristo Velato* (Veiled Christ) that is housed in the Cappella Sansevero (see p45).

Extending out from Sala IX, the once-impressive hanging gardens are still closed for restoration, although they are sometimes opened for the Maggio dei Monumenti (p10). Otherwise, head to the picture-perfect garden to the left of the palace's main ground-floor entrance. Entry is free and there are bay views to boot.

Designed by Domenico Fontana and completed two long centuries later in 1841, the palace also houses the **Biblioteca Nazionale** (National Library; ☎ 081 781 2 31; ⏰ 9am-7pm Mon-Fri, to 1pm Sat), which includes at least 2000 papyri discovered at Herculaneum and fragments of a 5th-century Coptic Bible. Entry to the library requires photo ID.

♥ TEATRO SAN CARLO // SHOUT FOR AN ENCORE AT A REVAMPED LANDMARK

Even if Puccini and pirouettes don't tickle your fancy, a night at Italy's biggest and oldest **opera house** (Map pp62-3; ☎ box office 081 797 23 31; www.teatrosancarlo.it; Piazza Trieste e Trento, Via San Carlo 98; ⏰ box office 10am-7pm Tue-Sat; 🚇 R2 to Via San Carlo) is a magical experience. Freshly restored, its six gilded levels and pitch-perfect acoustics set an enchanting scene for world-class opera and ballet. Which is just as well; Neapolitan audiences are notoriously demanding and tickets are not easy to come by as most are snapped up by season ticket holders.

The original 1737 theatre burnt down in 1816 before rising from the ashes courtesy of Antonio Niccolini, who'd added the neoclassical facade a few years earlier.

The opera season here runs from January to December, with a midseason break in July and August. Reckon on €50 for a place in the sixth tier and €100 for a seat in the stalls. If you're under 30 (and can prove it) last-minute tickets are available one hour before performances for €15. Ballet tickets range from €35 to €130.

In summer some opera performances are staged in the courtyard of the Castel Nuovo and at the ancient Parco Archeologico di Baia (p82).

At the the time of writing, the future of the 40-minute **guided tours** (☎ 081 553 45 65; adult/student & disabled €5/3) remained unclear. Contact the tourist office for updates.

♥ CASTEL NUOVO // SCOUR A CASTLE FOR FRESCOES, RUINS AND VIEWS

Known as the Maschio Angioino (Angevin Keep) by the locals, this hulking

SANTA LUCIA & CHIAIA

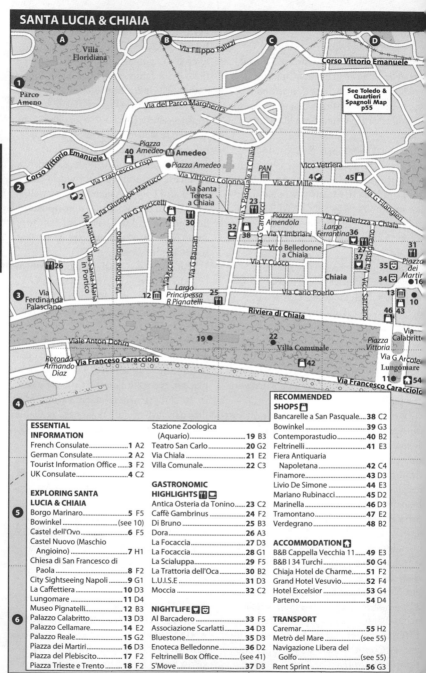

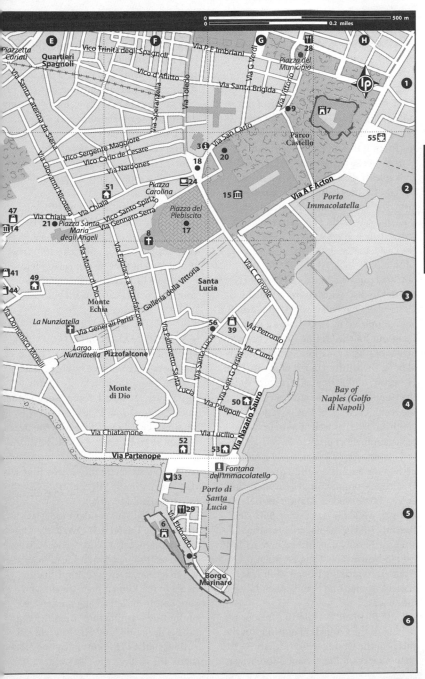

NAPLES

13th-century **castle** (Map pp62-3; ☎ 081 795 58 77; Piazza del Municipio; adult/EU under 18yr & over 65yr €5/free; ☼ 9am-7pm Mon-Sat; ⊕ R2 to Piazza del Municipio) is a striking icon.

When Charles I of Anjou took over Naples and the Swabians' Sicilian kingdom, he found himself in control not only of his new southern Italian acquisitions, but also of possessions in Tuscany, northern Italy and Provence (France). It made sense to base the new dynasty in Naples, rather than Palermo in Sicily, and Charles launched an ambitious construction program to expand the port and city walls. His plans included converting a Franciscan convent into the castle that still stands in Piazza del Municipio.

Christened the Castrum Novum (New Castle) to distinguish it from the older Castel dell'Ovo and Castel Capuano, it was completed in 1282. It was a popular hang-out for the leading intellectuals and artists of the day – Giotto repaid his royal hosts by painting much of the interior. However, of the original structure only the Cappella Palatina remains; the rest is the result of Aragonese renovations two centuries later, as well as a meticulous restoration effort prior to WWII.

The two-storey Renaissance triumphal arch at the entrance – the Torre della Guardia – commemorates the victorious entry of Alfonso I of Aragon into Naples in 1443, while the stark stone **Sala dei Baroni** (Hall of the Barons) is named after the barons slaughtered here in 1486 for plotting against King Ferdinand I of Aragon. Its striking ribbed vault fuses ancient Roman and Spanish late-Gothic influences.

Only fragments of Giotto's frescoes remain in the **Cappella Palatina**, on the splays of the Gothic windows. Above the chapel's elegant Renaissance doorway is a beautiful Catalan-style rose window. To the left of the chapel, the glass-floored **Sala dell'Armeria** (Armoury Hall) showcases Roman ruins discovered during restoration works on the Sala dei Baroni. Among the finds are the remains of a private swimming pool, as well as skeletons dating to the medieval period.

All this forms part of the museum, spread across several halls on three floors. The 14th- and 15th-century frescoes and sculptures on the ground floor are of the most interest.

The other two floors mostly display paintings, either by Neapolitan artists, or with Naples or Campania as subjects, covering the 17th to the early 20th centuries. Worth seeking out is Guglielmo Monaco's 15th-century bronze door, complete with a cannonball embedded in it.

♣ BORGO MARINARO // CLIMB A CASTLE, THEN TOAST TO IT

An evocative combo of bobbing boats, seaside dining and cocktail-sipping night owls, the small, rocky **Borgo Marinaro** (Map pp62-3; ⊕ C25 to Via Partenope) is where – according to legend – the heartbroken siren Partenope washed ashore after failing to seduce Ulysses with her song. It's also where the Greeks first settled the city in the 7th century BC, calling the island Megaris.

Its most famous resident today is the hulking **Castel dell'Ovo** (Castle of the Egg; Map pp62-3; ☎ 081 240 00 55; Borgo Marinaro; ☼ 9am-6pm Mon-Fri, to 1pm Sat & Sun). According to legend, it owes its improbable name to the Roman poet Virgil, who supposedly buried an egg on the site, ominously warning that when the egg breaks the castle (and Naples) will fall.

Built in the 12th century by the Normans, the castle is the city's oldest. Its particular position had long been appreciated – originally by the Roman general Lucullus, who had his villa here – and it became a key fortress in the defence of Campania. It was subsequently used by the Swabians, Angevins and Alfonso of Aragon, who modified it to suit his military needs.

Today the castle hosts regular art exhibitions and is worth the climb for that perfect sea-view shot alone.

VIA CHIAIA // WINDOW-SHOP AND STRUT YOUR STUFF

Join the perma-tanned locals for a fix of people watching, window shopping and *palazzo* gazing on this **pedestrianised street** (Map pp62–3; CS to Piazza Trieste Trento). Linking Piazza Trieste e Trento with Piazza dei Martiri (and Santa Lucia with Chiaia), it's a particular hit with evening *flâneurs*, not to mention home to the 16th-century **Palazzo Cellamare** (Map pp62–3) at No 149. Built as a summer residence for Giovan Francesco Carafa, the *palazzo* later hosted Bourbon monarchy guests, including Goethe and Casanova. Towards the western end of the street you pass under what looks like a triumphal arch but is, in fact, a bridge built in 1636 to connect the hills of Pizzofalcone and Mortella. Past the arch, turn right into blue-ribbon Via Gaetano Filangieri and continue up to Via dei Mille, where sharply garbed locals and shops mix it with flouncy Liberty (Italian Art Nouveau) architecture.

PIAZZA DEI MARTIRI // SIP, SHOP, BROWSE AND BE SEEN

If Chiaia is Naples' drawing room, then **Piazza dei Martiri** (Map pp62–3; C25 to Piazza dei Martiri) is its showpiece chaise longue. Anyone worth their Gucci shades heads here for espresso at **La Caffettiera** (Map pp62–3; 081 764 42 43, Piazza dei Martiri 30; daily) and a fix of book browsing, flirtatious glances and (more) espresso at bookshop-cum-hang-out **Feltrinelli** (p97).

The piazza's centrepiece is Enrico Alvino's 19th-century monument to Neapolitan martyrs, with four lions representing the anti-Bourbon uprisings of 1799, 1820, 1848 and 1860. On the southwestern flank of the square, at No 30, **Palazzo Calabritto** (Map pp62–3) is a Luigi Vanvitelli creation, while around the corner, Via Calabritto is the city's golden shopping strip, home to fashion slaves, catwalk threads and legendary local tailor **Finamore** (see the boxed text, p98).

LUNGOMARE // CATCH (OR LOSE) YOUR BREATH BY THE SEA

Bay vistas and gorgeous sun-kissed joggers make for an enticing stroll along the **lungomare** (seafront; Map pp62–3; C25 to Via Partenope), despite the roaring traffic. A 2.5km seaside stretch running the length of Via Partenope and Via Francesco Carrociolo (the latter is car-free on Sunday morning!), it's particularly romantic at dusk, when Capri and Mt Vesuvius take on a soft orange hue

Separating the Lungomare from Riviera di Chiaia is the **Villa Comunale** (Map pp62–3; Piazza Vittoria; 7am-midnight; C25 to Riviera di Chiaia), a long, leafy park designed by Luigi Vanvitelli for private Bourbon frolicking. Its bountiful booty of fountains include the **Fontana delle Paperelle** (Duck Fountain), which replaced the famous *Toro Farnese* after its transferral to the Museo Archeologico Nazionale (p54) in 1825.

The park's most famous resident is the **Stazione Zoologica** (Aquario; Map pp62–3; 081 583 32 63; www.szn.it; Viale Aquario 1; adult/

NAPLES

NAPLES

child €1.50/1; ⊙ 9am-6pm Tue-Sat, 9.30am-7.30pm Sun Mar-Oct, 9am-5pm Tue-Sat, to 2pm Sun Nov-Feb; 🚌 C25 to Riviera di Chiaia), Europe's oldest aquarium. Housed in a stately neoclassical building designed by Adolf von Hildebrandt, it's home to 200 species of marine flora and fauna from the city's bay.

♥ MUSEO PIGNATELLI // INDULGE IN ART AT A FORMER ROTHSCHILD PAD

When Ferdinand Acton, a minister at the court of King Ferdinand IV (1759–1825), asked Pietro Valente to design Villa Pignatelli in 1826, Valente whipped up this striking Pompeiian lookalike, now the **Museo Pignatelli** (Map pp62-3; ☎ 081 761 23 56; Riviera di Chiaia 200; adult/EU 18-25yr/EU under 18yr & over 65yr €2/1/free; ⊙ 8.30am-2pm Wed-Mon; 🚌 C25 to Riviera di Chiaia). Bought and extended by the Rothschilds in 1841, it became home to the Duke of Monteleone, Diego Aragona Pignatelli Cortes, in 1867, before his granddaughter Rosina Pignatelli donated it (and its treasures) to the state. Last entry is one hour before close.

An aristocratic spectacle of opulent furniture, art and hunting paraphernalia (including a collection of royal whips), its highlights include Meissen and Viennese porcelain in the Salotto Verde (Green Room), and a leather-lined smoking room. The 1st floor features mainly 18th- to 20th-century Neapolitan paintings and busts from the Banco di Napoli's extensive art collection, including Francesco Solimena's masterpiece *Agar e l'angelo* (Hagar and the Angel; 1695–99).

The adjoining **Museo delle Carrozze** contains a collection of 19th- and 20th-century carriages but remains closed for restoration.

VOMERO, CAPODIMONTE & LA SANITÀ

All roads might lead to Rome, but three Neapolitan funiculars lead to Vomero, a hilltop neighbourhood where quasi-anarchy is replaced with mild-mannered *professori*, Liberty villas and the stunning Certosa di San Martino.

Northeast of Vomero, former royal hunting ground Capodimonte boasts its own cultural jewel in Palazzo Reale di Capodimonte, where names like Caravaggio, Botticelli and Warhol grace its regal rooms.

In stark contrast, the impoverished Sanità district (squeezed between Via Foria and Via Santa Teresa degli Scalzi directly south of Capodimonte) is a strangely bewitching mix of *bassi* (one-room, ground-floor houses), baroque staircases and ancient catacombs. It's also where local comic legend Totò was born (at Via Santa Maria Antesaecula 109, to be precise!).

♥ VILLA FLORIDIANA & MUSEO NAZIONALE DELLA CERAMICA DUCA DI MARTINA // ROMANTIC VIEWS AND A CERAMICS-CRAMMED LOVE PAD

While the lush, manicured **gardens** (Map pp68-9; Via Domenico Cimarosa 77; admission free; ⊙ 8.30am-1hr before sunset; Ⓜ Vanvitelli) are worth the trip for the lofty views alone (think city, sea and Capri), the cultural highlight here is the **National Museum of Ceramics** (Map pp68-9; ☎ 081 578 84 18; adult/EU 18-25yr/EU under 18yr & over 65yr €2.50/1.25/free; ⊙ 8.30am-2pm Wed-Mon). Housed in the stately Villa Floridiana – a gift from King Ferdinand I to his second wife, the Duchess of Floridia – its 6000-piece collection features priceless Chinese Ming (1368–1644) ceramics and Japanese Edo (1615–1867) vases on the lower floor. The top floor is dedicated to European ceramics, including some sumptuous Meissen pieces, as well as a smattering of paintings from greats such as Francesco Solimena, Francesco De Mura and Vincenzo Camuccini. At the time of research, the middle floor and its collection of Renaissance majolica pottery were set to reopen in 2010 after restoration works. Last entry is one hour before close.

🌿 **CERTOSA DI SAN MARTINO //
FALL FOR A MONASTERY OF
MASTERPIECES**
The Certosa di San Martino and its **Museo Nazionale di San Martino** (Map pp68-9; ☎ 848 80 02 88; Largo San Martino 5; adult/EU 18-25yr/EU under 18yr & over 65yr €6/3/free; ⊗ 8.30am-7.30pm Thu-Tue; Ⓜ Vanvitelli, funicular Montesanto to Morghen) are absolutely superb and must sees. What was once a Carthusian monastery is now home to one of the most extensive collections of Neapolitan art and history,

NAPLES

RICCARDO DALISI & THE ART OF BENEVOLENCE

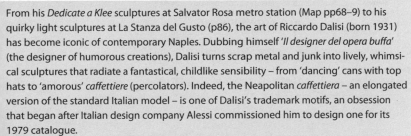

From his *Dedicate a Klee* sculptures at Salvator Rosa metro station (Map pp68–9) to his quirky light sculptures at La Stanza del Gusto (p86), the art of Riccardo Dalisi (born 1931) has become iconic of contemporary Naples. Dubbing himself '*Il designer del opera buffa*' (the designer of humorous creations), Dalisi turns scrap metal and junk into lively, whimsical sculptures that radiate a fantastical, childlike sensibility – from 'dancing' cans with top hats to 'amorous' *caffettiere* (percolators). Indeed, the Neapolitan *caffettiera* – an elongated version of the standard Italian model – is one of Dalisi's trademark motifs, an obsession that began after Italian design company Alessi commissioned him to design one for its 1979 catalogue.

Despite a string of other famous commissions for the likes of Zanotta, Fiat and Bisazza, Dalisi has always eschewed diva demands, preferring humility, humanity and a social conscience. Graduating as an architect in 1957, he first achieved fame as a pioneer of Italy's anti-design movement in the 1960s, which decried consumerist thinking in design in favour of individuality, spontaneity and an acknowledgement of every person's creative potential. By the 1970s, the artist was running *design povero* (poor design) workshops for underprivileged Neapolitan youth, teaching them how to turn scrap metal into works of art. His more recent collaboration with locals from the rough-and-ready Sanità district reached fruition with the birth of a successful, functioning workshop inside a deconsecrated neighbourhood church, giving work and hope to youth otherwise vulnerable to criminal careers.

As you'd expect, a visit to the artist's own **studio** (Map pp68-9; ☎ 081 68 14 05; studiodalisi@libero.it; Calata San Francesco 59; admission free; ⊗ 9am-2pm Mon-Fri, call ahead; 🚌 C28 to Via Aniello Falcone) is a wonderful experience, its collection of rooms packed to the rafters with charismatic prototypes, works-in-progress and roll upon roll of Dalisi's own paintings and illustrations (the recycling theme continues here, with Dalisi only using recycled paper, much of which comes from schools). The gentle *maestro* also offers free three-, four- or five-day workshops (book a week ahead), though it's worth considering that Dalisi does not speak English. And while all visitors are welcome at the studio, don't forget to call ahead and book a time with Dalisi's assistant, Carla Rabuffetti, first.

NAPLES

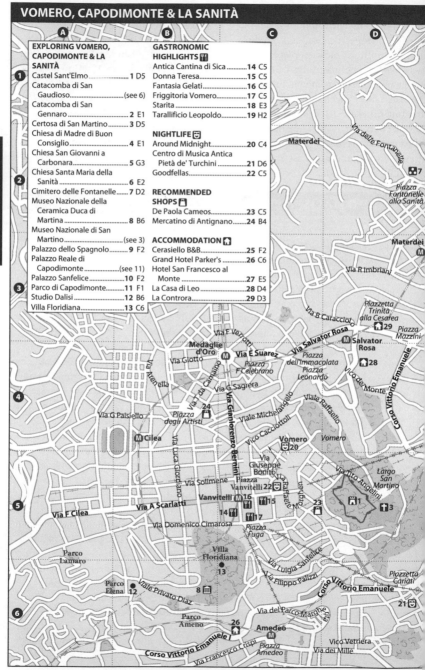

VOMERO, CAPODIMONTE & LA SANITÀ

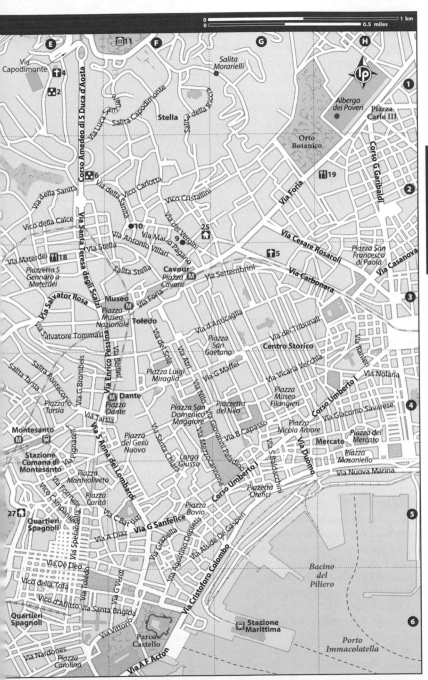

NAPLES

all of it wisely collected by its resident monks.

Originally built by Charles of Anjou in 1325, the *certosa* (charterhouse) has been decorated, adorned and altered over the centuries by some of the greats of Italian art and architecture, most importantly Giovanni Antonio Dosio in the 16th century and baroque master Cosimo Fanzago a century later.

It's worth noting that some of the exhibitions may close down for some part of the day, so it's a good idea to phone ahead and check if you're especially keen on seeing a particular part of the museum. Last entry is 1½ hours before close.

The Church

The monastery's church and the rooms that flank it contain a feast of frescoes and paintings by some of Naples' greatest 17th-century artists. In the *pronaos* (a small room flanked by three walls and a row of columns), Micco Spadaro's frescoes of Carthusian persecution seem to defy perspective as figures sit with their legs hanging over nonexistent edges. Elsewhere throughout the chapel you'll discover works by Francesco Solimena, Massimo Stanzione, Giuseppe de Ribera, Luca Giordano and Battista Caracciolo.

The Cloisters

Adjacent to the church, the elegant **Chiostro dci Procuratori** is the smaller of the monastery's two cloisters. A grand corridor on the left leads to the larger **Chiostro Grande** (Great Cloister), considered one of Italy's finest. Originally designed by Giovanni Antonio Dosio in the late 16th century and added to by Fanzago, it's a sublime composition of Tuscan-Doric porticoes, garden and marble statues. The sinister skulls mounted on the balustrade were a light-hearted reminder to the monks of their own mortality.

Sezione Navale

Just off the Chiostro dei Procuratori is the recently inaugurated **Naval Museum**, whose two exhibition halls focus on the history of the Bourbon navy from 1734 to 1860. The collection features a series of detailed scale models of late 18th- and 19th-century warships used by the former royals, as well as original navy weaponry. The true highlight, however, is the small collection of original royal barges, among them a gilded, canopied number used by Charles VII and a beautifully carved 18th-century gift to Ferdinand IV from Turkish sultan Selim III.

Sezione Presepiale

One of the many museum highlights is the **Sezione Presepiale**, which houses a whimsical collection of rare Neapolitan *presepi* carved in the 18th and 19th centuries. These range from the minuscule – a nativity scene in an ornately decorated eggshell – to the colossal Cuciniello creation, which covers one wall of what used to be the monastery's kitchen. Angels fly down to a richly detailed landscape of rocky houses, shepherds and local merrymakers, all made out of wood, cork, papier-mâché and terracotta.

Quarto del Priore

The **Prior's Quarter** in the southern wing houses the bulk of the picture collection, as well as one of the museum's most famous pieces, Pietro Bernini's tender *La Vergine col Bambino e San Giovannino* (Madonna and Child with the Infant John the Baptist).

NAPLES

Immagini e Memorie di Napoli

A pictorial history of Naples is told in the section **Images and Memories of Naples**. Here you'll find portraits of historic characters (Don Pedro de Toledo in Room 33, Maria Carolina di Borbone in Room 43); antique maps, including a 35-panel copper map in Room 45; and rooms dedicated to major historical events such as the Revolt of the Masaniello (Room 36) and the plague (Room 37). Room 32 boasts the beautiful Tavola Strozzi (Strozzi Table), whose fabled depiction of 15th-century maritime Naples is one of the city's most celebrated historical records.

♥ CASTEL SANT'ELMO //
SPOT LANDMARKS ATOP A
SKYSCRAPING CASTLE

Barely 100m west of the Certosa, the star-shaped **Castel Sant'Elmo** (Map pp68-9; ☎ 081 578 40 30; Via Tito Angelini 22; admission €3; ⏰ 8.30am-7.30pm Thu-Sat, Mon & Tue, 9am-6.30pm Sun; Ⓜ Vanvitelli, funicular Montesanto to Morghen) was originally a church dedicated to St Erasmus (from which the name Elmo is derived). Some 400 years later, in 1349, Robert of Anjou turned it into a castle before Spanish viceroy Don Pedro de Toledo had it further fortified in 1538. Used as a military prison until the 1970s, the castle's interior is now usually off-limits, so unless you're determined on catching the views from the rooftop (which can be similarly enjoyed from the Certosa), we suggest you save your euros.

♥ PARCO E PALAZZO REALE DI
CAPODIMONTE // HEAD UP A HILL
FOR AN EPIC CULTURAL FEAST

A rambling oasis above the maddening city, the 130-hectare **Parco di Capodimonte** (Map pp68-9; ⏰ 9am-1hr before sunset; 🚌 R4 to Via Miano) makes for a blissful chill, with lakes, a wood, and various 18th-century buildings, including former royal porcelain workshop **Palazzo Porcellane**. Designed by Ferdinando Sanfelice in 1742 as a royal hunting reserve, the park's main attraction, however, is the grandiose **Palazzo Reale di Capodimonte** (Map pp68-9; ☎ 081 749 91 11; Parco di Capodimonte; adult/EU 18-25yr/EU under 18yr & over 65yr €7.50/3.75/free, adult 2-5pm €6.50; ⏰ 8.30am-7.30pm Thu-Tue). Last entry is 1½ hours before close.

Home to one of Italy's finest art collections, the building itself was originally planned as a hunting lodge for Charles VII of Bourbon. But it seems Charles's plans kept getting grander and by the time the place was finished in 1759, Naples had a new palace. Just as well, really, for when Charles inherited his mother Elisabetta Farnese's hefty art collection, space was at a premium.

During the decade of French rule (1806–15), the colossal *palazzo* became the official residence of Joseph Bonaparte and Joachim Murat.

Today, the museum is spread over three floors and 160 rooms. The 1st floor is dominated by the Galleria Farnese and the Appartamento Reale (Royal Apartment); the 2nd floor contains the Galleria delle Arti a Napoli; while the top floor is dedicated to modern art. Consider forking out €4 for the insightful audioguide.

To do the whole museum in one day is impossible – you'd need at least two to start getting to grips with the place. For most people, though, a full morning is sufficient for a shortened best-of tour.

First-floor highlights include family portraits of the Farnese by Raphael and Titian in Room 2 and Masaccio's celebrated *Crocifissione* (Crucifixion; 1426) in Room 3. Botticelli's *Madonna col Bambino e Due Angeli* (Madonna with Baby and Angels; Room 6), Bellini's

Trasfigurazione (Transfiguration; Room 8) and Parmigianino's *Antea* (Room 12) are all must-see pieces, while Joachim Beukelaer's voluptuous 16th-century market scenes will whet your appetite in Room 18. In Room 20, a glum-looking Hercules is torn between a stern-looking Virtue and a fun-loving Vice in Annibale Carracci's 16th-century painting *Ercole al bivio* (Hercules at the Crossroads).

The **Galleria delle Cose Rare** (Gallery of Rare Objects) is home to Cardinal Alessandro Farnese's gold-embossed, blue majolica table service. The nifty centrepiece depicting Diana the huntress can be used as a goblet by taking off the stag's detachable head.

A study in regal excess, the 1st-floor **Appartamento Reale** (Royal Apartment) occupies Rooms 31 to 60. Sumptuous rooms positively heave with valuable Capodimonte porcelain, heavy curtains and shiny inlaid marble. The Salottino di Porcellana (Room 52) is an extraordinary example of 18th-century chinoiserie, its walls and ceiling crawling with whimsically themed porcelain 'stucco'. The Appartamento Reale is also home to Volaire's *Eruzione del Vesuvio dal Ponte Maddalena* (Eruption of Vesuvius from the Bridge of Maddalena).

The 2nd floor is packed to its elegant rafters with works produced in Naples between the 13th and 18th centuries. The first room you come to, however, is lined with a series of epic 16th-century Belgian tapestries depicting episodes from the Battle of Pavia.

Simone Martini's work *San Ludovico di Tolosa* (1317) is brilliantly displayed in Room 66. Considered the museum's finest example of 14th-century art, Martini's golden work portrays the canonisation of Ludovico, brother of King Robert of Anjou.

The piece that many come to Capodimonte to see, *Flagellazione* (Flagellation; 1607–10) hangs in reverential solitude in Room 78, at the end of a long corridor. Caravaggio's arresting image of Jesus about to be flogged was originally painted for the de Franchis family chapel in the Chiesa di San Domenico Maggiore. And, like his other great Neapolitan work *Le Sette Opere di Misericordia* (The Seven Acts of Mercy; see p45), its intensity and revolutionary depiction of light were to have a huge influence on his contemporaries.

Continue through the 28 rooms that remain on the 2nd floor for works by Ribera, Giordano, Solimena and Stanzione. The small gallery of modern art on the 3rd floor is worth a quick look – for Andy Warhol's poptastic Mt Vesuvius if nothing else.

But you're not finished yet. On the ground floor, the **Gabinetto Disegni e Stampe** (Drawing and Print Room) contains some 27,000 pieces, including several sketches by Michelangelo and Raphael. And did we mention the basement exhibition space, home to temporary exhibitions of mostly contemporary art?

♣ CATACOMBA DI SAN GENNARO // GLIMPSE ANCIENT FRESCOES IN A HOLY UNDERGROUND OTHERWORLD

An evocative otherworld of tombs, corridors and broad vestibules, Naples' oldest and most sacred **catacombs** (Map pp68-9; ☎ 081 741 10 71; Via Capodimonte 16; admission €5; ⊙ guided tours 9am, 10am, 11am, noon, 2pm, 3pm Tue-Sat, 9am, 10am, 11pm, noon Sun; 🚌 R4 to Via Capodimonte) became a Christian pilgrimage site when San Gennaro's body was interred here in the 5th century. Naples' bishops were also buried here until the 11th century. Scan the crumbling walls for 2nd-century Christian frescoes and 5th-century mosaics, including the oldest known portrait of San Gennaro.

The ticket office is in a small ivy-clad building to the left of the **Chiesa di Madre di Buon Consiglio** (Map pp68–9; ☎ 081 741 00 06; Via Capodimonte 13; ☉ 8am-12.30pm & 5-7pm Mon-Sat, 9am-1pm & 5-7pm Sun), a snack-sized replica of St Peter's in Rome completed in 1960. Tours of the catacombs go for around an hour and usually only depart if there are more than two people.

❦ CIMITERO DELLE FONTANELLE // GET THE CREEPS AT A CULTISH UNDERGROUND CEMETERY

Creaking with the skulls and bones of some 40,000 Neapolitans, the ghoulish **Fontanelle Cemetery** (Map pp68–9; ☎ 081 549 03 68; Piazza Fontanelle alla Sanità 154; ☉ 10am-noon Mon-Fri; Ⓜ Museo) was first used during the plague of 1656, before becoming the city's main burial site during the cholera epidemics of 1835 and 1974.

At the end of the 19th century it became a cult spot for the worship of the dead, in which locals would adopt a skull and pray for its soul (see p240). When condensation formed on the skull, it was seen a sign of good fortune for its custodian. Dry bones, however, were seen as a sign of impending doom. Some custodians were so attached to their skeletal friend that they would encase it in a glass shrine for protection.

Although normally only open during the Maggio dei Monumenti (May of the Monuments; p10), the site does open sporadically, so call ahead and ask for updates.

❦ CHIESA SANTA MARIA DELLA SANITÀ & CATACOMBA DI SAN GAUDIOSO // ARRESTING PAINTINGS MEET MACABRE RITUALS

Topped by a striking green-and-yellow tiled dome, the 17th-century **Chiesa Santa Maria della Sanità** (Map pp68–9; ☎ 081 544 13 05; www.santamariadellasanita.it; Via della Sanità 124; ☉ 8.30am-1.30pm & 5-7.30pm Mon-Sat, 8.30am-1.30pm Sun; Ⓜ Cavour) boasts canvases by greats like Andrea Vaccaro, Luca Giordano and Giovan Vincenzo Forlì, as well as two contemporary sculptures by Riccardo Dalisi (see the boxed text, p67).

Below the high altar, a dramatic double staircase frames the 5th-century Cappella di San Gaudioso, entrance to the unmissable **catacombs** (adult/child €5/3; catacombs tours ☉ 9.30am, 10.15am, 11am, 11.45am, 12.30pm). Burial site of San Gaudioso, a North African bishop who died in Naples in AD 452, these eerie chambers reveal traces of mosaics and frescoes from various periods; the earliest is from the 5th century, while later examples are from the 17th and 18th centuries. But it's not so much the art that strikes you as the somewhat grisly history to which the catacombs attest.

The damp walls reveal two medieval methods of burying the dead. The first involved burying the corpse in the foetal position in the belief that you should depart this world as you enter it. The second method, favoured by the 17th-century rich, was to be buried upright in a niche with one's head cemented to the wall. Once sapped of fluids, the headless body would be buried and the skull set over a fresco of the dearly departed.

Tours of the catacombs last about 45 minutes. English-language tours should be booked around four days ahead.

NAPLES

☙ PALAZZO DELLO SPAGNUOLO // REVEL IN A THEATRICAL ASCENT

In baroque-rich Naples, even stair-cases can be an event and the recently restored masterpiece gracing the court-yard of the **palazzo** (Map pp68-9; Via dei Vergini 19; Ⓜ Cavour) is one of the city's showstopping best. Designed by Ferdi-nando Sanfelice and dating from 1738, its double-ramped, five-arched flights are a wildly theatrical affair. Indeed, the staircase is so dramatic that it fea-tures in several film classics, including Luigi Zampa's *Processo alla Città* (A City Stands Still) and Vittorio de Sica's *Giudizio Universal* (Judgement Day). Believe it or not, horses once used the stairs, providing door-to-door service for lazy cavaliers.

If Sanfelice's sweeping architectural statement leaves you stair-crazy, a quick walk north will lead you to his debut effort inside the **Palazzo Sanfe-lice** (Map pp68-9; Via della Sanità 2). Upon its completion in 1726 the double-ramped diva became the talk of the town, and from then on there was no stopping Sanfelice, who perfected his dramatic staircase design in various *palazzi* across the city.

While neither of these two buildings is technically open to the public, the porter should let you through if you ask nicely. Porters generally work office hours, so avoid the early afternoon if you want to find someone there.

☙ CHIESA SAN GIOVANNI A CARBONARA // SWOON OVER CHISELLED FEATURES

Built on the site of an Angevin *carbon-arius* (waste disposal and incineration site), the **Chiesa San Giovanni a Car-bonara** (Map pp68-9; ☎ 081 29 58 73; Via Carbonara 5; ☿ 9am-6pm Mon-Sat; Ⓜ Cavour) is a Gothic

church, chapel and cloister complex famed for its priceless booty of sculpture. Ferdinando Sanfelice's 18th-century dou-ble-flight staircase leads up to the church, in which the colossal mausoleum of King Ladislas soars 18m behind the main altar. Fusing Renaissance and Gothic styles, it was a collaborative effort between Andrea de Firenze, Tuscan sculptors and north-ern Italian artists.

Behind the monument, the circular **Cappella Caracciole del Sole** features colourful 15th-century frescoes and Leonardo da Besozzo's tomb for Gianni Caracciolo, the ambitious lover of King Ladislas' sister Queen Joan II of Naples. Caracciolo's increasing political power led the queen to plot his demise and in 1432 he was stabbed to death in the Cas-tel Capuano.

Other important works include the Cappella Caracciolo di Vico (renowned for showcasing early-16th-century Ro-man style in southern Italy), the *Monu-mento Miroballo* by Tommaso Malvito and Jacopo dell Pila and the colourful 14th-century Cappella Somma, complete with mannerist frescoes and an exquisite 16th-century altar executed by Anni-bale Caccarello and Giovan Domenico d'Auria.

MERGELLINA & POSILLIPO

Located at the western end of the Lungo-mare, Mergellina exudes an air of faded grandeur with its Liberty *palazzi* and slightly scruffy seafront. Kitsch marina chalets sell gelato to lovestruck teens, while, close by, hydrofoils head out to the islands.

Further west, on the headland dividing the Bay of Naples from the Bay of Poz-zuoli, Posillipo is a verdant, blue-ribbon neighbourhood of sprawling villas, secret

MERGELLINA & POSILLIPO

ESSENTIAL INFORMATION
Tourist Information Office...... 1 B1
US Consulate............................... 2 D1

EXPLORING MERGELLINA & POSILLIPO
Parco Vergiliano....................... 3 B2
Porticciolo.................................. 4 B3

GASTRONOMIC HIGHLIGHTS
Chalet Ciro Mergellina............. 5 B3
Di Girolamo Giuseppe 6 B2
Salvatore 7 B4

RECOMMENDED SHOPS
Anna Matuozzo.......................... 8 B2

ACCOMMODATION
Hotel Ausonia............................. 9 C2
Hotel Paradiso........................10 A3

swimming coves and the urban oasis of Parco Virgiliano.

🐚 PORTICCIOLO // LICK YOURSELF SILLY BY THE SEA

Once home to the area's fishing fleet, Mergellina's **marina** (Map p75; Via Francesco Caracciolo; Ⓜ Mergellina) is now a crowd-pulling combo of anchored yachts and kitsch Neapolitan chalets, neon-lit seaside gelaterie and bars. Pick up an ice-cream brioche at Chalet Ciro Mergellina (p91) and soak up the postcard view of bay, *castello* (castle) and volcano.

🐚 PARCO VERGILIANO // PEER INTO A GIANT ROMAN TUNNEL

Wedged between a railway bridge and the cliffs of Posillipo hill, this off-the-radar **park** (Map p75; ☎ 081 66 93 90; Salita dell Grotta 20; ⏱ 9am-1hr before sunset Tue-Sun; Ⓜ Mergellina) boasts a rather steep flight of steps leading up to the world's longest Roman tunnel, a 700m-long affair once linking Naples to Pozzuoli. While you can't walk through it, peering into its dark, draughty abyss is nonetheless a thrill.

Make it to the top of the steps and pay tribute at the tomb of Virgil, who died in

Brindisi in 19 BC. Legend has it that the Roman poet's remains were carted to Naples and buried in this Augustan-era vault.

Also buried in the park is the 19th-century poet Giacomo Leopardi.

❦ PARCO VIRGILIANO // ESCAPE UP A BREATHTAKING HILL

Playground of the city's well-heeled denizens, this 9600 sq metre **park** (Map pp78-9; Viale Virgilio; 🕙 9.30am-11.30pm; 🚍 140 to Via Posillipo) sits high above the shimmering sea on the westernmost tip of posh Posillipo hill. Kick back on a terrace and soak up the views; from Capri to the south, Nisida, Procida and Ischia to the southwest, to the Bay of Pozzuoli and Bagnoli to the west. (History buffs may know that the tiny island of Nisida is where Brutus reputedly conspired against his over-achieving nemesis Julius Caesar.) The trendy Posillipo **market** (see the boxed text, p96) takes place outside the main gates on Thursday.

CAMPI FLEGREI

Stretching west of Posillipo Hill to the Tyrrhenian Sea, the oft-overlooked Campi Flegrei (Phlegrean Fields) counterbalances its ugly urban sprawl with steamy active craters, lush volcanic hillsides and priceless ancient ruins. While its Greek settlements are Italy's oldest, its Monte Nuovo is Europe's youngest mountain. Gateway to the region is the port town of Pozzuoli, home to archaeological must-sees and handy for ferries to Ischia and Procida.

POZZUOLI & SURROUNDS

Founded around 530 BC by political exiles from the Aegean island of Samos, Pozzuoli (ancient Dikaiarchia) came into its own under the Romans, who in 194 BC colonised it, renamed it Puteoli (Little Wells), and turned it into a major port. It was here that St Paul is said to have landed in AD 61, that San Gennaro was beheaded and that screen goddess Sophia Loren spent her childhood. A bout of bradeyism (the slow upward and downward movement of the earth's crust) saw Pozzuoli's seabed rise 1.85m between 1982 and 1984, rendering its harbour too shallow for large vessels.

Indeed, geological curiosities surround the town, from the sizzling Solfatara Crater 1.2km to the east to novice mountain Monte Nuovo 3km to the west.

A SCANDALOUS ADDRESS

Few buildings fire up the local gossipmongers like Posillipo's seaside **Palazzo Donn'Anna** (Map pp78-9; Largo Donn'Anna 9; 🚍 140 to Via Posillipo). Incomplete, semiderelict yet strangely beautiful, it takes its name from Anna Carafa, for whom it was built as a wedding present from her husband, Ramiro Guzman, the Spanish viceroy of Naples. When Guzman hotfooted it back to Spain in 1644 he left his wife heartbroken in Naples. She died shortly afterwards and architectural whiz-kid Cosimo Fanzago gave up the project. The grand yet forlorn heap sits on the site of an older villa, La Sirena (The Mermaid), reputed setting for Queen Joan's scandalous sex orgies and crimes of passion (rumour has it that fickle Joan dumped her lovers straight into the sea). Exactly which Queen Joan is up for debate. Some believe her royal nastiness was Joan I (1326–82). Daughter of Charles, Duke of Calabria, her list of alleged wicked deeds includes knocking off her husband. Others place their bets on Joan II (1373–1435). Sister of King Ladislao, her appetite for men remains the stuff of saucy legend. Palazzo Donn'Anna is not open to the public.

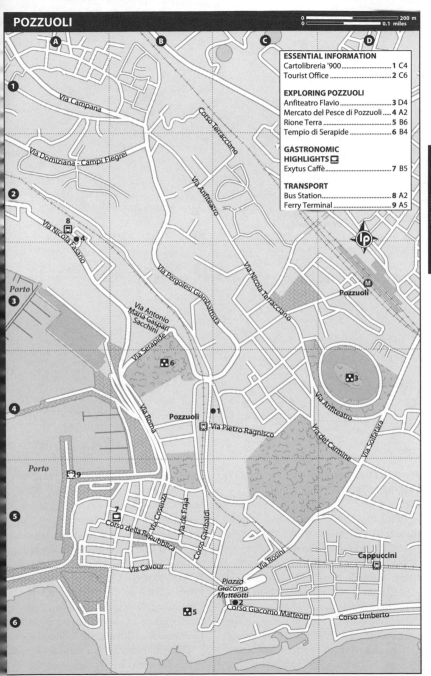

POZZUOLI

0 — 200 m
0 — 0.1 miles

ESSENTIAL INFORMATION
Cartolibreria '900.............................. **1** C4
Tourist Office **2** C6

EXPLORING POZZUOLI
Anfiteatro Flavio **3** D4
Mercato del Pesce di Pozzuoli **4** A2
Rione Terra **5** B6
Tempio di Serapide **6** B4

GASTRONOMIC HIGHLIGHTS
Exytus Caffè **7** B5

TRANSPORT
Bus Station.. **8** A2
Ferry Terminal **9** A5

NAPLES

Via Campana

Corso Terracciano

Via Domiziana - Campi Flegrei

Via Anfiteatro

Via Nicola Fasano

Porto

Via Pergolesi Giambattista

Via Nicola Terracciano

Pozzuoli

Via Antonio Maria Gaspari Sacchini

Via Serapide

Via Roma

Pozzuoli

Via Pietro Ragnisco

Via Anfiteatro

Via del Carmine

Via Solfatara

Porto

Via Cosenza

Via de Fraja

Corso Garibaldi

Corso della Repubblica

Via Cavour

Via Rosini

Cappuccini

Piazza Giacomo Matteotti

Corso Giacomo Matteotti

Corso Umberto

NAPLES

CAMPI FLEGREI

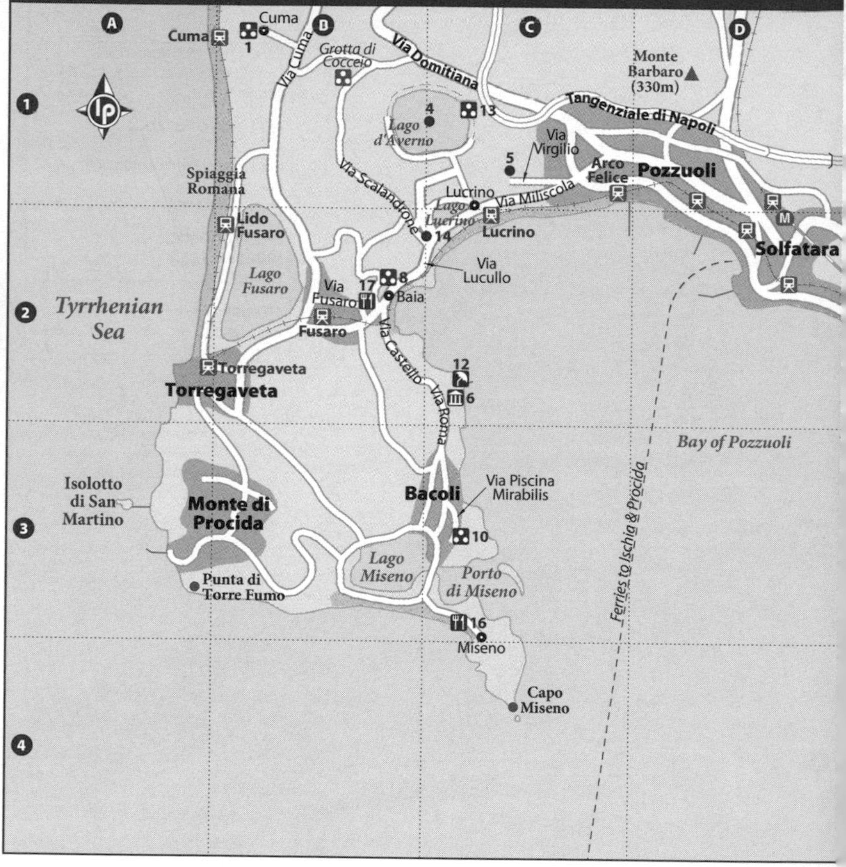

Map labels: Cuma, Grotta di Cocceio, Via Domitiana, Monte Barbaro (330m), Tangenziale di Napoli, Lago d'Averno, Via Virgilio, Arco Felice, Pozzuoli, Spiaggia Romana, Via Scalandrone, Lucrino, Lago Lucrino, Via Miliscola, Lucrino, Solfatara, Lido Fusaro, Lago Fusaro, Via Fusaro, Via Lucullo, Tyrrhenian Sea, Baia, Torregaveta, Fusaro, Via Castello, Via Roma, Bay of Pozzuoli, Isolotto di San Martino, Monte di Procida, Bacoli, Via Piscina Mirabilis, Punta di Torre Fumo, Lago Miseno, Porto di Miseno, Ferries to Ischia & Procida, Miseno, Capo Miseno

☙ ANFITEATRO FLAVIO // WALK THE SET OF ANCIENT REALITY SHOWS

In its heyday, Italy's third-largest **amphitheatre** (Map p77; ☎ 081 526 60 07; Via Terracciano 75; adult/18-24yr/under18yr & over 65yr €4/2/free; ☺ 9am-1hr before sunset Wed-Mon; ® Cumana to Pozzuoli, Ⓜ Pozzuoli) could hold over 20,000 bloodthirsty spectators, who would pour in to cheer on mock naval battles (yes, the stadium was occasionally flooded for fun), and indulge in a little *schadenfreude* as lions chased those captive Christians. Planned by Nero and completed by Vespasian (AD 69–79), the ancient stadium's best-preserved remains lie under the main arena. Wander among the fallen columns and get your head around the complex mechanics involved in hoisting the caged wild beasts up to their waiting victims through the overhead 'skylights'. In AD 305 seven Christian martyrs were thrown to the animals by the emperor Diocletian. They survived, only to be later beheaded. One of the seven was San Gennaro, the patron saint of Naples.

The Anfiteatro hosts a summer season of theatre and concerts – contact the

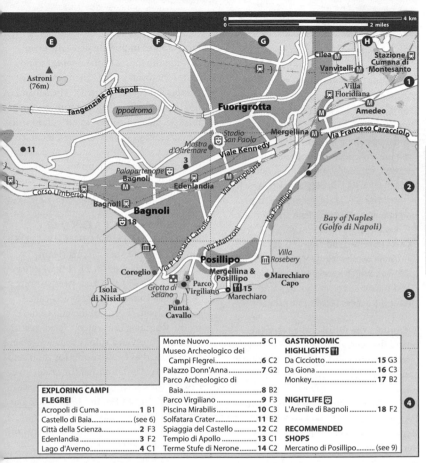

NAPLES

tourist office for information (see the boxed text, p80).

🌿 RIONE TERRA // SINK INTO A VERITABLE TIME MACHINE

Rising 33m above sea level at the western end of the seafront, **Rione Terra** (Map p77; ☎ 848 80 02 88; Largo Sedile di Porto; adult/6-18yr/under 6yr & over 65yr €3/2/free; ☼ vary; ℞ Cumana to Pozzuoli, Ⓜ Pozzuoli) is Pozzuoli's oldest quarter and its ancient acropolis. Beneath the current cluster of 17th-century buildings lies an archaeological treasure trove of roads, shops and even a brothel dating back to the days when the town was the ancient port of Puteoli. You can walk down the *decumanus maximus*, check out ancient taverns, peer into millers' shops (complete with intact grindstones) and decipher graffiti written by the poet Catallus in a dingy slaves' cell. Archaeologists made the startling find after volcanic activity in the 1970s forced a mass evacuation of the quarter. Above ground, Pozzuoli's 16th-century Duomo is built around an ancient Capitolium, itself lavishly restructured by Lucius Cocceius in the Augustan age.

NAPLES

Before exploring the Campi Flegrei, it's worth stopping at the helpful **tourist office** (Map p77; ☎ 081 526 66 39; Piazza Giacomo Matteotti 1a; ⊙ 9am-2pm & 2.30-3.40pm Mon-Fri Oct-May, 9am-1pm & 4-7.30pm daily Jun-Sep) in Pozzuoli to pick up tourist information and maps of the area. An easy five-minute walk downhill from the metro station, the tourist office also sells the good-value €4 cumulative ticket, which covers the Temple of Serapis and the archaeological sites of Baia and Cuma.

Also useful is bookshop **Cartolibreria '900** (Map p77; ☎ 081 526 13 63; Via Pergolesi 38c/d; ⊙ 9am-1pm & 4-8pm Mon-Sat), which stocks great books and information on the area and has internet access (€0.60 per hr).

Contact the tourist office (see the boxed the text, above) before visiting, as opening hours and public accessibility can be erratic.

❦ POZZUOLI MARKETS // COMPARE MARKETS, OLD AND NEW

Begin your market tour at the **Tempio di Serapide** (Temple of Serapis; Map p77; Via Serapide; ▣ Cumana to Pozzuoli, Ⓜ Pozzuoli). Badly damaged by centuries of seismic bradeyism and occasionally flooded by sea water, this sunken square just east of the port wasn't a temple at all but rather an ancient *macellum* (town market). Named after a statue of the Egyptian god Serapis found here in 1750, its ancient toilets (at either side of the eastern apse) are considered works of historical ingenuity.

An easy 300m walk to the northwest, the atmospheric **Mercato del Pesce di Pozzuoli** (Pozzuoli Fish Market; Map p77; Via Nicola Fasano; ⊙ 7.30am-1.30pm Tue-Sun) is the town's modern-day equivalent and a fab spot

for an appetising morning stroll. Good weather brings in the best catches, with local staples including *pesce azzurro*, *pesce bandiera* (sailfish), *seppie* (squid), *polipi* (octopus), *alici* (anchovies) and *gamberoni* (giant prawns). The second of the two aisles is a fragrant, mouth-watering spectacle of robust salami and *salsiccie* (sausages), plump cheeses, local fruits and vegetables, and crunchy *casareccio* bread. Peckish? Stock up for an impromptu picnic on nearby Monte Nuovo (see the boxed text, opposite).

❦ SOLFATARA CRATER // LET MOTHER NATURE UNNERVE YOU

Unnerving and surreal, this steamy **crater** (Map pp78-9; ☎ 081 526 23 41; Via Solfatara 161; adult/5-10yr €6/4; ⊙ 8.30am-1hr before sunset; ▣ Cumana to Pozzuoli, Ⓜ Pozzuoli) was called Foro Vulcani (home of the god of fire) by the Romans; the crater's acrid steam, bubbling mud and sulphurous water have been lauded as health cures for thousands of years. At the far end of the crater you can see the Stufe, two ancient grottos excavated at the end of the 19th century to create two brick *sudatoria* (sweat rooms). Christened Purgatory and Hell, they both reach temperatures of up to 90°C.

To get here, catch any city bus heading uphill from the metro station and ask the driver to let you off at Solfatara.

❦ CITTÀ DELLA SCIENZA // NURTURE THE EINSTEIN WITHIN

Part of a long-term redevelopment of the Bagnoli steelworks area 5km southeast of central Pozzuoli, the huge, interactive **Città della Scienza** (Science City; Map pp78-9; ☎ 081 242 00 24; www.cittadellascienza.it; Via Coroglio 104, Bagnoli; adult/4-18yr/under 4yr & over 65yr €7/5/free; ⊙ 9am-5pm Tue-Sat, 10am-7pm Sun Jun-Feb, 9am-5pm Mon-Sat, 10am-7pm Sun Mar-May; ▣ Cumana to Bagnoli, then ▣ C1) takes the 'geek' out of science. It's a particular hit with kids, who can get clued up on physics at the science gym, walk through constellations in the high-tech planetarium (€2) or just go plain silly pressing lots of funky buttons.

LUCRINO, BAIA & BACOLI

This string of towns spreads west from Pozzuoli along a built-up and inspiring coastal road. First up is Lucrino, where you'll find peaceful Lago d'Averno (the mythical entrance to hell) and a famous thermal spa centre. A further 3km southwest, Baia takes its name from Baios, a shipmate of Ulysses who died and was buried here. A glamorous Roman holiday resort with a sordid reputation, much of the ancient town is now under water (bradeyism again), though evocative ruins and a recently expanded archaeological museum help kickstart the imagination. A further 4km south is the sleepy fishing town of Bacoli, where the magical Piscina Mirabilis awaits.

❦ LAGO D'AVERNO // FIND PEACE AT HELL'S GATE

In Virgil's *Aeneid*, it is precisely from **Lago D'Averno** (Lake Averno; Map pp78-9; Via Lucrino Averno; ☒ Cumana to Lucrino) that Aeneas descends into the underworld. It's hard to imagine hell in such a soothing setting, with old vineyards and citrus groves lining this ancient crater. A popular walking track now circles the lake's entire perimeter, giving you more time to visualise bobbing ancient fleets – in 37 BC the Roman general Marcus Vipsanius Agrippa linked the lake to nearby Lago Lucrino and the sea, turning it into a strategic naval dockyard.

The battleships may have gone, but the lakeside ruins of the **Tempio di Apollo** (Temple of Apollo) remain. Built during the reign of Hadrian in the 2nd century AD, this thermal complex once boasted a domed roof almost the size of the Pantheon's in Rome. Today, only four great arched windows remain.

Lago D'Averno is an easy 1km walk north of Lucrino train station.

❦ TERME STUFE DI NERONE // PAMPER YOURSELF LIKE THE ANCIENTS

Your body will thank you after a trip to this much-loved **thermal spa complex** (Map pp78-9; ☎ 081 868 80 06; www.termestufedinerone.it, in Italian; Via Stufe di Nerone 37; admission incl massage €48; ☒ 8am-11pm Tue, Thu & Fri, to 8pm Mon,

THE NOVICE MOUNTAIN

It's not every week that a mountain just appears on the scene. But this is exactly what happened just west of Pozzuoli in 1538. It all began in the early 1530s, when the area began experiencing an unusual level of seismic activity. Meanwhile, locals began noticing a dramatic uplift of the land between Lago d'Averno, Monte Barbaro and the sea, which displaced the coast by several hundred metres. Little did they know that under them a **Monte Nuovo** (New Mountain; Map pp78-9; ☎ 081 804 14 62; Via Virgilio; ☒ 9am-1hr before sunset; ☒ Cumana to Arco Felice) was getting set for its grand debut. At 8pm on 29 September 1538, a crack appeared in the earth near the ancient Roman settlement of Tripergole, spewing out a violent concoction of pumice, fire and smoke over six days. By the end of the week, Pozzuoli had a new 134m-tall neighbour. Today, Europe's newest mountain is a lush and peaceful nature reserve. Off the tourist track, its shady sea-view slopes are the perfect spot for a chilled-out stroll or picnic.

Wed & Sat, to 3pm Sun Sep-Jun, 8am-8pm Mon-Sat, to 3pm Sun Jul & Aug; 🚇 Cumana to Lucrino). Built on the site of an ancient Roman prototype (spot the remnants in the bar), its muscle-melting combo of steamy grottos, thera-peutic mineral baths and pools, massage and beauty treatments (60-minute shiatsu massages are €50, body mud peels are €25), and botanically savvy grounds make for a blissful interlude. Book treatments online at least two days in advance, and don't forget to bring your own swimsuit, towel and flip-flops (thongs).

From Lucrino train station, walk 500m southwest along Via Miliscola before turning right into Via Stufe di Nerone. The entrance is 200m ahead. If you have your own wheels, on-site parking costs €2 for cars and €1.50 for scooters.

♥ MUSEO ARCHEOLOGICO DEI CAMPI FLEGREI // ENCOUNTER LOCAL HISTORY IN A TOWERING CASTLE

Bigger and better after a recent expan-sion, the Campi Flegrei's **Archaeologi-cal Museum** (Map pp78-9; ☎ 081 523 37 97; Via Castello; adult/18-24yr/under 18yr & over 65yr €4/2/free; 🕙 9am-1hr before sunset Tue-Sun; 🚇 Cumana to Fusa-ro, then 🚌 EAV to Baia) brims with local finds, including a bewitching Nymphaeum, dredged up from underwater Baiae and skilfully reassembled. Monuments conse-crated to the nymphs, nymphaeums were a popular spot to tie the proverbial knot. Other highlights include a bronze eques-trian statue of the Emperor Domitian (altered to resemble his more popular successor Nerva upon his deposition) and finds from Rione Terra (p79).

The museum sits in the **Castello di Baia** (Map pp78-9), built in the late 15th century by the Aragonese as a defence against possible French invasion. Later enlarged by Spanish viceroy Don Pedro de Toledo, it served as a military orphan-age for most of the 20th century. The bay views are sublime.

♥ PARCO ARCHEOLOGICO DI BAIA // WALK WHERE EMPERORS BATHED

In Roman times, these 1st-century BC **ruins** (Map pp78-9; ☎ 081 868 75 92; Piazza Alcide De Gaspero, off Via Lucullo, Bacoli; adult/18-24yr/under 18yr & over 65yr €4/2/free; 🕙 9am-1hr before sunset Tue-Sun; 🚇 Cumana to Fusaro, then 🚌 EAV to Baia) were part of a sprawling palace and spa complex. Emperors would entertain themselves and their guests in a series of lavishly decorated thermal baths that descended to the sea. Among the surviving salubri-ous snippets are exquisite floor mosaics, a beautifully stuccoed *balneum* (bathroom), an outdoor theatre and the impressive Tempio di Mercurio, its domed swim-ming pool filled with giant goldfish. In the summer months, the outdoor theatre is

A CHOICE DIP

Right below the Castello di Baia sits the wonderful **Spiaggia del Castello** (Castle Beach; Map pp78-9). A sandy double-sided affair, it's only accessible by **boat** (☎ 338 169 34 48; 🕙 8.30am-7pm Jun-Aug, to 6pm late Apr-May & early-mid Sep; one-way ticket €2.50, Sat, Sun & Aug €4) from a nearby jetty. To reach the jetty, catch the EAV bus to Baia and get off outside the FIART factory just south of town. Walk a further 200m south and turn left into the driveway at the curve. Past the green-and-yellow iron gate sit the car park and jetty, where you can hire a sundeck (€5) or umbrella (€5) for stylish waterside sunning. Avoid the weekend summer crowds by coming earlier in the week.

sometimes used for opera performances by the Teatro San Carlo (p61).

From the Fusaro station on the Cumana rail line, walk 150m north to Via Fusaro, from where Miseno-bound EAV buses run roughly every 30 minutes Monday to Saturday and every hour on Sunday to the site, and on to Bacoli, home of the Piscina Mirabilis (below).

♥ PISCINA MIRABILIS // TRACK DOWN A ROMAN MARVEL

An archaeological pièce de résistance, the **Piscina Mirabilis** (Marvellous Pool; Map pp78-9; ☎ 081 523 31 99; Via Piscina Mirabilis; ☺ vary; ® Cumana to Fusaro, then ⊟ EAV to Bacoli) lies tucked away in a Bacoli backstreet. To access it, contact custodian Signora Filomena at No 9, who has the key to what is the world's largest Roman cistern. Bathed in an eerie light and featuring 48 soaring pillars and a barrel-vaulted ceiling, it's more 'subterranean cathedral' that 'giant water tank'. The cistern was an Augustan-era creation, its 12,600 cu metre water supply serving the military fleet at nearby Miseno. Fresh water flowed into the cistern from the Serino river aqueduct, which was then raised up to the terrace with hydraulic engines, exiting through doors in the central nave. Engineers still marvel at its sophistication. Admission is free, but save face and tip the *signora* a euro.

CUMA

Founded in the 8th century BC by Greek colonists from the island of Euboea, ancient Cumae exerted a powerful sway on the ancient imagination.

♥ ACROPOLI DI CUMA // LISTEN OUT FOR THE SIBYL

The centre of the ancient settlement of Cuma was this **acropolis** (Map pp78-9; ☎ 081 854 30 60; Via Montecuma; admission €4; ☺ 9am-1hr before sunset; ® Cumana to Fusaro, then ⊟ EAV to Cuma). Situated at its base, the Tempio di Apollo (Temple of Apollo) was built on the site where Daedalus is said to have flown into Italy. According to Greek mythology, Daedalus and his son Icarus took to the skies to escape King Minos in Crete. En route Icarus flew too close to the sun and plunged to his death as his wax-and-feather wings melted from the heat. Last entry is one hour before close.

At the top of the acropolis stands the **Tempio di Giove** (Temple of Jupiter). Dating back to the 5th century BC, it was later converted into a Christian basilica, of which the remains of the altar and the circular baptismal font are visible.

The star attraction, however, is the haunting **Antro della Sibilla Cumana** (Cave of the Cumaean Sibyl). Hollowed out of the tufa bank, its 130m-long trapezoidal tunnel leads to an eerie vaulted chamber where the oracle was said to pass on messages from Apollo. The poet Virgil, probably inspired by a visit to the cave himself, writes of Aeneas coming here to seek the Sibyl, who directs him to Hades (the underworld), entered from nearby Lago d'Averno (p81). Less poetic are recent studies that maintain the tunnel was originally built as part of Cuma's defence system.

From the Fusaro Cumana station, walk 150m north to Via Fusaro, from where Cuma-bound EAV buses run roughly every 30 minutes Monday to Saturday and every hour on Sunday.

ELSEWHERE

Naples' northwest Fuorigrotta district is home to several entertainment venues, including the city's iconic fun park.

NAPLES

❦ EDENLANDIA // DITCH CULTURE FOR DODGEMS

Fabulously kitsch and loads of fun, Naples' major **amusement park** (Map pp78-9; ☎ 081 239 40 90; www.edenlandia.it, in Italian; Viale Kennedy 76; adult/child under 1.1m €2.50/free, per ride €2, unlimited-rides ticket €10; ☺ vary, call ahead; ⓡ Cumana to Edenlandia) boasts a plethora of attractions, including dodgem cars, a fairy-tale castle, a 3D cinema and a flight simulator. The €2.50 admission covers the cinema, variety show and children's theatre.

FESTIVALS & EVENTS

Festa di San Gennaro The faithful flock to the Duomo to witness the miraculous liquefaction of San Gennaro's blood on the Saturday before the first Sunday in May. Repeat performances take place on 19 September and 16 December.

Maggio dei Monumenti (☎ 081 247 11 23) A month-long cultural feast, with a bounty of concerts, performances, exhibitions, guided tours and other events across the city; May.

Napoli Teatro Festival Italia (www.teatro festivalitalia.it) More than three weeks of local and international theatre and performance art, staged in conventional and unconventional venues across the city; June.

Napoli Film Festival (www.napolifilmfestival. com, in Italian) Six days of local and international flicks and celluloid chat; June.

Madonna del Carmine Pilgrims and fireworks on Piazza del Mercato, in honour of the Chiesa di Santa Maria del Carmine's miraculous Madonna; 16 July.

Festa di Piedigrotta (www.festadipiedigrotta. it) Folk tunes, floats and fireworks mark this historic song fest, centred on the Chiesa di Piedigrotta in Mergellina; early to mid-September.

Pizzafest (www.pizzafest.info, in Italian) A celebration of Naples' most famous edible export, with local and international *pizzaioli* kneading it out for top honours; September.

GASTRONOMIC HIGHLIGHTS

Naples is one of Italy's gastronomic heavyweights, and the bonus of a bayside setting makes for some seriously memorable meals. While white linen, candlelight and €50 bills are readily available, some of the best bites await in the city's spit-and-sawdust trattorias, where three courses and house wine can cost under €15. Even cheaper is Naples' plethora of top-notch pizzerias and *friggitorie* (fried-food kiosks). Indeed, you could do a lot worse than picking up a €3 bag of fried goodies or a slice of margherita for a flavoursome lunch. On the downside, many eateries close for two weeks in August, so call ahead if visiting then. For the lowdown on local dishes, see p255.

CENTRO STORICO & MERCATO

❦ ANGELO CARBONE €

Map pp42-3; ☎ 081 45 78 21; Largo Regina Coeli 4-8; pastries from €1; ☺ 7am-8pm; Ⓜ Museo
Off the tourist trail but well on the radar of locals, this chintzy bar-pasticceria-*rosticceria* makes one seriously buttery *sfogliatella*, not to mention a heavenly *pasticcino crema e amarena* (a shortpastry bun filled with cherries and custard). Savoury options include satisfying *panini* (€2) and there's alfresco seating beside the frescoed porticos of the Chiesa Santa Maria Regina Coeli opposite.

❦ ATTANASIO €

Map pp42-3; ☎ 081 28 56 75; Vico Ferrovia 1-4; snacks from €1.20; ☺ 6.30am-7.30pm Tue-Sun; Ⓜ Garibaldi
So you thought a *sfogliatella* from Pintauro (p88) was crispy perfection? Bite into the piping-hot ricotta filling at this retro pastry pedlar and prepare to reas-

ess. But why stop there with so many trays of fresh, plump treats on show, from creamy *cannoli siciliani* to a runny, gummy *babà*. Savoury fiends shouldn't pass up the hearty *pasticcino rustico*, stuffed with *provola* cheese, ricotta and salami.

CHARCUTERIE €
Map pp42-3; ☎ 081 551 69 81; Via Benedetto Croce 3; Ⓜ Dante
Even the doors heave with gourmet grub at this jam-packed little deli. Fill your bags with everything from pasta, macaroons and *grappa* (Italian pomace brandy), to lemon-flavoured olive oil and chocolate-coated figs.

DA MICHELE €
Map pp42-3; ☎ 081 553 92 04; Via Cesare Sersale 1; pizzas from €4; Ⓨ 11am-11pm Mon-Sat; Ⓡ R2 to Corso Umberto I
Veteran pizza brat-pack member Da Michele keeps things plain and simple: unadorned marble tabletops, brisk service and two types of pizza – margherita or marinara. Both are delicious and guaranteed to turn you into a pizza snob. Just show up, take a ticket and wait your turn.

DI MATTEO €
Map pp42-3; ☎ 081 45 52 62; Via dei Tribunali 94; snacks €0.50, pizzas from €2.50; Ⓨ 9am-midnight Mon-Sat, closed 2 weeks Aug; Ⓡ CS to Via Duomo
Di Matteo's golden, velvety *crocchè* are like a culinary cuddle. In fact, the little street stall at this no-frills pizzeria sells some of the city's best fried snacks, from *pizza fritta* (fried pizza) to nourishing *arancini* (fried rice balls). If you're after a sit-down feed, head inside for trademark mallow lighting, surly waiters, and lip-smacking pizzas, best washed down with cold bottled beer.

EUROPA MATTOZZI €€€
Map pp42-3; ☎ 081 552 13 23; Via Campodisola Marchese 4; meals €45; Ⓨ closed Sun & 2 weeks Aug; Ⓡ R2 to Corso Umberto I
A dignified dining institution that has wowed the best of them – Anita Ekberg signed the plate in the window. Colourful ceramic plates line the walls, while seasonal classics line the menu. While the *antipasto misto* (mixed antipasto platter) makes for an inspiring prologue (we adore the delicate artichoke and potato frittata), trust your waiter's suggestions – whether it's the grilled squid with endive or the soothing pasta Genovese, you'll be toasting like a Swedish goddess. Book ahead.

GAY-ODIN €
Map pp42-3; ☎ 081 551 07 94; Via Benedetto Croce 61; Ⓨ 9.30am-8pm Mon-Sat, 10am-2pm Sun, closed Sun summer; Ⓜ Dante
Not so much a chocolatier as an institution, Gay-odin concocts some of the city's finest cocoa creations, including oh-so-Neapolitan chocolate *'cozze'* (mussels). For a punch to the palate, try the chocolate-coated coffee beans or the fiery *peperoncino-cioccolato* (chilli-chocolate) combo. This branch also sells Gay-odin's creamy-licious gelato.

LA CANTINA DELLA SAPIENZA €
Map pp42-3; ☎ 081 45 90 78; Via della Sapienza 40; meals €18; Ⓨ lunch Mon-Sat; Ⓜ Cavour
No culinary acrobatics here, just pared-down, just-like-mamma classics served to loyal locals – think *parmigiana di melanzane* (slices of baked aubergine with decadent layers of tomato and Parmesan) and succulent *salsiccia di maiale* (pork sausages). The *'di tutto un po' contorno* ('bit of everything' side dish) allows you to sample a wide variety of flavours, such as sweet pan-fried

NAPLES

peppers, while sweet tooths will be positively chuffed to know that the owner Gaetano whips up a different dessert every day.

🍴 LA STANZA DEL GUSTO €€€

Map pp42-3; ☎ 081 40 15 78; Via Santa Maria di Costantinopoli 100; set lunch €18, meals €45; ☺ cheese bar 11am-4pm & 7.30pm-midnight Tue-Sat, 7.30pm-midnight Mon, 11am-4pm Sun, upstairs restaurant 7.30pm-midnight Mon-Sat; Ⓜ Dante

Eclectic and buzzing, 'The Taste Room' has caused a stir with its mod-twist local grub. On the ground floor, the trendy 'cheese bar' is perfect for low-fuss vino sessions or a graze on rare cheeses and fab *zuppe* (soups), while the upstairs dining room is *the* spot for daring dishes like a *fegatini* (chicken liver) flan with strawberry salsa and variations on *baccalà* (salted cod). For a gastronomic adventure, opt for a tasting menu (€35 to €65). The small basement food shop stocks La Stanza's very own sauces, as well as take-home deli treats and wines.

🍴 PIZZERIA GINO SORBILLO €

Map pp42-3; ☎ 081 44 66 43; Via dei Tribunali 32; pizzas from €3; ☺ Mon-Sat; Ⓜ Dante

The clamouring crowds say it all: Gino Sorbillo is the Naples pizza king. We specify Gino because there are two other Sorbillo pizzerias on the same block, all from one family of 21 pizza-making siblings! Gino's pizzas are gigantic, wood-fired to perfection and best followed by a velvety *semifreddo*; we're addicted to the chocolate and *torroncino* (almond nougat) combo. Done, check out the converted condom vending machine in the basement, now dispensing Neapolitan lucky charms. It's one of several in-house works by artistic duo Ulderico & Ognissanti (see the boxed text, p52).

🍴 PIZZERIA VESI €

Map pp42-3; ☎ 081 29 99 95; Via dei Tribunali 388; pizzas from €2.50; ☺ 10.30am-5pm & 7pm-1am; 🚌 R2 to Corso Umberto I

If Gino Sorbillo (left) is closed, this popular pizzeria makes for a handy back-up plan. The pizzas are more than decent and there's warm-weather alfresco seating for voyeuristic noshing.

🍴 SCATURCHIO €

Map pp42-3; ☎ 081 551 70 31; Piazza San Domenico Maggiore 19; pastries from €1.30; ☺ 7.30am-8.30pm; Ⓜ Dante

In a city infamous for belt-busting temptations, this vintage *pasticceria* enjoys cult status. While you'll find all the local classics (including a particularly luscious *babà*), the star attraction is the *ministeriale*. A dark-chocolate medallion invented in the 19th century, the ingredients of its liqueur-laced ganache filling are a closely guarded secret. At the time of research, a frescoed tearoom was set to open upstairs.

🍴 TARALLIFICIO LEOPOLDO €

Map pp68-9; ☎ 081 45 11 66; Via Foria 212; snacks from €2; ☺ 8.30am-9pm; Ⓜ Cavour

Made with pepper, almonds and pork fat, oven-baked *tarallini mandorlati* (savoury almond biscuits) are dangerously moreish and readily available at this fourth-generation bakery-*pasticceria*. For a sugar hit try the buttery *taralli zuccherati* (sugared *taralli*); the ones without the icing sugar are best. *Taralli*'s traditional rivals are also available here, from *babà* to a wicked *cannoletto* crammed with chocolate butter cream and dipped in dark chocolate.

🍴 TRATTORIA MANGIA E BEVI €

Map pp42-3; ☎ 081 552 95 46; Via Sedile di Porto 92; meals €8; ☺ lunch only, closed Sat & Sun; 🚌 R2 to Corso Umberto I

Utterly unmissable, this loud and lively trattoria sees everyone from pierced stu-

ents to bespectacled *professori* squeeze
round the communal tables for brilliant
ome cooking at rock-bottom prices. Scan
he daily-changing menu, jot down your
hoices and prepare yourself for gems
uch as grilled *provola* cheese, juicy *salsic-
ia* (pork sausage) and *peperoncino*-spiked
riarielli (local broccoli). The *casareccio*
read is crunchy perfection and best
ashed down with a plastic cup of vino.

TOLEDO & QUARTIERI
SPAGNOLI

ANTICHE DELIZIE €
ap p55; ☎ 081 551 30 88; Via Pasquale Scura 14;
8am-8pm Mon-Sat; Ⓜ Montesanto

Hanging hams, succulent salami and the
est mozzarella in town: this legendary
eli is the perfect picnic pit stop. If it's
riday, don't miss the heavenly *capri-*
netti (goat's cheese stuffed with herbs).
Otherwise, taste test the *provolone del*
Monaco (a cheese seasoned in wine cel-
rs), pick up some *prêt-à-manger* anti-
asto or furnish the cellar with a bottle of
ocal Greco del Tufo.

CAFFÈ MEXICO €
ap p55; ☎ 081 549 93 30; Piazza Dante 86;
7am-8.30pm Mon-Sat; Ⓜ Dante

Naples' best (and best-loved) espresso
ar is a retro-tastic combo of old-school
aristas, orange espresso machine and
elvety, full-flavoured *caffè*. The espresso
ere is served *zuccherato* (sweetened), so
equest it *amaro* if you fancy a bitter hit.
or an in-the-know treat, request a *harem*
on *panna* (an Arabica bean espresso
opped with luscious cream and devoured
ith a teaspoon). There's another branch
: Piazza Garibaldi 70 (Map pp42–3).

FANTASIA GELATI €
ap p55; ☎ 081 551 12 12; Via Toledo 381; gelato
om €1.50; 7.30am-midnight; CS to Via Toledo

Head here for the city's finest gelato. The
heavenly, made-on-site flavours include
a dangerously dense *cuore nero* (dark
chocolate), bound to leave chocoholics
gagging for more. The *gelato caldo* (hot
gelato) flavours aren't actually warm –
just creamier. There's another handy
branch in Vomero (p90).

FRIGGITORIA FIORENZANO €
Map p55; ☎ 081 551 27 88; Piazza Monte-
santo; snacks from €1; 8am-10.30pm Mon-Sat;
Ⓜ Montesanto

Slap-bang in market country, this majolica-tiled veteran serves Italian-style
tempura such as crunchy deep-fried
aubergines and artichokes (in season),
and prosciutto-and-mozzarella-stuffed
crocchè. Wolf them down by the counter
or dive back into the market throng.

IL GARUM €€
Map p55; ☎ 081 542 32 28; Piazza Monteoliveto 2a;
meals €40; daily; R4 to Via Monteoliveto

The kind of place you keep coming back
to, this cosy *osteria* (wine bar that serves
food) blends whitewashed walls, linen-
clad tables and softly glowing wrought-
iron lanterns. Delicately flavoured,
revamped classics are the order of the
day in dishes like rigatoni with shred-
ded courgettes (zucchini) and mussels,
and an exquisite grilled calamari stuffed
with vegetables, cherry tomatoes and
Parmesan. All the cakes are made on the
premises and there's live Neapolitan music once or twice a week.

LA TAVERNA DEL
BUONGUSTAIO €
Map p55; ☎ 081 551 26 26; Via Basilio Puoti 8; meals
€16; Mon-Sat, lunch only Sun, closed Sun Jun-Sep;
CS to Via Toledo

A stroll through La Pignasecca (p57) is
bound to whet your appetite. Mercifully,

this low-fuss, Totò-loving, white-tiled dining room is a fork plunge away. Written menus are traded in for fast-talking, white-capped cooks who speed through the daily specials with seasoned dexterity. Don't stress! It's all fresh, faithful home cooking, from the moreish *fritto misto* (mixed fried seafood) to the sublime *spaghetti alle frutte di mare* (spaghetti with mussels and clams). A local favourite; it's best to book ahead.

🍴 NENNELLA €

Map p55; ☎ 081 41 43 38; Vico Lungo Teatro 103-105; meals €10; ⏰ Mon-Sat; 🚌 R2 to Piazza Trieste e Trento

Casareccio cooking and Neapolitan theatricality collide at loud, unmissable Nennella. Give your name and number of guests to joke-cracking Ciro and wait for the boisterous staff to call you in, boot camp style. Inside, roguish waiters shout orders across the floor, patriarchs propose toasts and Rolexed studs dine with Mafia mistresses. Tuck into crispy fried sardines, lip-smacking *spaghetti con lupine* (spaghetti with lupin) or *insalatona nennella* (rocket, bresaola and radish salad). If the queue is long, head one block north for a premeal swill at A Pigna d'Uva (p92).

🍴 PINTAURO €

Map p55; ☎ 348 7781645; Via Toledo 275; sfogliatella €1.50; ⏰ 8am-2pm & 2.30-8pm Mon-Sat Jun & Jul, 8am-2pm & 2.30-8pm Mon-Sat, 9am-2pm Sun Sep-May; 🚌 R2 to Piazza Trieste e Trento

Another local institution (even the owner looks like Sofia Loren's long-lost cousin), cinnamon-scented Pintauro sells perfect *sfogliatelle* to shopped-out locals. But don't stop there; it makes a mean *babà* to boot.

🍴 TRIPPERIA FIORENZANO €

Map p55; ☎ 349 7810146; Via Pignasecca 14; snacks from €2; ⏰ 8.30am-8.30pm Mon-Sat; Ⓜ Montesanto

Beneath languorous strips of hanging tripe, fifth-generation *trippaio* (tripe seller) Antonio and his wife busily prepare take-home orders for hurried housewives. Behind the counter, five tables and a neon blue shrine to Christ set the scene for sit-down adventures. Be brave and try the *zuppa di carne cotta* (tripe broth; €6) or the quintessentially Neapolitan tripe with tomato and basil. You might surprise yourself.

SANTA LUCIA & CHIAIA

🍴 ANTICA OSTERIA DA TONINO €

Map pp62-3; ☎ 081 42 15 33; Via Santa Teresa a Chiaia 47; lunch €12, meals €22; ⏰ lunch daily, dinner Fri & Sat; Ⓜ Amedeo

Just shy of 80, the quick-witted Tonino (nicknamed JR by his wife, who still runs the kitchen) is still going strong, just like his heirloom *osteria*. At the front, time-pressed *signore* pick up their takeaway orders and a bottle of red. At the few packed tables, Rubinacci suits, old-timers and the odd Nobel Prize winner (Dario Fo ate here) tuck into hearty, honest grub like *rigatoni ragù e ricotta* (rigatoni in a meat and ricotta sauce).

🍴 CAFFÈ GAMBRINUS €

Map pp62-3; ☎ 081 41 75 82; Via Chiaia 1-2; espresso at bar/sitting down €0.90/3, sfogliatella at bar/sitting down €1.50/4; ⏰ 7am-2am Sun-Fri, to 3am Sat; 🚌 R2 to Piazza Trieste e Trento

The grand Gambrinus is Naples' oldest and most venerable cafe. Oscar Wilde knocked back a few here and Mussolini had some of the rooms shut down to keep out left-wing intellectuals. Sure, the prices may be steeper, but sipping a spritz or nibbling on a pastry amid the

marble and chandeliers is a moment
worth savouring.

DI BRUNO €€€

Map pp62-3; ☎ 081 251 24 11; Riviera di Chiaia
213-214; meals €50; ☺ Tue-Sun; 🚌 C25 to Riviera
di Chiaia

Discerning palates flock here for uppercrust Italian fare, a 350-strong wine list
and impeccable service. Seafood is the
undisputed star, with offerings such as a
show-stopping *spaghetti ricci e cicinielli*
(spaghetti with sea urchin and whitebait)
guaranteed to please the picky. The pasta
is made from scratch, as are the desserts,
which may include a spectacular *tortina
di cioccolato* (chocolate tartlet), best accompanied by a glass of Barolo Chinato.

DORA €€€

Map pp62-3; ☎ 081 68 05 19; Via Ferdinando Palas-
ciano 30; meals €60; ☺ lunch Tue-Sun, dinner Mon-
Sat; 🚌 152 to Riviera di Chiaia

An empty seat is as rare as a mediocre
meal at this retro, tiled VIP favourite.
Tuck into seafood revelations like *linguine alla Dora* (al dente pasta pimped
with fresh anchovies, prawns, mussels
and *sparnocchie*, a prawn-like crustacean), always best preceded by an *antipasto misto*, which may include succulent
octopus salad and fried-to-perfection
calamaretti (baby squid) drizzled in
lemon juice. Best of all, veteran owner
Signora Consiglia breaks out into song
every night. Book ahead.

LA FOCACCIA €

Map pp62-3; ☎ 081 41 22 77; Vico Belledonne a
Chiaia 31; focaccias from €1.60; ☺ 11am-late Mon-
Sat, 5pm-late Sun, closed Aug; 🚌 C25 to Piazza dei
Martiri

The young, hip and the just plain starving cram into this funky spot for fat focaccia squares stacked with lip-smacking

combos such as artichokes and *provola*
cheese, or aubergine with pecorino and
smoked ham. Best of all, there isn't a mi-
crowave oven in sight! There's another
handy branch on Piazza del Municipio
(Map pp62–3).

LA SCIALUPPA €€€

Map pp62-3; ☎ 081 764 53 33; Borgo Marinaro 4;
meals €45; ☺ Tue-Sun; 🚌 152 to Via Partenope

Almost 150 years young and a hit with
Italian VIPs, La Scialuppa is a sound
choice for romantic harbourside noshing. Predictably, seafood is the menu's
winner, from the delicious *fritto misto* to
the vino-infused *risotto alla scialuppa*. In
the warmer months, the yacht-flanking
alfresco tables are prized possessions, so
book ahead.

LA TRATTORIA DELL'OCA €€

Map pp62-3; ☎ 081 41 48 65; www.trattoriadell
oca.it; Via Santa Teresa a Chiaia 11; meals €20;
☺ closed dinner Sun Oct-May; Ⓜ Amedeo

Refined yet relaxed, this intimate, softly
lit trattoria is divided into several dining
alcoves where wine bottles and vintage
Neapolitan prints line the walls. The daily changing menu celebrates beautifully
cooked classics, which may include *gnocchi al ragù* or a superb *baccalà* cooked
with succulent cherry tomatoes, capers
and olives.

L.U.I.S.E. €

Map pp62-3; ☎ 081 41 77 35; Piazza dei Martiri 68;
snacks from €1.20, meals €15; ☺ 7.30am-8.30pm
Mon-Sat, 8.30am-3.30pm Sun; 🚌 C25 to Piazza dei
Martiri

A chic little deli that's a gourmand's play-
pen, L.U.I.S.E. peddles everything from
plump local cheeses to homemade food-
stuffs and bottles of luscious wine. In the
back room, lunching nine-to-fivers tuck
into warming osso bucco, nourishing

NAPLES

risottos and homemade gnocchi. Busy travellers can take away, with freshly fried *pizza fritta*, crisp *arancini* and sugar-dusted *pasticcini crema amarena* (pastries filled with cherry cream).

🍽 MOCCIA €
Map pp62-3; ☎ 081 41 13 48; Via San Pasquale a Chiaia 21-22; pastries from €0.60; ⏰ Wed-Mon; 🚌 C25 to Riviera di Chiaia

With gleaming displays of dainty strawberry tartlets, liqueur-soaked *babà* and creamy gelato (try a watermelon and peach combo), no one is safe at this chichi pastry *pasticceria* – blow-waved matriarchs, peckish professionals or waif-thin Chiaia princesses. The almond *caprese* is the best in town, and best washed down with a potent espresso.

VOMERO, CAPODIMONTE & LA SANITÀ

🍽 ANTICA CANTINA DI SICA €€
Map pp68-9; ☎ 081 556 75 20; Via Gianlorenzo Bernini 17, meals €27; ⏰ Tue-Sun; Ⓜ Vanvitelli

While the softly lit vaulted ceilings and genteel vibe recall central Italy, this wonderful gastronomic hideaway is true to classic regional fare made with salutary attention to detail. The generous antipasto is an inspiring introduction (think tender tripe in fragrant tomato sauce and buttery *melanzana parmigiana*), while the *frittura mista* (mixed fried seafood) stays crispy to the last bite. The homemade desserts (try the velvety *cassata napoletana*) are equally inspired.

🍽 DONNA TERESA €
Map pp68-9; ☎ 081 556 70 70; Via Michele Kerbaker 58; meals €14; ⏰ Mon-Sat; Ⓜ Vanvitelli

This swing-a-cat-sized dining room – there are only eight tables – has an epic reputation for solid home cooking. Mamma Teresa's photo looks on approv-

ingly as regulars tuck into low-fuss classics like *pasta provola e melanzane* (pasta with *provola* cheese and aubergines) and *salsicce al sugo* (sausages with tomato sauce). The menu is limited, changes daily and pulls in the hordes, so book ahead or go early.

🍽 FANTASIA GELATI €
Map pp68-9; ☎ 081 578 83 83; Piazza Vanvitelli 22; gelato from €1.50; ⏰ 7.30am-midnight; Ⓜ Vanvitelli

This branch of Naples' king of gelato serves fresh, seasonal, icy perfection to Vomero's middle-class gluttons. Do not deprive your taste buds!

🍽 FRIGGITORIA VOMERO €
Map pp68-9; ☎ 081 578 31 30; Via Domenico Cimarosa 44; snacks from €0.20; ⏰ Mon-Sat; funicular Centrale to Fuga

The stuff of legend (it even boasts its own Facebook fan page), this spartan snack bar makes some of the city's finest *fritture* (deep-fried snacks). Crunch away on deep-fried aubergines, potatoes and *zeppole*, *frittatine di maccheroni* (fried pasta and egg) and *supplì di riso* (rice balls). Located opposite the funicular, it's a handy pit stop before legging it to the Certosa di San Martino.

🍽 STARITA €
Map pp68-9; ☎ 081 557 46 82; Via Materdei 28; pizzas from €3; ⏰ Tue-Sun; Ⓜ Materdei

They don't get more Neapolitan than this pizzeria, set in a washing-fringed street. The giant fork and ladle hanging on the wall were used by Sophia Loren in *L'Oro di Napoli,* and the kitchen made the *pizze fritte* sold by the actress in the film. While the 53 pizza varieties include a tasty *fiorilli e zucchini* (zucchini, zucchini flowers and *provola*), our allegiance remains to its classic marinara.

MERGELLINA & POSILLIPO

CHALET CIRO MERGELLINA €

Map p75; ☎ 081 66 99 28; Via Francesco Caracciolo; pastries from €1.50, gelato brioche €3.80; ⏰ 7am-?am Thu-Tue; Ⓜ Mergellina

This iconic seaside chalet sells everything from coffee and pastries to crêpes, but the reason to head here is for *brioche con gelato*, a sweetened bun stuffed with delectable ice cream and topped with a dollop of *panna* (cream). Pay inside, choose your flavours at the street-side counter, and then counter the cals with a bayside saunter.

DA CICCIOTTO €€

Map pp78-9; ☎ 081 575 11 65; Calata Ponticello a Marechiaro 32; meals €40; ⏰ daily; 🚌 140 to Via Posillipo

Perched on a cliff in the fishing village of Marechiaro, low-key yet elegant Cicciotto is a seasoned charmer. Edible highlights include a sublime carpaccio antipasto (thin slices of raw seafood drizzled with lemon juice and olive oil), lightly battered courgette flowers stuffed with ricotta and a *pacchetti* pasta dish served with local crab and cherry tomatoes. Desserts such as *crostata* with lemon cream, wild strawberries and Chantilly cream are equally mesmerising. There's a warm-weather terrace, and a free courtesy shuttle (☎ 338 380 3 75, in Italian) servicing various city hotels. Book ahead.

DI GIROLAMO GIUSEPPE €

Map p75; ☎ 081 66 44 98; Via Mergellina 55e; pizza al taglio from €1.50, pasta from €3; ⏰ 8am-3pm & ?-11pm; Ⓜ Mergellina

A lovable bakery-cum-snack bar with tasty eat-and-go grub; pop in for superb *pizza al taglio* (pizza by the slice), with combos including pumpkin, tomato, basil and olives. Other winners include

pizza fritta, focaccia, just-like-mamma-made *pasta al forno* and tray upon tray of luscious, gleaming *crostate* (tarts).

SALVATORE €€

Map p75; ☎ 081 68 18 17; Via Mergellina 4a; meals €40; ⏰ Thu-Tue; 🚌 140 to Via Mergellina

The key to happiness? Balmy nights, sea breezes and impeccable seafood. You're guaranteed at least the last two at this stylish veteran, with its *dolce vita* terrace and sofly lit interior. Here, culinary clichés make way for inspired gems such as *cecinielle* (fried fish patties), comforting *minestra in brodo* (thick noodle broth) and *seppie con uva passa* (baby squid with pine nuts and raisins).

CAMPI FLEGREI

DA GIONA €€

Map pp78-9; ☎ 081 523 46 59; Via Dragonara 6, Miseno; meals €30; ⏰ lunch & dinner May-Oct, lunch only Nov-Apr; Ⓡ Cumana to Fusaro, then 🚌 EAV to Miseno

Right on a sandy beach with views of Procida and Ischia, this retro, sun-bleached restaurant enjoys cult status in Naples (book ahead on weekends). The seafood dishes are simple, fresh and lingering, from the *antipasto misto* (which might include fried courgettes and prawns, marinated carpaccio and octopus salad) to an unforgettable *spaghetti alle vongole* (spaghetti with clams). If the weather's on your side, request a table on the raffish deck, and while away the hours with a local Falanghina.

EXYTUS CAFFÈ €

Map p77; ☎ 081 526 70 90 ; Corso della Repubblica 126, Pozzuoli; ⏰ 7.30am-1.30pm & 4pm-2am; Ⓡ Cumana to Pozzuoli, Ⓜ Pozzuoli

It might just be a tiny hole-in-the-wall (okay, technically, there are two holes in the wall), but Exytus is a street cafe

NAPLES

with a big reputation. Join the curbside crowd for espresso with perfect *schiuma zuccherata* (sugared froth), best enjoyed with a brilliant *cornetto* (croissant); we have a major crush on the *crema e amarena* (custard and cherry) combo.

❦ MONKEY €

Map pp78-9; ☎ 081 868 70 82; Via Lucullo 2, Baia; ⏱ 7am-3am; ⓡ Cumana to Fusaro, then ⓑ EAV to Baia

A quick walk from the Parco Archeologico di Baia, this piazza-side neighbourhood bar-geletaria combo dishes out a fine *aperitivo* spread nightly from 7pm (get in early). The real star, however, is the wickedly good gelato, served in waffle cones. Freshly made, the small selection of flavours is seasonal and regularly changing – the creamy *cioccolato* and delectable *nocciola* (hazelnut) are particularly fine.

NIGHTLIFE

BARS & ENOTECHE

Neapolitans aren't big drinkers and in the *centro storico*, many people simply buy a bottle of beer from the nearest bar and hang out on the streets. Here, bar hot spots include Via Cisterno dell'Olio, Piazza Bellini and Piazza del Gesù Nuovo, where a high concentration of students, artists and bohemians lend a energetic, live-and-let-live vibe. For a side serve of sea breeze, head to the bayside bars of Borgo Marinaro. Those after fashion-conscious vino sessions should sashay straight to Chiaia's sleek bars, famed for their evening *aperitivo* spreads (gourmet nibbles for the price of a drink, nightly from around 6.30pm to 9.30pm). Some of the best are on (and off) Vicolo Belledonne a Chiaia and Via Bisignano.

❦ A PIGNA D'UVA €

Map p55; ☎ 081 40 56 08; Vico Lungo Teatro Nuovo 31; ⏱ 9am-10pm Mon-Sat; ⓑ R2 to Piazza Trieste e Trento

It might look like a makeshift bar in a neighbour's garage, but this threadbare *enoteca* is a local darling. Selling the city's cheapest vino (wine by the plastic cup starts at €0.70, bottles around €2 to €3), it's a brilliant spot to soak up the neighbourhood vibe, with an eclectic cast of regulars spanning lefty artists to sing-song drunks. It's also a handy spot to sip a spritz before noshing at Nennella (p88).

❦ AL BARCADERO

Map pp62-3; ☎ 333 2227023; Banchina Santa Lucia 2; ⏱ 7am-2am May-Sep, to 6pm Oct-Apr weather permitting; ⓑ C25 to Via Partenope

Turn left down the steps as you walk towards Borgo Marinaro and you'll find this unpretentious waterfront bar. Grab a beer, plonk yourself by the water and gaze out at boat-rowing fishermen and a menacing Mt Vesuvius.

❦ ARET'A'PALM

Map pp42-3; ☎ 339 8486949; Piazza Santa Maria La Nova 14; ⏱ 6.30pm-2.30am; ⓑ CS to Via Diaz

Its name means 'behind the palm' in Neapolitan, and that's exactly where you'll find this soulful piazza-side bolt-hole, decked out in red velvet curtains and dimly lit mirrors. Slip in and rub shoulders with a laid-back crowd of artists, actors and academics, who flock here as much for the jazz and blues as fo the inspiring wine list.

❦ ENOTECA BELLEDONNE

Map pp62-3; ☎ 081 40 31 62; Vico Belledonne a Chiaia 18; ⏱ 10am-2pm & 7pm-2am Mon, 10am-2pm & 4.30pm-2am Tue-Sat, 7pm-2am Sun; ⓑ C25 to Riviera di Chiaia

Exposed-brick walls, ambient lighting and bottle-lined shelves set a cosy scene at Naples' best-loved wine bar. Swill, sip and eavesdrop over a list of well-chosen, mostly Italian wines, as well as a grazing menu that includes a moreish antipasto platter (€8) and bruschetta topped with grilled aubergines, peppers and marinated *friarielli* (€5).

❤ IL CAFFÈ ARABO

Map pp42-3; ☎ 081 442 06 07; Piazza Bellini; ☺ 11am-late; Ⓜ Dante

Backgammon boards, water pipes, and cafe nosh spanning hummus to *fuul* (a bean-based dip): this Italo-Arab bolt-hole is laid-back, raffish and the darling of artists, the theatre crowd and verified free spirits. The wine is the cheapest on the piazza and charismatic staffer Lucia can make you one seriously creamy *caffè aur* (coffee with cream and cocoa) on request.

❤ INTRA MOENIA

Map pp42-3; ☎ 081 29 07 20; Piazza Bellini 70; ☺ 10am-2am; Ⓜ Dante

Lattes and literature live in harmony at this free-thinking cafe-bookshop–publishing house, slap-bang on Piazza Bellini. Browse limited-edition books on Neapolitan culture, pick up a vintage-style postcard, or simply slip on that beret, sip a *prosecco* and act the intellectual. The house wine costs €4 a glass and there's a range of salads, pasta dishes and snacks for peckish bohemians.

❤ S'MOVE

Map pp62-3; ☎ 081 764 58 13; Vico dei Sospiri 10a; ☺ 6.30pm-2am Mon-Wed, to 3.30am Thu-Sun, closed Aug; 🚌 C25 to Riviera di Chiaia

Bulbous lamps and futuristic wall panels channel *Barbarella* at this perennially hip yet friendly Chiaia lounge bar. *Aperitivo*

is served between 7pm and 9pm, with DJs spinning nu-jazz, acid jazz, electro and funk every Thursday to Sunday. Liquid concoctions include a mighty mojito.

LIVE MUSIC & THEATRE

More than just mandolins and tenors, Naples boasts a swinging jazz scene, thought-provoking theatre and cultured classical ensembles. To see what's on, scan daily papers like *Corriere del Mezzogiorno* or *La Repubblica* (Naples edition), click onto www.turismoregione campania.it or ask at the tourist office. In smaller venues you can usually buy your ticket at the door; for bigger events try the box office inside Feltrinelli (Map pp62–3).

❤ AROUND MIDNIGHT

Map pp68-9; ☎ 081 742 32 78; www.aroundmid night.it, in Italian; Via Giuseppe Bonito 32a; admission free; ☺ 9pm-1am Wed-Sun, live music from 10.30pm, closed early Jul-Aug; Ⓜ Vanvitelli

One of Naples' oldest and most famous jazz clubs, this tiny swinging bolt-hole features mostly home-grown live gigs, with the occasional blues band putting in a performance. Best of all, you can nosh while you tap those toes. It's a good idea to book ahead if heading in Friday to Sunday, or for major midweek gigs.

❤ ASSOCIAZIONE SCARLATTI

Map pp62-3; ☎ 081 40 60 11; www.associaziones carlatti.it, in Italian; Piazza dei Martiri 58; 🚌 C25 to Piazza dei Martiri

Naples' premier classical-music association organises an annual program of chamber-music concerts in venues across the city. Local talent mixes it with foreign guests, which have included the Amsterdam Baroque Orchestra and St Petersburg's Mariinsky Theatre Orchestra.

❦ BLUESTONE

Map pp62-3; ☎ 081 423 84 55; www.bluestone
napoli.it, in Italian; Via Alabardieri 10; ✆ bar
6.30pm-2am Mon-Fri, to 3am Sat & Sun, restaurant
8am-midnight, to 12.30am Sat & Sun; 🚌 C25 to
Piazza dei Martiri

Soulless to some, über-glam to others,
this slinky restaurant-bar–live music
venue is the latest place to see and be
seen. Ditch the overpriced menu and
join the label-loving crowd for live gigs
spanning local singer-songwriters to imported jazz, gospel and rock. Check the
website for what's on when.

❦ CENTRO DI MUSICA ANTICA PIETÀ DE' TURCHINI

Map pp68-9; ☎ 081 40 23 95; www.turchini.it; Via
Santa Caterina da Siena 38; funicular Centrale to
Corso Vittorio Emanuele

Classical-music buffs are in for a treat
at this beautiful deconsecrated church.
Home to the historic Orchestra Cappella
della Pietà dei Turchini, it's an evocative
setting for concerts of mostly 17th- and
18th-century Neapolitan works. Tickets
cost about €10, and upcoming concerts
are listed on the venue's website.

❦ GALLERIA TOLEDO

Map p55; ☎ 081 42 50 37; www.galleriatoledo.org,
in Italian; Via Concezione a Montecalvario 34; tickets
from €14; ✆ box office 11am-2pm & 3-6pm Mon-Fri;
Ⓜ Montesanto

If it's cutting edge, independent or
experimental, chances are it's playing
at this cult-status theatre, tucked away
in the Quartieri Spagnoli. Gigs span
both local and global plays and live
music, with the odd offbeat arthouse
flick thrown in for good measure.
Phone bookings are taken (including
at weekends), with ticket pick-up at
the box office 30 minutes prior to the
performance.

❦ GOODFELLAS

Map pp68-9; ☎ 340 9225475; www.goodfellas
club.com; Via Morghen 34bis, admission free;
✆ 8pm-2am Sun, Mon & Wed-Fri, to 3am Sat, closed
Tue & Aug; Ⓜ Vanvitelli

Only a few years old, this barrel-vaulted
watering hole serves up infectious live
music (anything from rhythm and blues
to rock and jazz) nightly bar Tuesday
and Saturday. It's a hit with music aficionados, who'll warn you not to miss
a show by local bluesman–guitar whiz
Gennaro Porcelli and his Highway 61
(www.gennaroporcelli.com).

❦ L'ARENILE DI BAGNOLI

Map pp78-9; ☎ 081 570 60 35; www.arenilere
load.com, in Italian; Via Coroglio 14b, Bagnoli; admission varies; ✆ daily Apr-Sep weather permitting;
🚉 Cumana to Bagnoli

Best known for its posing, Campari-
sipping fashionistas, Naples' most famous beach club redeems itself with
gorgeous views, a magical atmosphere,
cultural events and a brilliant Tuesday-
night jam session (€10, includes one
drink, 10.30pm), which sees the top cats
of the Neapolitan music scene trading
licks and venting off.

RECOMMENDED SHOPS

Shopping in Naples is a highly idiosyncratic experience, dominated by specialist, family-heirloom businesses. For
Neapolitan tailors and high-end labels,
hit Chiaia's Via Calabritto, Via dei Mille
and Via Gaetano Filangieri. For antiques
explore Via Domenico Morelli in Chiaia
and Via Costantinopoli in the *centro
storico*. Also in the *centro storico*, check
out Via San Gregorio Armeno for its
presepi and buzzing Via Benedetto Croce
and Via San Biagio dei Librari for an
eclectic mix of offerings. For the ultimate

Neapolitan shopping experience, however, hit the legendary markets, home to everything from dirt-cheap kinky knickers to convincing Gucci fakes. Many shops close for two weeks in August.

CENTRO STORICO & MERCATO

ELIA'S VINTAGE

Map pp42-3; ☎ 081 291 589; Vicoletto San Domenico; R4 to Monteoliveto

Revamp your rack at this eccentric fashion bolt-hole, where vintage threads and accessories mix it with boho-chic one-offs designed and hand-sewn by Angela and her costume designer sister-in-law, Antonella. Expect anything from lusciously knitted scarves to ruffled felt necklaces and bags made from rockabilly beer caps. Even the jewellery pouches are whipped up using vintage fabric scraps.

KIPHY

Map pp42-3; ☎ 393 8703280; Vico San Domenico Maggiore 3; 10am-6.30pm Wed-Fri, to 4pm Tue & Sat; R4 to Via Monteoliveto

Named after a fabled ancient Egyptian perfume, this funky shop-cum-workshop sells pure, handmade slabs of soap that look as beautiful as they smell. Lined up under low-slung lights, varieties include a refreshing orange-and-cinnamon blend. The freshly made shampoos, creams and oils use organic, fair-trade ingredients and can be personally tailored. Best of all, products are gorgeously packaged, reasonably priced and made with love.

LA SCARABATTOLA

Map pp42-3; ☎ 081 29 17 35; Via dei Tribunali 50; 10.30am-2pm & 3.30-7.30pm Mon-Fri, 10am-8pm Sun; Dante

Not only have La Scarabattola's handmade sculptures of *magi* (wise men),

devils and Neapolitan folk figures featured in top exhibitions, they have some seriously VIP fans, including the Spanish royal family. Figurines aside, its line of sleek, contemporary ceramic creations (think Pulcinella-inspired placecard holders) makes for some urbane souvenirs. Best of all, you can even visit its nearby workshop (see the boxed text, p52) to watch the masters in action.

LIMONÈ

Map pp42-3; ☎ 081 29 94 29; Piazza San Gaetano 72; Cavour

For a taste of Napoli long after you've gone home, stock up on a few bottles of Limonè's organic, homemade *limoncello*. Ask nicely and you might get a sip for free. Other take-home treats include lemon pasta, lemon-infused grappa and a refreshing *crema di melone* (melon liqueur).

MANI DESIGN

Map pp42-3; ☎ 347 9532930; Via San Giovanni Maggiore Pignatelli 1b; Dante

Retail meets progressive creativity at Mani Design, where bimonthly exhibitions mean a steady stream of fresh, funky art and design. Past items have included contemporary Sicilian jewellery and frocks made from '70s ties, to sculptural pieces by Riccardo Dalisi (see the boxed text, p67). Dubbed a visionary by the local press, curator Simona Perchiazzi also stocks her own creations, which might include kimonos, felt brooches or svelte men's scarves.

TOLEDO & QUARTIERI SPAGNOLI

NAPOLIMANIA

Map p55; ☎ 081 41 41 20; Via Toledo 312; CS to Via Toledo

This offbeat shrine to local pop culture is the place for plastic Totò statues,

TO MARKET, TO MARKET

Porta Nolana (p52) and La Pignasecca (p57) are only two of Naples' loud and legendary markets. Stock up on cheap shoes, designer fakes and the odd vintage gem at the following favourites.

Bancarelle a San Pasquale (Map pp62-3; Via San Pasquale a Chiaia, Via Imbriani & Via Carducci; ☺ 8am-2pm Mon-Wed, Fri & Sat, closed Aug; 🚌 C25 to Riviera di Chiaia) Hit the stalls on Via Imbriani for hip threads, sarongs and avant-garde jewellery. The section between Via Carducci and Via San Pasquale is great for fish, spices, fruit and vegetables. Don't haggle.

Fiera Antiquaria Napoletana (Map pp62-3; Villa Comunale; ☺ 8am-2pm last 2 weekends of month, closed Aug; 🚌 C25 to Riviera di Chiaia) This waterfront antiques market sells vintage silverware, jewellery, furniture, paintings, prints and wonderful, overpriced junk.

La Duchessa (Map pp42-3; Via San Giuseppe Calasanzio and surrounding streets; ☺ 8am-2pm Mon-Sat, closed Aug; 🚌 R2 to Piazza Garibaldi) Gritty, multiethnic and obscenely cheap; head here for bargain denim, shoes, knickers, make-up and bootleg DVDs. Serious music buffs head in early to hunt for original, recent-release CDs and the odd hard-to-find special edition for as little as €3.

Mercatino di Antignano (Map pp68-9; Piazza degli Artisti; ☺ 8am-1pm Mon-Sat, closed Aug; Ⓜ Medaglie D'Oro) Up high in Vomero, this place is popular for bags, jewellery, linen, kitchenware, shoes, and new and end-of-season clothing.

Mercatino di Posillipo (Map pp78-9; Parco Virgiliano; ☺ 8am-1pm Thu; 🚌 140 to Viale Virgilio) Not the cheapest market, but the best for quality goods. Top buys include genuine designer labels (although the D&G and Louis Vuitton bags are fakes), women's swimwear, underwear and linen. It's only the African vendors who don't mind a haggle.

Mercato di Poggioreale (off Map pp42-3; Via Nuova Poggioreale; ☺ 8am-1pm Fri-Mon, closed Aug; 🚇 No 1 to Via Nuova Poggioreale) Set in the city's old slaughterhouse, this hugely popular market has 40 shoe stalls alone selling designer overstock and no-frills everyday brands. Equally fab are the cheap casual wear, suits, colourful rolls of fabrics and kitchenware.

Neapolitan 'survival kits', and jocks and tops with witty local slang.

♯ TALARICO

Map p55; ☎ 081 40 77 23; Vico Due Porte a Toledo 4b; 🚌 CS to Via Toledo

Mario Talarico and his nephews have turned the humble umbrella into a work of art. Sought after by international heads of state, each piece is a one-off, complete with mother-of-pearl buttons, a horn tip and a handle made from a single tree branch. While top-of-the-range pieces can fetch up to €300, there are more-affordable options that will keep the budget-conscious singing in the rain.

SANTA LUCIA & CHIAIA

♯ BOWINKEL

Map pp62-3; ☎ 081 764 07 39; Via Santa Lucia 25; 🚌 C25 to Via Partenope

The city's finest vintage prints, photographs, watercolour paintings and classic frames. If you can't find what you're looking for here, check out its sister branch at Piazza dei Martiri 24 (Map pp62-3; ☎ 08 764 43 44). Erudite owner Umberto speaks a smattering of English and will arrange shipments abroad.

♯ CONTEMPORASTUDIO

Map pp62-3; ☎ 081 247 99 37; Via Francesco Crispi 50; ☺ 4.30-8pm Mon, 10am-1.30pm & 4.30-8pm Tue-Fri, 10am-1.30pm Sat; Ⓜ Amedeo

A concrete-clad gallery stocking funky, experimental jewellery from Neapolitan Asad Ventrella: necklaces made of solid-silver *penne rigate* (penne pasta shapes), fat double-faced rings in titanium and aluminium and sharp-looking cufflinks for style-savvy gents.

🍃 FELTRINELLI

Map pp62-3; ☎ 081 240 54 11; Piazza dei Martiri; ⏰ 10am-9pm Mon-Thu, to 10pm Fri, to 11pm Sat, 10am-2pm & 4-10pm Sun; 🚌 C25 to Piazza dei Martiri

Pick up anything from Italian music CDs and DVDs to novels and coffee-table tomes at this three-level book and music store, complete with cafe and box office. There's a fair-sized English-language section to boot.

🍃 LIVIO DE SIMONE

Map pp62-3; ☎ 081 764 38 27; Via Domenico Morelli 5; 🚌 C25 to Piazza dei Martiri

The late Livio De Simone dressed the likes of Audrey Hepburn and Jackie O. Today his wife and daughter keep the vision alive with bold, bright, hand-printed *robe chemesier*s (shirt dresses) and matching purses, bags and shoes – it's Capri with a Japanese twist.

🍃 TRAMONTANO

Map pp62-3; ☎ 081 41 48 37; Via Chiaia 143-144; 🚌 C25 to Piazza dei Martiri

With fans including Woody Allen, Tramontano has an epic rep for exquisitely crafted Neapolitan leather goods, from butter-soft wallets to glam handbags and preppy-cool satchels. Famously at Christmas, a new model bag is released, inspired by a classic song…such as Patti Smith's 'Kimberley'.

🍃 VERDEGRANO

Map pp62-3; ☎ 081 40 17 54; Via Santa Teresa a Chiaia 17; ⏰ 10.30am-1pm & 5-7.30pm Tue-Sat, closed Mon morning Oct-late May, closed Sat afternoon late May-Sep; Ⓜ Amedeo

Give your *casa* that Mediterranean look with exquisitely patterned, hand-painted porcelain pots, vases, plates and decorative items. Prices are reasonable and there are some easy-to-pack smaller pieces for the trip home.

VOMERO, CAPODIMONTE & LA SANITÀ

🍃 DE PAOLA CAMEOS

Map pp68-9; ☎ 081 578 29 10; Via Annibale Caccavello 67; ⏰ 9am-8pm Mon-Sat, to 2pm Sun; funicular Centrale to Fuga

Head here for a beautiful range of finely carved cameos as well as coral necklaces, earrings, pendants and bracelets. Designs range from vintage to modern and there's no pressure to buy.

TRANSPORT

TO/FROM THE AIRPORT

AIRPORT // Capodichino (NAP; ☎ 081 789 62 59; www.gesac.it), 7km northeast of central Naples, is southern Italy's main airport, connecting Naples with most Italian and several European cities, as well as New York. Budget carrier Easyjet operates several routes to/from Capodichino, including London, Paris-Orly, Berlin and Geneva.

BUS // Airport shuttle Alibus (☎ 081 53 11 705) connects the airport to Piazza Garibaldi (Stazione Centrale) and Piazza del Municipio (€3, 45 minutes, every 30 minutes). Regular ANM (☎ 800 63 95 25) bus 3S (€1.10, 45 minutes, every 15 minutes) connects the airport to Piazza Garibaldi.

TAXI // Official fares to the airport are as follows: €21 from a seafront hotel or from Mergellina hydrofoil terminal; €18 from Piazza del Municipio; and €14.50 from Stazione Centrale.

GETTING AROUND

BUS // SITA (☎ 199 73 07 49; www.sitabus.it, in Italian) has services to Pompeii (40 minutes, half-

SARTORIAL NAPLES

Milan may be the hyped-up face of Italian style, but Naples is its heart and soul. The city's bespoke tailors are legendary and once drew the likes of early-20th-century Italian king Emmanuel III to their needles and threads.

The key to this success is traditional, handmade production, superlative fabrics and minute attention to detail and form. Suitwise, the look is more brat pack than power broker – slim-fit flexible cut, natural and unengineered shoulders (great for gesticulating), high-set armholes and the signature *barchetta* (little boat) breast pocket.

A classic Neapolitan shirt will often feature fine Italian, Swiss or Irish cottons, hand-stitched collar, yoke and sleeve, hand-sewn buttonholes and gathered pleating at the shoulder.

While most of the boutiques offer prêt-à-porter threads and accessories (including ready-made suits), creating a shirt or suit from scratch will usually involve a couple of fittings and anything from three to eight weeks. Finished items can be shipped overseas.

Credit card at the ready, hit these needle-savvy icons for a Neapolitan revamp:

Anna Matuozzo (Map p75; ☎ 081 66 38 74; www.annamatuozzo.it; Viale Antonio Gramsci 26) The softly spoken Signora Matuozzo was once the apprentice of Mariano Rubinacci. Now the *signora* and her daughters are famed for their bespoke shirts, which feature mother-of-pearl buttons and vintage hand stitching. Silk ties in luscious tones complete the elegant look. Fittings must be booked.

Finamore (Map pp62-3; ☎ 081 246 18 27; www.finamore.it, in Italian; Via Calabritto 16) Ready-to-wear and bespoke hand-sewn shirts in delectable shades such as royal blue, pastel pink and citrus green. There are ties and scarves to match.

Mariano Rubinacci (Map pp62-3; ☎ 081 41 57 93; www.marianorubinacci.it; Via Gaetano Filangeri 26) Beautiful, lightweight and precisely fitting suits from the granddaddy of Neapolitan tailoring. Former clients include Neapolitan film director Vittorio de Sica.

Marinella (Map pp62-3; ☎ 081 245 11 82; www.marinellanapoli.it; Piazza Vittoria 287) One-time favourite of Luchino Visconti and Aristotle Onassis, this is *the* place for prêt-à-porter and made-to-measure ties. Match them with an irresistible selection of luxury accessories, including shoes, shirts, sweaters and vintage colognes.

---

hourly), Sorrento (one hour 20 minutes, twice daily), Positano (two hours, twice daily), Amalfi (two hours, twice daily) and Salerno (every 25 minutes, one hour 10 minutes).

TRAIN // Naples is southern Italy's rail hub and on the main Milan–Palermo line. National rail company **Trenitalia** (☎ 89 20 21; www.trenitalia.com) runs regular services to Rome (2nd class €10.50 to €40, 80 minutes to three hours, up to 30 daily). **Circumvesuviana** (☎ 081 772 24 44; www.vesuviana.it; Corso Giuseppe Garibaldi) operates frequent services to Sorrento (€3.30, 70 minutes) via Ercolano

(€1.80, 20 minutes), Pompeii (€2.40, 40 minutes) and other towns along the coast, departing from Stazione Circumvesuviana (Map pp42–3). The Ferrovia Cumana and the **Circumflegrea** (☎ 800 00 16 16; www.sepsa.it), based at Stazione Cumana di Montesanto (Map p55) on Piazza Montesanto, 500m southwest of Piazza Dante, operate services to Pozzuoli (€1.10, every 25 minutes) and other Campi Flegrei towns beyond.

BOAT // Ferries for Palermo, Cagliari, Milazzo, the Aeolian Islands (Isole Eolie) and Tunisia leave from the **Stazione Marittima** (Map pp42–3). Purchase ckets at ferry company offices (see p305) or at a travel gent. **Metro del Mare** (www.metrodelmare. om) connects Bacoli and Pozzuoli to Naples and from here has services to Sorrento, Positano and Amalfi. rom Easter to October Amalfi, Positano, Salerno, apri, Naples and Sorrento are connected by ferry or ydrofoil.

AR // Naples is on the north–south Autostrada del ole, the A1 (north to Rome and Milan) and the A3 outh to Salerno and Reggio di Calabria).

ARKING // See Map pp34–5 for information on arking in Naples.

CITY TRAINS // Metronapoli (www.metro. a.it) operates three metro lines. Line 1 (yellow) and ne 2 (blue) are the most useful. Line 1 runs from ianturco to Garibaldi (Stazione Centrale) and on to ozzuoli. Line 2 runs from Piazza Dante to Vomero and n to the northern suburbs. Interchange at Museo (Line / Cavour (Line 2). Tickets (also valid on city buses, niculars and trams) can be purchased at kiosks, tobac- nists or from automated ticket machines at metro ations.

ITY BUSES // ANM (☎ 800 63 95 25; ww.anm.it, in Italian) buses serve the city and its riphery. Many routes pass through Piazza aribaldi, outside Stazione Centrale. This is where u'll find the ANM information kiosk. For useful utes, see p306).

TY FUNICULARS // Three services connect ntral Naples to Vomero, while a fourth connects Merg- lina to Posillipo.

TY TRAMS // Two lines run along the waterfront. he 1 connects Mercato di Poggioreale to Piazza del unicipio and Piazza Vittoria in Chiaia.

AXI // For a taxi you can call ☎ 081 55 13 06 or 081 570 70 70.

BAY OF NAPLES

· · · · · ·

uried for centuries beneath metres of olcanic debris, Naples' archaeologi- l sites are among the best-preserved d most spectacular Roman ruins in

existence. And it's here, in the dense urban sprawl stretching from Naples to Castellammare, that you'll find Italy's blockbuster finest: Pompeii and Herculaneum, as well as a host of lesser-known jewels, from salubrious ancient villas to the country's biggest vintage clothes market.

While Pompeii, Herculaneum and Oplontis are within easy walking distance of stations on the Naples–Sorrento Circumvesuviana train line, Stabiae and Boscoreale both require a bit more searching around (see the boxed text, p107).

As for Mt Vesuvius, it's an easy bus trip from Pompeii.

TRANSPORT

TRAIN // Circumvesuviana (☎ 081 772 24 44; www.vesuviana.it) operates frequent trains between Naples' Stazione Circumvesuviana (connected by concourse to Naples' central station) and Sorrento, stopping at both Ercolano (€1.80 from Naples, €1.90 from Sorrento) and Pompeii (€2.40 from Naples, €1.90 from Sorrento). To reach Ercolano's sights, including the ruins of Herculaneum, alight at Ercolano-Scavi station. For the ruins of Pompeii, hop off at Pompeii-Scavi-Villa dei Misteri station.

BUS // SITA (☎ 199 73 07 49; www.sitabus.it, in Italian) buses for Pompeii depart every 30 minutes from Naples (€2.40), beside the central train station (Stazione Centrale). From Pompeii, **Vesuviana Mobilità** (☎ 081 963 44 20) operates eight daily (10 daily in summer) return-trip buses (€8.90) to Mt Vesuvius. Two return daily services also depart from Ercolano (€7.80).

CAR // From Naples, the A3 runs southeast along the Bay of Naples. To reach the Ruins of Herculaneum, exit at Ercolano Portico and follow the signs to car parks near the site. Use the same exit for Mt Vesuvius, following the signs for the Parco Nazionale del Vesuvio. For Pompeii, use the Pompeii exit and follow signs to Pompei Scavi. Car parks (approximately €4 per hour) are clearly marked and vigorously touted.

NAPLES

EXPLORING THE BAY OF NAPLES

🌿 RUINS OF HERCULANEUM // EXPLORE AN EVOCATIVELY PRESERVED ROMAN VILLAGE

Unfairly upstaged by Pompeii's ancient offerings, the **Ruins of Herculaneum** (☎ 081 732 43 38; Corso Resina 6; adult/EU 18-25yr/ EU under 18yr & over 65yr €11/5.50/free, combined ticket incl Pompeii, Oplontis, Stabiae & Boscoreale €20/10/free; ⏱ 8.30am-7.30pm Apr-Oct, to 5pm Nov-Mar, last entry 90min before closing; 🚇 Circumvesuviana to Ercolano-Scavi) has a wealth of archaeological finds, from ancient ads and stylish mosaics, to carbonised furniture and terror-struck skeletons. Indeed, this superbly conserved Roman fishing town of 4000 inhabitants is smaller and easier to navigate than Pompeii, and can be explored with a map and audioguide.

From the site's main gateway on Corso Resina, head down the wide boulevard, where you'll find the new ticket office on the left. Pick up a free map and guide booklet here, and then follow the boulevard right to the actual entrance into the ruins themselves. Here you can hire the useful audioguide (€6.50, €10 for two) or pick up the insightful book *Herculaneum, The Excavations, Local History & Surroundings* (€10), published by Electra, from the bookshop.

Herculaneum's fate runs parallel to that of Pompeii. Destroyed by an earthquake in AD 62, the AD 79 eruption of Mt Vesuvius saw it submerged in a 16m-thick sea of mud that essentially fossilised the city. This meant that even delicate items, such as furniture and clothing, were discovered remarkably well preserved. Tragically, the inhabitants didn't fare so well; thousands of people tried to escape by boat but were suffocated by the volcano's poisonous gases. Indeed, what appears to be a moat around the town is in fact the **ancient shoreline**. It was here in 1980 that archaeologists discovered some 300 skeletons, the remains of a crowd that had fled to the beach only to be overcome by the terrible heat of clouds surging down from Vesuvius.

The town itself was rediscovered in 1709 and amateur excavations were carried out intermittently until 1874, with many finds being carted off to Naples to decorate the houses of the well-to-do or to end up in museums. Serious archaeological work began again in 1927 and continues to this day, although with much of the ancient site buried beneath modern Ercolano it's slow going. Indeed note that at any given time some houses will invariably be shut for restoration; at the time of writing these included the Terme Suburbane and the Casa dell'Atri a Mosaico.

Casa d'Argo & Casa dello Scheletro

As you begin your exploration northeas along Cardo III you'll stumble across **Argus House**. This noble pad would originally have opened onto Cardo II (as yet unearthed). Onto its porticoed, palm-treed garden open a *triclinium* and other residential rooms. Across the street sits the **Casa dello Scheletro** (House of the Skeleton), a modestly sized house boasting five styles of mosaic flooring, including a design of whit arrows at the entrance to guide the mos disorientated of guests. In the internal courtyard, don't miss the skylight, complete with the remnants of an ancient security grill. Of the house's mythically themed wall mosaics, only the faded ones are originals; the others now resid in the Museo Archeologico Nazionale (p54).

Terme Maschili

Just across the Decumano Inferiore (one of ancient Herculaneum's main streets), the **Male Baths** was the men's section of the **Terme del Foro** (Forum Baths). Note the ancient latrine to the left of the entrance before you step into the *apodyterium* (changing room), complete with bench for waiting patrons and a nifty wall shelf for sandal and toga storage. While those after a bracing soak would pop into the *frigidarium* (cold bath) to the left, the less stoic headed straight into the *tepadarium* (tepid bath) to the right. The sunken mosaic floor here is testament to the seismic activity preceding Mt Vesuvius's catastrophic eruption. Beyond this room lies the *caldarium* (hot bath), as well as an exercise area.

Decumano Massimo

At the end of Cardo III, turn right into the **Decumano Massimo**. This ancient High Street is lined with shops; frag

NAPLES

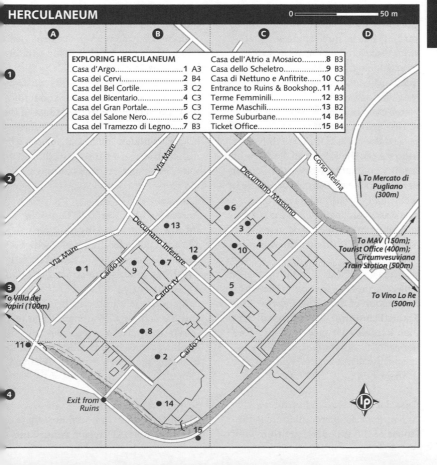

HERCULANEUM

0 ⸻ 50 m

EXPLORING HERCULANEUM

Casa d'Argo................................1 A3	Casa dell'Atrio a Mosaico...........8 B3
Casa dei Cervi...........................2 B4	Casa dello Scheletro...................9 B3
Casa del Bel Cortile..................3 C2	Casa di Nettuno e Anfitrite......10 C3
Casa del Bicentario...................4 C3	Entrance to Ruins & Bookshop..11 A4
Casa del Gran Portale...............5 C3	Terme Femminili.....................12 B3
Casa del Salone Nero...............6 C2	Terme Maschili.......................13 B2
Casa del Tramezzo di Legno.....7 B3	Terme Suburbane...................14 B4
	Ticket Office...........................15 B4

To Mercato di Pugliano (300m)

To MAV (150m); Tourist Office (400m); Circumvesuviana Train Station (500m)

To Vino Lo Re (500m)

To Villa dei Papiri (100m)

Exit from Ruins

ments of advertisements still adorn the walls, like that to the right of the **Casa del Salone Nero**. This ancient consumer information listed anything from from the weight of goods to their price.

Further east along Decumano Massimo, a crucifix found in an upstairs room of the **Casa del Bicentenario** (Bicentenary House) provides possible evidence of a Christian presence in pre-Vesuvius Herculaneum.

Casa del Bel Cortile & Casa di Nettuno e Anfitrite

Turning into Cardo IV from Decumano Massimo, you'll hit the **Casa del Bel Cortile** (House of the Beautiful Courtyard). Inside lie three of the 300 skeletons discovered on the ancient shore by archaeologists in 1980. Almost two millennia later, it's still a poignant sight to see the assumed mother, father and young child huddled together in the last, terrifying moments of their lives.

Next door awaits the **Casa di Nettuno e Anfitrite** (House of Neptune and Amfitrite), an aristocratic pad taking its name from the extraordinary mosaic in the *nymphaeum* (fountain and bath). The warm colours in which the sea god and his nymph bride are depicted hint at how lavish the original interior must once have been.

A quick walk further southwest along Cardo IV leads you to the women's section of the Terme del Foro, the **Terme Femminili**. Though smaller than its male equivalent, it boasts finer floor mosaics (note the beautifully executed naked figure of Triton in the *apodyterium*).

Casa del Tramezzo di Legno

Across the Decumano Inferiore is the **House of the Wooden Partition**, which unusually features two atria. It's likely that the atria belonged to two separate houses merged together in the 1st century AD. Predictably, the most famous relic here is a wonderfully well-preserved wooden screen, separating the atrium from the *tablinum*, where the owner talked business with his clients. The second room off the left side of the atrium features the remains of an ancient bed.

Casa dell'Atrio a Mosaico

Further southwest on Cardio IV, ancient mansion **House of the Mosaic Atrium** harbours extensive floor mosaics, although time and nature have left the floor buckled and uneven. Particularly noteworthy is the black-and-white chessboard mosaic in the atrium.

Backtrack up Cardo IV and turn right at Decumano Inferiore. Here you'll find the **Casa del Gran Portale** (House of the Large Portal), named after the elegant brick Corinthian columns that flank its main entrance. Step inside to admire some well-preserved wall paintings.

Casa dei Cervi

Accessible from Cardo V, **House of the Stags** is an imposing example of a Roman noble family's house which, before the volcanic mud slide, boasted a seafront address. Constructed around a central courtyard, the two-storey villa contains murals and some beautiful still-life paintings. Waiting for you in the courtyard is a diminutive pair of marble deer assailed by dogs, and an engaging statue of a drunken, peeing Hercules.

Terme Suburbane

Marking the site's southernmost tip is the 1st-century AD **Terme Suburbane**

(Suburban Baths), one of the best pre-served bath complexes in existence, with deep pools, stucco friezes and bas-reliefs looking down upon marble seats and floors. This is also one of the best places to observe the soaring volcanic deposits that literally smothered the ancient coastline.

If you're travelling to the *scavi* (ruins) by Circumvesuviana train (€1.80 from Naples, €1.90 from Sorrento), get off at Ercolano-Scavi station and walk 500m downhill to the ruins – follow the signs for the *scavi* down the main street, Via IV Novembre. En route you'll pass the **tourist office** (8.30am-6pm Mon-Sat early Apr-Oct, to 2pm Mon-Sat Nov-early Apr) on your right.

MAV (MUSEO ARCHEOLOGICO VIRTUALE) // GIVE YOUR MIND'S EYE A HELPING HAND

Need help conjuring up 'before' images of the region's ruins? The new **Virtual Archaeology Museum** (081 1980 6511; www.museomav.com; Via IV Novembre; adult/concession €7/5.50; 9am-5pm Tue-Sun; Circumvesuviana to Ercolano-Scavi) can help; its high-tech holograms and computer-generated footage bring ruins like Pompeii's forum and Capri's Villa Jovis back to virtual life. Ever so slightly gimmicky, it's undoubtedly a useful place to comprehend just how impressive those crumbling columns once were. It's also a fun place for kids, with everything from holographic images of Roman jewellery to an interactive table shedding light on themes from ancient art and marriage. While many of the digital information panels alternate languages automatically (including English), it's a good idea to read the free English information sheet available at reception before you 'step back in time'. It's an extra €2 to watch the 15-minute

documentary in the auditorium, also available in English.

Easy to reach, MAV is on the main street heading downhill from the train station.

MERCATO DI PUGLIANO // PIMP YOUR WARDROBE AT ITALY'S FINEST VINTAGE MARKET

Fashion fans shouldn't miss Italy's largest pre-loved clothing **market** (Via Pugliano; 9am-1pm Mon-Sat; Circumvesuviana to Ercolano-Scavi), which straddles Via Pugliano in the heart of Ercolano. Everyone from local teens to serious Tokyo stylists dives into the op-shops lining the street, where stock-standard junk mixes it with fabulous offbeat finds (killer cocktail dresses, vinyl LP handbags and the odd military jacket). One of the best outlets is **Old Star** (Via Pugliano 60); ask politely and you may be shown the rare stock upstairs. There's a number of cheap bakeries and food outlets along the strip, while the surrounding streets are awash with fresh produce stalls, fishmongers and suburban Neapolitan life at its cacophonous best.

From the Circumvesuviana Ercolano-Scavi station, walk downhill 400m to Prima Traversa Mercato. Turn right into it and you'll stumble onto Via Pugliano 200m later.

RUINS OF POMPEII // LOSE YOURSELF AT EUROPE'S MOST COMPELLING ARCHAEOLOGICAL SITE

Nothing piques human curiosity like a mass catastrophe and few beat the **ruins of Pompeii** (081 857 53 47; entrances at Porta Marina and Piazza Anfiteatro; Circumvesuviana to Pompeii-Scavi-Villa dei Misteri; adult/EU 18-25yr/EU under 18yr & over 65yr €11/5.50/free, combined ticket incl Herculaneum, Oplontis, Stabiae & Boscoreale

€20/10/free; 🕑 8.30am-7.30pm Apr-Oct, last entry 6pm, 8.30am-5pm Nov-Mar, last entry 3.30pm). A once-thriving Roman town frozen in its 2000-year-old death throes and conserved under a sea of volcanic pumice, Pompeii (Pompei in Italian) is a stark reminder of the malign forces that lie deep inside Vesuvius.

The site's appeal goes beyond tourism; from an archaeological point of view it's priceless. Much of its value lies in the fact that it wasn't simply blown away by Vesuvius in AD 79, rather it was buried under a layer of *lapilli* (burning fragments of pumice stone), as Pliny the Younger hints at in his celebrated account: 'Darkness came on again, again ashes, thick and heavy. We got up repeatedly to shake these off; otherwise we would have been buried and crushed by the weight'.

But as terrible as the eruption was, it could have been worse. Seventeen years earlier Pompeii had been devastated by an earthquake and much of the 20,000-strong population had been evacuated. Many had not returned by the time Vesuvius blew, but 2000 men, women and children perished nevertheless.

The origins of Pompeii are uncertain, but it seems likely that it was founded in the 7th century BC by the Campanian Oscans. Over the next seven centuries the city fell to the Greeks and the Samnites before becoming a Roman colony in 80 BC.

After its catastrophic demise, Pompeii receded from the public eye until 1594, when the architect Domenico Fontana stumbled across the ruins while digging a canal. Exploration proper didn't begin until 1748, however. Of Pompeii's original 66 hectares, 44 have now been excavated. Of course that doesn't mean you'll have unhindered access to every inch of the Unesco-listed site – expect to come across areas cordoned off for no apparent reason, a noticeable lack of clear signs and the odd stray dog. Audioguides are a sensible investment and a good guidebook will also help – try the €8 *Pompeii* published by Electa Napoli.

At the time of writing, the Casa dei Vettii and Terme Stabiane were closed for restoration. The Terme Suburbane, just outside the city walls, are visitable subject to prior booking at www.arethusa.net. It's here that you'll find

POMPEII TOURS

You'll almost certainly be approached by a guide outside the ticket office. Authorised guides wear identification tags. Reputable tour operators include the following:

Casting (☎ 081 850 07 49)

Gata (☎ 081 861 56 61)

Promo Touring (☎ 081 850 88 55)

Torres Travel (☎ 081 856 78 02; www.torrestravel.it)

Expect to pay €100 to €120 for a two-hour tour, whether you're alone, in a couple or in a group of up to 25 people.

For more information, contact the town's tourist office at **Porta Marina** (☎ 081 536 32 93; Piazza Porta Marina Inferiore 12; 🕑 8am-3.30pm Mon-Fri, 8.30am-2pm Sat, closed Sun Oct-Jul, 8am-6pm Mon-Sat, 8.30am-2pm Sun Aug & Sep) or in **central Pompeii** (☎ 081 850 72 55; Via Sacra 1; 🕑 8am-3.30pm Mon-Fri, 8.30am-2pm Sat, closed Sun all year).

NAPLES

POMPEII

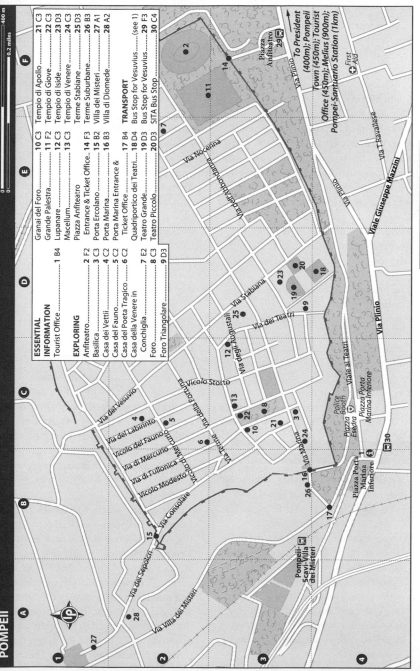

ESSENTIAL		Granai del Foro....................10 C3	Tempio di Apollo................21 C3
INFORMATION		Grande Palestra..................11 F2	Tempio di Giove..................22 C3
Tourist Office........................1 B4		Lupanare............................12 C3	Tempio di Iside..................23 D3
		Macellum............................13 C3	Tempio di Venere.............24 C3
EXPLORING		Piazza Anfiteatro	Terme Stabiane..................25 D3
Anfiteatro...............................2 F2		Entrance & Ticket Office..14 F3	Terme Suburbane..............26 B3
Basilica...................................3 C3		Porta Ercolano..................15 B2	Villa dei Misteri................27 A1
Casa dei Vettii......................4 C2		Porta Marina......................16 C2	Villa di Diomede...............28 A2
Casa del Fauno.....................5 C2		Porta Marina Entrance &	
Casa del Poeta Tragico.......6 C2		Ticket Office...................17 B4	**TRANSPORT**
Casa della Venere in		Quadriportico dei Teatri....18 D4	Bus Stop for Vesuvius......(see 1)
Conchiglia..........................7 E2		Teatro Grande...................19 D3	Bus Stop for Vesuvius.......29 F3
Foro.......................................8 C3		Teatro Piccolo...................20 D3	SITA Bus Stop...................30 C4
Foro Triangolare..................9 D3			

the erotic frescoes that scandalised the Vatican when they were revealed in 2001. The saucy panels decorate the changing rooms of what was once a private baths complex.

Porta Marina

The site's main entrance is at **Porta Marina**, the most impressive of the seven gates that punctuated the ancient town walls. A busy passageway now as it was then, it originally connected the town with the nearby harbour, hence the gateway's name. Immediately on the right as you enter the gate is the 1st century BC **Tempio di Venere** (Temple of Venus), formerly one of the town's most opulent temples.

The Forum

Continuing northeast along Via Marina you'll hit the grassy **foro** (forum). Flanked by limestone columns, this was the ancient city's main piazza and the buildings surrounding it are testament to its role as the city's hub of civic, commercial, political and religious activity.

At its southwestern end sit the remains of the **basilica**, the 2nd century BC seat

of the city's law courts and exchange. Their semicircular apses would later influence the design of early Christian churches. Opposite the basilica, the **Tempio di Apollo** (Temple of Apollo) is the oldest and most important of Pompeii's religious buildings. Most of what you see today, including the striking columned portico, dates to the 2nd century BC, although fragments remain of an earlier version dating to the 6th century BC.

At the forum's northern end is the **Tempio di Giove** (Temple of Jupiter), which has one of two flanking triumphal arches remaining, and the **Granai del Foro** (Forum Granary), now used to store hundreds of amphorae and a number of body casts that were made in the late 19th century by pouring plaster into the hollows left by disintegrated bodies. The **macellum** nearby was once the city's main meat and fish market.

Lupanare

From the market head northeast along Via degli Augustali to Vicolo del Lupanare. Halfway down this narrow alley is the **Lupanare**, the city's only dedicated brothel. A tiny two-storey building with five rooms on each floor, its collection of raunchy frescoes was a menu of sorts for its randy clientele.

Teatro Grande

Heading back south, Vicolo del Lupanare becomes Via dei Teatri. At the end you'll find the verdant **Foro Triangolare**, which would originally have overlooked the sea and the River Sarno. The main attraction here was, and still is, the 2nd century BC **Teatro Grande**, a 5000-seat theatre carved into the lava mass on which Pompeii was originally built. Behind the stage, the porticoed **Quadriportico dei Teatri** wa

TOP TIP

If visiting Pompeii's ruins in summer, bring a hat, sun block and plenty of water. If you've got small children, try to visit in the early morning or late afternoon when the sun's not too hot. Unfortunately, there's not much you can do about the uneven surfaces, which are a challenge for strollers. To do justice to the place, allow at least three or four hours, longer if you want to go into detail. And don't forget to bring a passport or ID card to claim discounts or to hire an audioguide.

VINTAGE VILLAS

Buried beneath the unappealing streets of Torre Annunziata, **Oplontis** was once a blue-ribbon seafront suburb under the administrative control of Pompeii. First discovered in the 18th century, only two of its houses have been unearthed, and only one, Villa Poppaea, is open to the public. This villa is a magnificent example of an *otium* villa (a residential building used for rest and recreation), thought to have belonged to Sabina Poppaea, Nero's second wife. Particularly outstanding are the richly coloured 1st-century wall paintings in the *triclinium* (dining room) and *calidarium* (hot bathroom) in the west wing. Marking the villa's eastern border is a garden with an impressive swimming pool (17m by 61m). The villa is a straightforward 300m walk from Torre Annunziate Circumvesuviana train station.

South of Oplontis, **Stabiae** stood on the slopes of the Varano hill overlooking what was then the sea and is now modern Castellammare di Stabia. Here at Stabiae you can visit two villas: the 1st-century-BC Villa Arianna and the larger Villa San Marco, said to measure more than 11,000 sq metres. Neither is in mint condition, but the frescoes in Villa Arianna suggest that it must once have been quite something. Both are accessible by bus from Via Nocera Circumvesuviana station.

Some 3km north of Pompeii, the **Antiquarium di Boscoreale** is a museum dedicated to Pompeii and its ancient environs. Historical artefacts are combined with life-size photos and reconstructions to show what the area was like 2000 years ago. At the time of writing, getting here involved a 2km walk from Pompeii-Scavi-Villa dei Misteri Circumvesuviana station. Contact the Pompeii tourist office for further details.

All three sites are covered by a single **ticket** (adult/EU 18-25yr/EU under 18yr & over 65yr €5.50/2.75/free), and opening times are standard: 8.30am to 7.30pm April to October, last entry 6pm, and 8.30am to 5pm November to March, last entry 3.30pm.

NAPLES

initially used for the audience to stroll between acts, and later as a barracks for gladiators. Next door, the **Teatro Piccolo** (also known as the Odeion) was once an indoor theatre renowned for its acoustics, while the pre-Roman **Tempio di Iside** (Temple of Isis) was a popular place of cult worship.

Terme Stabiane & Casa della Venere in Conchiglia

As it shoots eastward, Via Marina becomes Via dell'Abbondanza (Street of Abundance). Lined with ancient shops, this was the city's main thoroughfare and where you'll find the **Terme Stabiane**, a typical 2nd century BC bath complex. Entering from the vestibule, bathers would stop off in the vaulted *apodyterium* before passing through to the *tepidarium* and *caldarium*. Particularly impressive is the stuccoed vault in the men's changing room, complete with whimsical images of cupids and nymphs. At the time of writing, the bath complex was closed for restoration but due to reopen shortly.

Towards the northeastern end of Via dell'Abbondanza, **Casa della Venere in Conchiglia** (House of the Venus Marina) has recovered well from the WWII bomb that damaged it in 1943. Although unexceptional from the outside, it houses a gorgeous peristyle that looks onto a small, manicured garden. And it's here in the garden that you'll find the striking

NAPLES

Venus fresco after which the house is named.

Anfiteatro
Just southeast of the Casa della Venere in Conchiglia, gladiatorial battles thrilled up to 20,000 spectators at the grassy **anfiteatro**. Built in 70 BC, it's the oldest known Roman amphitheatre in existence. Over the way, lithe ancients kept fit at the **Grande Palestra**, an athletics field with an impressive portico dating to the Augustan period. At its centre lie the remains of a swimming pool.

Casa del Fauno
From the Grande Palestra, backtrack along Via dell'Abbondanza and turn right into Via Stabiana to view some of Pompeii's grandest houses. Turn left into Via della Fortuna and then right down Via del Labirinto to get to Vicolo del Mercurio and the entrance to **Casa del Fauno** (House of the Faun), Pompeii's largest private house. Covering an entire *insula* (city block) and boasting two atria at its front end (humbler homes had one), it is named after the delicate bronze statue in the *impluvium* (rain tank). It was here that early excavators found Pompeii's greatest mosaics, most of which are now in Naples' Museo Archeologico Nazionale (p54). Valuable on-site remainders include a beautiful, geometrically patterned marble floor.

A couple of blocks away, the **Casa del Poeta Tragico** (House of the Tragic Poet) features one of the world's first 'Beware of the Dog' (*Cave Canem*) warnings. To the north, the **Casa dei Vettii** on Via di Mercurio is home to a famous depiction of Priapus whose oversized phallus balances on a pair of scales…much to the anxiety of many a male observer.

Villa dei Misteri
From the Casa del Fauna, follow the road west and turn right into Via Consolare, which takes you out of the town through **Porta Ercolano**. Continue past **Villa di Diomede** and you'll come to the 90-room **Villa dei Misteri**, one of the most complete structures left standing in Pompeii. The dionysiac frieze, the most important fresco still on site, spans the walls of the large dining room. One of the largest paintings from the ancient world, it depicts the initiation of a bride-to-be into the cult of Dionysus, the Greek god of wine. A farm for much of its life, the villa's own vino-making area is still visible at the northern end.

If travelling to the *scavi* (ruins) by Circumvesuviana train (€2.40 from Naples, €1.90 from Sorrento), alight at Pompeii-Scavi-Villa dei Misteri station, located beside the main entrance at Porta Marina. Signs direct those arriving by car from the A3 to the *scavi*.

❦ MT VESUVIUS // SCALE A SLUMBERING TROUBLEMAKER
Since exploding into history in AD 79, Vesuvius has blown its top more than 30 times. The most devastating of these was in 1631, and the most recent in 1944. What redeems this lofty menace is the spectacular panorama from its **crater** (adult/under 18yr & over 65yr/under 8yr €6.50/4.50/free; ⏰ 9am-6pm Jul & Aug, to 5pm Apr-Jun, to 4pm Mar & Oct, to 3pm Nov-Feb, ticket office closes 1hr before the crater) – a breathtaking panorama that takes in sprawling city, sparkling islands, and the Monti Picentini, part of the Apennine mountains. Unbeknown to many, admission includes a free guided walk halfway around the crater. You'll find the guides at the entrance gate; ignore any requests for tips as they're obliged to guide you for free.

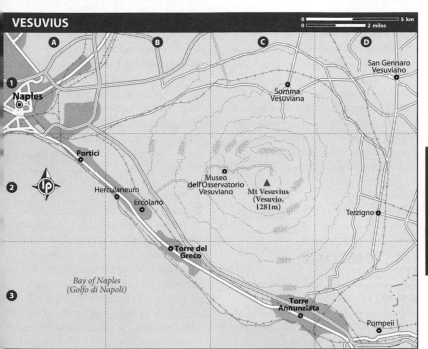

VESUVIUS

NAPLES

Whether arriving by bus or car, the end of the road is the summit car park and the ticket office. From here, a relatively easy 860m path leads up to the summit (allow 35 minutes), best tackled in trainers and with a sweater in tow (it can be chilly up top, even in summer).

The mountain itself was once higher than it currently stands, claiming a single summit rising to about 3000m rather than the 1281m of today. Its violent outburst in AD 79 not only drowned Pompeii in pumice and pushed the coastline back several kilometres but also destroyed much of the mountain top, creating a huge caldera and two new peaks.

Vesuvius itself is the focal point of the **Parco Nazionale del Vesuvio** (Vesuvius National Park; www.parconazionaledelvesuvio.it), which offers nine interesting nature walks around the volcano. A map of the trails is available from the ticket office (€2), with a free, smaller version available on the website.

Note that when the weather is bad the summit path is shut and bus departures are suspended.

About halfway up the hill, the **Museo dell'Osservatorio Vesuviano** (Museum of the Vesuvian Observatory; ☎ 081 610 84 83; www.ov.ingv.it; admission free; ☽ 9am-1pm Mon-Fri) tells the history of 2000 years of Vesuvius-watching.

The easiest way to reach Vesuvius is to get a bus from Pompeii up to the crater car park. **Vesuviana Mobilità** (☎ 081 963 44 20; www.vesuvianamobilita.it, in Italian) operates eight to 10 return-trip buses daily from both Piazza Anfiteatro and Piazza Porta Marina Inferiore. The journey time is one hour each way and return tickets cost €8.90, with a somewhat annoying 20-minute pit stop at a kiosk along the way. (Avoid the hard sell by bringing your own snacks and drinks.)

Two of the buses stop in Ercolano, departing from the bus stop on Via Panoramica (about 50m from the Ercolano-Scavi Circumvesuviana train station) at 8.25am and 12.45pm and returning at 2.40pm and 5.25pm. Return tickets are available on board and cost €7.80 for the 90-minute round trip.

If travelling by car, exit the A3 at Ercolano Portico and follow signs for the Parco Nazionale del Vesuvio.

GASTRONOMIC HIGHLIGHTS

♥ VINO LO RE €€
Off Map p101; ☎ 081 739 02 07; Corso Resina 261, Ercolano; meals €30; ✆ Tue-Sat, lunch only Sun, closed Aug; ⊞ Circumvesuviana to Ercolano-Scavi
In rough-and-tumble Ercolano, Vino Lo Re is a stylish, inviting haven, where vintage prints, bookshelves and funky tin lamps meet a fabulous wine list, clued-up staff and revamped regional grub. Start on a high note with the artful antipasto, whose row of 'tastings' may include a *polpettina di baccalà* (salted cod patty), *crocchetta di taleggio con porcino* (*taleggio* and porcini croquette) and a ricotta-filled courgette flower. Topping it all off are some delectable desserts (like a heavenly ricotta and chocolate flan served with warm chocolate sauce).

♥ MELIUS €
Off Map p105; ☎ 081 850 25 98; Via Lepanto 156-160, Pompeii; ✆ 8am-2pm & 4.30-8.30pm Mon-Sat, 8am-2pm Sun; ⊞ Circumvesuviana to Pompei-Santuario
Beef up the larder (or picnic hamper) at this luscious gourmet deli, where local

delicacies include fresh *mozzarella di bufala*, Graniano pasta, *sopressata Cilentana* (smoked salami from Cilento), citrusy Amalfi Coast marmalades and *liquore alla mela annurca*, a liqueur made using Annurca apples. For a self-catered treat, pick up some fragrant bread, a bottle of local Falanghina and some ready edibles; the peppery marinated aubergines and *pizza di scarole* (escarole pie) are equally divine.

♥ PRESIDENT €€
Off Map p105; ☎ 081 850 72 45; Piazza Schettini 12, Pompeii; meals €35; ✆ lunch & dinner Mar-Oct, closed Mon & dinner Sun Nov-Feb, closed 2 weeks Jan; ⊞ Circumvesuviana to Pompei-Santuario
With its dripping chandeliers, Bacharach melodies and breathtakingly gracious service, the President feels like a private dining room in an Audrey Hepburn film. Heading the charm is owner Paolo Gramaglia, whose passion for local produce is only matched by the menu's creative brilliance – the likes of aubergine *millefoglie* with Cetara anchovies, mozzarella *filante* (melted mozzarella) and grated *tarallo* biscuit presented like a wrapped-up *caramella* (lolly), or 'deconstructed' ricotta and pear cake with caramelised pear. The degustation menus (€40 to €70) are a gourmand's delight.

THE ISLANDS

3 PERFECT DAYS

❧ DAY 1 // SIMPLE PLEASURES ON PROCIDA

Enjoy a day of tranquillity, after the clamour and crowds of Naples, on the nearby island of Procida; a short ferry hop away. After a gentle stroll in the *centro storico* (historic centre), pull up a chair at picturesque Marina Corricella (p153) for a simple meal of fresh fish. Take an afternoon boat trip around the island's evocative hidden coves (p154). Stay overnight (see p275).

❧ DAY 2 // ISCHIA'S NATURE WALKS & BUBBLING SPAS

Catch another ferry to nearby Ischia. Head for the lush botanical gardens of La Mortella (p145) and wander the shady cool pathways surrounded by colourful exotic plants. Lunch near the beach at scenic Sant'Angelo (p146). In the afternoon catch a water taxi to Terme Cavascuro (see p146), the island's oldest natural spa, for an afternoon of restorative self-pampering. Catch a ferry to Capri and enjoy a romantic sunset from the deck.

❧ DAY 3 // GLAMOUR & GLITZ VERSUS NATURAL BEAUTY ON CAPRI

Wake up early before the day trippers arrive and join the local who's who brigade at the emblematic La Piazzetta square. Leave the surrounding sophisticated strut of shops behind as you head towards the nearby Giardini di Augusto terraced gardens (p122) and some of the best views in Capri. After lunch at one of our recommendations (see Gastronomic Highlights; p126), enjoy the beauty of the island's trails with either a country amble or a more demanding hike (see p118).

THE ISLANDS

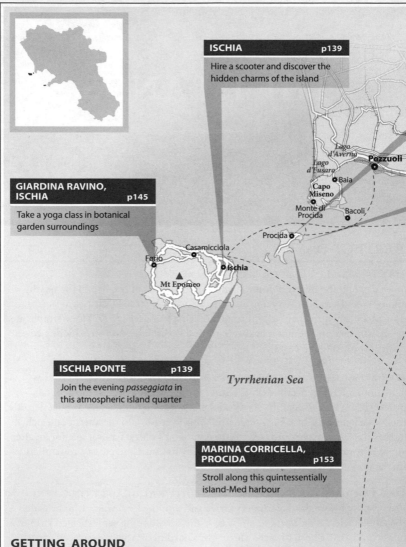

ISCHIA   p139

Hire a scooter and discover the hidden charms of the island

GIARDINA RAVINO, ISCHIA   p145

Take a yoga class in botanical garden surroundings

ISCHIA PONTE   p139

Join the evening *passeggiata* in this atmospheric island quarter

MARINA CORRICELLA, PROCIDA   p153

Stroll along this quintessentially island-Med harbour

Tyrrhenian Sea

Lago d'Averno · **Pozzuoli**
Lago d'Fusaro
Capo Miseno · Baia
Monte di Procida · Bacoli
Procida

Casamicciola
Forio
Mt Epomeo · Ischia

GETTING AROUND

Unless you travel by helicopter, ferries are the only way to go if you are visiting the Bay of Naples' islands of Procida, Ischia and Capri. Note that ferries departing from Positano and Amalfi operate solely from Easter to September. At other times of the year, you will have to catch the ferry or hydrofoil from Naples or Sorrento. All three islands have excellent public transport infrastructure and also provide scope for hiking and cycling.

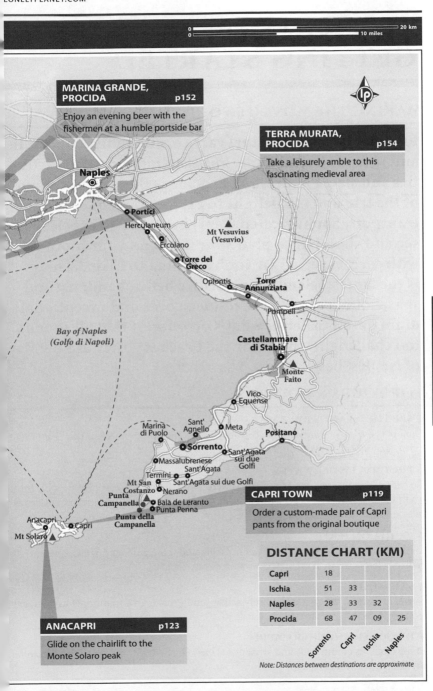

0 [========] [==========] 20 km
0 [========] [==========] 10 miles

MARINA GRANDE, PROCIDA   p152

Enjoy an evening beer with the fishermen at a humble portside bar

TERRA MURATA, PROCIDA   p154

Take a leisurely amble to this fascinating medieval area

Naples

Portici
Herculaneum
Ercolano
Torre del Greco
Oplontis
Torre Annunziata
Pompeii
Mt Vesuvius (Vesuvio)

Bay of Naples (Golfo di Napoli)

Castellammare di Stabia
Monte Faito

Vico Equense
Sant' Agnello
Meta
Positano
Marina di Puolo
Sorrento
Massalubrense
Sant'Agata
Sant'Agata sui due Golfi
Termini
Mt San Costanzo
Nerano
Punta Campanella
Baia de Leranto
Punta Penna
Punta della Campanella

Anacapri
Capri
Mt Solaro

CAPRI TOWN   p119

Order a custom-made pair of Capri pants from the original boutique

THE ISLANDS

ANACAPRI   p123

Glide on the chairlift to the Monte Solaro peak

DISTANCE CHART (KM)

	Sorrento	Capri	Ischia	Naples
Capri	18			
Ischia	51	33		
Naples	28	33	32	
Procida	68	47	09	25

Note: Distances between destinations are approximate

THE ISLANDS GETTING STARTED

MAKING THE MOST OF YOUR TIME

Procida, Ischia and Capri vary considerably, not just in ambience and landscape, but also in their sights, activities and size. Picturesque Procida is the smallest island of the trio and is a delight to explore by foot or public transport. Sophisticated Capri has more to experience, see and shop for, so plan your day (and your footwear!) with care, especially if you're hoping to hike. Ischia is the largest island, so prioritise beforehand: natural spas, botanical gardens, hidden coves and exceptional dining are a taster of what's on offer. If that all sounds too challenging, head for the beaches – they are the Bay of Naples' best.

TOP TOURS & COURSES

♥ SEE THE ISLANDS BY SEA
Explore Capri's stunning natural grottoes by boat, including the legendary *Grotta Azzurra*. (Banana Sports; ☎ 081 837 51 88; Marina Grande; p125)

♥ PROCIDA UNDERWATER
Go snorkelling in Procida's crystal-clear waters and discover the fabulous sea life beneath the waves (Procida Diving Centre; ☎ 081 896 83 85; www.vacanzeaprocida.it/framediving01-uk.htm; Via Cristoforo Colombo 6, Marina Chiaiolella; p154)

♥ ISCHIA ON FOOT
Join a group of walkers and stride out in Ischia under the guidance of an experienced geologist (Geo-Ausfluge; ☎ 081 90 30 58, www.eurogeopark.com; p145)

♥ SAIL AHOY
Travel in historic style with a leisurely sail around Procida in a traditional wooden galleon (☎ 081 896 90 63; Marina Corricella, Procida; p154)

♥ DISCOVER ANOTHER CAPRI
Enjoy fabulous countryside and sensational views by hiking Capri´s well-marked off-the-beaten-track trails (p118)

THE ISLANDS

GETTING AWAY FROM IT ALL

In Capri, most day trippers follow a classic route, which encompasses La Piazzetta and Anacapri. Ischia Porte and Ponte are similarly popular, while Procida's harbour and pretty marinas are this island's more crowded hot spots.

* **Wander the backstreets** Explore the streets surrounding Anacapri centre. Heading towards Monte Solaro, you'll discover a delightful landscape of overgrown allotments, contented cats and banks of dazzling wild flowers

* **Pick up a picnic** Go to one of the delis in Ischia Porte and head off to the 3km long and secluded Spiaggia dei Maronti beach (p146)

* **Rent a bike** Enjoy Procida's delightful rural countryside by an easygoing pedal around the island (p157)

LOCAL FESTIVALS

* **Capri Tango Festival** A skirt-swirling combo of music, dancing, exhibitions and tango classes (19 to 22 June)

* **Festa di Sant'Anna** (Ischia) The allegorical 'burning of the Castello Aragonese' on 26 July, with a hypnotic procession of boats and fireworks

* **Vinischia** (Ischia; www.vinischia.it, in Italian) Foodies flock to this four-day regional food and wine celebration in July

* **Settembrata Anacaprese** (Capri) Annual celebration of the grape harvest with gastronomic events and markets (1 to 15 September)

TOP SWIMMING SPOTS

* **PUNTA CARENA (CAPRI)**
The rocks by the *faro* (lighthouse) make natural diving platforms (p124)

* **SPIAGGIA DI CHIAIA (PROCIDA)**
Beautiful stretch of sand with warm shallow sea (p153)

* **SPIAGGIA DEI PESCATORI (ISCHIA)**
Picturesque seafront strip with clear rock-free water (p142)

* **PUNTA CARUSO (ISCHIA)**
Secluded rocky spot perfect for a solitary swim (p145)

* **GROTTA AZZURRA (CAPRI)**
Dive off the platform into the deep blue water by the cave's entrance (p125)

RESOURCES

* **Capri Online** (www.caprionline.it) Covers all aspects of Capri

* **Ischia Online** (www.ischiaonline.it) Good all-round website including sights, restaurants and hotels

* **Procida Tourism** (www.isoladiprocida.it) Includes an accommodation-booking service

* **Capri Information** (http://goitaly.about.com/od/capri/p/capri.htm) Comprehensive site on all aspects of the island

* **Anacapri** (www.anacapri-life.com) News and information about Anacapri

* **Capri Island** (www.capri.net) Includes listings, itineraries and ferry schedules

THE ISLANDS

TRANSPORT

BOAT // Ferries are the only way to go if you are visiting the islands. Note that ferries departing from Positano and Amalfi operate solely from Easter to September. At other times of the year, you will have to catch the ferry or hydrofoil from Naples or Sorrento. The information listed here refers to high-season crossings and is not comprehensive; check the respective websites and the Transport chapter (p303) for more detailed itineraries. Ferries leave from both the Beverello and adjacent Mergellina ports in Naples; there is a strip of booths with the times, berth numbers and costs clearly displayed. Overall, there is no need to book in advance. Just turn up around 35 minutes before departure in case there is a queue. Note that some companies require you to pay a small supplement for luggage, typically around €1.50. **Caremar** (☎ 081 837 07 00; www.caremar.it) operates up to 13 daily hydrofoils to/from Naples and Ischia (€16, 40 minutes), and five daily hydrofoils to/from Naples and Procida (€8.60, 30 minutes). It also operates slower ferries to Capri (€9.60, 1¼ hours, six daily). **SNAV** (☎ 081 837 75 77; www.snav.com) operates six daily hydrofoils to/from Naples and Capri (€16), and four daily hydrofoils to/from Naples and Procida (€13.60), while **Alilauro** (☎ 081 837 69 95; www.alilauro.it)

operates hydrofoils to/from Naples and Ischia (€16, nine daily, 40 minutes). **Neopolis** (☎ 081 552 72 09; www.caprinfo.it) and **Navigazione Libera del Golfo** (☎ 081 552 07 63; www.navlib.it) both operate up to four daily hydrofoils to/from Naples and Capri (€17). There are also ferries and hydrofoils that run virtually hourly from Sorrento to Capri during the high season, and less frequently the rest of the year. They are operated by several companies, all of which have kiosks in the Marina Piccola. See the Transport chapter for more details.

CAPRI

· · · · · ·

pop 13,100

A legendary idyll: Capri is a beguiling combination of fabled beauty and hedonistic appeal that has charmed Roman emperors, Russian revolutionaries and showbiz stars for decades. It's the perfect microcosm of Mediterranean appeal – a smooth cocktail of chichi piazzas and cool cafes, Roman ruins and rugged seascapes.

THE ISLANDS ACCOMMODATION

In Capri you can stay in celeb-style luxury, a stylish B&B or somewhere comfortable, modern and in the midrange bracket. Ischia and Procida have a wider price range, but all three are firmly seasonal, with the choicest accommodation getting booked up months in advance.

★ A classic Capri hotel since the '50s, **Hotel Gatto Blanco** (p272) oozes quality with shiny majolica tiles, sumptuous patios and a thoroughbred Persian cat

★ Relax on a hammock at Anacapri's rural retreat of **Villa Eva** (p272) surrounded by fruit and olive trees

★ A dreamy five-star resort, Ischia's **Messatorre Resort & Spa Agriturismo Serafino** (p275) is the ultimate in self-pampering bliss

★ A fashionably thought-out converted farmhouse, **Casa Giovanni da Procida** (p275) is surrounded by lush green gardens

★ Breathtaking panoramic views and fabulously elegant, Procida's **Casa sul Mare** (p275) is the quintessential boutique hotel

THE ISLANDS

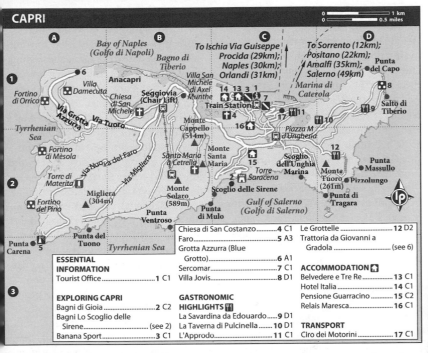

CAPRI

Chiesa di San Costanzo............4 C1
Faro...5 A3
Grotta Azzurra (Blue
    Grotto)..................................6 A1
Sercomar....................................7 C1
Villa Jovis.................................8 D1

**ESSENTIAL
INFORMATION**
Tourist Office...........................1 C1

EXPLORING CAPRI
Bagni di Gioia..........................2 C2
Bagni Lo Scoglio delle
    Sirene...............................(see 2)
Banana Sport............................3 C1

**GASTRONOMIC
HIGHLIGHTS**
La Savardina da Edouardo......9 D1
La Taverna di Pulcinella........10 D1
L'Approdo...............................11 C1

Le Grottelle............................12 D2
Trattoria da Giovanni a
    Gradola...........................(see 6)

ACCOMMODATION
Belvedere e Tre Re................13 C1
Hotel Italia............................14 C1
Pensione Guarracino..............15 C2
Relais Maresca......................16 C1

TRANSPORT
Ciro dei Motorini...................17 C1

THE ISLANDS

It's also a hugely popular day-trip destination and a summer favourite of holidaying VIPs. Inevitably, the two main centres, Capri Town and its up-hill rival Anacapri are almost entirely given over to tourism so you can expect prices to be high. But explore beyond the effortlessly cool cafes and designer boutiques, and you'll find that Capri retains an unspoiled charm with grand villas, overgrown vegetable plots, sun-bleached peeling stucco and banks of brilliantly coloured bougainvillea. All of this overlooks deep blue water that laps unseen into secluded coves and mysterious grottoes.

Already inhabited in the Palaeolithic age, Capri was briefly occupied by the Greeks before the Emperor Augustus made it his private playground, and Tiberius retired here in AD 27. Its modern incarnation as a tourist centre dates from the early 20th century.

ESSENTIAL INFORMATION

EMERGENCIES // Guardia Medica (Map p121; ☎ 081 838 12 39; Via Madonna delle Grazie 28, Capri Town) 24-hour medical emergency centre which can arrange transportation to the mainland; **Police Station** (Map p121; ☎ 081 837 42 11; Via Roma 70, Capri Town);

TOURIST OFFICES // Capri Tourism (www.capritourism.com) Anacapri (Map p124; ☎ 081 837 15 24; Via Giuseppe Orlandi 59, Anacapri; ⏲ 8.30am-8.30pm Jun-Sep, 9am-3pm Mon-Sat Oct-Dec & Mar-May); Capri Town (Map p121; ☎ 081 837 06 86; Piazza Umberto I, Capri Town; ⏲ 8.30am-8.30pm Jun-Sep, 9am-1pm & 3.30-6.45pm Mon-Sat Oct-May); Marina Grande (Map p117; ☎ 081 837 06 34; Quayside, Marina Grande; ⏲ 9am-1pm & 3.30-6.45pm Jun-Sep, 9am-3pm Mon-Sat Oct-May).

ORIENTATION

About 5km from the mainland at its nearest point, Capri is a mere 6km long and 2.7km wide. As you approach, there's a great camera shot of Capri Town with the dramatic slopes of Monte Solaro (589m) to the west, hiding the village of Anacapri.

All hydrofoils and ferries arrive at Marina Grande, the island's transport hub. From here the quickest way up to Capri Town is by funicular, but there are also buses and more costly taxis. On foot, it's a tough 2.3km climb along Via Marina Grande. At the top, turn left (east) at the junction with Via Roma for the centre of town or right (west) for Via Provinciale di Anacapri, which eventually becomes Via Giuseppe Orlandi as it leads up to Anacapri.

Pint-sized Piazza Umberto I is the focal point of Capri Town. A short hop to the east, Via Vittorio Emanuele leads down to the main shopping street, Via Camerelle.

Up the hill in Anacapri, buses and taxis drop you off in Piazza Vittoria, from where Via Giuseppe Orlandi, the main strip, runs southwest and Via Capodimonte heads up to Villa San Michele di Axel Munthe.

WALKING TOUR

Surprisingly for such a small place, Capri offers some memorable hiking. A network of well-maintained paths weaves its way across the island, leading through areas that even in the height of summer are all but deserted. The tourist office can provide you with walking maps.

Distance: 1.2km
Duration: 1¼ hours
This fine walk starts at the **Arco Naturale** (p123), a curious eroded limestone arch, which was part of a large grotto. (Note: for a tougher walk, do it in reverse, no – not backwards, but starting at the Belvedere di Tragara and ending up at the Arco Naturale, which involves an invigorating climb of steps.) At the end of Via Matermània, backtrack to **Le Grottelle** (p127) restaurant and take the nearby set of stairs. About halfway down you'll pass the **Grotta di Matermània**, a giant natural cave used by the Romans as a *nymphaeum* (shrine to the water nymph) and dedicated to the Mater Magna (Great Mother). You can still see a few traces of the mosaic wall decorated with shells. At the bottom, continue down the path as it follows the rocky coastline south. The striking flat-roofed red villa you eventually see on your left, on the Punta Massullo promontory, is **Villa Malaparte**, the former holiday home of Tuscan writer Curzio Malaparte (1898–1957), currently being restored by his great nephew after decades of neglect. Carrying on, the sea views become increasingly impressive as the path continues westward around the lower wooded slopes of **Monte Tuoro**. A few hundred metres further along and you will arrive at a staircase on your right, which leads up to the **Belvedere di Tragara** and some absolutely stunning views of the Isole Faraglioni.

To get back to the centre of Capri Town simply follow Via Tragara and its continuation Via Camerelle.

EXPLORING CAPRI

The name Capri comes, appropriately, from the ancient Greek kaprie (wild goat) and some would say that you need to be as sure footed and nimble as a goat to explore the island properly.

OTHER WALKS

ANACAPRI TO MONTE SOLARO
Distance: 2km
Duration: two hours
Rising 589m above Anacapri, **Monte Solaro** is Capri's highest point. To get to the top you can either take the *seggiovia* (chairlift) from Piazza Vittoria or you can walk. To do the latter take Via Axel Munthe and turn right up Via Salita per il Solaro. Follow the steep trail until you come to the pass known as **La Crocetta**, marked by a distinctive iron crucifix. Here the path divides: go right for the summit and its spectacular views over the Bay of Naples and Amalfi Coast; or go left for the valley of Cetrella and the picturesque hermitage of **Santa Maria a Cetrella** (generally open on Saturday afternoon until sunset).

If you don't fancy the walk up, do what many people do and take the chairlift up and walk down.

ANACAPRI TO BELVEDERE DI MIGLIERA
Distance: 2km
Duration: 45 minutes
A lovely, relaxing walk, this leads out to the **Belvedere di Migliera**, a panoramic platform with spectacular sea views.

The route couldn't be simpler: from Piazza Vittoria take Via Caposcuro and continue straight along its continuation Via Migliera. Along the way you'll pass fruit orchards, vineyards and small patches of woodland. Once at the Belvedere you can return to Anacapri via the **Torre di Materita** or, if you've still got the legs, continue up Monte Solaro. Note, however, that this is a tough walk graded medium-difficult by the Club Alpino Italiano (CAI; Italian Alpine Club).

CARENA TO PUNTA DELL'ARCERA, THE SENTIERO DEI FORTINI
Distance: 5.2km
Duration: three hours
Snaking its way along the island's oft-overlooked western coast, the **Sentiero dei Fortini** (Path of the Small Forts) is a wonderful, if somewhat arduous, walk that takes you from Punta Carena, the island's southwestern point, up to Punta dell'Arcera near the **Grotta Azzurra** in the north. Named after the three coastal forts (Pino, Mésola and Orrico) along the way, it passes through some of Capri's most unspoiled countryside.

THE ISLANDS

If time (or your pair of shoes) is tight, the island's sights may be visited by funicular, bus and/or taxi. The island has three distinct areas: sophisticated and downright good-looking Capri Town; more rural, low-key Anacapri; and the bustling Marina Grande, where, unless you travel by helicopter, you are more than likely to arrive.

CAPRI TOWN

With its whitewashed stone buildings and tiny, car-free streets, Capri Town seems more film set than real life. A diminutive model of upmarket Mediterranean chic, it's a pristine mix of luxury hotels, expensive bars, restaurants and designer boutiques. In summer the centre swells with crowds of camera-wielding day trippers and the designer-clad wealthy.

❦ PIAZZA UMBERTO I (AKA LA PIAZZETTA) // SEE-AND-BE-SEEN WITH THE IDLE RICH

Located beneath the clock tower and framed by swish cafes, this showy, open-air salon is central to your Capri experience, especially in the evening when the main activity in these parts is dressing up and hanging out. Be prepared, as the moment you sit down for a drink, you're going to pay handsomely for the grandstand views (around €6 for a coffee and €16 for a couple of white wines).

If it's before 8pm and you feel like a little exercise, trip up the stairs to the adjacent, baroque 17th-century **Chiesa di Santo Stefano** (Map p121; ☎ 081 837 00 72; Piazza Umberto I; ⏲ 8am-8pm), with its well-preserved marble floor (taken from Villa Jovis, see p122) and statue of San Costanzo, Capri's patron saint. Note the pair of languidly reclining patricians in the chapel to the south of the main altar, who seem to mirror some of the roués in the cafes outside. Beside the northern chapel is a reliquary with a saintly bone that reputedly saved Capri from the plague in the 19th century.

❦ LO SFIZIETTO // INDULGE IN ORGANIC (AND ADDICTIVE!) ICE CREAM

Located just off La Piazzetta, loosen your belt a notch and experience this cream of the crop gelateria. **Lo Sfizietto** (Map p121; ☎ 081 837 00 91; Via Longano 6) uses only organic ingredients with choices that include *cremolate* with 60% fresh fruit, *semifreddi* (a decadent cross between mousse and ice cream), and some unusual combinations like its namesake, *sfizietto* (caramel with pine nuts).

❦ LA PARISSIENNE // MADE-TO-MEASURE CAPRI PANTS

First opened in 1906 (yes, that is not a misprint!), and best known for introducing Capri pants in the 1960s, famously worn by Jacqueline Onassis, who bought them from here – **La Parissienne** (Map p121; ☎ 081 837 02 83; Piazza Umberto 1, 7) can run you up a made-to-measure pair within a day. Apparently Clark Gable was another Hollywood star who favoured the fashions here, particularly the Bermuda shorts, which (believe it or not) were considered quite raffish in their day.

❦ CERTOSA DI SAN GIACOMO // PONDER THIS MONASTERY'S VIOLENT PAST

To the east of La Piazzetta, take Via Vittorio Emanuele, which meanders down to the picturesque **Certosa di San Giacomo** (Map p121; ☎ 081 837 62 18; Viale Certosa 40; ⏲ 9am-2pm Tue-Sun), a 14th-century monastery generally considered to be the finest remaining example of Caprese architecture. The history is a harrowing one: it became the stronghold of the island's powerful Carthusian fraternity and was viciously attacked during Saracen pirate raids in the 16th century. A century later, monks retreated here to avoid the plague and were rewarded by an irate public (who they should have been tending), who tossed corpses over the walls. The monastery was eventually closed in the early 19th century and today houses a school, library, temporary exhibition space and a museum with some evocative 17th-century paintings. Be sure to look at the two cloisters, which have a real sense of faded glory (the smaller dates to the 14th century, the larger to the 16th century). There are also some soothing 17th-century frescoes in the church, which should hopefully

THE ISLANDS

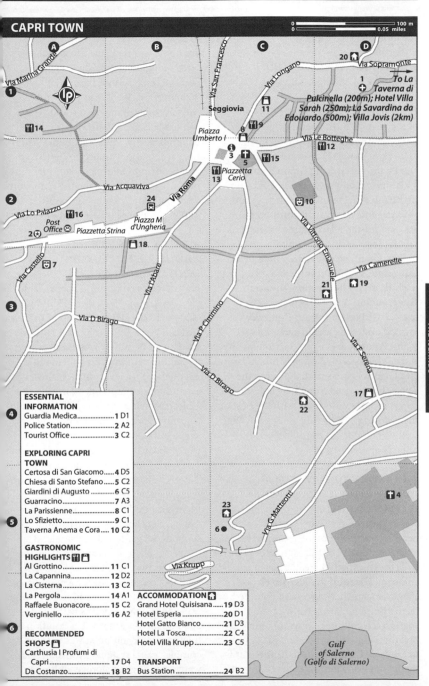

CAPRI TOWN

ESSENTIAL INFORMATION
Guardia Medica.................**1** D1
Police Station...................**2** A2
Tourist Office...................**3** C2

EXPLORING CAPRI TOWN
Certosa di San Giacomo...**4** D5
Chiesa di Santo Stefano...**5** C2
Giardini di Augusto..........**6** C5
Guarracino........................**7** A3
La Parissienne..................**8** C1
Lo Sfizietto......................**9** C1
Taverna Anema e Cora.....**10** C2

GASTRONOMIC HIGHLIGHTS
Al Grottino.......................**11** C1
La Capannina....................**12** D2
La Cisterna.......................**13** C2
La Pergola........................**14** A1
Raffaele Buonacore.........**15** C2
Verginiello.......................**16** A2

RECOMMENDED SHOPS
Carthusia I Profumi di Capri...**17** D4
Da Costanzo.....................**18** B2

ACCOMMODATION
Grand Hotel Quisisana......**19** D3
Hotel Esperia...................**20** D1
Hotel Gatto Bianco..........**21** D3
Hotel La Tosca.................**22** C4
Hotel Villa Krupp.............**23** C5

TRANSPORT
Bus Station......................**24** B2

THE ISLANDS

To La Taverna di Pulcinella (200m); Hotel Villa Sarah (250m); La Savardina da Edouardo (500m); Villa Jovis (2km)

Gulf of Salerno (Golfo di Salerno)

serve as an antidote as you contemplate the monastery's dark past.

☙ TAVERNA ANEME E CORE // CLASSY CLUBS FOR NEAPOLITAN SONG

Lying beyond a humble exterior is one of the island's most famous nightspots. **Taverna Aneme e Core** (Map p121; ☎ 081 837 64 61; Via Sella Orta 39E; ☾ closed Nov-Mar) is run by the charismatic Guido Lembo. This smooth and sophisticated bar-cum-nightclub attracts an appealing mixture of super chic and casually dressed punters here for the relaxed atmosphere and regular live music, including unwaveringly authentic Neapolitan guitar strumming (and song). Dress up and give it a whirl or stop by the more informal **Guarrancino** (Map p121; ☎ 081 837 05 14; Via Castello 7; ☾ closed Nov-Mar) atmospherically located under the arches and a former 17th-century olive oil production facility. It dates back to 1972 when brothers Brun and Gianni Lembo started playing the songs they learned from their father. Today you can warble along with the best of them during a lively sing-song show that sounds naff but has a heady good-time holiday atmosphere.

☙ GIARDINI DI AUGUSTO // ENJOY SCENIC VISTAS AND LOVELY GARDENS

Get away from the Capri crowds by heading southwest of the monastery where, at the end of Via Matteotti, you have the unexpected green oasis of the colourful **Giardini di Augusto** (Gardens of Augustus; Map p121; ☾ dawn-dusk). Founded by the Emperor Augustus, you should spend a few minutes contemplating the breathtaking view from here: gaze ahead to the Isole Faraglioni and the three dramatic limestone pinnacles that rise vertically out of the sea. Measuring 109m, 81m and 104m respectively, the stacks are home to a rare blue lizard that was once thought to be unique to the Faraglioni but has since been found on the Sicilian coast. While sadly beyond the capacity of even the most sophisticated camera lens, a photo from here should still impress the folks back home. From the gardens, pretty hairpin Via Krupp winds down to Marina Piccola and past a bust of Lenin overlooking the road from a nearby platform – no one seems to know who placed it here – or why!

☙ VILLA JOVIS // LEARN ABOUT ROMAN LUXURY (AND DECADENCE)

East of the town centre, a comfortable 2km walk along Via Tiberio, **Villa Jovis** (Jupiter's Villa; Map p117; ☎ 081 837 06 34; Via Tiberio; adult/EU citizen 18-25yr/EU citizen under 18yr & over 65yr €2/1/free; ☾ 9am–1hr before sunset) is sure to capture your imagination. Standing 354m above sea level, this was the largest and most sumptuous of the island's 12 Roman villas and was Tiberius' main Capri residence. Although not in great shape today, it is still very impressive size wise and wandering around will give you a good idea of the scale on which Tiberius liked to live. This vast pleasure complex famously pandered to the emperor's saucy desires, and included imperial quarters and extensive bathing areas set in dense gardens and woodland.

Spectacular but hardly practical, the villa's location posed major headaches for Tiberius' architects. The main problem was how to collect and store enough water to supply the villa's baths and 3000-sq metre gardens. The solution they eventually hit upon was to build a complex canal system to transport rainwater to four giant storage tanks; you

THE ISLANDS

TOP FIVE

CAPRI VIEWS

★ **Monte Solaro** (right)

★ **Belvedere di Tragara** (p118)

★ **Villa Jovis** (opposite)

★ **San Michele di Axel Munthe** (below)

★ **Giardini di Augusto** (opposite)

can still see the remains clearly today. Plumbers take note.

The stairway behind the villa leads to the 330m-high **Salto di Tiberio** (Tiberius' Leap; Map p117), a sheer cliff from where, says the story, Tiberius had out-of-favour subjects hurled into the sea. Although this could be a fabrication, the stunning views are real enough, especially if you suffer from vertigo.

A short walk from the villa, down Via Tiberio and Via Matermània, is the **Arco Naturale**, a huge rock arch formed by the pounding sea and another great photo opportunity.

ANACAPRI & AROUND

Traditionally Capri Town's more subdued neighbour, Anacapri is no stranger to tourism. But attention is largely limited to Villa San Michele di Axel Munthe and the souvenir stores on the main streets. Get off these and you'll discover that Anacapri is still, at heart, the laidback, rural village that it's always been.

♥ VILLA SAN MICHELE DI AXEL MUNTHE // ENJOY MATCHLESS VIEWS AND MAGNIFICENT SCULPTURES

The former home of self-aggrandising Swedish doctor Axel Munthe, **San Michele di Axel Munthe** (Map p124; ☎ 081 837 14 01; Via Axel Munthe; adult/under 12yr €5/free; ⚐ 9am-6pm May-Sep, 10.30am-3.30pm Nov-Feb, 9.30am-4.30pm Mar, 9.30am-5pm Apr & Oct) should be included on every visitor's itinerary. Built on the ruined site of a Roman villa, the gardens make a beautiful setting for a tranquil stroll with pathways flanked by immaculate flowerbeds. There are also superb views from here, plus some fine photo props in the form of Roman sculptures. If you are here between July and September, you may be able to catch one of the classical concerts that take place in the gardens. Check the **Axel Munthe Foundation** (☎ 081 837 14 01; www.sanmichele. org) website for the current program and reservation information.

Beyond the villa, Via Axel Munthe continues to the 800-step stairway leading down to Capri Town. Built in the early 19th century, this was the only link between Anacapri and the rest of the island until the present mountain road was constructed in the 1950s. Throughout history, the people of Capri and Anacapri have been at loggerheads and they are always ready to trot out their respective patron saints to ward off the *mal'occhio* (evil eye) of their rivals.

♥ SEGGIOVIA DEL MONTE SOLARO // TAKE A CHAIRLIFT TO HEAVENLY VIEWS

A fast and painless way to reach Capri's highest peak, the **Seggiovia del Monte Solaro** (Map p124; ☎ 081 837 14 28; single/return €5/6.50; ⚐ 9.30am-5pm Mar-Oct, 10.30am-3pm Nov-Feb) chairlift whisks you to the mountain peak in a tranquil beautiful ride of just 12 minutes. The views from the top are outstanding – on a clear day you can see the entire Bay of Naples, the Amalfi Coast and the islands of Ischia and Procida. If all that camera clicking has worked up an appetite, there's a cafeteria here that serves snacks, drinks and ice creams.

THE ISLANDS

☙ CHIESA DI SAN MICHELE // ADAM AND EVE IN EARTHLY PARADISE

If you appreciate the colour, intricate patterns and historical tradition of antique majolica tiles, consider a speedy visit to the **Chiesa di San Michele** (Map p124; ☎ 081 837 23 96; Piazza San Nicola; adult/under 12yr €1/free; ⏰ 9.30am-7pm Apr-Oct, 9.30am-3pm Nov-Mar), where Adam and Eve are vividly depicted, along with a bizarre animal menagerie, including a unicorn, bull, several goats and an elephant, in a glorious octagonal 18th-century majolica-tiled floor.

☙ FARO // SWIM FROM THE ROCKS BESIDE THE LIGHTHOUSE

Rising above Punta Carena, Capri's rugged southwesterly point, is the **faro** (Map p124), Italy's second-tallest and most powerful lighthouse. The rocks nearby are a great place to swim in the summer with lots of rocks to dive (safely) from and clear turquoise water. If this sounds like something you'd take the plunge and do, then hop on the bus that runs from the centre of Anacapri every 20 minutes to the *faro* in summer (and every 40 minutes in winter; if you are a real chill seeker).

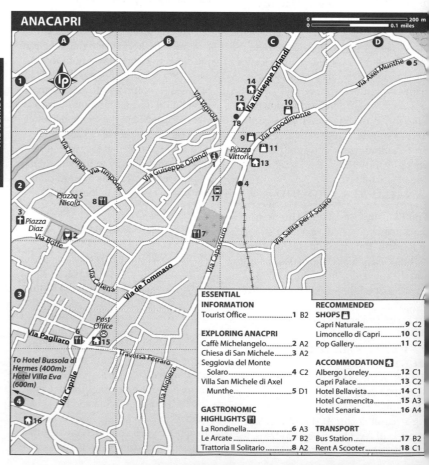

ANACAPRI

0 ————— 200 m
0 ————— 0.1 miles

☙ CAFFÈ MICHELANGELO // ANACAPRI'S VERY OWN MINI PIAZZETTA!

It's not that flashy, but the position of the delightful **Caffè Michelangelo** (Map p124; Via Giuseppe Orlandi 138) on a street flanked by tasteful shops and near two lovely piazzas makes it a perfect spot for indulging in a little people-watching-cum-cocktail time. Large cushioned chairs and a raised terrace add to the kick-back appeal.

MARINA GRANDE

Capri's main port is a shabbily attractive place with little evidence of the glitz that awaits up the hill. There are no real sights here, aside from the island's oldest church: the 5th-century **Chiesa di San Costanzo** (Map p117; ☎ 081 837 70 28; Via Marina Grande), which is a short walk away from the main harbour. This whitewashed *chiesa* is dedicated to the island's patron saint, who settled on the island after escaping a vicious storm en route from Constantinople to Rome. It was originally built over an earlier Roman construction, although the Byzantine version you see today is the result of a 10th-century makeover. If you're desperate for a swim, there's a 200m-long pebble beach to the west of the port.

☙ SEA SPORTS // CAPTAIN A BOAT OR DON A WETSUIT

The marina is the hub of Capri's thriving water-sports business. On the eastern edge of the waterfront, **Sercomar** (Map p117; ☎ 081 837 87 81; www.caprisub.com; Via Colombo 64; ☉ closed Nov) offers various diving packages, costing from €100 for a single dive (maximum of three people) to €350

THE ISLANDS

GROTTA AZZURRA

Capri's single most famous attraction is the **Grotta Azzurra** (Blue Grotto; Map p117; adult/EU citizen under 18yr & over 65yr €10.50/free; ☉ 9am–1hr before sunset), a stunning sea cave illuminated by an other-worldly blue light.

Long known to local fishermen, it was rediscovered by two Germans – writer Augustus Kopisch and painter Ernst Fries – in 1826. Subsequent research, however, revealed that Emperor Tiberius had built a quay in the cave around AD 30, complete with a *nymphaeum*. You can still see the carved Roman landing stage towards the rear of the cave.

Measuring 54m by 30m and rising to a height of 15m, the grotto is said to have sunk by up to 20m in prehistoric times, blocking every opening except the 1.3m-high entrance. And it's this that's the key to the magical blue light. Sunlight enters through a small underwater aperture and is refracted through the water; this, combined with the reflection of the light off the white sandy seafloor, produces the vivid blue effect to which the cave owes its name.

The easiest way to visit is to take a boat tour from Marina Grande. A return trip will cost €18.50, comprising a return motorboat to the cave, the rowing boat into the cave itself and admission fee; allow a good hour. The singing 'captains' are included in the price, so don't feel any obligation if they push for a tip.

The grotto is closed if the sea is too choppy and swimming in the cave is forbidden although you can swim outside the entrance – get a bus to Grotta Azzurra, take the stairs down to the right and dive off the small concrete platform.

for a four-session beginners course. Operating out of a kiosk on the private Pontile beach (to the west of the ferry ticket booths), **Banana Sport** (Map p117; ☎ 081 837 51 88; ☯ mid-Apr–Oct) hires out five-person motorised dinghies for €75 for two hours or €175 for the day (from 9.30am to 5.30pm) allowing you to explore the island's more secluded coves and grottoes. You can also pick up a boat to the popular swimming spot **Bagno di Tiberio**, a small inlet west of Marina Grande. It's said that Tiberius once swam here, although he wouldn't have had to pay €8.50 to access the private beach as you will.

MARINA PICCOLA

Little more than a series of private bathing facilities, Marina Piccola is on the southern side of the island, directly south of Marina Grande. A short bus ride from Capri Town, or a downhill 15-minute walk, it has a 50m-long public pebble beach hemmed in by the **Scoglio delle Sirene** (Rock of the Sirens) at the western end and the **Torre Saracena** (Saracen Tower) at the other. The swimming's not great, although the two rocks rising out of the water about 10m offshore make excellent diving boards. You can hire canoes at **Bagni di Gioia** (Map p117; ☎ 081 837 77 02) and **Bagni Lo Scoglio delle Sirene** (Map p117; ☎ 081 837 02 21) for around €14 per hour for a double canoe or €8 for a single.

GASTRONOMIC HIGHLIGHTS

Traditional Italian food served in traditional Italian trattorias is what you'll find on Capri. Prices are high but drop noticeably the further you get from Capri Town.

The island's culinary gift to the world is *insalata caprese*, a salad of fresh tomato, basil and mozzarella bathed in olive oil. Look out for *caprese* cheese, a cross between mozzarella and ricotta, and *ravioli caprese*, ravioli stuffed with ricotta and herbs.

Many restaurants, like the hotels, close over winter.

CAPRI TOWN & AROUND

☙ AL GROTTINO €€
Map p121; ☎ 081 837 05 84; Via Longano 27; pizzas from €6, meals €35; ☯ closed Nov-Mar
Two minutes' walk from La Piazzeta down a narrow alley; you can expect a queue here. A real old timer, dating from 1937, it was a renowned VIP dining spot in the '50s and '60s and continues to lure locals and visitors with traditional Neopolitan dishes like *ravioli al ragú* (ravioli in a meat, garlic sauce) and *pennette alla rucola* (small pasta tubes with a ruculo-based topping). The small dining space is seriously traditional, right down to the decorative *chianti* bottles.

☙ L'APPRODO €€
Map p117; ☎ 081 837 89 90; Piazzeta Ferraro 8, Marina Grande; pizzas from €6, meals €25
If you have arrived on the ferry with an appetite, head here; a three-minute walk to the left from where you disembark. You can easily fill up on the superb antipasti spread (€10). The pizzas are also tasty and varied; try the *Sfilatino* with ricotta, ham and mozzarella. Seafood is pricier, but the fish is as fresh as the day's catch and includes spiny lobster grill and seafood risotto. There are picturesque views over the colourful fishing boats and nets from the sprawling outdoor terrace, with little to remind you of Capri's fabled glitz up the hill.

LA CAPANNINA €€€

Map p121; ☎ 081 837 07 32; Via Le Botteghe 12;
meals €50; ☟ mid-Mar–Oct

Dating back to the 1930s, this is the island's most famous traditional trattoria and a long-time favourite on the celebrity circuit. Set up to look like a Hollywood version of a rustic eatery – pink tablecloths, hanging copper pots and carved wooden chairs – it serves a classic island menu of comfort food including high-quality seafood pasta, *ravioli capese*, grilled meat and fresh fish, including the speciality *linguine allo scorfano* (flat ribbons of pasta with scorpion fish).

LA CISTERNA €€

Map p121; ☎ 081 837 56 20; Via M Serafina 5; meals 25; ☟ closed Feb

Named after and housed in a 2000-year-old Roman cistern, this unpretentious trattoria (right down to the kitsch paintings on the wall) has been family run for several generations. Currently owned by the larger-than-life Salvatore, whose memorable picture adorns the bottles of house wine, it serves solid traditional dishes such as pasta with beans, veal outlets braised in lemon and wood-fired pizzas. Rumbling tummies won't go hungry – the portions are huge.

LA PERGOLA €€

Map p121; ☎ 081 837 74 12; Via Traversa Lo Palazzo
; meals €30; ☟ Thu-Tue Nov-Sep

A step up from the average island trattoria, La Pergola's vine-shaded terrace and sea views provide a sublime setting for the delicious, innovative food. The menu comprises all the Capri classics, plus a number of more innovative dishes such as *paccheri con cozze, patate e peperoncino* (large pasta rings with mussels, potatoes and chilli) and ravioli *verde* (green) in a creamy lemon sauce. It's hard to find; persevere and follow the signs.

LA SAVARDINA DA EDOUARDO €€

Map p117; ☎ 081 837 63 00; Via Lo Capo 8; meals €30; ☟ daily Jul & Aug, closed Tue Mar-Jun & Sep-Oct, closed Nov-Feb

You'll build up a hearty appetite as you stroll up to this laid-back restaurant surrounded by citrus trees in the Capri countryside. But as you collapse on the open-air terrace and look out to Ischia in the hazy distance, you'll appreciate the effort. The food is great, too. Dishes are made with local produce and are unapologetically simple. For proof try the *papardelle con ragùdi coniglio* (pasta with rabbit sauce) followed by succulent lamb chops.

LA TAVERNA DI PULCINELLA €€

Map p117; ☎ 081 837 64 85; Via Tiberio 7; pizzas around €7, meals €22; ☟ Apr-Oct

Thousands of tourists trudge past this down-to-earth trattoria-cum-pizzeria every day on their way up to Villa Jovis. Very few stop off to eat – perhaps put off by the sight of waiters in Punchinello (Pulcinella) costumes. Islanders know better and come here for their takeaway pizzas. And with good reason – they're the best on the island. If you're really hungry, go for the *Vesuvio*, a delicious combination of ricotta cheese, ham, mushrooms and peppers.

LE GROTTELLE €€

Map p117; ☎ 081 837 57 19; Via Arco Naturale 13; meals around €28; ☟ Apr-Oct

This is a great place to impress your partner. Not so much for the food, which is decent enough – think simple pasta dishes followed by grilled fish, chicken or rabbit – but for its atmospheric setting. About 150m from the Arco Naturale (p118), it's got two dining areas, one set in a cave, the other, more appealing, on a

THE ISLANDS

terrace perched above a wooded hillside that slopes dramatically down to the sea.

☙ RAFFAELE BUONACORE €

Map p121; ☎ 081 837 78 26; Via Vittorio Emanuele 35; treats €2-4.50; ◷ Mar-Oct

Ideal for a quick fill-up, this popular snack bar does a roaring trade in savoury and sweet treats, including frittatas, *panini* (bread rolls), pastries, waffles and ice cream. Hard to beat, though, are the delicious *sfogliatelle* (cinnamon-infused ricotta in a puff-pastry shell) and the feather-light speciality *caprilu al limone* (lemon and almond cakes) for just €0.70.

☙ VERGINIELLO €

Map p121; ☎ 081 837 09 44; Via Lo Palazzo 25; pizzas from €5, meals €20; ◷ closed Nov

Head for the post office, then down the steps to find this nearest thing to a budget diner in Capri Town. Verginiellio has a no-frills feel with two small square dining rooms and a hard-working team of harried waiters. Offering grandstand views over Marina Grande, the food is earthy and reliable. Of the pasta dishes, the *ravioli caprese* and *spaghetti alle cozze* (spaghetti with mussels) are worth trying; or go for a grilling with lamb chops or steak.

ANACAPRI & AROUND

☙ LA RONDINELLA €€

Map p124; ☎ 081 837 12 23; Via Guiseppe Orlandi 295; meals €28

La Rondinella has a relaxed, rural feel and remains one of Anacapri's most consistently good restaurants; apparently Graham Greene had a favourite corner table here. The menu features a number of Italian classics such as *saltimbocca alla Romana* (veal slices with ham and sage). For something different try chef Michele's *linguine alla ciammura*, a deli-

cious pasta dish with a creamy white sauce of anchovies, garlic and parsley. Top it all off with a slice of *torta di mandorle* (chocolate and almond tart).

☙ LE ARCATE €€

Map p124; ☎ 081 837 33 25; Via de Tommaso 24; meals €30

This is the restaurant that the locals recommend – and frequent. An unpretentious place with hanging baskets of ivy, sunny yellow tablecloths and well-aged terracotta tiles, it specialises in delicious *primi* (first courses) and pizzas. A real show stopper is the *risotto con polpa di granchio, rughetta e scaglie di parmigiano* (risotto with crab meat, rocket and shavings of Parmesan).

☙ TRATTORIA DA GIOVANNI A GRADOLA €

Map p117; Grotta Azzurra; meals €18; ◷ Apr-Oct

This laid-back, sand-between-your-toes trattoria is just beyond the swish bathing facilities at the Grotta Azzurra. The setting is lovely for a summer lunch – basic wooden tables on a narrow terrace overlooking the deep blue sea – and the food straightforward. Menu stalwarts include *parmigiana di melanzane* (baked eggplant with tomato and Parmesan), fried fish and *pasta e fagioli* (pasta and bean stew).

☙ TRATTORIA IL SOLITARIO €

Map p124; ☎ 081 837 13 82; Via Giuseppe Orlandi 96; pizzas from €4.50, meals around €20; ◷ Apr-Oct

This is the nearest you will get to being invited to someone's home. Tables are set in a small backyard with lemon trees and children's toys in the corner and the whole ambience is one of unhurried holiday time. The unremarkable menu lists the usual island fare – pasta and seafood, grilled meat and pizzas – but the helpings

(Continued on page 137)

THE ISLANDS

THE BEST OF
NAPLES & THE
AMALFI COAST

Whether you are falling for the figures in a Caravaggio masterpiece, savouring silky cozze (mussels) to the sound of lapping sea, or stumbling across a secret ancient marvel, Naples and its fabled bay rarely fail to seduce. Get set to fall head over Gucci heels for this impressively cultured, lip-lickingly delicious and scandalously good-looking region.

ABOVE Explore the ruined treasures of the Anfiteatro Flavio (p78) at Campi Flegrei

THE BEST MUSEUMS

1 MUSEO ARCHEOLOGICO
NAZIONALE // NAPLES
A world historical heavyweight, the National Archaeological Museum (p54) is an engrossing time machine. Featuring precious artefacts from Pompeii, Herculaneum, Rome and beyond, it documents all facets of ancient life.

2 PALAZZO REALE DI
CAPODIMONTE // NAPLES
A one-time residence of Joseph Bonaparte and Joachim Murat, the Royal Palace of Capodimonte (p71) is one of Europe's finest art repositories. Travel from medieval to modern with names like Botticelli, Titian, de Ribera and Merz.

JEAN-BERNARD CARILLET

3 CERTOSA DI SAN MARTINO // NAPLES

Naples' most visible building (p67) since the 14th-century was home to Carthusian monks. Avid hoarders with a weakness for lavish interiors, the monks filled their lofty abode heaves with cultural treasures.

4 MUSEO ARCHEOLOGICO DI PITHECUSAE // ISCHIA

The antithesis of a stuffy academic museum, the location of this archaeological treasure trove (p144) has a location that's as evocative as the collection.

5 MUSEO DELLA CARTA // AMALFI

Dig out that fountain pen, this museum (p188) will tempt you to ditch the emails for good. Learn the history of paper making from animal-hide parchment to exquisite handmade paper with beautiful watermarks and ragged edges.

TOP LEFT The magnificent Certosa di San Martino **BOTTOM LEFT** The striking exterior of the Museo Archeologico Nazionale **BOTTOM RIGHT** One of the many rooms at Palazzo Reale di Capodimonte

THE BEST RESTAURANTS

1 DORA // NAPLES

When it comes to Dora (p89), the word 'institution' is no hyperbole. Here, frozen seafood is a foreign concept and only flawless produce makes it to the table. And despite the enviable reputation and famous fans, Dora keeps it real with its corner TV and crooning matriarch.

2 LA STANZA DEL GUSTO // NAPLES

Thick-rimmed black glasses and an intellectual air give Mario Avallone that 'film critic' look. He's actually a former accountant, self-taught cook and the man behind this whimsical foodie hot spot (p86), which boasts rare cheeses, twisted local classics and a thrilling wine list.

133

3 DA CICCIOTTO // MARECHIARO, NAPLES

Ferries slide across the bay beyond the terrace. Old-school waiters present you with just-caught fish and a healthy serve of Latin charm. Tucked away just beyond the city chaos, this tiny trattoria (p91) has a way of making you feel that life is perfect.

4 DA COSTANTINO // POSITANO

This family-run restaurant (p182) has some of the best lofty dining views of Positano and the coast in the region. The food is also up there with the best, with home-made pasta dishes, superb pizzas and charcoal-grilled speciality entrees.

5 LA PERGOLA // CAPRI

The epitome of Capri dining (p127), with a terrace surrounded by lemon groves overlooking a lush green landscape and the Bay of Naples twinkling tantalisingly on the horizon.

⊃P LEFT *Insalata caprese* (salad of tomato, basil and mozzarella, bathed in olive oil) **BOTTOM LEFT** ctopus salad **BOTTOM RIGHT** *Spaghetti alle vongole* (spaghetti with clams)

THE BEST WALKS

---
1 VIA TRIBUNALI // NAPLES

The ancient city's *decumanus maior* (high street; p40) is urban intoxication; a hearty *ragù* of raucous pizzerias, old-school delis and *enoteche* (wine bars), crumbling churches and loud, scooter-riding teens. Grab a *pizza fritta* (fried pizza) from one of the street stalls and dive in.

---
2 LUNGOMARE // NAPLES

Start from the Giardini Pubblici below Palazzo Reale and follow the sea past neo-classical *palazzi*, a muscle-bound castle and the palm-fringed gardens of Villa Comunale. Those who make it to the Lungomare's western end (p65) are rewarded with ice-cream chalets and romantic kitsch.

ENRICO CARACCIOLO/ PHOTOLIBRARY

3 PARCO NAZIONALE DEL CILENTO E VALLO DI DIANO // CILENTO

This largely unknown park (p214) is superb for walking enthusiasts. The landscape is enticingly untamed and diverse with forests of silver birch and oak, vivid green valleys, craggy mountains and magical flora and fauna.

4 SENTIERO DEI FORTINI // CAPRI

Away from the high-octane glamour of Capri's town centre lies an island that has remained unchanged for centuries. Snaking around the little-known western coast, the Sentiero del Fortini (Path of the Small Forts; p119) passes secluded coves and three ruined forts.

5 RAVELLO TO MINORI // RAVELLO

High in the mountains, picturesque Ravello makes a great base camp for hikes (p194). For scenery and the relief of a steady descent, head for coastal Minori.

TOP LEFT Coastline scenery on the Sentiero dei Fortini walk **BOTTOM LEFT** Rural hamlet near Minori
BOTTOM RIGHT You'll see the striking Castel dell'Ovo on the Lungomare walk

TOP The breathtaking Certosa di San Lorenzo
RIGHT Soak away the pain at Parco Termale
Aphrodite Appollon, near Terme Cavascuro

THE BEST HIDDEN TREASURES

1 PISCINA MIRABILIS // CAMPI FLEGREI, NAPLES

Only in Naples do you need to track down an apron-strung pensioner to access one of the world's archeological wonders. Find her and she'll lead you down the street, swing open a gate, and let you into a Roman cistern (p83) so vast and impressive that the ancients dubbed it the 'Marvellous Pool'.

2 TERME CAVASCURO // ISCHIA

There is something evocative about bathing in a spa (p146) that has been a favourite bubbling spot since Roman times. As well as the grottoes, waterfalls and warm thermal waters, there's a natural sauna here.

3 CERTOSA DI SAN LORENZO // PADULA

This extraordinary middle-of-nowhere monastery (p213) will blow your mind with its lavish monumental proportions; the cloisters extend over an area that is only a grass blade short of Rome's Colosseum.

4 GROTTA DI CASTELCIVITA // PARCO NAZIONALE DEL CILENTO

This extraordinary series of caverns (p212) is a movie-set wonderland of colours, shapes and atmosphere. Inhabited since the Palaeolithic era, the gap-toothed chambers are punctuated by shapely stalactite and stalagmite formations, and some pure-crystal accretions.

(Continued from page 128)

are large and the quality high. The pizzas include a vast *pizza bianche* choice which is handy if you're tiring of tomatoes.

RECOMMENDED SHOPS

Boasting more designer boutiques per square metre than almost anywhere else on earth, Capri's shopping scene is conservative and expensive. Along the two main strips, Via Vittorio Emanuele and Via Camarelle, you'll find most of the fashion big guns as well as a number of jewellery and shoe shops. Look out, also, for the ceramic work and anything lemony, in particular, lemon-scented perfume and *limoncello*, a sweet lemon liqueur.

♥ CAPRI NATURALE
Map p124; ☎ 081 837 47 19; Via Capodimonte 15, Anacapri; ☉ Apr-Oct

One of the better shops along touristy Via Capodimonte, Capri Naturale sells a limited range of women's fashions. Expect whisper-thin linen frocks in delphinium blue or dip-dyed lavender and a small selection of handmade sandals. Everything is made locally and prices are reasonable, all things considered.

♥ CARTHUSIA I PROFUMI DI CAPRI
Map p121; ☎ 081 837 03 68; Viale Parco Augusto 2C, Capri Town

Legend has it that Capri's famous floral perfume was discovered in 1380 by the

CELEBRITY ISLAND

THE ISLANDS

A byword for Mediterranean chic, Capri has long enjoyed a reputation as a celebrity haunt.

The first big name to decamp here was Emperor Tiberius in AD 27. A man of sadistic sexual perversions, at least if the Roman author Suetonius is to be believed, he had 12 villas built on the island, including the vast Villa Jovis (p122). He also left deep scars and until modern times his name was equated with evil by islanders. When the Swedish doctor Axel Munthe first began picking about the Roman ruins on the island in the early 20th century and built his villa on the site of a Tiberian palace, locals would observe that it was all *'roba di Tiberio'* – Tiberius' stuff.

But more than Tiberius' capers, it was the discovery of the Grotta Azzurra in 1826 that paved the way for Capri's celebrity invasion. As news of the spectacular cave spread so artists, intellectuals, industrialists and writers began to visit, attracted by the island's isolated beauty and, in some cases, the availability of the local lads. An early habitué, Alfred Krupp, the German industrialist and arms manufacturer, was involved in a gay scandal, while author Norman Douglas and French count Jacques Fersen set all manner of tongues wagging.

The island also proved an escape for Russian revolutionaries. In 1905 the author Maxim Gorky moved to Capri after failing to topple the Russian Tsar and five years later Lenin stopped by for a visit.

In the course of the early 20th century the Chilean poet Pablo Neruda and German author Thomas Mann visited regularly; British writers Compton Mackenzie and Graham Greene lived here for extended periods; and Britain's wartime singer Gracie Fields retired here.

Today it's the Hollywood stars and international models who keep Capri's reputation alive and its overworked paparazzi in business.

Prior of the Certosa di San Giacomo. Caught unawares by a royal visit, he arranged a floral display of the island's most beautiful flowers for the queen. Three days later he went to change the water in the vase only to discover that it had acquired a mysterious floral odour. This became the base of the perfume that's now sold at this smart laboratory outlet.

🌳 DA COSTANZO

Map p121; ☎ 081 837 80 77; Via Roma 49, Capri Town; 🕑 Mar-Nov

In 1959 Clarke Gable stopped off at this tiny, unpretentious shoe shop on the main street to get himself a pair of hand-made leather sandals (to go with those Bermuda shorts he picked up earlier; see p120). The shop's still going, selling a bewildering range of colourful styles to a mixed crowd of passers-by and shoe aficionados. Prices start at around €90, which is a small investment for gleaning a piece of Hollywood history.

🌳 LIMONCELLO DI CAPRI

Map p124; ☎ 081 837 29 27; Via Capodimonte 27, Anacapri; 🕑 Oct-Apr

Don't be put off by the gaudy yellow display; this historic shop stocks some of the island's best *limoncello*. In fact, it was here that the drink was first concocted. Apparently, the grandmother of current owner Vivica made the tot as an after-dinner treat for the guests in her small guesthouse. Nowadays, the shop produces some 70,000 bottles each year, as well as lemon and orange chocolate (recommended), lemon marmalade and lemon honey. They ship all over the world.

🌳 POP GALLERY

Map p124; ☎ 081 978 05 13; Via Capodimonte 24, Anacapri; 🕑 Apr-Oct

Grown weary of that ubiquitous lemon motif? Then this cutting-edge new showroom will delight and inspire with its modern sculptures and objets d'art by Italian artists. The faux abalone pieces are particularly ingenious, as are the sculpted heads with their bad-hair day industrial foam bouffant hairdos in vivid colours.

TRANSPORT

BOAT // Sam Helicopter (☎ 0828 35 41 55; www.capri-helicopters.com) Unless you're prepared to pay €1300 for a helicopter transfer from Naples' Capodichino Airport, you'll arrive in Capri by boat. The two major ferry routes to Capri are from Naples and (more seasonally) Sorrento, although there are also connections with Ischia and the Amalfi Coast (Amalfi, Positano and Salerno). For more information on ferries and hydrofoils to the island see p116 and p303.

BUS // Sippic (☎ 081 837 04 20; Bus Station, Via Roma, Capri; €1.40) runs regular buses to/from Marina Grande, Anacapri and Marina Piccola. It also operates buses from Marina Grande to Anacapri and from Marina Piccola to Anacapri. **Staiano Autotrasporti** (☎ 081 837 24 22; Bus Station, Via Tommaso, Anacapri; €1.40) Buses serve the Grotta Azzurra and Faro di Punta Carena.

CAR & SCOOTER // Between March and October you can only bring a vehicle to the island if it's registered outside Italy – but there's really no need, as buses are regular and taxis plentiful. There are scooters for hire from **Ciro dei Motorini** (Map p117; ☎ 081 837 80 18; Via Marina Grande 55, Marina Grande; per hr/day €15/60) and at **Rent A Scooter** (Map p124; ☎ 081 837 38 88; Piazza Barile 20, Anacapri; per hr/day €15/65).

FUNICULAR // Funicular (🕑 6.30am-12.30am Jun-Sep, to 9.30pm Apr-May, to 9pm Oct-Mar) The first challenge facing visitors is how to get from Marina Grande to Capri Town. The most enjoyable transport is the funicular. Tickets (€1.40) are available from the booths to the west of the port or, at the top, from the funicular station. You will enjoy the views and the ride past lemon groves.

ISCHIA

· · · · · ·

pop 61,640

The volcanic outcrop of Ischia is the most developed and largest of the islands in the Bay of Naples. It is a bubbling concoction of sprawling spa towns, buried necropolis, rheumatic Germans and spectacular scenery, with forests, vineyards and picturesque small towns. Ischia only attracts a fraction of the day trippers that head for Capri daily from Naples in the summer. Perhaps someone should tell them that the beaches are a lot better here.

Most visitors head straight for the north-coast towns of Ischia Porto, Ischia Ponte, Casamicciola Terme, Forio and Lacco Ameno. Of these, Ischia Porto boasts the best bars, Casamicciola the worst traffic and Ischia Ponte and Lacco Ameno the most appeal.

On the calmer south coast, the car-free perfection of Sant'Angelo is a languid blend of a cosy harbour, sunning cats and nearby bubbling beaches. In between the coasts lies a less-trodden landscape of dense chestnut forests loomed over by Monte Epomeo; Ischia's highest peak.

The island was an important stop on the trade route from Greece to northern Italy in the 8th century, but has since seen its fair share of disaster. The 1301 eruption of the now-extinct (and unfortunately named) Monte Arso forced the locals to flee to the mainland where they remained for four years. Five centuries later, in 1883, an earthquake killed more than 1700 people and razed the burgeoning spa town of Casamicciola to the ground. To this day, the town's name signifies 'total destruction' in the Italian vernacular.

ESSENTIAL INFORMATION

EMERGENCIES // **Police Station** (☎ 081 99 10 65; Via Casciaro 22, Ischia Porto) **Tourist Office** (✆ 081 507 42 11; Corso Sogliuzzo 72, Ischia Porto; ⊙ 9am-2pm & 3-8pm Mon-Sat)

ORIENTATION

Ischia sits 19km southeast of Pozzuoli and 33km southeast of Naples. Ferries and hydrofoils reach Casamicciola Terme and Ischia Porto. The latter is Ischia's major gateway and tourist hub. The island's main bus station is a one-minute walk west of the pier, with buses servicing all other parts of the island. East of the pier, shopping strip Via Roma eventually becomes Corso Vittoria Colonna and heads southeast to Ischia Porto.

EXPLORING ISCHIA

A narrow coastal band of development rings the thickly forested and mainly vertiginous slopes of the island's heartland. This is not the place for verdant open meadows and rambling walks, although there are excellent guided geological hikes available (see p145). Land is at a premium in Ischia and the main circular highway can get clogged with traffic in the height of summer. This, combined with the penchant the local youth have for overtaking on blind corners, means that you may feel safer riding the excellent network of buses or hopping in a taxi to get around. Out of season, a hire car or scooter is a comfortable and convenient option. For more information, see Getting Around (p151).

ISCHIA PORTO & ISCHIA PONTE

Although technically two separate towns, Ischia Porto and Ischia Ponte are

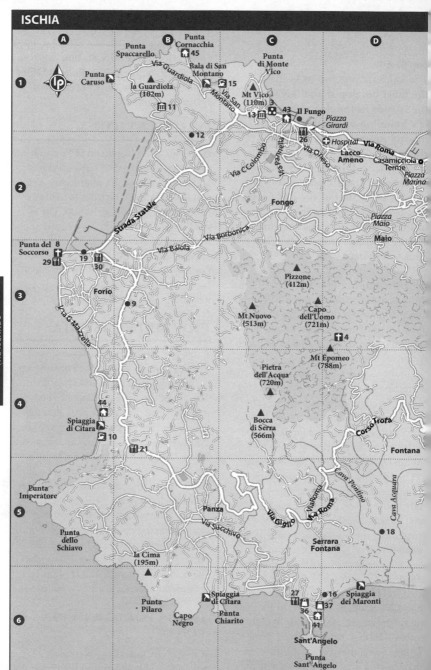

ISCHIA

THE ISLANDS

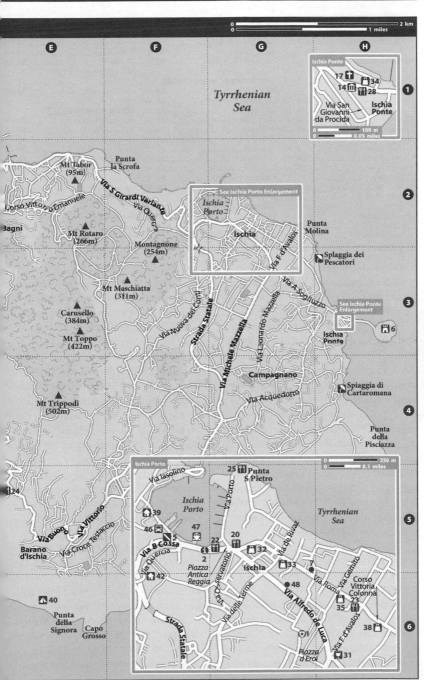

THE ISLANDS

bookends to one long, sinuous sprawl of pastel-coloured buildings, sprawling terrace bars and gelaterias, and palm-fringed shops and hotels.

The ferry port itself was a crater lake, opened up to sea at the request of Spanish King Ferdinand II in 1854. While the story goes that he couldn't stand the stench of the lake, his request was more likely inspired by the prospect of increasing shipping tax revenue. The harbour is fringed by a string of restaurants serving fresh seafood. Head further east and you'll hit the heart-stealing **Spiaggia dei Pescatori** (Fishermen's Beach), a compelling scene of brightly painted fishing boats, bronzed flesh, lurid beach umbrellas and mothers on balconies calling in their chubby kids for lunch.

🌱 SACRED ISCHIA // ENJOY A SPOT OF SWEET (AND SPIRITUAL) RESPITE

Check out the 18th-century baroque extravaganza of **Chiesa di San Pietro** (cnr Corso Vittoria Colonna & Via Gigante, Ischia; ⊗ 8am-12.30pm & 4-7.30pm), which has a fetching convex facade, semicircular chapels and

an elevated terrace sprinkled with flirty teens and gossipy *signore* (women). Grab an ice cream from the nearest gelateria and absorb the cheerful atmosphere.

Still further along the shore stands the 15th-century watchtower Torre del Mare, now bell tower to Ischia's cathedral **Santa Maria della Scala** (Via Mazzella, Ischia Ponte; ⊗ 8am-12.30pm & 4.30-8pm). The current church, designed by Antonio Massinetti and completed in 1751, stands on the site of two older churches, one built in the 13th century and the other in the 17th century. Step inside its peeling interior and you'll find the original 14th-century baptismal font, a Romanesque wooden crucifix and a wistful 18th-century canvas by Giacinto Diano.

🌱 MUSEO DEL MARE // EXPLORE MARITIME HISTORY THROUGH THE AGES

If you are an old salt at heart (or have a penchant for model ships), don't miss Ischia's maritime museum, the **Museo del Mare** (☎ 081 98 11 24; Via Giovanni da Procida 2, Ischia Ponte; adult/child under 12yr €2.75/free; ⊗ 10.30am-12.30pm Nov-Jan & Mar, 10.30am-

12.30pm & 3 7pm Apr-Jun & Sep-Oct, 10.30am-12.30pm & 6.30-10pm Jul & Aug, closed Feb), with its lovingly documented exhibits. Objects include cult ex-votos from sailors to saints, ancient urns, beautifully crafted model ships and revealing photographs of island life in the 20th century, including the arrival of Ischia's very first American car in 1958 – and you can just imagine what a celebratory occasion that must have been.

🎖 CASTELLO ARAGONESE // CASTLE, CATHEDRAL, CONVENT – AND CRYPT

Head for the elegant 15th-century **Ponte Aragonese**, which connects the town to the sprawling **Castello Aragonese** (☎ 081 99 28 34; Rocca del Castello; adult/10-20yr/under 10yr €10/6/free; ⏲ 9am-7pm Apr-Oct, 10am-5pm Nov-Mar), perched high and mighty on a rocky islet. While Syracusan tyrant Gerone I built the site's first fortress in 474 BC, the bulk of the current structure dates from the 1400s, when King Alfonso of Aragon gave the older Angevin fortress a thorough makeover, building the fortified bastions, current causeway and access ramp cut into the rock.

Further up lie the sunbaked, stuccoed ruins of the 14th-century **Cattedrale dell'Assunta**, which collapsed under British cannon fire in 1809. The 11th-century **crypt** below features snippets of 14th-century frescoes inspired by Giotto. Better preserved is the 18th-century **Chiesa dell'Immocolata** with its Greek-cross plan and dome studded with curved tympanum windows. Commissioned by the adjoining **Convento delle Clarisse** (Convent for Clarisse nuns), it was left in its minimalist state after building funds ran out. When the nuns' own lives expired, they were left to decompose sitting upright on stone chairs in the macabre **Cimitero delle Monache Clarisse,** as a grisly reminder of mortality. Heading back into daylight and further up the islet you will find the elegant, hexagonal **Chiesa di San Pietro a Pantaniello** and sombre **Carcere Borbonico**, one-time prison pad for leading figures of the Risorgimento (the 19th-century Italian unification movement), such as Poerio, Pironti, Nusco and Settembrini.

LACCO AMENO

In the 1950s and 1960s, French starlets and European royalty came to play at the legendary Terme Regina Isabella spa resort. The stars may have gone but one local icon remains, sprouting out of the sea: the iconic **Il Fungo** (The Mushroom) is a 10m volcanic rock formation spat out by Monte Epomeo thousands of years ago.

According to legend, the martyred Restituta was washed ashore on nearby San Montano Beach in the 4th century on a boat steered from Tunisia by a seaworthy angel. Every May, residents re-enact her arrival on the beach.

🎖 AREA ARCHEOLOGICA DI SANTA RESTITUTA // A TANTALISING GLIMPSE OF ANCIENT CULTURE

Beneath the pretty-in-pink church of **Chiesa di Santa Restituta**, rebuilt after the 1883 earthquake, be sure to visit the fascinating **Area Archeologica** (☎ 081 98 05 38; Piazza Restituta; admission €3; ⏲ 9.30am-12.30pm & 5-7pm Mon-Sat, 9.30am-12.30pm Sun, closed Nov-Mar). Excavations undertaken between 1951 and 1974 have uncovered parts of an ancient Greek kiln, Roman temple and street, 4th-century burial amphorae and an early Christian basilica. Rows of cabinets display other ancient objects, from Roman bracelets and votive gifts to

THE ISLANDS

a 3300-year-old stove from Procida. The ground-floor collection goes back to the future, with exquisite 17th-century *pastori* (nativity scene figurines), colourful 18th-century ceramics, high camp clerical garb and the 18th-century wooden statue of Santa Restituta still used in the annual procession in the Bay of San Montano. You can borrow an informative, handwritten guide to the excavations from the ticket desk.

♥ MUSEO ARCHEOLOGICO DI PITHECUSAE // ARCHAEOLOGY MEETS PAPARAZZI PICS

Housed in the elegant Villa Arbusto, former home of local celeb Angelo Rizzoli, the **Museo Archeologico di Pithecusae** (☎ 081 99 61 83; www.pithecusae. it; Corso Angelo Rizzoli 210, Lacco Ameno; adult/under 12yr €5/free; ⏰ 9.30am-1pm & 3-7pm Oct-May, 9.30am-1pm & 4-8pm Jun-Sep, closed Mon), enjoys a heady historical location – overlooking Monte Vico, site of the ancient settlement and acropolis of Pithecusae. Check out the museum's fascinating collection of important finds from the island's Hellenic settlement, ranging from imported earthenware to parts of the acropolis itself. A highlight is the legendary 7th-century Nestor's Cup in Sala (Room) II bearing one of the oldest known Greek inscriptions, which appropriately celebrates the wine of Ischia.

If this is a bit too much of a cultural heavyweight, the museum also houses the frivolous sidekick of the **Museo Angelo Rizzoli**, which pays homage to the man who turned humble little Lacco into a celebrity hotspot in the 1950s. Cool paparazzi shots and clippings of a Hitchcock-esque Rizzoli and his famous pals decorate rooms once host to the likes of Gina Lollabrigida, Grace Kelly and Federico Fellini. Equally striking are the villa's gardens, complete with lemon trees, fountain, a children's playground and star-worthy views towards the Campi Flegrei.

♥ NEGOMBO // A MAGNIFICENT SPA RESORT AND SECLUDED BEACH

Recover from museum fatigue at the nearby **Negombo** (☎ 081 98 61 52; www.negombo.it; Baia di San Montano, Lacco Ameno; admission all day €25, from 1pm €20, from 4.30pm €13, from 5pm €5; ⏰ 8.30am-7pm Apr-Oct). Part spa resort, part botanical wonderland with more than 500 exotic plant species, the Negombo's combination of Zen-like thermal pools, hammam, contemporary sculpture and private beach on San Montano Bay draws a younger crowd than many other Ischian spa spots. There's a Japanese labyrinth pool for weary feet, a decent *tavola calda* (snack bar), and a full range of massage and beauty treatments. Those arriving by car or scooter can park all day on site (car €3.60, scooter €2). For a free dip in the bay, follow the signs to the *spiaggia* (beach) out the front of Negombo.

FORIO & THE WEST COAST

The largest town on the island and apparently the favoured destination of Tennessee Williams and Truman Capote in the 1950s, Forio is home to some of the best restaurants on the island, as well as good beaches, a couple of stunning botanical gardens and, on the western edge of town, the dazzlingly white **Chiesa di Santa Maria del Soccorso** (Via Soccorso 1, Forio; ⏰ 10am-sunset), which was originally part of a 14th-century Augustinian monastery; its side chapel and dome were added in 1791 and 1854 respectively, the latter rebuilt after the 1883 earthquake. Most beautiful are the 18th-century mismatched majolica tiles adorning the semicircular staircase out the front. From here, the views are heavenly.

♥ BOTANICAL GARDENS // SEEK TRANQUILLITY IN BEAUTIFUL GARDENS

The vision of local botanist, Giuseppe D'Ambra who has travelled collecting plants since the 1960s, do check out the 2430-hectare **Giardina Ravino** (☎ 081 99 77 73; www.ravino.it; SS 270, Forio; adult/under 12yr €8/4; ☺ 9am-sunset, closed Tue & Thu), which opened in 2008 as a homage to the not-so-humble cacti. There is a diverse collection here, as well as other succulent plants, many of which apparently have homeopathic qualities. You can join a guided walk every Saturday at 5.30pm. The gardens are also the site of concerts, art and craft exhibitions, and twice weekly yoga classes (watch where you lay your mat!).

Designed by Russell Page and inspired by the Moorish gardens of Granada's Alhambra in Spain, **La Mortella** (☎ 081 8 62 20; www.lamortella.it; Via F Calese 39, Forio; adult/under 12yr €10/5; ☺ 9am-7pm Tue, Thu, Sat & Sun Apr-Nov) is recognised as one of Italy's finest botanical gardens and well worth a couple of hours of your time. Stroll among terraces, pools, palms, fountains and more than 1000 rare and exotic plants from all over the world. The latter includes the huge water lily *Victoria Amazonica* with flowers that turn from white to crimson red. This veritable Eden was established by the late British composer Sir William Walton and his Argentinian wife, Susana, who made it their home in 1949. His life is commemorated in a small museum and his music wafts over the loudspeakers at the elegant cafe. There are classical music concerts here in the spring and autumn.

♥ GUIDED HIKES // JOIN A FASCINATING NATURE WALK

Geo-Ausfluge; ☎ 081 90 30 58, English spoken; www.eurogeopark.com

Unlike Capri and Procida, Ischia is not an island that is easily accessible to hikers. If you are interested in exploring the hinterland, Italian geologist

THE ISLANDS

TOP FIVE

ISCHIA BEACHES

★ **Spiaggia dei Maronti** (p146) Long, sandy and very popular, the sand here is warmed by natural steam geysers. Reach it by bus from Barano, by water taxi from Sant'Angelo or on foot along the path leading east from Sant'Angelo.

★ **Il Sorgeto** (p146) Catch a water taxi from Sant'Angelo or reach it on foot from the town of Panza. Waiting at the bottom is an intimate cove complete with bubbling thermal spring. Perfect for a winter dip.

★ **Spiaggia dei Pescatori** (p115) Wedged in between Ischia Porto and Ischia Ponte is the island's most atmospheric and popular seaside strip; perfect for families.

★ **Baia di San Montano** Due west of Lacco Ameno, this gorgeous bay is the place for warm, shallow, crystal-clear waters. You'll also find the **Negombo spa park** (opposite).

★ **Punta Caruso** (p115) Located on Ischia's northwestern tip, this secluded rocky spot is perfect for a swim in clear, deep water. To get here, follow the walking path that leads off Via Guardiola down to the beach. Not suitable for children or when seas are rough.

Aniello Di Lorio conducts a choice of walks throughout the island ranging from three to five hours (€17 to €26) with various collection points in Ischia (10am), including Casamicciola and Panza. Note that the walks are primarily conducted in German and Italian, but some English is spoken and, even if you do not understand all the explanations, you will still have the opportunity of exploring some beautiful parts of the island that may be otherwise difficult to access.

❦ LA COLOMBAIA // GIVE A SALUTE TO CINEMA HISTORY

One of the joys of coming here is the untamed rural surroundings; there's also a tangible lived-in feel about **La Colombaia** (☎ 081 333 21 47; www.colombaia.org; Via F Calise 130, Forio; admission €6; ☼ 10am-2pm & 3-7pm Aug-Dec), a handsome neo-Renaissance villa. Little wonder, perhaps, as this is the former bachelor pad of flamboyant Italian film director Luchino Visconti. Born into one of Milan's wealthiest families in 1906, his 1969 film *The Damned*, about a wealthy German family that turns fascist, received an Academy Award nomination for best screenplay. His recently restored home now houses an arts foundation, which includes a documentary library focussing on Visconti and cinema history, as well as costumes, set pieces and stills from his films. It's also a venue for the **Ischia Film Festival** (opposite) and regularly holds edgy and interesting exhibitions.

❦ GIARDINI POSEIDON // SOAK AND SPLASH AT A SPA COMPLEX

South of Forio, spa lovers can enjoy sprawling **Giardini Poseidon** (Poseidon Gardens; ☎ 081 908 71 11; www.giardiniposeidon.it; Via Mazzella, Spiaggia di Citara; day pass €28; ☼ 9am-

6.30pm Apr, 8.30am-7pm May-Oct, closed Nov–mid-Apr). There is a wide choice of treatments and facilities available, including massages, saunas, Jacuzzis, various health treatments and terraced pools spilling down the volcanic cliffside. If it's all too stressful, settle for the dazzling private beach below.

SANT'ANGELO & THE SOUTH COAST

Tiny Sant'Angelo attracts a voguish crowd with its chic boutiques, seafront restaurants and great beaches. Quiet lanes spill down the hill to fashionable Piazzetta Ottorino Troia, where tanned Italians sip Campari soda and take in late-night summer music concerts. Keeping an eye on it all is the great hulking *scoglio* (rock), joined to the village by a long sandbar sprinkled with fishing boats, beach umbrellas and *bagnini* (lifeguards). From the pier, catch a brightly painted water taxi to the sandy **Spiaggia dei Maronti** (one way €5) or the intimate cove of **Il Sorgeto** (one way €7), with its steamy thermal spring. Sorgeto can also be reached on foot down an albeit poorly signposted path from the village of Panza.

❦ TERME CAVASCURO // ENJOY AN ATMOSPHERIC SPA EXPERIENCE

Experience an earthy natural spa by catching a water taxi to Cavascura (one way €3.50) and follow the signs 300m down a rocky gorge to **Terme Cavascuro** (☎ 081 99 92 42; www.cavascura.it; Via Cavascura 1, Spiaggia dei Maronti, Sant'Angelo; basic thermal bath €10, mud & thermal bath €25; ☼ 8.30am-1.30pm & 2.30-6pm mid-Apr–mid-Oct, closed mid-Oct–mid-Apr). Wedged between soaring cliffs, this historic no-frills outdoor spa is Ischia's oldest. Soak in old Roman baths hewn into the cliff, sweat it out in a grotto, then (for an extra fee) top it all off with a mud wrap (€20), manicure (€13) or massage (€26). The sulphurous waters are reputedly beneficial for rheumatic, bronchial and skin conditions.

A spectacular, if partly strenuous, 2km walk above the coast from Sant'Angelo also reaches the spa, passing on its way the faded luxury of **Parco Termale Aphrodite Apollon** (☎ 081 99 92 19; www.aphrodite.it; Via Petrelle, Sant'Angelo; admission €25; ☺ 8am-6pm mid-Apr–Oct, closed Nov–mid-Apr). Beyond its ivy-clad entrance is a rambling complex of gyms, saunas, lush terraced gardens and 12 differently heated pools, including one for hydrocycling. Beauty treatments include tailored kinesiology therapies (€60), aquatic therapies (€60) and regenerating mud showers (€22). Buffed and balanced, flaunt that new bod at the beach bar below.

☝ MONTE EPOMEO // CLIMB THE MOUNTAIN THEN GO TO CHURCH

Lace up those hiking boots and set out on a roughly 2.5km (50-minute) uphill walk from the village of Fontana, which will bring you to the top of **Monte Epomeo** (788m). Formed by an underwater eruption, it boasts superlative views of the Bay of Naples. The little church near the top is the 15th-century **Cappella di San Nicola di Bari**, where you can check out the pretty majolica floor. The adjoining hermitage was built in the 18th century by an island governor who, after narrowly escaping death, swapped politics for poverty and spent the rest of his days here in saintly solitude. Have a peek inside then head back down the hill thankful that your saintliness doesn't exclude good wining and dining, Capri style.

☝ WATERSPORTS & SAILING // DABBLE IN A LITTLE SEASPORT AND DIVING

If diving takes your fancy, **Captain Cook** (☎ 335 636 26 30; www.captaincook.it; Via Iasolino 106, Ischia Porto; ♿) has equipment for hire and runs courses for all levels and ages. A single dive will cost from €40. **Westcoast Boat Hire** (☎ 081 90 86 04; www.westcoastischia. it; Porto di Forio; hire from €100) provides full-day hire of motorised boats and dinghies (with or without a sailor). This is a particularly good idea in August when the more popular beaches are crowded and you are desperate to find a quiet sandy cove all to yourself (or selves).

FESTIVALS & EVENTS

Ischian festivals are all about the good life – food, wine, film and a little laidback jazz to while away those summer evenings.

Ischia Film Festival (www.ischiafilmfestival. it) Serves up free flicks and exhibitions in star locations around the island, including Castello Aragonese, Villa Arbusto and La Colombaia, usually in June.

Vinischia (www.vinischia.it, in Italian) Foodies flock to this four-day celebration of regional food and wine, with free tastings and concerts along the Lungomare Aragonese, usually in June and early July.

Festa di Sant'Anna The allegorical 'burning of the Castello Aragonese' takes place on the feast day of St Anne on 26 July, with a hypnotic procession of boats and fireworks.

Ischia Jazz Festival (www.ischiajazzfestival.com, in Italian) Ischia's annual jazz festival pumps out five days of smooth Italian sax with a dash of foreign acts, usually in September.

GASTRONOMIC HIGHLIGHTS

While seafood is an obvious speciality on the island, Ischia is also famed for its rabbit, which is bred on inland farms.

Another local speciality is *rucolino*, a green, liquorice-flavoured liqueur made from *rucola* (rocket) leaves.

☙ BAR DE MAIO €
☎ 081 99 18 70; Piazza Antica Reggia 9, Ischia Porto; ice cream €2

This bar has been raising the locals' cholesterol levels since 1930 with a delicious selection of ultracreamy ice creams, plus coffee, cocktails and snacks. Sit on the square with your cone; this central piazza is a prime people-watching spot. According to residents, this is the best ice-cream parlour on the island – they should know.

☙ CANTINE DI PIETRATORCIA €€
☎ 081 90 72 32; www.pietratorcia.it; Via Provinciale Panza 267, Forio; meals €30; ☙ Apr-Oct

Enjoying a bucolic setting among tumbling vines, wild fig trees and rosemary bushes, this A-list winery is a foodie's nirvana. Tour the old stone cellars, sip a local drop and eye up the delectable degustation menu. Offerings include fragrant bruschetta and cheeses, hearty Campanian sausages and spicy *salumi* (cold meats). Full dinners are also available if booked in advance.

☙ DA CICCIO €
☎ 081 199 13 14; Via Porto 1, Ischia Porto; snacks from €1; ☙ year-round

Just the spot for ferry-weary arrivals, this much-loved bar does light meals, luscious pastries and dangerously good *gelati*. Eat in or take away, the *calzone* (pizza folded over to form a pie) stuffed with spinach, pinenuts and raisins (€1.20) is divine.

☙ GRAN CAFFÈ VITTORIA €
☎ 081 199 16 49; Corso Vittorio Colonna 110, Ischia Porto; pastries €2

At the smarter end of the port, this elegant, wood-panelled cafe has been spoiling customers and waistlines for more than 100 years with its irresistible cakes, pastries, coffees and cocktails, all served by old-school, bow-tied waiters.

☙ IL FOCOLARE €€
☎ 081 90 29 44; Via Creajo al Crocefisso, Barano d'Ischia; meals €25; ☙ 8-11pm Mon-Fri, noon-3pm & 8-11pm Sat & Sun, closed Wed Nov-Mar

A good choice for those seeking a little turf instead of surf, this is one of the island's best loved restaurants. Family run, homey and rustic, it has a solidly traditional meat-based menu with steaks, lamb cutlets and specialities, including *coniglio all'Ischitana* (typical local rabbit dish with tomatoes, garlic and herbs) and *tagliatelle al ragu di cinghiale* (ribbon-shaped pasta with wild boar ragout). On the sweet front, the desserts are home-made and exquisite. Owner Riccardo D'Ambra is a leading local advocate of the Slow Food Movement (see the boxed text, opposite).

☙ LA BAIA EL CLIPPER €€€
☎ 081 333 42 09; Via Porto 116, Ischia Porto; meals €40

With its romantic setting at the entrance to the port, this restaurant continues to draw in the crowds. Now run by the second generation, the waiters are friendly, the service slick. Today's catch is proudly displayed in the entrance; try the *linguine con gamberetti e rucola* (with shrimp and rocket), one of the more interesting specialties. Dress up – it's that kind of place.

☙ LA BROCCA €
☎ 081 90 00 51; Via Roma 24, Lacco Ameno; meals €17; ☙ Jan-Oct

Tired of sand in your sandwiches? This no-fuss trattoria is located just across the road from the beach and serves simple, superlative seafood to locals and the occasional wised-up tourist. Mamma cooks out the back, *nonna* polishes the cutlery and the exuberant sun-kissed son serves fabulous seafood straight off the boat. Tuck a napkin into your collar and try the juicy spaghetti with mussels.

☙ LO SCOGLIO €€

☎ 081 99 95 29; Via Cava Ruffano 58, Sant'Angelo; meals €28; ⊗ closed Jan-Mar & mid-Nov–mid-Dec
The most dramatically located restaurant in Sant'Angelo fortunately has not allowed the setting to usurp the quality of the cuisine. Jutting out over the sea beside a picture-perfect beach cove, this is a great place for sunsets and seafood. Excellently prepared mussel soup, grilled bass and butterfly noodles with salmon are examples of the fishy fare on offer. The service is brisk and efficient. Sunday lunchtime is a popular weekly event.

☙ RISTORANTE DA CICCIO €€

☎ 081 99 16 86; Via Luigi Mazzella 32, Ischia Ponte; meals €25; ⊗ closed Nov & Tue Dec-May & Oct
Sublime seafood and charming host Carlo make this atmospheric place winner.

ISCHIA ON A FORK

Ischian restaurateur Carlo Buono gives the low-down on classic island cuisine:

'Fresh, seasonal ingredients are the cornerstone of Ischian cooking, from silky olive oil to plump *pomodorini* (cherry tomatoes). Like Neapolitan cooking, the emphasis is on simple, uncomplicated home cooking using premium produce. Traditionally, there are two types of Ischian cuisine: coastal and mountain. For centuries, the fishermen of Lacco Ameno and Sant'Angelo would barter with the farmers of Barano and Serrara Fontana, who'd offer wine, vegetables, pork and rabbit in exchange for the fishermen's catch.

'Indeed, rabbit is a typical Ischian meat and we're seeing a revival of the traditional *fossa* (pit) breeding method, where rabbits are bred naturally in deep *fosse* instead of in cages. The result is a more tender, flavoursome meat. Leading this renaissance is local Slow Food advocate Riccardo D'Ambra, whose famous trattoria Il Focolare (see opposite) is well known for its rabbit and rustic mountain dishes. Definitely worth eating on the island is a popular Sunday dish called *coniglio all'ischitana* (Ischia-style rabbit), which is prepared with olive oil, unpeeled garlic, chilli, tomato, basil, thyme and white wine.

'Like the land, the sea is seasonal, so the seafood that we cook depends on the time of year. Typical local fish include *pesce bandiera* (sailfish), the flat *castagna*, *lampuga* and *palamide* (a small tuna). A popular way of cooking it is in *acqua pazza* (crazy water). Traditionally prepared on the fishing boats, it's a delicate sauce made with *pomodorini*, garlic and parsley. Fried fish is also very typical; a fresh serve of *frittura di mare* (mixed fried seafood) drizzled in lemon juice is just superb. May to September is *totano* (squid) season and a great time to try *totani imbotti* (squid stuffed with olives, capers and breadcrumbs, and stewed in wine).

'Equally wonderful is fresh, wood-fired *casareccio* bread. Soft and dense on the inside and crunchy on the outside, it's perfect for doing the *scarpetta* (wiping your plate clean) or for filling with salami or *parmigiano* cheese. If you have any room left, track down a slice of *torta caprese*, a moist chocolate and almond cake. *Buon appetito*.'

THE ISLANDS

Highlights include *tubattone* pasta with clams and pecorino cheese, a zesty mussel soup topped with fried bread and *peperoncino* (chilli) and a delicious chocolate and almond cake. Tables spill out onto the pavement in the summer, from where there are fabulous castle views. There is an good Campanian wine list.

☙ UMBERTO A MARE €€€

☎ 081 99 71 71; Via Soccorso 2, Forio; meals €46; ☾ Mar-Dec

In the shadow of the Spanish mission–style Soccorso church, this waterside restaurant has the choice of low-key cafe-bar for light snacks, or more formal restaurant where the menu changes according to season. Highlights include long thick tubes of pasta with tuna, fresh tomatoes and *peperoncino*, penne with lobster and asparagus and a delicate *al profumo di mare* (lightly grilled freshly caught fish). The orange sorbet dessert comes highly recommended.

☙ ZI CARMELA €

☎ 081 99 84 23; Via Schioppa 27, Forio; meals €20; ☾ Apr-Oct

Dating back several decades, this restaurant has a lovely terrace decorated with copper pans, ceramic mugs and strings of garlic and chillies. Locals in the know come here for seafood dishes such as the *fritturina e pezzogne* (a local white fish baked with potatoes and herbs in the wood-fired pizza oven) or *tartare di pulamito al profumo d'arancia* (tartar of local fish with citrus). Undecided taste buds can go for the €28 four-course set menu.

NIGHTLIFE

Ischia is not Ibiza. That said, the area around Ischia Porto has the best buzz, with a handful of bars and clubs that stay open way past cocoa time.

☙ BAR CALISE

☎ 081 99 12 70; Piazza degli Eroi 69, Ischia Porto; ☾ 7pm-3am Thu-Sun

One of the oldest bars on the island, located near the harbour, the atmosphere here is one of languid gentility. Waistcoated waiters serve cocktails and coffees to a background of live Latin, swing and folk music.

RECOMMENDED SHOPS

Ischia's shopping is centred on Via Roma and the web of narrow streets leading to Ischia Ponte. From floss-thin bikinis to decadent jars of *babà* (sponge soaked in rum), there's enough shopping on these cobbled stones to shift your credit card into overdrive. For a more low-key experience, explore the tiny boutiques and art galleries in Sant'Angelo and Forio.

☙ ADAM

☎ 081 98 22 05; Via Roma 102, Ischia Porte

Fancy a suit of armour for the hallway back home? Pick one up at this offbeat ode to all things vintage Italian. It's all here, from antique Ischian urns and handmade Punchinello dolls to shining vintage pistols. Take a detour through the leafy back garden, complete with giant lemons, sleepy turtles and one very determined pussycat.

☙ ANTICA MACELLERIA DI FRANCESCO ESPOSITO

☎ 081 98 10 11; Via delle Terme 2, Ischia Porte

This century-old deli is gourmet foodie heaven. Drop in from 8am for fresh mozzarella and wood-fired *casareccio* bread, plus a lip-smacking choice of cheeses, prosciutti, homemade *peperoncino* salami and marinated peppers. In fact, everything you need for a picnic on the beach, including the bottle of obligatory *falanghina* (dry white wine).

THE ISLANDS

♥ ISCHIA SAPORI

☎ 337 97 24 65; Via Luigi Mazzella 5, Ischia Ponte

If you thought *rucola* was just a tasty green leaf for salads, think again: this savvy little produce shop is the home of *rucolino*, a local, liquorice-flavoured digestive made with none other than the green weed itself (no, not that one). The recipe is a closely guarded secret, but the liquid is yours for the taking. The shop also sells its own wines, gourmet food stuffs, *limoncello*-soaked *babà*, olive-oil soaps, and fragrances, all reasonably priced and gorgeously packaged with trademark Italian flair.

♥ JUDITH MAJOR

☎ 081 98 32 95; Corso Vittoria Colonna 174, Ischia Porte

Despite the headmistressy name, this snazzy boutique is the exclusive stockist of Italian label Brunello Cucinelli. The look here is Polo Ralph Lauren with a sexy Italian twist. Cashmere sweaters, suave shirts, blazers and chic womens-wear. Shoes include Prada, Barrett and Alberto Guardiani for men and Stuart Weitzman and Pedro Garcia for women. Everything you'll need for a jaunt on the yacht.

♥ L'ISOLETTO

☎ 081 99 93 74; Via Chiaia delle Rose 36, Sant'Angelo

Stock up on a mouthwatering selection of local produce, from spicy *peperoncino*, rum-soaked *babà* and lemon-cream *cannoncelli* (pastry filled with lemon cream) to Ischian vino and the ubiquitous *limoncello*. Less tasteful – but deliciously kitsch – is the collection of tourist souvenirs, from seashell placemats to 3D souvenir wall plates.

♥ PERCORSI COMUNICANTI IN GALLERIA

☎ 081 90 42 27; Via Sant'Angelo 93, Sant'Angelo

Offering a welcome contemporary ceramic respite from smiling sun platters and souvenir ashtrays, this slick little gallery features bold, contemporary ceramics crafted by Neapolitan artist Massimiliano Santoro. A modest selection of Murano glass jewellery and designer silk kaftans further loosen the purse strings.

♥ RICCIO CALZATURE

☎ 081 98 41 99; Corso Vittoria Colonna 216, Ischia

Italian footwear sans the designer price tag. Men's, women's, formal and sporty, last season's stock is slashed by up to 50%. Fashion victims needn't fret. New-season stock is also available, at new-season prices. The choice isn't huge but definitely worth a browse, with names such as Diesel, Richmond, Miss Sixty and Cesare Paciotti in the mix.

TRANSPORT

For information on ferries and hydrofoils to the island see the Transport section earlier (p116) and the Transport chapter (p303).

BUS // The island's main bus station is located in Ischia Porto. There are two principal lines: the CS (Circolo Sinistro, or Left Circle), which circles the island anticlockwise, and the CD line (Circolo Destro, or Right Circle), which travels in a clockwise direction, passing through each town and departing every 30 minutes. Buses pass near all hotels and campsites. A single ticket, valid for 90 minutes, costs €1.30, an all-day, multi-use ticket is €4.50, while a two-day ticket is €6.50. Taxis and micro-taxis (scooter-engined three-wheelers) are also available.

CAR & SCOOTER // You can do this small island a favour by not bringing your car. If you want to hire a car or scooter for a day, there are plenty of hire companies, although razor-thin roads and holiday traffic make driving a car here stressful; a scooter is a better option. **Fratelli del Franco** (☎ 081 99 13 34; Via A de Luca 127, Ischia Ponte) In addition to hiring out cars (from €30 per day) and scooters (€25 to €35), it also has mountain bikes (around €10 per day). You can't take a hired vehicle off the island.

PARKING // If you are hiring a car in high season, parking is going to be a headache. Go for a Smart car if you can, which takes up minimal space. There is a small carpark at the entrance of Sant'Angelo and Ischia Porte and Ponte both have signposted central carparks (per hour €1.50).

PROCIDA

· · · · · ·

The Bay of Naples' smallest island is also its best-kept secret. Dig out your paintbox, this soulful blend of hidden lemon groves, weathered fishermen and pastel-hued houses is memorably picturesque. Mercifully off the mass-tourist radar, Procida is like the original Portofino prototype and refreshingly real. August aside – when beach-bound mainlanders flock to its shores – its narrow sun-bleached streets are the domain of the locals: wiry young boys clutch fishing rods, weary mothers clutch wiry young boys and wizened old seamen swap tales of malaise. Here, the hotels are smaller, fewer waiters speak broken German and the islanders' welcome lacks that seasoned smarminess.

On Marina Grande, tumbledown cottages in hues of pinks, whites and yellow crowd the waterfront as an evocative first introduction to the island. Under strung wet washing, fishermen mend their nets while waiters serve their catch in well-worn restaurants.

Even in the height of summer, Procida doesn't attract the number of tourists welcomed by its more famous neighbours. Nightlife hasn't caught on here yet either. Procida is an island for those seeking to both escape the crowds and discover the best lemon *granita* (crushed ice flavoured with lemon juice) this side of Sorrento.

ESSENTIAL INFORMATION

TOURIST OFFICES // Graziella Travel Agency (☎ 081 896 91 91; Via Roma 117; ☯ closed Sun) While not technically a tourist office, this agency provides a free map, advice on accommodation as well as bicycle and scooter hire.

EXPLORING PROCIDA

If you have the time, Procida is an ideal island to explore on foot. The most compelling areas (and where you will also find most of the hotels, bars and restaurants) are Marina Grande, Marina Corricella and Marina di Chiaiolella. Beaches are not plentiful here, apart from the Lido di Procida where, aside from August, you shouldn't have any trouble finding some towel space on the sand.

♥ ABBAZIA DI SAN MICHELE ARCANGELO // SECRET CHAPELS, CATACOMBS AND SHIPWRECKED SAILORS

Soak in the dizzying bay views before exploring the adjoining **Abbazia di San Michele Arcangelo** (☎ 081 896 76 12; Via Terra Murata 89; admission €2; ☯ 9.45am-12.45pm Mon-Sat year-round, plus 3.30-6pm May-Oct). Built in the 11th century and remodelled between the 17th and 19th centuries, this one-time Benedictine abbey is a small museum with some arresting pictures done in gratitude by shipwrecked sailors, plus a church and a maze of catacombs that lead to a tiny secret chapel.

THE ISLANDS

❦ MARINAS & BEACHES //
FALL FOR PICTURE-PERFECT HARBOURS AND BEACHES

From panoramic Piazza dei Martiri, the village of **Marina Corricella** tumbles down to its marina in a waterfall of pastel colours: pinks, yellows and whites.

Fishing boats are painted in still more colours, alongside piles of fishing nets, sleek cats and, in the summer, a sprawl of terrace cafes and restaurants. The international hit film *Il Postino* was partly filmed here; it really *is* a magical spot – don't miss it.

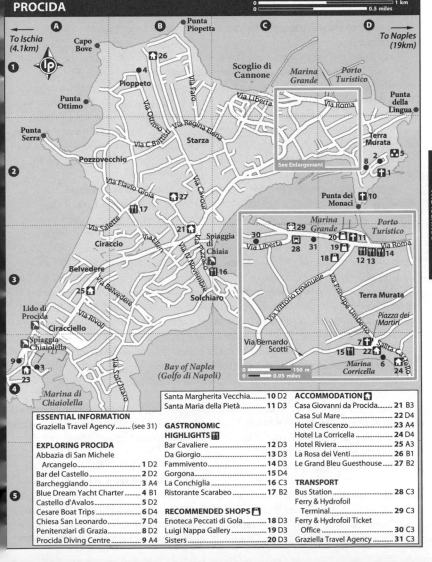

THE ISLANDS

AN EVOCATIVE WALK

Distance: 2.5km
Duration: 1¼ hours

This gentle walk starts at the Marina Grande. Turn left towards the distinctive domed church **Santa Maria della Pietà**. Just beyond here, turn right on Via Vittorio Emanuele, a narrow main thoroughfare lined with shops and crowded with hanging washing. After around 200m, turn left at Via Principe Umberto, a more residential street which climbs steeply. After around 500m you arrive at **Piazza dei Martiri**, where you can stop for a breather and admire the view of the captivating village of **Corricella** below.

Carry along this road (Salita Castello) as it continues to climb beside the crumbling 16th-century **Castello d'Avalos**, until you reach the canons on your right. You are now in Procida's ancient Terra Murata area. Turn left through the tunnel, **Porta Romantica**, and follow signs to the Belverdere. Turn right on Via San Michelle through the **Porta di Mezzomo** and, if you feel like a cappuccino or ice cream stop at the hole-in-the-wall **Bar del Castello**, halfway up. Turn left at the top of this street and continue to the Belvedere. Ignore the graffiti and feast your eyes instead on the spectacular view of the Bay of Naples with Vesuvius looming threateningly on the horizon.

Double back around 20m and follow signs to the **Abbazia di San Michele Arcangelo**; the chapel here dates from the 7th century. Head for the back of the chapel up Via Concetta Bacca and Via Canalone from where you have a good view of the abandoned church, **Santa Margherita Vecchia**. Double back through a small tunnel flanked by simple houses with steep steps and bulging walls. Continue down Via Guarrancino and return via Porta di Mezzomo. Around 50m further on take the steep steps to your right continuing down to the otherworldly former moat of the where the rock has taken on swirling and surreal formations. Emerge at the former **Penitenziari di Grazia** prison and take the path down to join the road that meets Piazza dei Martiri. Turn left at the steps to the marina. Walk along this lovely picturesque beach with the nets drying in the sun until you reach some steep steps on your right. Take Via Bernado Scotti on your left past orchards and high walls and turn right at the T-junction past the 18th century **Chiesa San Leonardo**. You have now arrived at the turn off to Via Principe Umberto from where you can retrace your steps to the marina.

Further south, off Via Pizzaco, a steep flight of steps leads down to sand-brushed **Spiaggia di Chiaia**, one of the island's most beautiful beaches and home to **La Conchiglia** (p156).

All pink, white and blue, crescent-shaped **Marina di Chiaiolella** was once the crater of a volcano. Today it features a yacht-stocked marina, old-school eateries and a relaxed laid-back charm. From the pier, you can catch a brightly painted water taxi to reach several superb beaches in the surrounding area (from €6).

☘ DIVING & BOATS // MAKE THE MOST OF THOSE CRYSTAL CLEAR WATERS

Procida is surrounded by crystal clear water, perfect for diving. If you fancy a dunk, head for **Procida Diving Centre**

THE ISLANDS

(☎ 081 896 83 85; www.vacanzeaprocida.it/frame diving01-uk.htm; Via Cristoforo Colombo 6, Marina di Chiaiolella) located right on the marina. A well-established outfit, it organises dives and courses, and hires out equipment. Depending on your level, there are four diving sites in Procida: Punta Pizzaco (intermediate to experienced); Secca delle Formiche (beginner-intermediate); Capo Bove (beginner); and Punta Solchiaro (intermediate). The price ranges from €45 for a single dive to €130 for a snorkelling course with more advanced open-water diving and rescue courses also on offer.

On the harbour at Marina Corricella, ask for friendly Cesare in your best Italian. Look for his colourful boats with his name blazoned across the side or, if all else fails, check at one of the beach bars – he won't be far away. Cesare runs some great **boat trips** (per 2½ hours €24) as well as half-day trips in a traditional galleon for €95 (minimum 25 people). **Barcheggiando** (☎ 081 810 19 34; Marina Chiaiolella) hires out motor boats and *gommoni* (wooden boats) from €100 per day.

If you have grander 'champagne on the deck' kind of ideas, you can always charter a yacht from **Blue Dream Yacht Charter** (☎ 081 896 05 79, 339 572 08 74; www.bluedreamcharter.com; Via Ottimo 3, Pioppeto) from €70 per person per day.

FESTIVALS & EVENTS

Procession of the Misteri Good Friday sees a colourful procession when a wooden statue of Christ and the Madonna Addolarata, along with life-sized tableaux of plaster and papier-mâché illustrating events leading to Christ's crucifixion, are carted across the island. Men dress in blue tunics with white hoods, while many of the young girls dress as the Madonna.

Il Vento del Cinema (www.ilventodelcinema. it) An annual five-day festival of art-house cinema and English-language workshops run by prolific film makers. See the website for festival dates.

GASTRONOMIC HIGHLIGHTS

Prime waterfront dining here needn't equal an overpriced disappointment, with portside trattorias serving fresh classic fare. Several inland trattorias use homegrown produce and game in their cooking. Try the zesty *insalata al limone*, a lemon salad infused with chilli oil. Marina Grande is the place to kick back with the fishermen at one of the earthy local bars.

🍴 BAR CAVALIERE €
☎ 081 810 10 74; Via Roma 76, Marina Grande; pastries from €1
Procida's prime pastry shop has a delicious range of cakes, pastries and sweet treats. All the rage is the *lingua di bue* (ox tongue), flaky pastry shaped like a tongue and filled with *crema pasticcera* (custard). Also advertises as a cocktail bar – who are you kidding?

🍴 DA GIORGIO €
☎ 081 896 79 10; Via Roma 36, Marina Grande; meals €12; 🕐 Mar-Oct
These folk try hard to please with a reasonable menu, welcoming window boxes and inexpensive beer. The menu holds few surprises, but the ingredients are fresh, zesty and in evidence, like the bruised cherry tomatoes that top the *gnocchi alla sorrentina* (gnocchi in a tomato, basil and pecorino cheese sauce) and the freshly grated Parmesan.

🍴 FAMMIVENTO €€
☎ 081 896 90 20; Via Roma 39, Marina Grande; meals €25; 🕐 closed Sun night, Mon & Nov-Mar
Get things going with the *frittura di calami* (fried squid), then try the *fusilli*

THE ISLANDS

carciofi e calamari (pasta with artichokes and calamari). For a splurge, go for the house speciality of *zuppa di crostaci e moluschi* (crustacean and mollusc soup). The €14 menu will put a waddle in your step.

✪ GORGONA €

☎ 081 810 10 60; Via Marina Corricella; meals €20; ⊗ Mar-Oct

Along this unpretentious marina, with its old fishing boats, piles of fishing nets and sleek, lazy cats, any restaurant will provide you with a memorable dining experience. This place is a tad pretentious with its fake figurehead looming over the dining room, but the smoked seafood dishes are particularly good, including swordfish and tuna steaks.

✪ LA CONCHIGLIA €€

☎ 081 896 76 02; Via Pizzaco 10; meals €25; ⊗ Mar-Oct

The views from here are pure holiday-brochure magic: turquoise water lapping below with the pastel Marina Corricella glowing gently in the distance. A more elegant restaurant than most on the island, tuck into gems such as *spiedini di mazzancolle* (prawn kebabs) and a superb *spaghetti alla povera* (spaghetti with *peperoncino*, green capsicum, cherry tomatoes and anchovies). To get here, take the steep steps down from Via Pizzaco or book a boat from Corricella.

✪ RISTORANTE SCARABEO €€

☎ 081 896 99 18; Via Salette 10; meals €27; ⊗ daily Dec-Oct, Sat & Sun only Dec-Feb

Behind a veritable jungle of lemon trees lies the venerable kitchen of Signora Battinelli. With husband Francesco, she whips up classics such as *fritelle di basilico* (fried patties of bread, egg, Parmesan and basil) and home-made eggplant and

provola ravioli (€9). They breed their own rabbits, make their own *falanghina* and it's all yours to devour under a pergola of bulbous lemons.

RECOMMENDED SHOPS

Low-key Procida isn't a shopping heavyweight. Good buys include ceramics, wine and local art.

✪ ENOTECA PECCATI DI GOLA

☎ 081 810 19 99; Via Vittorio Emanuele 13, Marina Grande

Provocatively called 'Sins of the Throat', this slick little bottle shop stocks the best of Campanian vino and a smattering of other Italian drops. The friendly owner will advise you (in Italian!) of the best local wines and the best deals. *Limoncello* and a wide choice of traditional and more modern flavoured grappas is also available.

✪ LUIGI NAPPA GALLERY

☎ 081 896 05 61; Via Roma 50, Marina Grande

Nappa's paintings are fresh and contemporary with a Procidan theme. And there can be few places in the world that are more picturesque than this pretty-in-pastels island. His sculpture and jewellery are also offbeat and original with bright colours and abstract designs. The prices are a similar one-off – surprisingly low, given the individuality and quirky show-stopping appeal.

✪ SISTERS

☎ 081 896 03 33; Via Roma 154, Marina Grande

Go Med with the vividly hand-painted ceramic jugs, platters, coasters, lemon squeezers and seriously dishy coffee cups. If it all seems a bit risky (or heavy) for the baggage handlers, then go for a lightweight vintage photograph of Procida instead; they make for soulful souve-

THE ISLANDS

nirs providing a glimpse of the island in
grainy bygone days.

TRANSPORT

For information on ferries and hydrofoils to the island, see the Transport
section earlier (p116) and the Transport
chapter (p303).

BUS // There is a limited bus service (€0.80), with four
lines radiating from Marina Grande. Bus L1 connects the
port and Via Marina di Chiaiolella.

HIRE // Graziella Travel Agency (☎ 081
896 95 94; www.isoladiprocida.it; Via Roma 117) Organises bicycle hire (per half-/full day €5/8). The best way
to explore the island – a mere 4 sq km – is on foot or by
scooter or bike. Small, open micro-taxis can also be hired
for two to three hours for around €35, depending on your
bargaining prowess.

THE AMALFI COAST

3 PERFECT DAYS

❧ DAY 1 // EXPLORE THE COAST BY FERRY
Wake up in picturesque Positano (p178) and head for Marina Grande and a cappuccino overlooking the bodies beautiful and bobbing fishing boats. Peruse the fashions, duck into the church and stroll around the cliff to Spiaggio Fornillo for lunch. Catch a ferry to pretty Amalfi (p186) and spend the afternoon exploring the colourful *duomo* (cathedral), the museums, the medieval backstreets and the *pasticcerie*. Have dinner and drinks in lovely, low-key Atrani (p186).

❧ DAY 2 // EXHILARATING HIKES AMID STUNNING SCENERY
Hiking trails here wend their way through compelling coastal routes and countryside. Energetic souls can stride out on the poetically named Sentiero degli Dei (Walk of the Gods; p180) high up in the hills. It takes six hours so is breathtaking in all senses of the word. If this sounds a tad daunting, there are some delightful shorter walks available; tourist offices and bookshops can provide maps.

❧ DAY 3 // RENT A CAR FOR THE DAY AND HEAD FOR THE WILD WEST
Rent a car from Sorrento (p171) and take in fabulous mountains and seascapes in this little-known western corner. Leave town on the minor coastal road through groves of olives and lemon trees. Dip down to the beach at Marina di Puolo, admire the view of Capri from the belvedere in Massa Lubrense (p172) and head for dramatic Punta della Campanella (p176) for more killer views. Bypass Termini and continue to Nerano, from where you can walk to Baia di Leranto beach (one hour), before continuing to tranquil Sant'Agata sui due Golfi (p173) and doubling back to Sorrento.

SORRENTO

· · · · · ·

pop 16,547
Gateway to the sirens' domain, Sorrento is a working Italian city as well as a bustling resort town. While the modern vernacular architecture is, overall, flat-roofed and characterless, the medieval centro storico (historic centre) exudes southern Italian charm, its winding cobbled lanes interspersed with small piazze and churches. Unusually, despite its reputation as a package-holiday resort, Sorrento has no real beach.

Dating from Greek times and known to Romans as Surrentum, Sorrento's main selling point is its fabulous location. Straddling cliffs that overlook the Bay of Naples to Mt Vesuvius, it's ideally situated for exploring the surrounding area: to the south, the best of the peninsula's unspoilt countryside and, beyond that, the Amalfi Coast; to the north, Pompeii and the archaeological sites; offshore, the fabled island of Capri.

If you are here in midsummer, consider escaping the crowds by heading to the green hills around Sorrento. Known as the land of the sirens, in honour of the mythical maiden-monsters who were said to live on Li Galli (a tiny archipelago off the peninsula's southern coast), the area to the west of Massa Lubrense is among the least developed and most beautiful in the country.

ESSENTIAL INFORMATION

EMERGENCIES // Police Station (☎ 081 807 53 11; Via Capasso 11)
TOURIST INFORMATION // Tourist Office (☎ 081 807 40 33; Via Luigi De Maio 35; ☯ 8.45am-6.15pm Mon-Sat Sep-Jul, 8.45am-6.15pm Mon-Sat, 8.45am-12.45pm Sun Aug) In the Circolo dei Forestieri (Foreigners' Club).

THE AMALFI COAST ACCOMMODATION

Ranging from sumptuously restored *palazzi* to exquisite B&Bs, the Amalfi Coast has some of the classiest accommodation in Italy. Just be sure to book ahead in summer and remember that most hotels firmly close their shutters from around November to Easter. For information on accommodation throughout the Naples and Amalfi Coast region, see the Accommodation chapter, p263.

★ The five-star sea views and genial owner make Positano's **Pensione Maria Luisa** (p281) a perennial budget favourite

★ A former monastery, Amalfi's **Hotel Luna Convento** (p284) has an addictive air of tranquillity, although there's nothing monastic about the colourful, large rooms

★ Lush green views, organic homemade produce and cool, comfortable rooms make **Agriturismo Serafino** (p282) a superb farmhouse stay

★ An infinity pool in an 11th-century *palazzo* just has to be a winning combo. Ravello's **Hotel Caruso** (p285) ticks all the right boxes for comfort, mod cons and evocative Moorish surroundings

★ Exuding homey warmth, decorative flair and a eye for good art, **Casa Astarita** (p276) is a B&B winner in Sorrento

THE AMALFI COAST

THE AMALFI COAST

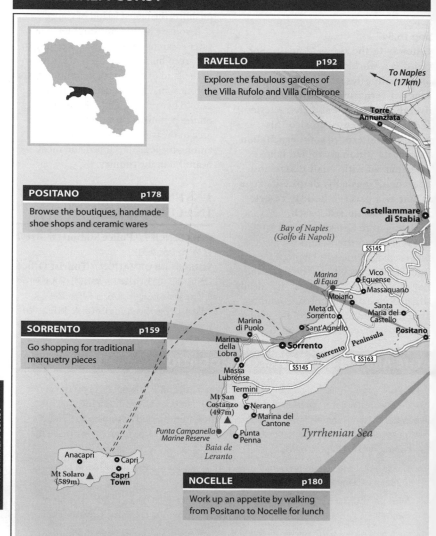

RAVELLO   p192

Explore the fabulous gardens of
the Villa Rufolo and Villa Cimbrone

To Naples
(17km)

Torre
Annunziata

POSITANO   p178

Browse the boutiques, handmade-
shoe shops and ceramic wares

Castellammare
di Stabia

*Bay of Naples
(Golfo di Napoli)*

SS145

Marina
di Equa

Vico
Equense

Massaquano

Moiano

Meta di
Sorrento

Santa
Maria del
Castello

Positano

Marina
di Puolo

Sant'Agnello

SORRENTO   p159

Go shopping for traditional
marquetry pieces

Marina
della
Lobra

Sorrento

Sorrento Peninsula

SS145

SS163

Massa
Lubrense

Termini

Mt San
Costanzo
(497m)

Nerano

Marina del
Cantone

Tyrrhenian Sea

Punta Campanella
Marine Reserve

Punta
Penna

*Baia de
Leranto*

Anacapri

Capri

NOCELLE   p180

Work up an appetite by walking
from Positano to Nocelle for lunch

Mt Solaro
(589m)

**Capri
Town**

GETTING AROUND

To reach the Amalfi Coast from Naples, hop on the Circumvesuviana railway from Piazza Garibaldi
to Sorrento. The train also stops at Pompeii. Right across from the Sorrento train station, there is a
stop with regular buses to Positano, Amalfi and Salerno. From April to September a choice of ferries
and hydrofoils also connect the major resorts on the Amalfi Coast. For ultimate flexibility, consider
renting a car in Sorrento; if you're game, undertake the famous coastal Blue Ribbon Drive.

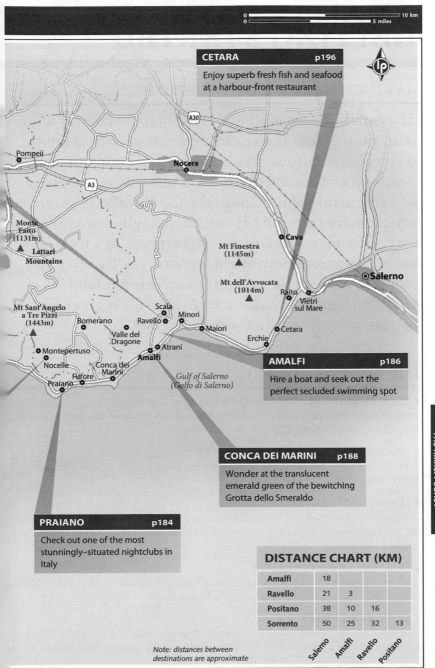

CETARA p196

Enjoy superb fresh fish and seafood at a harbour-front restaurant

AMALFI p186

Hire a boat and seek out the perfect secluded swimming spot

CONCA DEI MARINI p188

Wonder at the translucent emerald green of the bewitching Grotta dello Smeraldo

PRAIANO p184

Check out one of the most stunningly-situated nightclubs in Italy

DISTANCE CHART (KM)

	Salerno	Amalfi	Ravello	Positano
Amalfi	18			
Ravello	21	3		
Positano	38	10	16	
Sorrento	50	25	32	13

Note: distances between destinations are approximate

THE AMALFI COAST

AMALFI COAST GETTING STARTED

MAKING THE MOST OF YOUR TIME

The Amalfi Coast is all about drama; the coastal mountains plunge into the sea in a stunning vertical landscape of precipitous crags, forests and resort towns. Positano and Amalfi are both fabulously picturesque and colourful, while mountain-top Ravello is another gem: a more tranquil place with a tangible sense of history. Consider well-connected Sorrento as a base and, in the summer, luxuriate in ferry travel. Bicycles and scooters can also be useful for exploring inland, as can your two legs: the walking trails provide a great way of getting away from the coastal clamour.

TOP TOURS & COURSES

❦ HOW TO MAKE REAL ITALIAN GELATI
Learn to make deliciously authentic Italian gelati at this cream-of-the-crop gelateria. (Map p164; Gelateria David; ☎ 081 807 36 49; Via Marziale 19, Sorrento)

❦ MOONLIGHT BOAT TRIPS AND DIVES
Enjoy blissful views of a Positano sunset from the sea or dive to explore the watery depths. (Map p179; Blue Star; ☎ 089 81 18 88; Spiaggia Grande, Positano)

❦ LEARN TO SPEAK ITALIAN
Converse with the locals and take Italian classes in between your Sorrento sightseeing. (Map p164; Centro Linguistico Internazionale Sorrento Lingue; ☎ 081 807 55 99; www.sorrentolingue.com; Via San Francesco 8, Sorrento)

❦ ITALIAN COOKERY CLASSES
Cook your favourite Italian-mamma dishes in beautiful mountain-top Ravello. (Map p193; ☎ 089 85 70 19; www.mammaagata.com; Piazza San Cosma 9, Ravello)

❦ DISCOVER THE SEA
Experience another world and choose from a range of snorkelling and scuba-diving courses in Sorrento. (Map p164; ☎ 081 877 48 12; www.sorrentodivingcenter.it; Via Marina Piccola 63, Sorrento

THE AMALFI COAST

GETTING AWAY FROM IT ALL

While the main Amalfi Coast resorts are crowded in summer, it doesn't take too much effort (unless you are hiking, of course) to escape the crowds and the cars.

* **Seafood in a quiet marina** Enjoy that morning's catch at a seafood restaurant in picturesque Marina della Lobra (p173)
* **A tranquil snorkel (or sunbathe)** Head underwater at the stunning Punta Campanella Marine Reserve (p176), or sunbathe solo on the beach
* **A scenic coastal stroll** Explore the delightful trails that lead from the pretty town of Praiano to the sea (p184)

FOOD FESTIVALS

* **Sagra del Tonno** In the second half of July, the fishing folk of Cetara (p196) celebrate their main catch at this tuna festival
* **Sfogliatella festival** The irresistible *sfogliatella* (ricotta-stuffed flaky pastry) originated in Conca dei Marini (p188), where you can eat your fill of it on the first Sunday in August
* **Gustaminori** Food lovers on the coast gather in Minori (p195) in early September for the town's annual food jamboree
* **Sagra della Castagna** Chestnuts appear in various guises – roasted, and in jam, nut cakes and pancakes – at this festival in Scala (see the boxed text, p194) during the last three weeks of October
* **Sagra delle Zeppole** In late December Positano (p178) revels in *zeppole* (fried doughnuts served with custard cream).

TOP BEACHES

❦ BAIA DE LERANTO
A spectacular beach at the tip of the Sorrento Peninsula (see the boxed text, p174)

❦ BAGNI REGINA GIOVANNA
A picturesque sweep of sand set among the ruins of a Roman villa (p167)

❦ SPIAGGIA DEL FORNILLO
Walk around the cliffs from Positano to this attractive, lively cove (p181)

❦ MARINA DI PRAIA
A tempting inlet in Praiano with a small stretch of sand and crystal-clear water (above)

❦ MINORI
A great family beach in the centre of town (p195)

ONLINE RESOURCES

* **Sorrento Info** (www.sorrentoinfo.com) Sorrento webcam
* **Positano Online** (www.positanoonline.it) General tourist information about Positano, including accommodation, special events, activities and restaurants
* **Sorrento Online** (www.sorrento-online.com) Same as the above, but about Sorrento
* **Sorrento Service** (www.sorrentoservice.com) Overall guide to Sorrento, including events and commercial services, including car hire
* **Amalfi Coast Web** (www.amaflicoastweb.com) Guide to places to stay, restaurants, shops and services throughout the Amalfi coast

THE AMALFI COAST

SORRENTO

To Capri

Marina
Grande

Bay of Naples
(Golfo di Napoli)

To Naples

Marina San
Francesco

Marina Piccola

Marina
Piccola

0   200 m
0   0.1 miles

To Nube D'Argento
(100m); Nerfola Residence
(100m); La Tonnarella (400m); Hotel
Desiré (400m); Hotel Elios (450m);
Bagni Regina Giovanna (2km);
Santa Fortunata (2km);
Sant'Agata sui due
Golfi (6km); Massa Lubrense (6km);
Marina del Cantone (14km)

To Seven Hostel
(2km); Castellammare di
Stabia (17km); SS145;
Naples (48km)

Post
Office

Piazza
Angelina
Lauro

Piazza
Tasso

Villa
Comunale
Park

Piazza
Sant'Antonino

Circumvesuviana
Train Station

Via Renato

Via Marziale

Via degli Aranci

Via Marziale

Corso Italia

Via Fuorimura

Via Enrico
Caruso

Via Correale

Via Correale

Via Capasso

Via Rota

Viale
Nizza

Via Califano

Via Luigi De Maio

Via San Francesco

Via V Veneto

Via Marina Grande

Via Marina Piccola

Via Tasso

Via San Nicola

Via Accademia

Via San Cesareo

Corso Italia

Via Fuoro

Vico Fuoro

Via degli Aranci

Via Pietà

ORIENTATION

Piazza Tasso, bisected by Sorrento's main street, Corso Italia, is the centre of town. It's about a 300m walk northwest of the Circumvesuviana train station, along Corso Italia. From Marina Piccola, where ferries and hydrofoils dock, walk south along Via Marina Piccola, then climb about 200 steps to reach the piazza. Corso Italia becomes the SS145 on its way east to Naples and, heading west, changes its name to Via Capo.

EXPLORING SORRENTO

The town centre is compact and all the main sights (of which there are surprisingly few) are within walking distance of Piazza Tasso. Corso Italia (closed to traffic in the centre from 10am to 1pm and from 7pm to 7am) runs parallel and is a major hub for shops, restaurants and bars, as well as the focus of the town's passeggiata on balmy summer evenings. Sorrento lacks great beaches, so you may want to consider a hotel with a pool (see the Accommodation chapter, p276).

☙ CENTRO LINGUISTICO INTERNAZIONALE SORRENTO LINGUE // LEARN ITALIAN WHILE IN HOLIDAY MODE

There is something very appealing about rattling off your shopping list in faultless Italian; especially, given that most English-speaking tourists here never graduate much beyond *buongiorno* or (the more advanced) *buonasera*. The excellent **Centro Linguistico Internazionale Sorrento Lingue** (☎ 081 807 55 99; www. sorrentolingue.com; Via San Francesco 8) is one of the longest-established language schools on the Amalfi Coast, attracting students from all over the globe. A typical week-long beginner's course comprises four hours of lessons a day, which gives you plenty of time to practise while sightseeing. Prices start at €196 for one week of tuition.

☙ OLD TOWN // EXPLORE THE ATMOSPHERIC HISTORIC CENTRE

The bustling old town centres on Corso Italia, but duck into the side streets and you will find narrow lanes flanked by traditional green-shuttered buildings, interspersed with the occasional *palazzo,* piazza or church. Souvenir shops and trattorias also jostle for space in this backstreet tangle of cobbles, as well as some real surprises, such as the exquisite frescoed terrace of the 15th-century **Sedile Dominava** (Via San Cesareo), crowned by a domed *trompe l'œil* cupola. Originally a meeting point for the town's medieval aristocracy, today it houses a working men's club where bronzed pensioners sit around playing cards.

Just behind Piazzo Tasso a stunning natural phenomenon is on view from Via Fuorimura. The so-called **Il Vallone dei Mulino** (Valley of the Mills) is a deep cleft in the mountain that dates from a volcanic eruption 35,000 years ago. Sorrento was once bounded by three gorges, but today this is the only one that remains. It is named after the ancient wheat mills that were once located here, the ruins of which are still clearly visible.

♥ RELIGIOUS SORRENTO // ENJOY TRANQUIL RESPITE IN SACRED SURROUNDINGS

To get a feel for Sorrento's history, stroll down Via Pietà from Piazza Tasso and past two medieval palaces en route to the **duomo** (cathedral; ☎ 081 878 22 48; Corso Italia; ☻ 8am-noon & 4-8pm), with its striking exterior fresco, triple-tiered bell tower, four classical columns and elegant majolica clock. Take note of the striking marble bishop's throne (1573) and the beautiful wooden choir stalls decorated in the local *intarsio* (marquetry) style. The cathedral's original structure dates to the 15th century, but it has been altered several times, most recently in the early 20th century when the current façade was added.

On nearby Via San Francesco, check out one of Sorrento's most beautiful churches, the **Chiesa di San Francesco** (☎ 081 878

12 69; Via San Francesco; ☻ 8am-1pm & 2-8pm daily), with its distinct architectural styles: two sides are lined with 14th-century crossed arches, the other two with round arches supported by octagonal pillars. The church is most famous, however, for its summer program of concerts featuring world-class performers from the classical school. If this strikes a chord, check out the program at the tourist office.

The oldest church in town doubles as a quasi-museum: the **Basilica di Sant'Antonino** (☎ 081 878 14 37; Piazza Sant'Antonino; ☻ 9am-noon & 5-7pm), named after the patron saint of Sorrento, houses Roman artefacts, medieval paintings and the oddity of two whale ribs. Apparently the much-loved saint performed numerous miracles, including one in which he rescued a child from a whale's stomach. The saint's bones lie beneath the baroque interior in an 18th-century crypt.

♥ BOAT RENTAL & DIVES // EXPLORE HIDDEN COVES, BEACHES AND SEABEDS

Seek out the best beaches by rented boat. **Sic Sic** (☎ 081 807 22 83; www.nauticasicsic.com; Marina Piccola; ☻ May-Oct) rents out a variety of boats, starting at around €32 per hour or €95 per day. Operating out of Marina Piccola, the **Sorrento Diving Center** (☎ 081 877 48 12; www.sorrentodivingcenter.it; Via Marina Piccola 63; ⅏) organises daily dives and a series of courses. For eight- to 11-year-olds, a half-day course costs €80, for adults €95. For qualified divers a single dive (up to 45 minutes) will cost around €45, including equipment hire.

♥ MUSEO BOTTEGA DELLA TARSIA LIGNEA // WONDER AT THESE MARQUETRY MASTERPIECE

Since the 18th century, Sorrento has been famous for its *intarsio* furniture, made with elaborately designed inlaid wood. Some wonderful examples can be found in this **museum** (☎ 081 877 19 42; Via an Nicola 28; admission €8; ☻ 10am-1pm & 3pm-pm Mon-Sat), housed in an 18th-century palace, complete with beautiful frescoes. There's also an interesting collection of paintings, prints and photographs depicting the town and surrounding area in the 19th century. If you're interested in purchasing an updated *intarsio* piece, check out Gargiulo & Jannuzzi (p171), one of the longest-established specialist shops in town. And, yes, if that cute rocking chair is too large to fit in your baggage – it does arrange shipping.

☙ GELATERIA DAVID // MAKE YOUR OWN ITALIAN ICE CREAM
Impress your dinner-party pals with your homemade Italian *gelateria* by taking a course at this **gelaterie** (☎ 081 807 5 49; Via Marziale 19). The third generation in the ice-cream business, David runs classes (€7) that last around an hour and culminate in your very own *gelateria* certificate. Times vary according to demand, so call or drop by to organise; David speaks excellent English. His specialities include the deliciously one-off 'Sorrento moon', with almond and lemons, and *veneziana*, a lemon, orange and mandarin sorbet; he also makes all the traditional flavours.

☙ MUSEO CORREALE // ENJOY THIS HISTORIC PRIVATE COLLECTION
Located to the east of the city centre, the **Museo Correale** (☎ 081 878 18 46; www.museocorreale.com; Via Correale 50; admission €8; ☻ 9am-pm Wed-Mon) is well worth a visit whether you are into embroidery, a clock collector or an archaeological egghead. In addition to the rich assortment of 17th-

and 19th-century Neapolitan art and crafts, there are Japanese, Chinese and European ceramics, clocks, furniture, and, on the ground floor, Greek and Roman artefacts. The bulk of the collection, along with the 18th-century villa home, was generously donated to the city in the 1920s by aristocratic counts Alfredo and Pompeo Correale. Allow yourself at least a couple of hours for a visit here, and do wander around the gardens with their breathtaking coastal views and rare plants and flowers.

☙ VILLA COMUNALE PARK // VESUVIUS VIEWS FROM THE PARK
Another great place for views is the **Villa Comunale** (☻ 8am-8pm mid-Oct–mid-Apr, to midnight mid-Apr–mid-Oct), directly across the Bay of Naples from Mt Vesuvius. A popular park to while away the sunset hours, it's a lively spot, with benches, operatic buskers and a small bar. For parents with energetic toddlers, there's a playground just east of Piazza Tasso, the **Giardino Sorrento** (Via Califano; ☻ 9am-1pm & 4.30-11pm summer, 9am-5pm winter; ⌖).

☙ BAGNI REGINA GIOVANNA // BATHE SURROUNDED BY EVOCATIVE ROMAN RUINS
Sorrento, famously, lacks a decent beach, although both Marina Piccola and Marina Grande do have small stretches of dark sand and jetties sporting the ubiquitous umbrellas and deck chairs. Far more appealing is the **Bagni Regina Giovanna**, a rocky beach about 2km west of town, set among the ruins of the Roman Villa Pollio Felix. It's a picturesque spot with clear, clean water and it's possible to walk here (follow Via Capo), although you'll save your swimming (and sunbathing) strength if you get the SITA bus headed for Massa Lubrense.

THE AMALFI COAST

FESTIVALS & EVENTS

Sant'Antonino The city's patron saint, Sant'Antonino, is remembered annually with processions and huge markets. The saint is credited with having saved Sorrento during WWII when Salerno and Naples were heavily bombed; 14 February.

Settimana Santa (Holy Week; see p10) Famed throughout Italy; the first procession takes place at midnight on the Thursday preceding Good Friday, with robed and hooded penitents in white; the second occurs on Good Friday, when participants wear black robes and hoods to commemorate the death of Christ.

Sorrento Festival World-class classical concerts are held in the cloisters of the Chiesa di San Francesco (p166) between July and September. Ask at the tourist office.

GASTRONOMIC HIGHLIGHTS

The centre of town is full of bars, cafes, trattorias, restaurants and even the odd kebab takeaway. Many of these, particularly those with waistcoated waiters stationed outside, are unashamed tourist traps serving bland food at inflated prices. But not all are and it's perfectly possible to eat well. If you've got your own wheels there are some superb restaurants dotted around the nearby countryside, including one of Italy's top restaurants in Sant'Agata sui due Golfi.

A local speciality to look out for is *gnocchi alla sorrentina* (potato gnocchi baked in tomato sauce with mozzarella).

❦ ANGELINA LAURO €

☎ 081 807 40 97; Piazza Angelina Lauro 39-40; self-service meal €12; ⊙ daily Jul-Aug, Wed-Mon Sep-Jun

Owner Rafael is a congenial host at this brightly lit, roomy place that has a passing resemblance to a college canteen. No matter: it hits the spot for a filling, inexpensive self-service lunch. Simply grab a tray and choose from the daily selection of pastas, meats and vegetable side dishes. You can order a la carte too, but it is more costly and, frankly, not as good.

❦ GARDEN €€

☎ 081 878 11 95; Corso Italia 50-52; meals €25; ⊙ closed Jan-Mar

Downstairs this is a sophisticated wine bar where you can enjoy local and Italian wines by the glass accompanied by slices of prosciutto and cheese. The upstairs terrace is the namesake garden, with tables set under draping wisteria and bordered by a dazzle of plants and trees. The menu includes all the mainstay pasta dishes, including a recommended seafood pasta and, for undecided tastebuds, the refreshingly simple, fresh and familiar spaghetti with tomato and basil.

❦ IN BUFALITO €€

☎ 338 163 29 21; Via Fuoro 21; meals €25; ⊙ close Nov-Feb

Owner Franco Coppola (no relation to that movie man) exudes a real passion for showcasing local produce and the restaurant is a member of the Slow Food Movement. A mozzarella bar as well as a restaurant, In Bufalito boasts a menu including delights such as Sorrento-style cheese fondue, buffalo meat carpaccio and *salsiccia* (local sausage) *e broccoli*. Cheese tastings are a regular event, along with photographic and art exhibitions and occasional live music. This is a very special place with a great ambience: don't miss it

❦ IL GIARDINIELLO €

☎ 081 878 46 16; Via Accademia 7; pizzas from €3.50, meals €18

Elderly owner Franco also waits the tables and claims that his family restaurant was Sorrento's first. Certainly the decor has a timeless feel, with its mishmash of

THE AMALFI COAST

religious prints, faded family pics, questionable landscapes and the occasional cracked ceramic plate. Tuck into hearty classics like *pasta e fagioli* (pasta and white beans), *ravioli con spicaci e ricotta* (ravioli stuffed with spinach and ricotta cheese) and *calami in cassuola* (squid with tomato sauce, garlic, chilli peppers and parsley).

LA FENICE €€
☎ 081 878 16 52; Via degli Aranci 11; meals €24; ⊗ closed Mon

It's too large and bright for a romantic dinner for two, but locals continue to recommend this place for its down-to-earth, well-prepared dishes, particularly the seafood, like mussels with garlic and parsley, and grilled squid. The menu is bafflingly long and includes seven choices of risotto and some braver international dishes, like king prawns in a curry sauce. Allergies are sensitively catered to, with soy-based and wheat-free dishes available.

MONDO BIO €
☎ 081 807 56 94; Via degli Aranci 146; snacks/pasta .3/6.50; ⊗ 8.30am-8.30pm Mon-Sat

Flying the banner for organic vegetarian food, this bright shop-cum-restaurant serves a limited range of meat-free dishes and snacks. The menu, chalked up outside, changes daily, but typical dishes include *zuppa di soia verde* (soybean soup) and *polpette di tofu* (tofu balls). Seating is limited to just four tables, but you can always peruse the shop's shelves if you have to wait.

O'PARRUCCHIANO €€
☎ 081 878 13 21; Corso Italia 67; meals €25; ⊗ closed Wed

One of the longest-standing restaurants in town, dating from the late 19th century – the dining-room interiors here are truly sumptuous, lined by richly patterned historic tiles and original stone walls. Giant rubber plants and other foliage give the cavernous upper floor a veritable Kew Gardens feel. Try the cannelloni (said to have been invented here) or the *gnocchi alla sorrentina*, the ubiquitous Sorrentine speciality; vegetarians will enjoy the delicious *pasta e fagioli*. Check out the delectable desserts from the display cabinet near the entrance.

PHOTO €€
☎ 081 877 36 86; Via Correale 19-21; meals €40

With its modish look and regular photo projections, Photo is a far cry from Sorrento's traditional trattorias. Part bar and part restaurant, it serves several menus with dishes ranging from sushi-style raw fish to new takes on Italian classics – think Angus beef carpaccio with rocket salad and Parmesan shavings. The wine list is also interesting, with a limited selection of local labels. In winter a DJ adds to the modern vibe.

RISTORANTE IL BUCO €€€
☎ 081 878 23 54; Rampa Marina Piccola 5; meals €55; ⊗ Feb-Dec, closed Wed

Even the most disgruntled critic would be hard pressed to describe this Michelin-starred restaurant as a hole, as the name translates. Housed in a monks' former wine cellar, it is a refined restaurant offering far from monastic cuisine. The emphasis is on innovative regional cooking, so expect modern combos such as pasta with rockfish sauce or *treccia* (local cheese) and prawns served on a bed of capers with tomato and olive sauce. In summer there's outdoor seating near one of the city's ancient gates. Reservations are recommended.

THE AMALFI COAST

NIGHTLIFE

You can do the whole drinking trip in Sorrento: down pints of lager while watching Sky sport on a big screen; quaff local wines in wood-panelled wine bars or sip cocktails in swish cafes; you can people-watch over an aperitif at square-side bars or linger over wine while pondering Vesuvius across the water.

☙ BOLLICINE

☎ 081 878 46 16; Via dell' Accademia 9; ☾ 6pm-1am daily Jul & Aug, Tue-Sun Sep-Jun

An unpretentious wine bar with a dark, woody interior and boxes of bottles cluttering the floor. The wine list includes all the big Italian names and a selection of interesting local labels. If you can't decide what to go for, the amiable barman will happily advise you. There's also a small menu of *panini* (sandwiches), bruschetta and one or two pasta dishes.

☙ CAFÈ LATINO

☎ 081 878 37 18; Vico I Fuoro 4A; ☾ 10am-1am Apr-Sep

Think locked-eyes-over-cocktails time. This is the place to impress your partner with cocktails (from €7) on the terrace, surrounded by orange and lemon trees. Sip a Mary Pickford (rum, pineapple, *grenadino* and maraschino) or a glass of chilled white wine. If you can't drag yourselves away, you can also eat here (meals around €30).

☙ ENGLISH INN

☎ 081 807 43 57; Corso Italia 55

The vast upstairs terrace under the stars is a delight and attracts a primarily expat crowd, here for the Strongbow cider and Guinness on tap. A hip-swinging vibe continues late into the night, while the bacon-and-eggs breakfast is a suita-

ble reviver (and handy to know if you've grown weary of *cornetti* (croissants) in the morning).

☙ FAUNO BAR

☎ 081 878 11 35; Piazza Tasso; ☾ Dec-Oct

On Piazza Tasso, this elegant cafe covers half the square and offers the best people-watching in town. It serves stiff drinks at stiff prices – cocktails start at around €8.50. Snacks and sandwiches are also available (from €7).

☙ FAUNO NOTTE CLUB

☎ 081 878 10 21; www.faunonotte.it; Piazza Tasso 1

A direct competitor of the more established Teatro Tasso, the Fauno offers 'a fantastic journey through history, legends and folklore'. In other words, 500 years of Neapolitan history set to music. Sing along to the Masaniello Revolt (see p226) and other folkloristic episodes.

☙ TEATRO TASSO

☎ 081 807 55 25; www.teatrotasso.com; Piazza Sant'Antonino

The southern Italian equivalent of a cockney music hall, Teatro Tasso is home to the *Sorrento Musical* (€28), a sentimental revue of Neapolitan classics such as 'O Sole Mio' and 'Trona a Sorrent'. The 75-minute performance starts at 9.30pm Monday to Saturday from March to October.

RECOMMENDED SHOPS

The pedestrian-only *centro storico* is the place to shop. Ignore the replica football shirts and souvenir tat and look out for inlaid wood and *limoncello* (lemon liqueur; plus tastings) instead.

Unless otherwise stated, the following shops open all day until late in summer and close for lunch in winter.

THE AMALFI COAST

❦ CLAUDIO GARGIULO

☎ 081 807 18 02; Corso Italia 261

Expect to be tempted to ditch the Apple and weigh down your luggage with a few antique majolica tiles instead. There are piles all over this Aladdin's cave of a showroom, ranging in price from a reasonable €10, to €30 for the older signed ones. There are also paintings, Tiffany-style lamps and antiques.

❦ FATTORIA TERRANOVA

☎ 081 878 12 63; Piazza Tasso 16

Fattoria Terranova is an *agriturismo* (farm stay; see p280) near the village of Sant'Agata sui due Golfi in the hills to the south of Sorrento. It produces everything that you'll find for sale in this, its in-town shop – wine, olive oil, preserves and marmalades, vegetables in olive oil, and dried herbs.

❦ GARGIULO & JANNUZZI

☎ 081 878 10 41; Viale Enrico Caruso 1

Dating from 1863, this old-fashioned warehouse-cum-shop is a classic. Elderly shop assistants will guide you through the three floors of locally made goods ranging from ceramic crockery to inlaid cabinets, embroidered lace and pottery. The prices are as good as you will get anywhere in town, and the choice is certainly superior. Shipping can be arranged.

❦ LA RAPIDA

☎ 338 877 77 05; Via Fuoro 67; ⏰ 9am-1pm & 5-8pm Apr-Oct, 9am-1pm & 3.30-8pm Nov-Mar

There are numerous shops selling leather sandals in the *centro storico*, but head to the far end of Via Fuoro and you'll find this tiny cobbler. An old-fashioned shop, it doesn't have a huge range, but the quality's as good as anyone's and the prices (from €30) are generally better. It

also does repairs, so if your stiletto heel has snapped or you've lost a crucial button, this is your place.

❦ PIAZZA ITALIA

☎ 081 510 82 55; Corso Italia 193-197

Italy's version of the Spanish smash-hit chain, Zara, this store has contemporary, well-priced clothes for guys and girls, plus accessories, including colourful belts, bags and hats. Shoes range from trendy trainers to wedge sandals and thigh-length *Avengers*-style boots. Although the fashions are geared for the pencil thin, some of the floaty beach gear may accommodate those who don't stint on their daily quota of gelati.

❦ STINGA

☎ 081 878 11 30; www.stingatarsia.com; Via Via Luigi de Maio 16

Well worth seeking out, this place sells distinctive inlaid-wood items made in Sorrento by the same family of craftsmen (and women) for three generations. The pieces are highly original, especially in their use of colour and design. A small box, exquisitely inlaid and patterned, will cost in the range of €32. Fine jewellery, including coral pieces, is also on display.

TRANSPORT

CAR & MOTORCYCLE // Coming from Naples and the north, take the A3 autostrada until Castellammare di Stabia; exit there and follow the SS145 southeast. Renting a car provides the optimum flexibility and Sorrento is an excellent base for exploring the Amalfi Coast and the lesser-known villages and countryside inland. If you want to hire a car (or scooter) you'll be spoilt for choice. The big international operators are here – **Avis** (☎ 081 878 24 59; www.avisautonoleggio.it; Viale Nizza 53), **Hertz** (☎ 081 807 16 46; www.hertz.it; Via degli Aranci 9) – as well as a host of local outfits. At **Peninsula Rental** (☎ 081 877 46 64; Corso Italia 259) you

THE AMALFI COAST

THE AMALFI COAST

can pick up a scooter for €25 for five hours and cars from €45 per day. **Jolly Service & Rent** (☎ 081 877 34 50; www.jollyrent.eu; Via degli Aranci 180) has smart cars from €50 a day and 50cc scooters from €25.

PARKING // In midsummer, finding a parking spot can be a frustrating business, particularly as much of the parking on the side streets is for residents only and the city centre is closed to traffic for much of the day. There are well-signposted car parks near the ferry terminal, on the corner of Via degli Aranci and Via Renato and heading west out of town near Via Capo (€2 per hour).

BOAT // Sorrento is the main jumping-off point for Capri and also has excellent ferry connections to Ischia, Naples and Amalfi coastal resorts. **Alilauro** (☎ 081 878 14 30; www.alilauro.it) runs up to seven daily hydrofoils from Naples to/from Sorrento (€9, 35 minutes). Slower **Metrò del Mare** (☎ 199 60 07 00; www.metrodelmare.com) covers the same route (€6.50, one hour, four daily). **Linee Marittime Partenopee** (☎ 081 704 19 11; www.consorziolmp. it; Via Guglielmo Melisurgo 4, Naples) Runs hydrofoils from Sorrento to Capri from April to November (€13.50, 23 daily). For more ferry information, see the Transport chapter, p305.

BUS // **Curreri** (☎ 081 801 54 20; www.curreri viaggi.it) runs six daily services to Sorrento from Naples Capodichino airport. Buses depart from outside the arrivals hall and arrive in Piazza Angelina Lauro. Buy tickets (€10) for the 75-minute journey on the bus. There are also plenty of private agencies that will arrange airport transfers for around €80. **Marozzi** (☎ 080

579 01 11; www.marozzivt.it) operates two weekday buses to/from Rome. **SITA** (☎ 199 73 07 49; www. sitabus.lt, in Italian) buses serve Naples, the Amalfi Coast and Sant'Agata, leaving from the bus stop across from the entrance of the Circumvesuviana train station. Buy tickets at the station bar or from shops bearing the blue SITA sign.

TRAIN // Sorrento is the last stop on the **Circumvesuviana** (☎ 081 772 24 44; wwww.vesuviana. it) train line from Naples. Trains run every half-hour for Naples (one hour 10 minutes), via Pompeii (30 minutes) and Ercolano (50 minutes). Invest in a Unico Costiera card (see the boxed text, left).

UNICO COSTIERA

If you plan to do much travelling by SITA bus and/or Circumvesuviana train, then it saves money and hassle to invest in a Unico Costiera card, available for durations of 45 minutes (€2), 90 minutes (€3), 24 hours (€6) or 72 hours (€15). Aside from the SITA buses, the 24- and 72-hour tickets also allow you to hop on the City Sightseeing tourist bus, which travels between Amalfi and Ravello and Amalfi and Maiori.

WEST OF SORRENTO

· · · · · ·

The countryside west of Sorrento is emblematic of southern Italy. Tortuous roads wind their way through hills covered in olive trees and lemon groves, passing through sleepy villages and tiny fishing ports. There are magnificent views at every turn, the best from the high points overlooking Punta della Campanella, the westernmost point of the Sorrento Peninsula. Offshore, Capri seems no more than a Frisbee-throw away.

MASSA LUBRENSE

The first town you come to as you follow the coast west from Sorrento is Massa Lubrense. Situated 120m above sea level, it's a disjointed place, comprising a small town centre and 17 *frazioni* (fractions or hamlets) joined by an intricate network of paths and mule tracks. For those without a donkey, there are good road connections and SITA buses regularly run between them. There's a small **Tourist Office** (☎ 081 533 90 21; www.massalubrense.

t; Viale Filangieri 11; 9.30am-1pm daily & 4.30-8pm Mon, Tue & Thu-Sat), which can provide bus timetables and maps.

CHIESA DI SANTA MARIA DELLA GRAZIA // BASK IN THE HEAVENLY VIEWS

Don't forget your camera, as there are fabulous views over Capri from the town's central Largo Vescovado. On its northern flank stands the former cathedral, the 16th-century **Chiesa di Santa Maria della Grazia** (Largo Vescovado; 7am-noon & 4.30-8pm), worth a quick look for the bright majolica-tiled floor, which would look *so* good in your kitchen back home.

MARINA DELLA LOBRA // EXPLORE HIDDEN COVES BY BOAT

From the square it's a 2km descent to **Marina della Lobra** (a 20-minute downhill walk, and a wheezing 40-minute ascent), a pretty little marina backed by ramshackle houses and verdant slopes. The marina is a good place to rent a boat, the best way of reaching the otherwise difficult-to-get-to bays and inlets along the coast. Of the hire companies, **Coop Marina della Lobra** (081 808 93 80; www.marinalobra.com; per hr from €30) is a reliable operator.

GASTRONOMIC HIGHLIGHTS

FUNICULI FUNICULÁ €€

ia Fontanelle 16, Marina della Lobra; meals €24; Apr-Oct

You can find this great bar-restaurant on the seafront at Marina della Lobra. Unsurprisingly, the menu is dominated by seafood, but there are also meal-in-one salads and the usual array of grilled-meat dishes. The helpings are huge and the food is delicious. For proof try the *ubettoni con cozze, rucola e parmigiano* small pasta tubes with mussels, rocket and Parmesan). Expanding midriffs can behave with a fresh-fruit dessert.

LA TORRE €€€

 081 80 89 56; Piazzetta Annunziata 7, Massa Lubrense; meals €42; Apr-Feb

This delightful laid-back restaurant on a tranquil square serves mouth-watering traditional cuisine with an emphasis on seafood. The menu changes seasonally, but you can usually depend on classics like *tonani con patate* (tuna with potatoes), *parmigiana di melanzane* (baked aubergine with tomatoes and Parmesan) and *scialatielli ai frutti di mare* (pasta with seafood). Eat alfresco on the terrace.

TRANSPORT

BUS // From the Circumvesuviana train station in Sorrento, SITA (199 73 07 49; www.sitabus.it, in Italian) buses depart hourly.

CAR & MOTORCYCLE // By car, Massa Lubrense is an easy 20-minute drive from Sorrento.

PARKING // Parking is mainly a matter of trawling the streets; there are some meters in the centre (€1.30 per hour).

SANT'AGATA SUI DUE GOLFI

Perched high in the hills above Sorrento, Sant'Agata sui due Golfi is the most famous of Massa Lubrense's 17 *frazioni*. Boasting spectacular views of the Bay of Naples on one side and the Gulf of Salerno on the other (hence its name, St Agatha on the two Gulfs), it's a tranquil place that manages to retain its rustic charm despite a fairly heavy hotel presence. For information on the village and surrounding countryside, stop by the small **Tourist Office** (081 533 01 35; www.santagatasuiduegolfi.it; Corso Sant'Agata 25; 9am-1pm & 5.30-9pm Apr-Oct) on the main square.

HIKING THE PENINSULA

Forming a giant horseshoe between **Punta della Campanella** and **Punta Penna**, the beautiful **Baia de Leranto** is generally regarded as the top swimming spot on the Sorrento Peninsula. To get there you have two alternatives: you can either get a boat or you can walk from the village of Nerano, the steep descent forming part of a longer 6.5km hike from nearby Termini.

This picturesque path is just one of 20 (for a total of 110km) that cover the area. These range from tough all-day treks such as the 14.1km **Alta Via dei Monti Lattari** from the Fontanelle hills near Positano down to the Punta della Campanella, to shorter walks suitable for all the family.

Tourist offices throughout the area can provide maps detailing the colour-coded routes. With the exception of the Alta Via dei Monti Lattari, which is marked in red and white, long routes are shown in red on the map; coast-to-coast trails in blue; paths connecting villages in green; and circular routes in yellow. On the ground, trails are fairly well marked, although you might find some signs have faded to near-indecipherable levels.

If you enjoy a walk, there's a picturesque 3km trail between Sorrento and Sant'Agata. From Piazza Tasso venture south along Viale Caruso and Via Fuorimura to pick up the Circumpiso footpath, marked in green on the walking maps available from tourist offices. The walk should take approximately one hour.

♥ RELIGIOUS VIEWS // FROM HEADY VIEWS TO EXQUISITE ALTARS

The Carmelite convent of **Deserto** (☎ 081 878 01 99; Via Deserto; ☽ 8.30am-12.30pm & 2.30-4.30pm Oct-Mar, 8.30am-12.30pm & 4-9pm Apr-Sep) is located 1.5km uphill from the village centre, so read on carefully before striding out. It was founded in the 17th century and is still home to a closed community of Benedictine nuns. While of moderate interest (unless you are one of the nuns), it is the 360-degree views that should make that knee-wearying hike worthwhile. Back down in the centre, you can recover in the cool of the village's 17th-century parish church, the **Chiesa di Sant'Agata** (Piazza Sant'Agata; ☽ 8am-1pm & 5-7pm), famed for its 17th-century polychrome marble altar, an exquisite work of inlaid marble, mother-of-pearl, lapis lazuli and malachite.

GASTRONOMIC HIGHLIGHTS

Sant'Agata has a surprisingly sophisticated culinary choice, given its size.

♥ LO STUZZICHINO €

☎ 081 533 00 10; Via Deserto 1a; meals €18, pizzas from €5; ☽ closed Jan

Just down the road from the village church, this laid-back restaurant-cum-pizzeria has a gregarious host in owner Paolo de Gregorio. Try the specialty: *pasta e patate con provolone de Monaco* (pasta and potatoes with provolone) or *minestra maritata con le verdure di stagione* (seafood stew with seasonal vegetables). The rare *gamberetti* (prawns) *di Crapolla* taste better than they sound. There's outdoor summer seating, and the simple interior has wine racks and a corner TV.

THE AMALFI COAST

♥ RIOSTORANTE DON ALFONSO 1890 €€€

☎ 081 533 02 26; Corso Sant'Agata 11; meals €115-125; ⌚ closed Mon & Tue, except Tue night Jun-Sep, closed Jan–early Mar & Nov-Dec; ℗ ⌘

This Michelin two-star restaurant is generally regarded as one of Italy's finest. Dishes are prepared with produce from the chef's own 6-hectare farm in nearby Punta della Campanella, the dining hall is a picture of refined taste, and the international wine list is one of the country's most extensive and best. The menu changes seasonally, but hallmark dishes include lightly seared tuna in red-pepper sauce and pasta with clams and courgettes. Booking well in advance is essential.

TRANSPORT

BUS // From Sorrento's Circumvesuviana train station, SITA (☎ 199 73 07 49; www.sitabus.it, in Italian) buses depart hourly.

CAR // By car, follow the SS145 west from Sorrento for about 7km until you see signs off to the right.

PARKING // There is generally street parking available, although August can be busy, especially in the evening.

THE BLUE RIBBON DRIVE

Stretching from **Vietri sul Mare** to **Sant'Agata sui due Golfi**, near Sorrento, the **SS163** (nicknamed the Nastro Azzurro or Blue Ribbon) is one of Italy's most dramatic roads. Commissioned by Bourbon king Ferdinand II and completed in 1853, it wends its way along the Amalfi Coast's entire length, snaking round impossibly tight curves, over deep ravines and through tunnels gouged out of sheer rock. It's a magnificent feat of civil engineering. It's also a severe test of driving skill and courage, a white-knuckle, 50km ride that will pit you against the extraordinary ability of the local bus drivers. The price for those sublime views is numerous switchbacks and plunging drops to the sea, frequently with only waist-high barriers between you and oblivion.

Originally designed for horse-drawn carriages, the road can get very narrow, particularly on hairpin bends. To avoid blocking oncoming buses, check the circular mirrors on the roadside and listen for the sound of klaxons – if you hear

THE AMALFI COAST

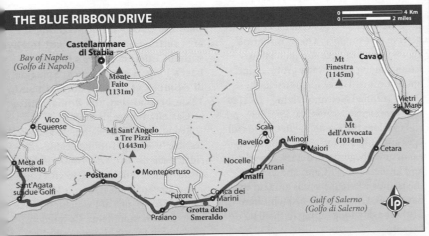

THE BLUE RIBBON DRIVE

THE AMALFI COAST

one slow right down as it will invariably be followed by a coach. Avoid peak season (July and August) and morning, lunchtime and evening rush hours. The trick to driving the coast is to stay calm, even when your toddler throws up all over the back seat or your partner tells you to look at the view while you're inching around a blind corner.

MARINA DEL CANTONE

From Massa Lubrense, follow the coastal road round to **Termini**. Stop a moment to admire the views before continuing on to **Nerano**, from where a beautiful hiking trail leads down to the stunning **Baia de Leranto** and **Marina del Cantone**. This unassuming village with its small pebble beach is not only a lovely, tranquil place to stay but also one of the area's prime dining spots, a magnet for VIPs, who regularly boat over from Capri to eat here – Bill Gates, Roman Abramovich, Michael Douglas and Catherine Zeta Jones are all recent visitors.

☙ PUNTA CAMPANELLA MARINE RESERVE // A FASCINATING NATURAL MARINE RESERVE

A popular diving destination, these protected waters are part of an 11 sq km reserve that supports a healthy marine ecosystem, with flora and fauna flourishing among underwater grottoes and ancient ruins. To see for yourself, the PADI-certified **Nettuno Diving** (☎ 081 808 10 51; www.sorrentodiving.com; Via A Vespucci 39; ♿) runs various underwater activities for all ages and abilities, including snorkelling excursions, beginners courses, cave dives and immersions off Capri and Li Galli, the islands where the sirens are said to have lived. Costs start at €20 (children €12) for a day-long outing to the Baia de Leranto.

☙ LO SCOGLIO // EXCLUSIVE SEAFOOD, SETTING – AND FELLOW GUESTS

The only one of the marina's restaurants directly accessible from the sea, **Lo Scoglio** (☎ 081 808 10 26; Marina del Cantone; meals €50) is a favourite of visiting celebs. The situation is certainly memorable – a glass pavilion built around a kitsch fountain on a wooden jetty – and the food is top-notch (and priced accordingly). Although you can eat *fettucine al bolognese* and steak here, you'd be sorry to miss the superb seafood. Menu tempters include a €24 antipasto of raw seafood and *spaghetti al riccio* (spaghetti with sea urchins).

TRANSPORT

BUS // From the Circumvesuviana train station in Sorrento, SITA (☎ 199 73 07 49; www.sitabus.it, in Italian) runs regular buses between Sorrento and Marina del Cantone.

EAST OF SORRENTO

· · · · · ·

More developed and less appealing than the coast west of Sorrento, the area to the east of town is not totally without interest. There's the district's longest sandy beach, Spiaggia di Alimuri, at Meta di Sorrento and, 12km beyond that, the Roman villas at Castellammare di Stabia.

Rising above Castellammare and accessible by an eight-minute **cable-car ride** (adult/under 18yr/19-26yr return €7/3/3.50; about 30 daily Apr-Oct) from the town's Circumvesuviana train station is Monte Faito (1131m), one of the highest peaks in the Lattari mountains. Covered in thick beech forests, the summit offers some lovely walking and sensational views.

♥ VICO EQUENSE // WANDER THE HOME OF PIZZA BY THE METRE

Known to the Romans as Aequa, Vico Equense (Vico) is a small cliff-top town about 10km east of Sorrento and just five stops away via the Circumvesuviana train. Largely bypassed by international tourists, it's a laid-back, authentic place worth a quick stopover, if only to sample some of the famous pizza by the metre (see right). General information on the area's attractions is available from the helpful **Tourist Office** (☎ 081 801 57 52; www.vicoturismo.it; Piazza Umberto I; ☽ 9am-2pm & 3-8pm Mon-Sat, 9.30am-1.30pm Sun Mar-Oct, 9am-2pm & 3-5pm Mon-Sat Nov-Feb) in the main square.

The town is easy to explore on foot. From Piazza Umberto I, the 19th-century focal point, take Corso Filangieri along to the small *centro storico*. Here, on a small balcony overlooking the village of Marina di Equa, you'll find the **Chiesa dell'Annunziata** (☎ 081 879 80 04; Via Vescovado; ☽ 10am-noon Sun), Vico's former cathedral and the only Gothic church on the Sorrento Peninsula. Little remains of the original 14th-century structure other than the lateral windows near the main altar and a few arches in the aisles. In fact, most of what you see today, including the chipped pink-and-white facade, is 17th-century baroque. In the sacristy, check out the portraits of Vico's bishops, all of whom are represented here except for the last one, Michele Natale, who was executed for supporting the ill-fated 1799 Parthenopean Republic (see p228). His place is taken by an angel with its finger to its lips, an admonishment to the bishop to keep his liberal thoughts to himself.

♥ RISTORANTE & PIZZERIA DA GIGINO // EAT WHERE IT ALL BEGAN

☎ 081 879 83 09; Via Nicotera 15; pizza per metre €12-26; ☽ noon-1am

Run by the five sons of pizza king Gigino Dell'Amura, who was the very first to introduce pizza by the metre to the world, this barn-like pizzeria produces kilometres of pizza each day in three huge ovens to the right of the entrance. There's a large selection of toppings and the quality is superlative. Although it seats around 200, you still may have to wait for a table.

♥ HISTORIC HAMLETS // FROM UNSPOILT VILLAGES TO STUNNING VIEWS

Dotted around Vico's surrounding hills are a number of ancient hamlets, known as *casali*. Untouched by mass tourism, they offer a glimpse into a rural way of life that has changed little over the centuries. You will, however, need wheels to get to them. From Vico, take Via Roma and follow Via Rafaelle Bosco, which passes through the *casali* before circling back to town. Highlights include **Massaquano** and the **Capella di Santa Lucia** (open on request), famous for its 14th-century frescoes; **Moiano**, from where an ancient path leads to the summit of **Monte Faito**; and **Santa Maria del Castello**, with its fabulous views towards Positano.

Three kilometres to the west of Vico, **Marina di Equa** stands on the site of the original Roman settlement, Aequa. Among the bars and restaurants lining the popular pebble beaches you can still see the remains of the 1st century AD Villa Pezzolo, as well as a defensive tower, the Torre di Caporivo, and the Gothic ruins of a medieval limestone quarry.

THE AMALFI COAST

AMALFI TOWNS

······

TRANSPORT

BOAT // There are excellent ferry connections between the coastal towns and islands from April to October. From Positano, **Alicost** (☎ 089 87 14 83; Largo Scario 5, Amalfi) operates services to/from Salerno (€8.50, five daily), Ischia (€19, one daily) and Capri (€15.50, five daily), and **Metrò del Mare** (☎ 199 44 66 44; www.metrodelmare.com) sails to/from Naples (€14, four daily), Sorrento (€9, five daily), Amalfi (€6, six daily) and Salerno (€11, three daily).

POSITANO

pop 3872
Positano is the coast's most picturesque and photogenic town, with steeply stacked houses tumbling down to the sea in a waterfall of sun-bleached peach, pink and terracotta colours. No less colourful are its near-vertical streets and steps lined with wisteria-draped hotels, smart restaurants and fashionable boutiques.

Look beyond the facades and the fashion, however, and you will find reassuring signs of everyday reality – crumbling stucco, streaked paintwork and even, on occasion, a faint whiff of drains. There's still a southern Italian holiday feel about the place as well, with sunbathers eating pizza on the beach, kids pestering parents for gelati and chic women from Milan checking out the boutiques. *Moda Positano* was born here in the '60s and the town was the first in Italy to import bikinis from France.

John Steinbeck visited in 1953 and wrote in an article for *Harper's Bazaar*: 'Positano bites deep. It is a dream place that isn't quite real when you are there

and becomes beckoningly real after you have gone'. There certainly is something special about the place and this is reflected, predictably, in the prices, which tend to be higher here than elsewhere on the coast.

The **Police Station** (☎ 089 87 50 11) is at the corner of Via Guglielmo Marconi and Viale Pasitea. You'll find the **Tourist Office** (☎ 089 87 50 67; Via del Saracino 4; ☯ 8am-2pm & 3.30-8pm Mon-Sat Apr-Oct, 9am-3pm Mon-Fri Nov-Mar) at the foot of the Chiesa di Santa Maria Assunta steps.

ORIENTATION

Positano is split in two by a cliff bearing the Torre Trasita. West of the tower is the smaller, less crowded Spiaggia del Fornillo beach area and the less expensive side of town; east is Spiaggia Grande backing up to the town centre.

Navigating is easy, if steep. Via Guglielmo Marconi, part of the main SS163 coastal road, forms a huge horseshoe around and above the town, which cascades down to the sea. From it, one-way Viale Pasitea makes a second, lower loop, ribboning off Via Guglielmo Marconi from the west towards the town centre then climbing back up as Via Cristoforo Colombo to rejoin Via Guglielmo Marconi and the SS163. Branching off the bottom of Viale Pasitea, Via dei Mulini leads down to Spiaggia Grande.

Getting around town is largely a matter of walking. If your knees can take the slopes, there are dozens of narrow alleys and stairways that make walking relatively easy and joyously traffic-free.

EXPLORING POSITANO

Positano's most memorable sight is its unforgettable townscape – a vertiginous stack of pastel-coloured houses cascad-

POSITANO

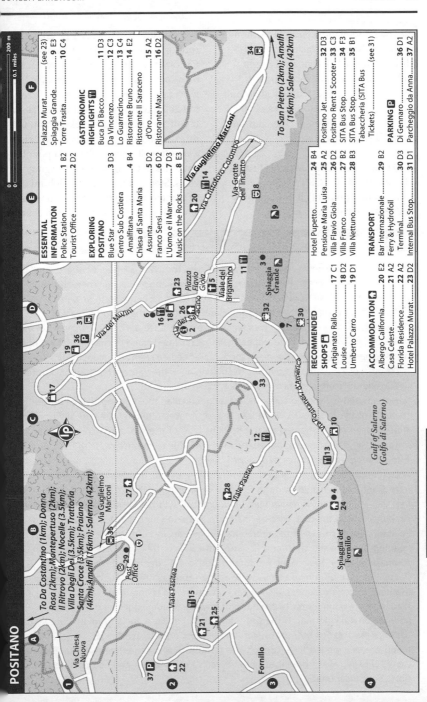

THE AMALFI COAST

ing down to **Spiaggia Grande**. Although it's no-one's dream beach, with greyish sand covered by legions of bright umbrellas, the water's clean and the setting is memorable. Hiring a chair and umbrella on the fenced-off areas costs around €18 per person per day, but the crowded public areas are free.

🌱 CHURCHES & PALACES // FROM CHERUBS TO COCKTAILS

It's the centre point of all those photos you've taken and graces just about every postcard of town: rising above the rooftops, the ceramic-tiled dome of the **Chiesa di Santa Maria Assunta** (Piazza Flavio Gioia; ⊙ 8am-noon & 3.30-7pm daily) is the most famous and – let's face it – pretty much the only major sight in Positano. If you are visiting at a weekend you will probably have the added perk of seeing a wedding; it's one of the most popular churches in the area for exchanging vows. Step inside to see a delightful classical interior with pillars topped with gilded Ionic capitals and winged cherubs

WALK WITH THE GODS

Probably the best-known walk on the Amalfi Coast, the 12km, six-hour **Sentiero degli Dei** (Walk of the Gods) follows the steep paths linking Positano to Praiano. The walk commences at **Via Chiesa Nuova**, just north of the SS163 road, in the northern part of Positano. Head to the right of the church and climb the steps at the end of the narrow road. Cross over and take the steps to your left, where you will see the official beginning of the route marked by red and white stripes; these are repeated along the path, usually daubed on rocks and trees, although some of these have become worn and might be difficult to make out. For a less arduous climb at the beginning of the trail, catch a bus from Positano to **Nocelle** and start from there (the walk is marked).

Not advised for vertigo sufferers, it's a spectacular, meandering trail along the pinnacle of the mountains where caves and terraces plummet dramatically from the cliffs to deep valleys framed by the brilliant blue of the sea. It can sometimes be foggy in the dizzy heights, but that somehow adds to the drama, with the cypresses rising through the mist like dark sword blades.

Don't miss the huge hole in the centre of the cliff at **Montepertuso**, as if some irate giant had punched through the slab of limestone. The local legend is a holier one: apparently the Virgin Mary, in a contest with the Devil, made the hole by simply touching the rock with her hand. In **Praiano** you can catch a bus back to Positano, but if you want the more challenging version of this hike then, instead of heading down to the coast and Praiano, turn left to the (signposted) small town of **Bomerano**, at the foot of the mountains between Sorrento and Amalfi.

You can pick up a map of this walk at the tourist office. Route details are also available in Lonely Planet's *Walking in Italy* guide, or hiking maps can be downloaded at www.amalficoastweb.com and www.grottedellangelo.sa.it. Another reliable regional hiking map is the CAI (Club Alpino Italiano; Italian Alpine Club) *Monti Lattari, Penisola Sorrentina, Costiera Amalfitana: Carta dei Sentieri* (€8) at 1:30,000. If you prefer a guided hike, contact the **Comunità Montana Peninsula Amalfitana** (☎ 089 87 63 54), which organises guided walks in the region and can provide information about local trails.

peeking from above every arch. Above the main altar is a 13th-century Byzantine Black Madonna and Child.

Just west of here and now a luxury hotel, **Palazzo Murat** (☎ 089 875 51 77; www.palazzomurat.it; Via dei Mulini 23) may be beyond your budget to stay, but you can still visit the stunning flower-filled courtyard, have a drink in the vine-draped patio and contemplate the short, tragic life of flamboyant Joachim Murat, the 18th-century French king of Naples who had the palace built as a summer residence for himself and his wife, Caroline Bonaparte.

♣ MUSIC ON THE ROCKS // DON THE GLAD RAGS FOR PARTY TIME
Unless the idea of parading up and down with a cashmere sweater draped over your shoulders turns you on, Positano's nightlife, overall, is not going to do much for you. More piano bar than warehouse, it's genteel, sophisticated and safe. An exception is the town's only genuine nightspot and one of the best clubs on the coast, **Music on the Rocks** (☎ 089 87 58 74; www.musicontherocks.it; Via Grotte dell'Incanto 51; admission €10-25) is dramatically carved into the tower at the eastern end of Spiaggia Grande. Join the good-looking crowd and some of the region's top DJs spinning mainstream house and reliable disco.

♣ FRANCO SENESI // ADMIRE EXCEPTIONAL MODERN ART
Nestled between the colourful boutiques and lemon-themed ceramics shops, **Franco Senesi** (☎ 089 87 52 57; www.francosenesifineart.com; Via dei Mulini 19) is a light and airy exhibition space with several rooms showcasing over 20 Italian modern artists and sculptors. You can walk around here without being hassled, admiring (and buying?) art works that are sufficiently varied to suit most tastes. They

range from exquisite life drawings to colourful surrealistic landscapes and edgy abstract sculptures. Shipping can be arranged.

♣ BLUE STAR // VISIT THE SIRENS' ISLANDS BY BOAT
Operating out of a kiosk on Spiaggia Grande, **Blue Star** (☎ 089 81 18 89; www.bluestarpositano.it; Spiaggia Grande; ☼ 9am-8pm Easter-Nov) hires out small motorboats for around €55 per hour. Consider heading for the archipelago of Li Galli, the four small islands where, according to Homer, the sirens lived. At Gullo Lungo, near a watchtower you will spy a crumbling villa, the former home of Rudolf Nureyev. The company also organises excursions to Capri and the Grotta dello Smeraldo (see p188). A similar company, **L'Uomo e il Mare** (☎ 089 81 16 13; www.gennaroesalvatore.it; ☼ 9am-8pm Easter-Nov) is operated by an English-Italian couple from a kiosk near the ferry terminal. It offers a range of tours including Capri and Amalfi day trips (€80, including lunch) and a romantic sunset cruise, complete with champagne (€24), to Li Galli.

♣ CENTRO SUB COSTIERA AMALFITANA // MEMORABLE MOONLIGHT DIVES
Over on Spiaggia del Fornillo, **Centro Sub Costiera Amalfitana** (☎ 089 81 21 48; www.centrosub.it; ⚓) is the place to go if you are into diving (€60 for two hours). This well-respected local outfit also offers lessons for adults and children over eight years, as well as night dives and full days with snacks on board.

♣ VIA POSITANESI D'AMERICA // TAKE A PRETTY SEASIDE STROLL
This is a pretty, short and undemanding walk with (hooray!) an acceptable

number of steps. Facing the sea, head right of Spiaggia Grande, where you will spy a staircase that leads to Via Positanesi d'America. Walk past the Torre Trasita, one of the coast's many medieval watchtowers built to warn inhabitants of pirate raids and now a private residence. Continue as the path passes dramatic rock formations and tiny inlets of turquoise water and bobbing boats until you reach the attractive Spiaggia di Fornillo with its welcoming terrace bar serving cold drinks and gelati.

GASTRONOMIC HIGHLIGHTS

Unfortunately, your Positano experience is unlikely to include the best meal of your trip. Most restaurants, bars and trattorias are unashamedly touristy, geared to turning over numbers rather than turning out top-quality food. This doesn't mean that you can't eat well here, more that you will have to pay a premium to do so. Overall, the nearer you get to the seafront, especially to Spiaggia Grande, the more expensive everything becomes. Many places close over winter, making a brief reappearance for Christmas and New Year.

☙ BUCA DI BACCO €
☎ 089 81 14 61; Viale del Brigantino 35-37; snacks around €5

This is the most convenient snack bar for sunbathers on Spiaggia Grande. You'll find the usual range of calorific snacks including well-stuffed *panini*, slices of pizza, crepes, *cornetti* and reliably good ice creams. Seating is limited, but no worries: you can always picnic on the nearby steps or sand. Drinks and cocktails are also served.

☙ DA COSTANTINO €
☎ 089 87 57 38; Via Montepertuso; meals €20, pizzas from €4; ☙ closed Wed

You will certainly work up an appetite on the steep climb up to Costantino's. One of the few authentic trattorias in Positano (OK, technically it's in Montepertuso), it serves honest, down-to-earth Italian grub. The house speciality, apart from the amazing views, is *scialatielli* (ribbon pasta) served with aubergines, tomato and mozzarella. There are also excellent pizzas and a selection of failsafe grilled meats.

☙ DA VINCENZO €€
☎ 089 87 51 28; Viale Pasitea 172-178; meals €35; ☙ Apr-Nov, closed lunch Tue Jul & Aug

Superbly prepared dishes are served here by the third generation of restaurateurs. The emphasis is on fish dishes, which range from the adventurous, like grilled octopus tentacles skewered with deep-fried artichokes, to seasonal pasta dishes like spaghetti with broad beans and fresh ricotta. Enjoy twanging Neapolitan guitarists during the summer months and be sure to try co-owner Marcella's legendary desserts, which are widely considered to be the best in town.

☙ DONNA ROSA €€
☎ 089 81 18 06; Via Montepertuso 97-99; meals €38 ☙ Wed-Mon Apr-Dec

This is where locals in the know come to eat homemade pasta and superb seafood. Once a humble trattoria and now run by two sisters, it has evolved into an elegant romantic restaurant with some of the best food – and views – on the coast. Particularly sought after is the handmade pasta, such as *fusilli al ragù con salsiccia e mozzarella* (pasta twists with meat sauce, sausage and mozzarella) or *scialatielli zucchini e vongole* (eggless pasta with clams and courgettes). The desserts are also excellent, particularly the hot chocolate soufflé. Book ahead.

♥ LO GUARRACINO €€

☎ 089 87 57 94; Via Positanesi d'America; meals €30, pizzas from €8.50; ☺ Mar-Dec

It's difficult to beat the location of this cliff-side restaurant. On the scenic path connecting Positano's two beaches, it's a memorable place to eat even if you're more likely to remember the unfettered sea views than the straightforward food. The menu is seafood heavy, with dishes such as grilled swordfish and *tagliatelle verdi ai frutti di mare* (green pasta with seafood). If those don't appeal there are also pizzas and steaks. It's a popular spot, so if possible book ahead.

♥ RISTORANTE BRUNO €€

☎ 089 87 53 92; Via Cristoforo Colombo 157; meals €28; ☺ closed lunch Thu & Feb-Oct

Although the decor is unimaginative, the food here is anything but average. Bag a table across the street and you can enjoy *the* view of Positano while enjoying specialties of the house such as the antipasto of marinated fish with vegetables, orange and Parmesan, followed by a *primo* of linguine with clams, courgettes and *pecorino* cheese. For a main course keep it simple with grilled fish and a wedge of local lemon. The wine list offers an ample choice of Italian labels.

♥ RISTORANTE IL SARACENO D'ORO €€

☎ 089 81 20 50; Viale Pasitea 254; meals €25, pizzas from €5; ☺ Mar-Oct

There is something so typically Italian about the setup of this restaurant, where waiters have to dash to and fro across the road with their dishes. But in the evening the traffic is light and the wacky layout will only add to the delight of eating here. The pizza and pasta choices are good; the *contorni* excellent (the grilled-vegetable antipasto makes a good choice

for vegetarians). Splurge on the legendary profiteroles in chocolate sauce for dessert. The complimentary end-of-meal glass of *limoncello* is a nice touch.

♥ RISTORANTE MAX €€

☎ 089 87 50 56; Via dei Mulini 22; meals €40; ☺ Mar-Nov

Here you can peruse the art work while choosing your dish. This established restaurant is popular with local ladies who lunch, with a menu including set meals and specials of the day, such as ravioli with clams and asparagus, and zucchini flowers stuffed with ricotta and salmon. Cooking courses are available in summer.

RECOMMENDED SHOPS

You can't miss Positano's colourful boutiques – everywhere you look, shop displays scream out at you in a riot of exuberant colour. After a while, though, your eyes may glaze over at the sameness of the clothes on sale. The humble lemon also enjoys star status; it's not just in *limoncello* and lemon-infused candles, but emblazoned on tea towels, aprons and pottery.

♥ ARTIGIANATO RALLO

☎ 089 81 17 11; Viale Pasitea 96; ☺ 10am-9.30pm Apr-Oct, to 6pm Nov-Mar

Run by the third generation of a Sorrentine shoemaker's family, this small shop sells an attractive range of handmade leather sandals in various funky and traditional designs and colours. If you don't see anything you fancy you can always have a pair made to order. Prices start at around €35 and the quality is fantastic.

♥ LOUISE

☎ 089 87 51 92; Via dei Mulini 22; ☺ Oct-May

Positano's most famous shop is a riot of brilliant floral-patterned dresses, shirts,

THE AMALFI COAST

skirts and scarves in predominantly blue and green (who said they should never be seen?). These distinctive garments have been designed and made here for 40 years under the watchful eye of Louise, the doyenne of Positano fashion. You should be able to pick up a wonderful feather-light dress for around €60.

♨ UMBERTO CARRO

☎ 089 87 53 52; Viale Pasitea 98; ☾ Oct-May
On offer here is a sumptuous display of locally produced ceramics to stress you – and your hand luggage – at check-in time; a better bet is to go for the shipping option. The colours and designs are subtle and classy, and a wide range of pieces is available, ranging from magnificent urns to minute eggcups and quirky, brightly coloured ceramic animals and ornaments.

TRANSPORT

BOAT // Positano has excellent ferry connections to the coastal towns and islands from April to October. Ferries all sail from/to the terminal to the west of Spiaggia Grande. **Linee Marittime Partenopee** (☎ 081 704 19 11; www.consorziolmp.it; Via Guglielmo Melisurgo 4, Naples) runs ferries/hydrofoils from Capri to Positano (€16.50/14.50), and **Positano Jet** (☎ 089 87 50 32; Spaggia Grande, Positano) operates three daily hydrofoils to Capri (€17).

BUS // About 16km west of Amalfi and 18km from Sorrento, Positano is on the main SS163 coastal road. In fact, it's just beneath the road, so if you arrive by bus you might have to ask the driver where to get off. There are two main bus stops: coming from Sorrento and the west, it's opposite Bar Internazionale; arriving from Amalfi and the east, it's at the top of Via Cristoforo Colombo. To get into town from the former, follow Viale Pasitea; from the latter, take Via Cristoforo Colombo. When departing, buy bus tickets at Bar Internazionale or, if headed east, from the *tabaccheria* (tobacconist) at the bottom of Via Cristoforo Colombo. **SITA** (☎ 199 73 07 49; www.sitabus.it, in Italian) runs frequent buses to/from Amalfi

and Sorrento. The local **Flavia Gioia** (☎ 089 81 30 77; Via Cristoforo Colombo 49) buses follow the lower ring road every half-hour. Stops are clearly marked and you can buy your ticket (€1.10) on board. The Flavia Gioia buses pass by both SITA bus stops. There are also 17 daily buses up to Montepertuso and Nocelle.

CAR & MOTORCYCLE // By car, take the A3 autostrada to Vietri sul Mare and then follow the SS163 coastal road. To hire a scooter, try **Positano Rent a Scooter** (☎ 089 812 20 77; Viale Pasitea 99; per day from €50). Don't forget that you will need to produce a driving licence and passport.

PARKING // Parking here is no fun in summer. There are some parking meters (€3 per hour) and a handful of expensive private car parks. **Parcheggio da Anna** (Viale Pasitea 173; per day €18) is located just before the Pensione Maria Luisa, at the top of town. Nearer the beach and centre, **Di Gennaro** (Via Pasitea 1; per day €23) is near the bottom of Via Cristoforo Colombo.

PRAIANO

An ancient fishing village and low-key summer resort, Praiano is the archetypal coastal community. With no centre as such, its whitewashed houses pepper the verdant ridge of Monte Sant'Angelo as it slopes towards Capo Sottile. Formerly an important silk-production centre, it was a favourite of the Amalfi doges (dukes), who made it their summer residence.

EXPLORING PRAIANO

Praiano is 120m above sea level, and exploring equals lots of steps. There are also several trails that start from town, including a scenic walk – particularly stunning at sunset – that leaves from beside the San Gennaro church and descends to the **Spiaggia della Gavitelli** beach to the west of town, carrying on to the medieval defensive Torre di Grado. To the east of the centre lies the pretty Marina di Praia (see opposite). In the upper village the 16th-century **Chiesa di San Luca** (☎ 089 87 41 65; Via Oratorio 1) features an impressive majolica floor, paintings by the 16th-century artist Giovanni Bernardo Lama and a late 17th-century bust of St Luke the Evangelist.

❦ MARINA DI PRAIA // CHECK OUT THE PICTURESQUE MARINA

But it's for the small beach that most people stop off here. From the SS163 (next to the Hotel Continentale) a steep path leads down the cliffs to a tiny inlet with a small stretch of coarse sand and very tempting water; the best is actually off the rocks just before you get to the bottom. In what were once fishermen's houses, you'll also find a couple of bars and a very decent fish restaurant. You can also rent boats from here.

❦ AFRICANA // GO NIGHTCLUBBING IN A CAVE

Another famous club in these parts is located just west of Marina di Praia. **Africana** (☎ 089 81 11 71; ☻ Fri & Sat May–Sep) has a cave setting and glass dance floor over the grotto could well provide the most memorable boogie of your life. Shuttle buses run regularly from Positano,

Amalfi and Mairori during summer. Check at the tourist office for a timetable.

If you want to see the cave up close and personal, swim in from just below the club's entrance.

❦ DA ARMANDINO // BEACHSIDE DINING ON FRESH, FRESH FISH

If you're a seafood lover, head for this widely acclaimed restaurant located in a former boatyard on the beach in Marina di Praia. **Da Armandino** (☎ 089 87 40 87; Via Praia 1; meals €35; ☻ Apr–Nov) is great for fish fresh off the boat. There is a menu, but you'd do as well just to agree to whatever the waiter suggests as the dish of the day – it's all excellent. *Contorni* such as *melanzane ripiene* (aubergine stuffed with rice) and *zucchini alla scapece* (marinated courgettes) are mainstays. The holiday atmosphere and appealing setting – at the foot of sheer cliffs towering up to the main road – round things off nicely.

FURORE

Marina di Furore, a tiny fishing village, was once a busy little commercial centre, although it's difficult to believe

NOCELLE

A tiny, still relatively isolated mountain village, Nocelle (450m) commands some of the most spectacular views on the entire coast. A world apart from touristy Positano, it's a sleepy, silent place where not much ever happens and none of the few residents would ever want it to.

If you want to stay, consider delightful **Villa degli Dei** (☎ 0898 12 35 10; www.villadegli dei.com; r €78-156; ☒), located past the **Trattoria Santa Croce** (☻ lunch & dinner summer), an excellent low-key restaurant in the main part of the village. Keep walking until you see the ceramic sign by the entrance.

The easiest way to get to Nocelle is by local bus from Positano (€1.10, 30 minutes, 17 daily). If you're driving, follow the signs from Positano. Hikers tackling the Sentieri degli Dei (see the boxed text, p180) might want to stop off as they pass through.

that today. In medieval times, its unique natural position freed it from the threat of foreign raids and provided a ready source of water for its flour and paper mills.

Originally founded by Romans fleeing barbarian incursions, it sits at the bottom of what's known as the fjord of Furore, a giant cleft that cuts through the Lattari mountains. The main village, however, stands 300m above, in the upper Vallone del Furore. A one-horse place that sees few tourists at any time of the year, it exudes a distinctly rural air despite the colourful murals and unlikely modern sculpture.

To get to upper Furore by car, follow the SS163 and then the SS366 signposts to Agerola; from Positano, it's 15km. Otherwise, regular SITA buses depart from the bus terminus in Amalfi (€1.10, 30 minutes, 17 daily).

AMALFI

pop 5527

It is hard to grasp that pretty little Amalfi, with its sun-filled piazzas and small beach, was once a maritime superpower with a population of more than 70,000. For one thing, it's not a big place – you can easily walk from one end to the other in about 20 minutes. For another, there are very few historical buildings of note. The explanation is chilling – most of the old city, and its populace, simply slid into the sea during an earthquake in 1343.

Today, although the resident population is a fairly modest 5000 or so, the numbers swell significantly during summer, when day trippers pour in by the coach load. Just around the headland, neighbouring **Atrani** is a picturesque tangle of whitewashed alleys and arches centred on a lively, lived-in piazza and popular beach.

Amalfi's **Tourist Office** (☎ 089 87 11 07; www.amalfitouristoffice.it; Corso delle Repubbliche Marinare 33; ⏱ 8.30am-1.30pm & 3-5.15pm Mon-Fri, 8.30am-noon Sat Sep-Jun, 8.30am-1.30pm & 3-7.15pm Mon-Fri, 8.30am-noon Sat Jul & Aug) is good for bus and ferry timetables.

ORIENTATION

Buses and boats drop you off at Amalfi's main transport hub, Piazza Flavio Gioia. From here cross the road and duck through to Piazza del Duomo, the town's focal square, with its majestic cathedral. Most of the hotels and restaurants are in the tangled lanes either side of the main strip, Via Lorenzo d'Amalfi, and its continuation, Via Capuano, which snake north from the cathedral. On the seafront, Corso delle Repubbliche Marinare follows the coast east, becoming Via Pantaleone Comite as it bends round to the Saracen tower on the headland. Continue down the other side, through the tunnel and off to the right for Atrani.

EXPLORING AMALFI

To try a glean a sense of the town's medieval history, get off the main street and explore the narrow parallel streets with their covered porticos and historic shrine niches. Amalfi also has a beautiful seaside setting; it's the perfect spot for long, lingering lunches.

For all its seafaring history, Amalfi is not a great place to swim. The town's beach, Spiaggia Grande, consists of about 150m of coarse sand and is not very appealing, even though it's highly popular with visitors, who throng to the private bathing facilities off Corso delle Repubbliche Marinare. About a 15-minute walk away, Atrani's small, dark-sand beach is a more tempting option.

♥ CATTEDRALE DI SANT'ANDREA // OGLE THIS ICONIC STRIPY CATHEDRAL

You can't miss Amalfi's fabulous **cathedral** (☎ 089 87 10 59; Piazza del Duomo; ⏰ 9am-7pm Apr-Jun, to 9pm Jul-Sep, 9.30am-5.15pm Oct & Mar, 10am-1pm & 2.30-4.30pm Nov-Feb), an imposing sight at the top of its sweeping flight of stairs. Like Rome's famous Spanish steps, the steps are usually crowded with idle tourists, boisterous students and chattering locals and make a great 'wish-you-were-here' holiday-pic backdrop.

The cathedral dates in part from the early 10th century, and its striking stripy facade has been rebuilt twice, most recently at the end of the 19th century. Although the building is a hybrid, the Sicilian Arabic-Norman style predominates, particularly in the two-tone masonry and the 13th-century bell tower. The huge bronze doors also merit a look – the first of their type in Italy, they were commissioned by a local noble and made in Syria before being shipped to Amalfi. Less impressive is the baroque interior, although the altar

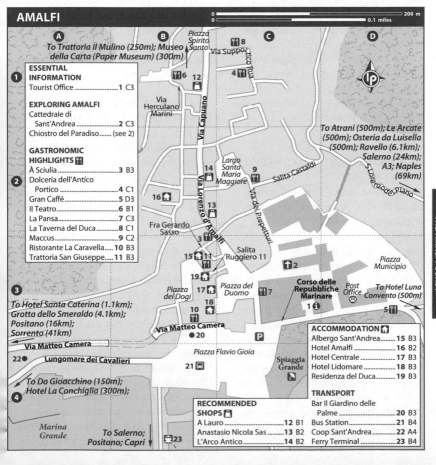

AMALFI

0 — 200 m
0 — 0.1 miles

ESSENTIAL INFORMATION
Tourist Office 1 C3

EXPLORING AMALFI
Cattedrale di Sant'Andrea 2 C3
Chiostro del Paradiso .... (see 2)

GASTRONOMIC HIGHLIGHTS 🍴
À Sciulia 3 B3
Dolcería dell'Antíco Portico 4 C1
Gran Caffè 5 D3
Il Teatro 6 B1
La Pansa 7 C3
La Taverna del Duca 8 C1
Maccus 9 C2
Ristorante La Caravella 10 B3
Trattoria San Giuseppe 11 B3

ACCOMMODATION 🏠
Albergo Sant'Andrea 15 B3
Hotel Amalfi 16 B2
Hotel Centrale 17 B3
Hotel Lidomare 18 B3
Residenza del Duca 19 B3

TRANSPORT
Bar Il Giardino delle Palme 20 B3
Bus Station 21 B4
Coop Sant'Andrea 22 A4
Ferry Terminal 23 B4

RECOMMENDED SHOPS 🛍
A Lauro 12 B1
Anastasio Nicola Sas 13 B2
L'Arco Antico 14 B2

To Trattoria Il Mulino (250m); Museo della Carta (Paper Museum) (300m)

Piazza Spirito Santo
Via Suppor...
Via Capuano
Via Herculano Marini
Largo Santa Maria Maggiore
Via Lorenzo d'Amalfi
Fra Gerardo Sasso
Salita Castaldi
Via del Prepotturi
Salita Ruggiero 11
Piazza del Duomo
Piazza dei Dogi
Corso delle Repubbliche Marinare
Post Office
Piazza Municipio
To Atrani (500m); Le Arcate (500m); Osteria da Luisella (500m); Ravello (6.1km); Salerno (24km); A3; Naples (69km)
S Lorenzo de Piano
To Hotel Luna Convento (500m)

To Hotel Santa Caterina (1.1km); Grotta dello Smeraldo (4.1km); Positano (16km); Sorrento (41km)

Via Matteo Camera
Lungomare dei Cavalieri
To Da Gioacchino (150m); Hotel La Conchiglia (300m);
Marina Grande
To Salerno; Positano; Capri
Piazza Flavio Gioia
Spiaggia Grande

THE AMALFI COAST

features some fine statues and there are some interesting 12th- and 13th-century mosaics. In high season, entrance to the cathedral between 10am and 5pm is through the adjacent Chiostro del Paradiso, meaning that you have to pay an entrance fee of €2.50.

To the left of the cathedral's porch, the **Chiostro del Paradiso** (☎ 089 87 13 24; adult/child €2.50/1; ⊙ 9am-7pm Jun-Oct, to 1pm & 2.30-4.30pm Nov-May) is well worth the small admission charge. Built in 1266 to house the tombs of Amalfi's prominent citizens, it's a magical Moorish-style cloister: 120 marble columns support a series of tall, slender Arabic arches around a central garden. From the cloisters, go through to the Basilica del Crocefisso, where you'll find various religious artefacts displayed in glass cabinets, and some fading 14th-century frescoes. Beneath lies the 1206 crypt containing the remains of Sant'Andrea.

♣ MUSEO DELLA CARTA // EXPLORE A HISTORICAL PAPER HEAVYWEIGHT

Amalfi's fascinating **Paper Museum** (☎ 089 830 45 61; www.museodellacarta.it; Via delle Cartiere; admission €4; ⊙ 10am-6.30pm Apr–mid-Nov, to 3pm Tue, Wed & Fri-Sun rest of yr) is housed in a 13th-century paper mill (the oldest in Europe). It lovingly preserves the original paper presses, which are still in full working order, as you'll see during the 15-minute guided tour (in English). Afterwards you may well be inspired to pick up some of the stationery that is sold in the gift shop and just perfect for that travel journal you keep vowing to write. You can also buy paper products via the museum website, including handmade-paper wedding invitations (you supply the printing details).

♣ DA GIOACCHINO // CRUISE THE WATERS IN STYLE

If you're absolutely intent on going for a swim, you're better off hiring a boat. You'll find a number of operators along Lungomare dei Cavalieri, including **Da Gioacchino** (☎ 328 649 41 92; www.amalfi boats.it; Spiaggia del Porto, Lungomare dei Cavalieri), run by charismatic ex-chef Gioacchino Esposito. You can hire a boat without a skipper – no nautical licence is required. Gioacchino can help you decide which kind of boat would be best, depending on time and distance, and direct you to quiet coves and beaches. There are also organised excursions along the coast and to the islands, including to Capri, Ischia, Procida, Maiori and Cetara. Prices begin at around €50 for two hours' boat hire.

♣ GROTTA DELLO SMERALDO // A HAUNTING NATURAL GROTTO

Four kilometres west of Amalfi, Conca dei Marini is home to one of the coast's most popular sights. Named after the eerie emerald colour that emanates from the water, the **Grotta dello Smeraldo** (admission €6; ⊙ 9am-4pm Mar-Oct, to 3pm Nov-Feb) is well worth a visit. Stalactites hang down from the 24m-high ceiling, while stalagmites grow up to 10m tall. Each year, on 24 December and 6 January, skin-divers from all over Italy make their traditional pilgrimage to the ceramic *presepe* (nativity scene) submerged beneath the water.

SITA buses regularly pass the car park above the cave entrance (from where you take a lift or stairs down to the rowing boats). Alternatively, **Coop Sant'Andrea** (☎ 089 87 31 90; www.coopsantandrea.it; Lungomare dei Cavalieri 1) runs two daily boats from Amalfi (€14 return) at 9am and 3.30pm. Allow 1½ hours for the return trip.

GASTRONOMIC HIGHLIGHTS

Inevitably, most of the restaurants in and around Amalfi's centre cater to the tourist trade. But that shouldn't put you off, as standards are generally high and it's rare to eat badly. Most places serve pizza, the best cooked in traditional wood-fired ovens (look for signs advertising *forno a legna*), and a range of pasta, grilled meat and seafood. The Amalfi drinking scene is fairly subdued, revolving around streetside cafes and bars. It gets a tad more boisterous in Atrani, but it's hardly hard-core.

🍴 À SCIULIA €
☎ 339 5893608; Via Fra Gerardo Sasso 2; granitas €5; 🕙 10am-2am Mar–mid-Nov
For the best lemon *granita* in town, head for this brightly coloured hole-in-the-wall. You'll also find sorbets, smoothies, yoghurts and fruit salads, all made on the premises and all truly delicious. Yoghurts cost around €4.50.

🍴 DOLCERÍA DELL' ANTÍCO PORTICO €
☎ 089 87 11 43; Via Supportico Rua 10; cakes from €3
Located under the arches, this place is run by celebrated pastry chef Tiziano Mita, who has worked in Paris and Milan and at the revered Palazzo Sasso in Ravello. Mita applies a contemporary twist to traditional sweet treats, like *sfogliatella* in the form of a *trullo* (conical roofed building unique to Puglia). Olive-oil biscuits, almond pastries and lemon cream cake are similarly delicate and delicious.

🍴 GRAN CAFFÉ €
☎ 089 87 10 47; Corso delle Repubbliche Marinare 37; snacks around €4.50, salads from €6
There is something very Italian riviera about this gracious traditional cafe, which dates from 1936. White-canopied tables with large, cushioned bamboo chairs are set on the wide seafront promenade, while the interior is formal and elegant. Among the light eats there's a choice of 12 salads, including smoked salmon (€8) and *caprese* (€6).

🍴 IL TEATRO €€
☎ 089 87 24 73; Via Herculano Marini 19; meals €25; 🕙 Thu-Tue Feb-Dec
This down-to-earth trattoria is tucked away in the atmospheric backstreets of the *centro storico*. The old-fashioned interior has a series of arches and walls decorated with black-and-white photos and assorted bric-a-brac. Seafood features heavily in dishes such as *ravioli al salmone* (ravioli with salmon) or, a speciality, *pesce spada il teatro* (swordfish in a tomato, caper and olive-oil sauce). But there's also plenty of meat and some good vegetarian options, including ribbon style *scialatielli* pasta with tomatoes and aubergines.

🍴 LA PANSA €
☎ 089 87 10 65; Piazza del Duomo 40; cornetti & pastries from €1.50; 🕙 closed Tue
A stuck-in-a-time-warp cafe on Piazza del Duomo where black-bow-tied waiters serve a great Italian breakfast – freshly made *cornetti* and deliciously frothy cappuccino. If you don't fancy a *cornetto*, there are any number of cakes and pastries to choose from, all made on the premises and all absolutely irresistible.

🍴 LA TAVERNA DEL DUCA €€
☎ 089 87 27 55; Piazza Spirito Santo 26; pizzas from €7, meals €35; 🕙 closed Thu
Grab a chair on the square at this popular restaurant with its fishy reputation. Specials vary according to the catch of the day but might include *carpaccio di*

THE AMALFI COAST

baccalà (thin strips of raw salted cod) or linguine with scampi. Or go for a pasta dish like *pasta fagioli e cozze* (with mussels and beans). There's an excellent antipasti spread ranging in price from €7 for just vegetables (and there are plenty) to €10 including seafood. The interior is elegant, with candles on the tables and tasteful oil paintings on the walls.

♥ LE ARCATE €€

☎ 089 87 13 67; Largo Orlando Buonocore, Atrani; pizzas from €6, meals €25; ☒ closed Mon; ☒

On a sunny day, it's hard to beat the dreamy location – at the far eastern point of the harbour overlooking the beach – with Atrani's ancient rooftops and church tower behind you. Huge white parasols shade the sprawl of tables, while the dining room is a stone-walled natural cave. Pizzas are served at night, while daytime fare includes risotto with seafood and grilled swordfish; the food is good, but it's a step down from the setting.

♥ MACCUS €€

☎ 089 873 63 85; Largo Santa Maria Maggiore 1-3; meals €40, set menu €14; ☒ closed Tue

The evocative piazza setting, complete with ancient church tower, and an elegant, intimate interior set Maccus apart. The menu, which changes according to the chef's morning shop, features plenty of seafood, such as meaty swordfish served with tomato and olive oil or *paccheri* (big tubes of pasta) with scorpion fish. Desserts are original and tasty – try the Coppa Maccus, a rich mix of sponge, mascarpone, rum, *torrone* and amaretto.

♥ OSTERIA DA LUISELLA €€

☎ 089 87 10 87; Piazza Umberto I, Atrani; meals €30; ☒ closed Wed

All the right ingredients are here: great food, great people-watching, and an atmospheric setting. Situated under the arches in Atrani's Piazza Umberto I, this *osteria* serves excellent regional fare with an emphasis on seafood. The menu often changes, but if they're on, the warm seafood salad and the *cassuola* (octopus stew) are scrumptious. Vegetarians might go for the *caporalessa*, a tasty baked concoction of aubergines, tomatoes and cheese. The wine is good and the service laid-back but efficient.

♥ RISTORANTE LA CARAVELLA €€€

☎ 089 87 10 29; Via Matteo Camera 12; meals €60, tasting menu €75; ☒ Wed-Mon Jan–mid-Nov

One of the few places in Amalfi where you pay for the food rather than the location, which in this case is far from spectacular – sandwiched between the rushing traffic of the road and the old *arsenale*. But that doesn't worry the discreet, knowledgeable crowd who eat here. The food is regional with either a nouvelle zap, like black ravioli with cuttlefish ink, scampi and ricotta, or unabashedly simple, like the catch of the day served grilled on lemon leaves. Wine aficionados are likely to find something to try on the 15,000-label list.

♥ TRATTORIA IL MULINO €

☎ 089 87 22 23; Via delle Cartiere 36; meals €20, pizzas around €6

Near the Museo della Carta, this is about as authentic a trattoria-pizzeria as you'll find in Amalfi. A TV-in-the-corner, kids-running-between-the-tables sort of place, it's not the restaurant to impress your partner. But if you just want to eat some good, hearty pasta and simple grilled meat or fish, it'll do just fine. The *scialatielli alla pescatore* (ribbon pasta with prawns, mussels, tomato and parsley) is much recommended, as is the *calamari in cassualoa* (squid stew). Service is pretty slow, but prices are fair.

THE AMALFI COAST

☙ TRATTORIA SAN GIUSEPPE €€
☎ 089 87 26 40; Salita Ruggiero II 4; meals €24, pizzas from €6; ⊘ closed Thu

Enjoying an atmospheric location hidden away under an arch in Amalfi's labyrinthine alleyways, this trattoria has the best pizzas in town, some say. Certainly they're good (although not exceptional), with toppings ranging from the traditional *margherita* to marine combos such as clams, prawns and anchovies. Whole-wheat *(integrale)* pizza bases are also, unusually, available, as well as some pasta and seafood dishes. Outside tables may be scented by the smell of antique drains; if so, head into the fan-cooled interior.

RECOMMENDED SHOPS

You'll have no difficulty loading up on souvenirs here – Via Lorenzo d'Amalfi is lined with garish shops selling local ceramic work, artisanal paper gifts and *limoncello*. Prices are set for tourists, so don't expect many bargains.

☙ A LAURO
☎ 089 87 21 13; Via Capuano 27

For a change there's nothing to eat or drink in this shop. But it is a wonderland of inexpensive and quirky gifts and souvenirs, including shell mobiles (from €3), miniature figurines, model boats, coloured glass ornaments, jazzily coloured fabric and leather bags, plus quirky hats and frivolous accessories.

☙ ANASTASIO NICOLA SAS
☎ 089 87 10 07; Via Lorenzo d'Amalfi 32

Unless you're flying to Australia, gourmet goodies can make excellent gifts. Here, among the hanging hams, you'll find a full selection, ranging from local cheese and preserves to coffee, chocolate, *limoncello* and every imaginable shape of

pasta. There's also a collection of fruit-scented soaps and natural shampoos, perfumes and moisturisers.

☙ L'ARCO ANTICO
☎ 089 873 63 54; Via Capuano 4; ⊘ closed Jan & Feb

Amalfi's connection with paper making dates back to the 12th century, when the first mills were set up to supply the republic's small army of bureaucrats. Now little is made here, but you can still buy it and the quality is still good. This attractive shop sells a range of paper products, including beautiful writing paper, leather-bound notebooks and huge photo albums.

TRANSPORT

BOAT // **Alilauro** (☎ 081 497 22 67; www.alilauro.it; Stazione Marittima, Naples) operates ferries from Naples to Amalfi (€13.50, two daily). **Linee Marittime Partenopee** (☎ 081 704 19 11; www.consorziolmp.it; Via Guglielmo Melisurgo 4, Naples) runs frequent daily hydrofoils/ferries from Amalfi to Capri (€17/15). **Metró del Mare** (☎ 199 44 66 44; www.metrodelmare.com) operates summer-only services between Naples and Amalfi (€15, six daily).

BUS // Located in Piazza Flavio Gioia, SITA (☎ 199 73 07 49; www.sitabus.it, in Italian) runs at least 12 buses a day from Piazza Flavio Gioia to Sorrento (via Positano), and also to Ravello, Salerno and Naples. You can buy tickets and check current schedules at **Bar Il Giardino delle Palme** (Piazza Flavio Gioia), opposite the bus stop.

CAR & MOTORCYCLE // If driving from the north, exit the A3 autostrada at Vietri sul Mare and follow the SS163. From the south, leave the A3 at Salerno and head for Vietri sul Mare and the SS163.

PARKING // Parking is a problem in this town, although there are some parking places on Piazza Flavio Gioia near the ferry terminal (€3 per hour), as well as on the coastal road. Failing this, head for the modern residential part of town, away from the sea, for onstreet (free) parking – if you can find it.

THE AMALFI COAST

RAVELLO

pop 2500

Sitting high in the hills above Amalfi, Ravello is a refined, polished town almost entirely dedicated to tourism. Boasting impeccable bohemian credentials – Wagner, DH Lawrence and Virginia Woolf all spent time here – it's today known for its ravishing gardens and stupendous views, the best in the world according to former resident Gore Vidal, and certainly the best on the coast.

Most people visit on a day trip from Amalfi – a nerve-tingling 7km drive up the Valle del Dragone – although to best enjoy its romantic, otherworldly atmosphere you'll need to stay overnight here. On Tuesday morning there's a lively street market in Piazza Duomo, where you'll find wine, mozzarella and olive oil, as well as discounted designer clothes.

The **Tourist Office** (☎ 089 85 70 96; www.ravellotime.it; Via Roma 18bis; ♥ 10am-8pm) has some general information on the town, plus walking maps.

EXPLORING RAVELLO

Even if you have absolutely no sense of direction and a penchant for going round in circles, it's difficult to get lost in this town; everything is clearly signposted from the main Piazza Duomo. Explore the narrow backstreets, however, and you will discover glimpses of a quieter, traditional lifestyle: drystone walls fronting simple homes surrounded by overgrown gardens, neatly planted vegetable plots and languishing cats.

❧ CATHEDRAL // THE SPIRITUAL HEART OF TOWN

Forming the eastern flank of Piazza Duomo, the **cathedral** (Piazza Duomo; ♥ 8.30-1pm & 4.30-8pm) was originally built in 1086 but has since undergone various makeovers. The facade is 16th century, even if the central bronze door, one of only about two dozen in the country, is an 1179 original; the interior is a late 20th-century interpretation of what the original must once have looked like. Of particular interest is the striking pulpit, supported by six twisting columns set on marble lions and decorated with flamboyant mosaics of peacocks, birds and dancing lions. Note also how the floor is tilted towards the square – a deliberate measure to enhance the perspective effect. To the right of the central nave, stairs lead down to the cathedral **museum** (admission €2) and a modest collection of religious artefacts.

❧ VILLAS & GARDENS // HEAVENLY GARDENS WITH HEADY VIEWS

To the south of the cathedral, the 14th-century tower marks the entrance to **Villa Rufolo** (☎ 089 85 76 57; adult/under 12yr & over 65yr €6/3; ♥ 9am-sunset), famous for its beautiful gardens and not to be missed, even if the nearest you get to gardening is growing cress on soggy cotton wool. Created by a Scotsman, Scott Neville Reid, in 1853, they are indeed magnificent, commanding superb views and packed with exotic colours, artistically crumbling towers and luxurious blooms. On seeing them on 26 May 1880, Wagner was moved to write: 'The enchanted garden of Klingsor [setting for the second act of the opera *Parsifal*] has been found'. Today the gardens are used to stage concerts during the town's classical music festival, which could well be a highlight of your trip, if the timing is right (see opposite). The villa itself was built in the 13th century for the wealthy Rufolo dynasty and was home to several popes as well as King Robert of Anjou.

THE AMALFI COAST

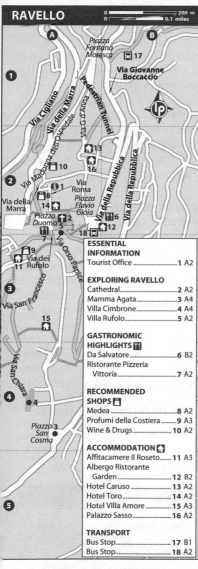

RAVELLO

0   200 m
0   0.1 miles

from an awe-inspiring terrace lined with fake classical busts. Something of a bohemian retreat in its early days, Villa Cimbrone was used by Greta Garbo and her lover Leopold Stokowski as a secret hideaway.

🌳 RAVELLO FESTIVAL // A SUMMER FESTIVAL OF WORLD-CLASS CLASSICAL CONCERTS

Between June and mid-September the **Ravello Festival** (☎ 089 85 83 60; www. ravellofestival.com) turns much of the town centre into a stage. Events ranging from orchestral concerts and chamber music to ballet performances, film screenings and exhibitions are held in atmospheric outdoor venues, most notably the famous overhanging terrace in the Villa Rufolo gardens.

However, you don't have to come in high summer to catch a concert. Ravello's program of classical music begins in March and continues until late October. It reaches its crescendo in June and September with the International Piano Festival and Chamber Music Weeks. Performances by top Italian and international musicians are world class, and the two venues (Villa Rufolo and the Convento di Santa Rosa in Conca dei Marini) are unforgettable. Tickets, bookable by phone, fax or online, start at €20. For further information and reservations, contact the **Ravello Concert Society** (☎ 089 85 81 49; www.ravelloarts.org).

🌳 MAMMA AGATA // LEARN THE SECRETS OF TRADITIONAL ITALIAN DISHES

Apparently Humphrey Bogart made a tradition out of having Mamma Agata's lemon cake (made with *limoncello*) for breakfast when she was cooking for a wealthy American family here back in

Some way east of Piazza Duomo the early 20th-century **Villa Cimbrone** ☎ 089 85 80 72; adult/under 12yr & over 65yr €6/3; 9am-sunset) is also worth a wander, if not or the villa itself (now an upmarket hotel) then for the fabulous views from the delightful gardens. They're best admired

THE AMALFI COAST

the '60s. Other guests of this Hollywood-connected couple included Richard Burton, Frank Sinatra and Audrey Hepburn. Today Mamma Agata offers private cooking classes in her home, producing simple, exceptional food using primarily organic ingredients. A one-day demonstration cooking class at **Mamma Agata** (☎ 089 85 70 19; www.mammaagata.com; Piazza San Cosma 9; €190) will culminate with tasting what's taught on a lovely sea-view terrace.

GASTRONOMIC HIGHLIGHTS

Surprisingly, Ravello doesn't offer many good eating options. It's easy enough to find a bar or cafe selling overpriced *panini* and pizza but not so simple to find a decent restaurant or trattoria. There are a few good hotel restaurants, most of which are open to nonguests, and a couple of excellent restaurants, but not much else. The places listed below get very busy in summer, particularly at lunchtime, and prices are universally high.

❤ DA SALVATORE €€
☎ 089 8572 27; www.salvatoreravello.co; Via della Republicca 2; meals €25; ✆ closed Mon
Located just before the bus stop and the Albergo Ristorante Garden, Da Salvatore

has nothing special by way of decor, but the view – from both the dining room and the large terrace – is very special indeed. Dishes include creative options like tender squid on a bed of pureed chickpeas with spicy *peperoncino*. In the evening, part of the restaurant is transformed into an informal pizzeria, serving some of the best wood-fired pizza you will taste anywhere this side of Naples. Very friendly and low-key, the place is frequented by more locals than tourists.

❤ RISTORANTE PIZZERIA VITTORIA €€
☎ 089 85 79 47; Via dei Rufolo 3; meals €30
Another place with exceptional pizza; here there are some 22 choices on the menu, including the Ravellese, with cherry tomatoes, mozzarella, basil and courgettes. Other dishes include sliced octopus on green salad with olive oil and lemon, and an innovative chickpea and cod antipasto. The atmosphere is one of subdued elegance, with a small outside terrace and grainy historical pics of Ravello on the walls.

RECOMMENDED SHOPS

Limoncello and ceramics are the mainstays of the Amalfi Coast souvenir trade and you'll find both sold here.

THE AMALFI COAST

RAVELLO WALKS

Ravello is the starting point for numerous walks – some of which follow ancient paths through the surrounding Lattari mountains. If you've got the legs for it you can walk down to **Minori** via an attractive route of steps, hidden alleys and olive groves and passing the picturesque hamlet of Torello en route. This walk kicks off just to the left of Villa Rufolo and should take you no more than around 45 minutes. Alternatively, you can head the other way, to Amalfi, via the ancient village of **Scala**. Once a flourishing religious centre with more than a hundred churches, Scala is now a sleepy place where the wind whistles through empty streets, and gnarled locals go patiently about their daily chores. In the central square, the Romanesque **duomo** (Piazza Municipio; ✆ 8am-noon & 5-7pm) retains some of its 12th-century solemnity. Ask at the Ravello tourist office for more walking information.

❦ **MEDEA**

☎ 089 858 62 83; www.medeaceramiche.com; Via della Marra 14; ⊗ 9am-11pm daily May-Oct, to 5pm Mon-Fri Nov-Apr

If you're after something ceramic but are fed up with the ubiquitous range of gaudy yellow fruit bowls then look no further. At this gallery-cum-laboratory-cum-shop you'll find an interesting selection of original, handmade vases, lamps, animals, figurines, plates and tiles. Particularly outstanding are the huge red and black vases by ceramic artist Ugo Marano. And if you're wondering, yes, they cost a bomb – for a 1.7m-high vase expect to fork out in the region of €12,000.

❦ **PROFUMI DELLA COSTIERA**

☎ 089 85 81 67; www.profumidellacostiera.it; Via Trinità 37; ⊗ 8.30am-7pm Apr-Oct, to 5.30pm Nov-Mar

The *limoncello* produced and sold here is made with local lemons. Known to experts as *sfusato amalfitano*, they're enormous – about double the size of a standard lemon. The tot is made according to traditional recipes, so there are no preservatives and no colouring. And it's not just the owners who say so – all bottles carry the IGP (Indicazione Geografica Proteta; Protected Geographical Indication) quality mark.

❦ **WINE & DRUGS**

☎ 089 85 83 63; Via Roma 64

Despite the tongue-in-cheek name, no mind-altering substances are sold here, only *limoncello* and a good selection of local and international wines. There are also complimentary daily tastings. Other products include olive oil and aged (24-year-old) balsamic vinegar. There's another branch in town, but this is the smaller, friendlier option.

TRANSPORT

BUS // SITA (☎ 199 73 07 49; www.sitabus.it, in Italian) operates hourly buses from Amalfi departing from the bus stop on the eastern side of Piazza Flavio Gioia. From the bus stop in Ravello, walk through the short tunnel to Piazza Duomo. Many, but not all, buses stop en route at Scala.

CAR // By car, turn north about 2km east of Amalfi.

PARKING // Vehicles are not permitted in Ravello's town centre, but there's plenty of space in supervised car parks on the perimeter.

MINORI

About 3.5km east of Amalfi, or a steep kilometre-long walk down from Ravello (see the boxed text, opposite), Minori is a small, workaday town, popular with holidaying Italians. Scruffier than its refined coastal cousins Amalfi and Positano, it's no less dependent on tourism yet seems more genuine, with its festive seafront, pleasant beach and noisy traffic jams.

If you want to pick up walking maps then head for the small **Tourist Office** (☎ 089 87 70 87; www.proloco-minori.sa.it; Via Roma 30; ⊗ 9am-noon & 5-8pm Mon-Sat, 9-11am Sun) on the seafront.

❦ **VILLA ROMA ANTIQUARIUM // VISIT A TYPICAL ROMAN HOLIDAY HOME**

Minori's one treasure is the **Villa Roma Antiquarium** (☎ 089 85 28 93; Via Capodipiazza 28; admission free; ⊗ 9am-7pm Jun-Aug, to 6.30pm May & Sep, to 6pm Apr & Oct, to 5.30pm Mar & Nov, to 5pm Feb & Dec, to 4.30pm Jan), the finest Roman ruins on the coast. Overshadowed by modern housing blocks, the 1st-century villa is a typical example of the sort that Roman nobles built as holiday homes in the period before Mt Vesuvius's AD 79 eruption. Maximise your time by concentrating on the best-preserved rooms that surround the garden on the lower

THE AMALFI COAST

THE AMALFI COAST

level. By the entrance there's also a moderately interesting two-room museum exhibiting various artefacts, including a collection of 6th century BC to 6th century AD amphorae. It makes for a nice pit stop on a driving tour of the coast.

CETARA

Just beyond **Erchie** and its beautiful beach (look for the mass of scooters parked by the side of the road), Cetara is a picturesque, tumbledown fishing village with a reputation as a gastronomic hot spot. Since medieval times it has been an important fishing centre and today its deep-sea tuna fleet is considered one of the Mediterranean's most important. At night, fishermen set out in small boats (known as *lampare*) armed with powerful lamps to fish for anchovies. Recently, locals have resurrected the production of what is known as *colatura di alici,* a strong anchovy essence believed to be the descendant of *garum,* the Roman fish seasoning. If you want to stay overnight, or for more information, visit the small **Tourist Office** (☎ 328 015 63 47; Piazza San Francesco 15; ☺ 9am-1pm & 5pm-midnight).

♥ SAGRA DEL TONNO // A THOROUGHLY FISHY FESTIVAL

Each year, in late July or early August, the village pays homage to its main meal tickets in the *sagra del tonno,* a festival dedicated to tuna and anchovies. If you can time your visit accordingly, there are plenty of opportunities for tasting, as well as music and other general festivities. Further details are available from the tourist office (see above). If you miss the festival, no worries, you can pick up a jar of the fishy specialities (usually preserved in olive oil) at local food shops and delis.

♥ AL CONVENTO // SIMPLY THE BEST RESTAURANT IN TOWN

For the money, you'll probably not eat better anywhere else on the coast. With tables set on a lovely shaded terrace above Cetara's main street (follow the signs up the steps), **Al Convento** (☎ 089 26 10 39; Piazza San Francesco 16; meals €20; ☺ daily mid-May–Sep, closed Wed Oct–mid-May) is an excellent spot to tuck into some local fish specialities. You can eat *tagliata di tonna alle erbe* (strips of lightly grilled tuna with herbs) as an antipasto, or anchovies prepared in various ways. Particularly delicious is the *spaghetti con alici e finocchietto selavatrico* (spaghetti served with anchovies and wild fennel). For dessert you must try the deliciously decadent chocolate cake with ricotta and cream.

VIETRI SUL MARE

Marking the end of the coastal road, Vietri sul Mare (Vietri) is the ceramics capital of Campania. Production dates back to Roman times, but it took off on an industrial scale in the 16th and 17th centuries with the development of high, three-level furnaces. The unmistakable local style – bold brush strokes and strong Mediterranean colours – found favour in the royal court of Naples, which became one of Vietri's major clients. Later, in the 1920s and '30s, an influx of international artists (mainly Germans) led to a shake-up of traditional designs. There's a moderately helpful **Tourist Office** (☎ 089 21 12 85; Piazza Matteotti; ☺ 10am-1pm & 5-8pm Mon-Fri, 10am-1pm Sat) near the entrance to the *centro storico.* Vietri's small and not unattractive historic centre is packed with decorative tiled-front shops selling ceramic wares of every description.

♥ MUSEO DELLA CERAMICA // GET THE CERAMICS HISTORY LOW-DOWN

For more on Vietri's ceramics past, head to this **museum** (☎ 089 21 18 35; Villa Guerriglia; admission free; 🕒 8am-1.15pm & 2-3pm Tue-Sat, 9am-1pm Sun), in the nearby village of Raito. Housed in a lovely villa surrounded by a park, the museum has a comprehensive collection, including pieces from the so-called German period (1929–47), when the town attracted an influx of artists, mainly from Germany.

♥ CERAMICA ARTISTICA SOLIMENE // HIT A CERAMICS SHOPOHOLIC'S HEAVEN

The most famous ceramics shop in town, **Ceramica Artistica Solimene** (☎ 089 21 02 43; www.solimene.com; Via Madonna degli Angeli 7) is a vast factory outlet selling everything from eggcups to ornamental mermaids, mugs to lamps. Even if you don't go in it's worth having a look at the shop's extraordinary glass and ceramic facade. It was designed by Italian architect Paoli Soleri, who studied under the famous Californian 'organic' architect Frank Lloyd Wright.

THE AMALFI COAST

SALERNO & THE CILENTO

3 PERFECT DAYS

🌱 DAY 1 // FROM ANCIENT HISTORY TO BEACHSIDE DINING

Wander the crumbling backstreets of Salerno's small *centro storico* (historic centre; p204) in the morning and enjoy a midmorning cappuccino in a typical hung-with-washing piazza. Hop on a train or drive to Paestum (p207) for an early lunch and an afternoon visiting its magical temples. In the evening continue south to Agropoli (p217) for sunset and dinner by the beach.

🌱 DAY 2 // ENJOY CILENTO'S SCENIC SHORES

Stretch your legs with a morning stroll along Agropoli's sweeping promenade. Visit the castle and pretty *centro storico* (p216) before continuing south along this dramatic coastline of hidden coves and high cliffs. Stop for a swim, a snack or a stroll at small Italian resorts like Acciaroli (p218), a favourite of Ernest Hemingway's, ending the day in the picturesque coastal town of Palinuro (p220).

🌱 DAY 3 // EXPLORE HIDDEN CAVES AND GROTTOES

It's not half as famous as its Capri cousin, but Palinuro's Grotta Azzurra (Blue Grotto; p220) is just as spectacular. Next, head inland into the Parco Nazionale del Cilento and two otherworldly caves, the Grotta di Castelcivita (p212), one of the largest cave complexes in Europe, and the equally tantalising Grotta dell'Angelo (p213) in Pertosa, where your tour includes the added adventure of a boat ride. Stay overnight at one of the park's superb *agriturismi* (farm-stay accommodation; p288).

SALERNO

· · · · · ·

pop 56,749

Salerno may seem like a bland big city after the Amalfi Coast's glut of postcard-pretty towns, but the place has a charming, if gritty, individuality with its compact centro storico and pleasant seafront promenade. One of Campania's five regional capitals and a major port, it was left in tatters by the heavy fighting that followed the 1943 landings of the American Fifth Army.

Concentrate your time in the *centro storico*, where medieval churches share space with neighbourhood trattorias, neon-lit wine bars and trendy tattoo parlours. Salerno is also a major transport hub and you might well find yourself passing through en route to Paestum (p207) and the Cilento coast.

Originally an Etruscan and later a Roman colony, Salerno flourished with the arrival of the Normans in the 11th century. Robert Guiscard made it the capital of his dukedom in 1076 and, under his patronage, the Scuola Medica Salernitana was renowned as one of medieval Europe's greatest medical institutes. The city recently invested €12.5 million in various urban regeneration programs centred on the *centro storico*, under the watchful eye of Oriol Bohigas, who was similarly involved in Barcelona's earlier makeover.

ESSENTIAL INFORMATION

EMERGENCIES // Police station (☎ 089 61 31 11; Piazza Amendola 16)
TOURIST INFORMATION // Tourist Office (☎ 089 23 14 32; Piazza Vittorio Veneto 1; ⏲ 9am-2pm & 3-8pm Mon-Sat Sep-Jun, 9am-2pm & 3-8pm Mon-Sat, 9am-12.30pm & 5-7.30pm Sun Jul & Aug)

ORIENTATION

Salerno's train station is on Piazza Vittorio Veneto, at the eastern end of town. Many intercity buses stop here and there are a number of hotels nearby. Salerno's

SALERNO & THE CILENTO ACCOMMODATION

While Salerno doesn't have a great choice of accommodation, the Cilento coastal region and park have a refreshingly diverse range of places to lay your head. Mountain-top, discreet *palazzi*, breezy beachfront hotels and ecofriendly *agriturismi* should cater to most tastes – and prices are considerably lower than those on the Amalfi Coast. For a fuller listing of options, see the Salerno section of the Accommodation chapter, p286.

★ Decorative painted furniture, canopy beds and quirky artwork and decor…B&B **Antichi Feudi** (p289) guarantees a memorable stay

★ Surrounded by rolling hills, grapevines and grazing pastures, **Agriturismo i Moresani** (p288) is a stunningly positioned Cilento *agriturismo*

★ Paestum's **Calypso** (p286) serves organic food, organises spiritual retreats and has suitably inspiring surroundings

★ Overlooking the sea at Santa Maria di Castellbate, **Villa Sirio** (p288) combines old-world elegance with modern panache

★ There's an appealing historic feel about Castellbate's **Albergo il Castello** (p287), with its original tile work and lofty beamed ceilings

SALERNO & THE CILENTO

SALERNO & THE CILENTO

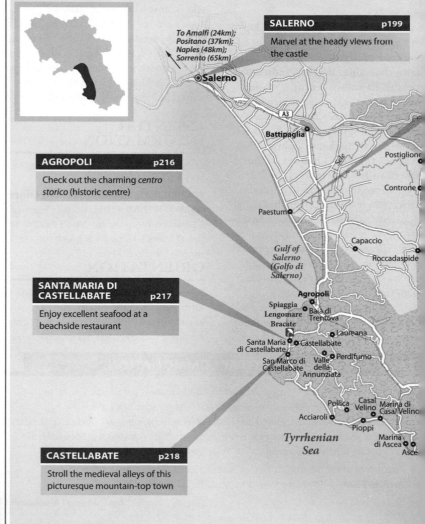

SALERNO   p199
Marvel at the heady views from the castle

To Amalfi (24km);
Positano (37km);
Naples (48km);
Sorrento (65km)

AGROPOLI   p216
Check out the charming *centro storico* (historic centre)

SANTA MARIA DI CASTELLABATE   p217
Enjoy excellent seafood at a beachside restaurant

CASTELLABATE   p218
Stroll the medieval alleys of this picturesque mountain-top town

GETTING AROUND

Salerno is on the ferry route from Naples and Sorrento, plus the Amalfi coastal resorts and islands in the summer. The main Cilento coastal resorts can be reached by train and/or bus; however, renting a car will provide the flexibility to explore the smaller villages and the magnificent Parco Nazionale del Cilento e Vallo di Diano (Cilento National Park and the Valley of Diana) inland, where the bus service is sporadic and many smaller villages are only accessible by car.

SALERNO & THE CILENTO

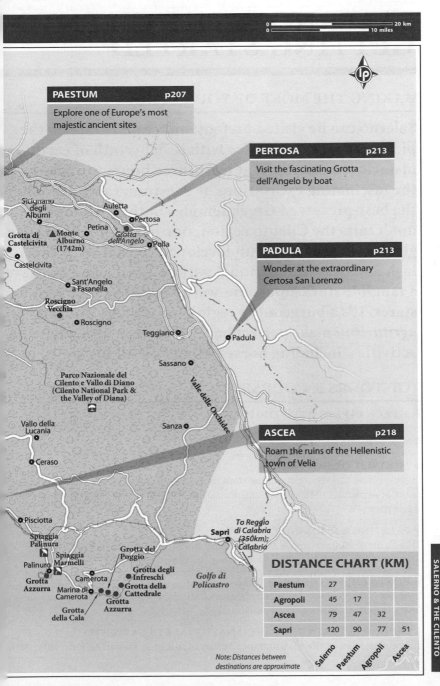

PAESTUM p207

Explore one of Europe's most majestic ancient sites

PERTOSA p213

Visit the fascinating Grotta dell'Angelo by boat

PADULA p213

Wonder at the extraordinary Certosa San Lorenzo

ASCEA p218

Roam the ruins of the Hellenistic town of Velia

Parco Nazionale del Cilento e Vallo di Diano (Cilento National Park & the Valley of Diana)

To Reggio di Calabria (350km); Calabria

Golfo di Policastro

DISTANCE CHART (KM)

	Salerno	Paestum	Agropoli	Ascea
Paestum	27			
Agropoli	45	17		
Ascea	79	47	32	
Sapri	120	90	77	51

Note: Distances between destinations are approximate

SALERNO & THE CILENTO

SALERNO & THE CILENTO GETTING STARTED

MAKING THE MOST OF YOUR TIME

Salerno can be visited on foot, but concentrate on the picturesque *centro storico* with its labyrinth of earthy historic streets. Allow at least three hours to explore the fascinating excavations at Paestum, ranked among the best-preserved Greek temples in the world. And don't miss the Cilento region, one of this area's unsung glories, with a largely undeveloped coastal strip and a lush and beautiful national park. The villages here have a tangible stuck-in-a-time-warp feel, so be prepared for stares. It's a burgeoning region for walkers, too, and *agriturismi* make perfect bases. They can also advise on activities, including horse-riding and hiking trails.

TOP TOURS & COURSES

♥ WRECK DIVING WITH THE PROS
Explore the hulks of ships and planes in deep-sea dives off the Cilento coast. (☎ 338 237 46 03; www.cilentosub.com; Via San Francesco 30, Agropoli; p217)

♥ MOONLIT OCEAN TRIP
Enjoy a romantic evening under the stars with a boat trip from the Cilento coastal resort of Acciaroli to Marina de Casal Velino. (☎ 0974 90 00 50; www.cilentoexplorer.com; Marina de Casal Velino; p219)

♥ PAINTING & COOKING COURSES
Take an art or culinary course surrounded by stunning nature at this choice *agriturismo*. (☎ 0974 90 20 86; www.agriturismoimoresani.com; Casal Velino; p288)

♥ BOAT TRIP TO THE GROTTOES
Visit five Capo Palinuro grottoes by boat, including the famous Grotta Azzurra. (Da Alessandro; ☎ 347 654 09 31; www.costieradelcilento.it; p220)

♥ GUIDED TREKS IN THE PARCO NAZIONALE DEL CILENTO
Hike surrounded by the wild, untamed beauty of this little-known national park. (p214)

SALERNO & THE CILENTO

GETTING AWAY FROM IT ALL

Much of the charm of this pristine corner of Italy lies in the fact that, unlike the Amalfi Coast, the lack of manicured glamour equals a lack of coach loads of tourists – although holidaying Italians descend here in droves during August.

★ **Hunt for wildflowers** Head to the area around Sassano, famed for its Valle delle Orchidee (Valley of the Orchids; see the boxed text, p213)

★ **Explore the castles, churches and backstreets** An extraordinary mountain-top Teggiano (see the driving tour, p211)

★ **Take a picnic** Enjoy the wide shingle beach at the tiny fishing village of Pioppi (p218)

TOP BEACHES

★ **SANTA MARIA DI CASTELLABATE**
Home to two fine sweeps of sand (p218)

★ **SPIAGGIA PALINURO**
Wide, sandy beach sporting an energetic, young vibe (p220)

★ **MARINA DE CASAL VELINO**
Delightful family-style beach with kids' activities (p218)

★ **BAIA DI TRENTOVA**
Beautiful bay and beach with crystal clear shallow waters (p216)

★ **ASCEA**
Some 5km of powder-soft sand fronting must-see ruins (p219)

ADVANCE PLANNING

If you're planning to visit the Parco Nazionale del Cilento, some preparation will stand you in good stead.

★ **Maps** If you are going to trek in the park or spend much time there, invest in a detailed trekking and road map. The *Parco Nazionale Cilento e Vallo di Diano* (1:50,000; €7), published by Matonti Editore, is a good choice.

★ **Plan your route** Even during the busier summer season, the sheer size of the park means that hikers are unlikely to meet others on the trail to swap tales and muesli bars – so getting lost could become lonely, not to mention dangerous, If you haven't done some essential planning before striding out.

★ **Book ahead** Don't just turn up at *agriturismi* or B&Bs in the park; chances are no one will be home, the bell won't work or grandpa won't have the right key. Tourism is recent in these parts – give it time and always reserve in advance.

RESOURCES

★ **Salerno City** (www.salernocity.com, in Italian) Comprehensive city website

★ **Salerno Province** (www.salernomemo.com, in Italian) Emphasis on sports and activities

★ **Agropoli** (www.comune.agropoli.sa.it, in Italian) General information and local news

★ **Paestum** (www.infopaestum.it) Information about the town and archaeological website

★ **Cilento** (www.discovercilento.com) Information on the park and coastal resorts

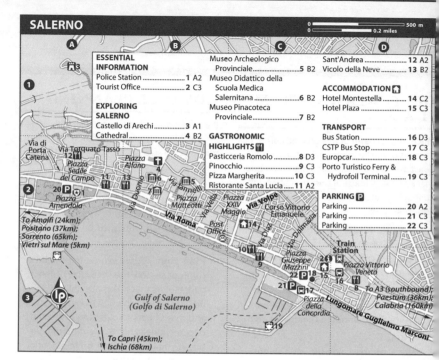

SALERNO

ESSENTIAL INFORMATION		
Police Station	1	A2
Tourist Office	2	C3

EXPLORING SALERNO		
Castello di Arechi	3	A1
Cathedral	4	B2

Museo Archeologico Provinciale 5 B2
Museo Didattico della Scuola Medica Salernitana 6 B2
Museo Pinacoteca Provinciale 7 B2

GASTRONOMIC HIGHLIGHTS		
Pasticceria Romolo	8	D3
Pinocchio	9	C3
Pizza Margherita	10	C3
Ristorante Santa Lucia	11	A2

Sant'Andrea	12	A2
Vicolo della Neve	13	B2

ACCOMMODATION		
Hotel Montestella	14	C2
Hotel Plaza	15	C3

TRANSPORT		
Bus Station	16	D3
CSTP Bus Stop	17	C3
Europcar	18	C3
Porto Turistico Ferry & Hydrofoil Terminal	19	C3

PARKING		
Parking	20	A2
Parking	21	C3
Parking	22	C3

main shopping strip, the car-free Corso Vittorio Emanuele, leads off northwest to the medieval *centro storico*. Running parallel is Corso Garibaldi, which becomes Via Roma as it heads out of the city towards Vietri sul Mare and the Amalfi Coast. Tree-lined Lungomare Trieste, on the waterfront, changes its name to Lungomare Guglielmo Marconi at the massive Piazza della Concordia on its way out of town, southeast towards Paestum.

EXPLORING SALERNO

Although Salerno is a sprawling town, you can easily visit it in one day, and on foot, as the main sights are concentrated in and around the *centro storico*. Don't miss the palm-flanked seafront promenade, one of the loveliest in the region. For shopping, head for the sophisticated

strut of shops on Via di Porta Catena, which leads westwards to the medieval market square of Piazza Sedile del Campo

🍴 CASTLES & CATHEDRALS // SPECTACULAR AND SPIRITUAL HIGHLIGHTS

Hop on bus 19 from Piazza XXIV Maggio to visit Salerno's most famous landmark, the forbidding **Castello di Arechi** (☎ 089 22 55 78; Via Benedetto Croce; ☷ 9am-3.30pm), dramatically positioned 263m above the city. Originally a Byzantine fort, it was built by the Lombard duke of Benevento, Arechi II, in the 8th century and subsequently modified by the Normans and Aragonese, most recently in the 16th century. The views of the city and Gulf of Salerno are spectacular from here, and you can also visit a moderately interesting permanent collection of ceramics, arms and coins. If you are visiting during the summer, check out the annual series of concerts staged here; the tourist office will have a program.

You can't miss the looming presence of Salerno's impressive **cathedral** (Piazza Alfano; ☺ 10am-6pm), located in the *centro storico* and widely considered to be the most beautiful medieval church in Italy. Built by the Normans in the 11th century and later aesthetically remodelled in the 18th century, it sustained severe damage in the 1980 earthquake. It is dedicated to San Matteo (St Matthew), whose remains were reputedly brought to the city in 954 and now lie beneath the main altar in the vaulted crypt.

Take special note of the magnificent main entrance, the 12th-century **Porta dei Leoni**, named after the marble lions at the foot of the stairway. It leads through to a beautifully harmonious atrium, overlooked by a 12th-century bell tower. Carry on through the huge bronze doors, cast in Constantinople in the 11th century. When you come to the three-aisled interior, you will see that it is largely baroque, with only a few traces of the original church. These include parts of the transept and choir floor and the two raised pulpits in front of the choir stalls.

In the right-hand apse, don't miss the **Cappella delle Crociate** (Chapel of the Crusades), containing stunning 13th-century mosaics and frescoes. It was so named because crusaders' weapons were blessed here. Under the altar stands the tomb of 11th-century pope Gregory VII.

♥ MUSEUMS OF SALERNO // FROM ROMAN RELICS TO MEDICINAL REMEDIES

The **Museo Archeologico Provinciale** (☎ 089 23 11 35; Via San Benedetto 28; admission free; ☺ closed for restoration) is the province's main archaeological museum and is a fascinating glimpse of how the city and surrounding region was influenced by the successive waves of settlers. Don't miss the highlight: a 1st-century-BC bronze head of Apollo, discovered in the Gulf of Salerno in 1930. One can only wonder at what else lies buried in the surrounding seabed. Check at the tourist office before turning up here, as, along with the Museo Didattico della Scuola Medica Salernitana (see below), the archaeological museum is closed for restoration, with no opening date available at the time of research.

Smock and beret enthusiasts may prefer to peruse the **Museo Pinacoteca Provinciale** (☎ 089 258 30 73; Via Mercanti 63; admission free; ☺ 9am-1pm & 2-3.15pm Tue-Sat, 9am-1pm Sun), located deep in the heart of the *centro storico*. Although fairly modest in size, this museum houses an interesting art collection dating from the Renaissance right up to the first half of the 19th century. There are some fine canvases by local boy Andrea Sabatini da Salerno, who famously worked on Rome's Sistine Chapel, and an assortment of works by foreign artists living in the area.

Situated within the ex-church of San Gregorio, the **Museo Didattico della Scuola Medica Salernitana** (Medical School of Salerno Museum; ☎ 089 24 12 92; Via Mercanti 72; admission free; ☺ closed for restoration) displays a collection of documents and illustrations recounting the fascinating history of Salerno's historic and illustrious medical school. Probably established in the 9th century, the school was the most important centre of medical knowledge in medieval Europe, reaching the height of its prestige in the 11th century. It was closed in the early 19th century.

GASTRONOMIC HIGHLIGHTS

Head to Via Roma in the lively medieval centre, where you'll find everything from traditional, family-run trattorias and gelaterias to jazzy wine bars, pubs and expensive restaurants. In summer, the seafront is a popular place for the evening *passeggiata* (stroll).

🌰 PASTICCERIA ROMOLO €

☎ 089 23 26 13; Corso Garibaldi 33; cakes from €1.50

Across from the train station, this sprawling *pasticceria* (pastry shop) dates from 1966 and the decor has changed little since. The cakes are similarly legendary in this town, with a mouthwatering display that includes *frollini* (fruit and chocolate tarts), *ameretti* (macaroons) and that all-time irresistible treat *sfogliatelle* (a flaky pastry cake filled with fresh ricotta). Fancy chocolates and a wide range of local and national wine are also on sale.

🌰 PINOCCHIO €€

☎ 089 22 99 64; Lungomare Trieste 56; meals €24; 🕑 closed Fri

Frequented by locals in the know, this restaurant dishes up groaning plates of no-nonsense local cuisine. Seafood is the speciality, but there's also a decent selection of fail-safe meats, including sausages, steak, and *scaloppine* (breaded veal) in a creamy mushroom sauce. Owners Rodolfo and Paula are a friendly couple and the dining space is comfortably informal with its kid's-room clutter of Pinocchio murals and mobiles. In summer, tables are set outside.

🌰 PIZZA MARGHERITA €

☎ 089 22 88 80; Corso Garibaldi 201; pizzas/buffet from €5/6.50, lunchtime menu €8

It looks like a bland, modern canteen, but this is, in fact, one of Salerno's most popular lunch spots. Locals regularly queue for the lavish lunchtime buffet that, on any given day, might include buffalo mozzarella, salami, mussels in various guises and a range of salads. If that doesn't appeal, the daily lunchtime menu (pasta, main course, salad and half a litre of water) is chalked up on a blackboard, or there's the regular menu of pizzas, pastas and main courses.

🌰 RISTORANTE SANTA LUCIA €€

☎ 089 22 56 96; Via Roma 182; meals €22; 🕑 closed Mon

The surrounding Via Roma area may be one of the city's trendiest, but there's nothing remotely flash about the delicious seafood served up here. Dishes such as *linguine ai frutti di mare* (flat spaghetti with seafood) and chargrilled cuttlefish may not be original but, cooked here, they taste quite exceptional – as do the uppercrust wood-fired pizzas. The buzzing atmosphere and friendly, efficient service add to the pleasure.

🌰 SANT'ANDREA €€

☎ 328 72 72 74; Piazza Sedile del Campo 58; meals €25

There's an earthy southern Italian atmosphere here, with tables (complete with red-and-white chequered cloths) sprawled on the historic market square with its old-fashioned barber shop and ancient houses decorated with washing hung out to dry. Choices are more innovative than you would expect and include seafood dishes such as squid with porcini mushrooms or cuttlefish accompanied by creamed vegetables. The white-truffle ice cream equals a sexy, sweet finale.

🍴 VICOLO DELLA NEVE €€

☎ 089 22 57 05; Vicolo della Neve 24; meals €25;
🕑 dinner Thu-Tue

A city institution, located on one of the
scruffiest streets in the city, Vicolo della
Neve is the archetypal *centro storico*
trattoria. It's got brick arches and fake
frescoes, the walls are hung with works
by local artists and the menu is unwaveringly authentic. There are pizzas and
calzones (pizzas folded over to form a
pie), *pepperoni ripieni* (stuffed peppers)
and a top-notch *parmigiana di melanzane* (baked eggplant with tomatoes and
Parmesan). It can get incredibly busy,
so be prepared to wait until a table becomes available.

TRANSPORT

BOAT // Metró del Mare (☎ 199 60 07 00;
www.metrodelmare.com) operates regular ferries
to/from Naples (€16, two daily) and Sorrento (€12, seven
daily). From April to October Linee Marittime
Partenopee (☎ 081 704 19 11; www.consorziolmp.
it; Via Guglielmo Melisurgo 4, Naples) and TraVel-
Mar (☎ 089 87 29 50; Largo Scario 5, Amalfi) run
frequent daily hydrofoils and ferries from Salerno to
various resorts and the islands. Approximate prices are
to/from Capri (€17.50/16), to/from Positano (€9/8.50,
10 daily) and to/from Amalfi (€ 7/6.50). Departures are
from the Porto Turistico, 200m down the pier from Piazza
della Concordia. You can buy tickets from the booths by
the embarkation point.

BUS // SITA (☎ 199 73 07 49; www.sitabus.it, in
Italian) buses for Amalfi depart at least hourly from
Piazza Vittorio Veneto, beside the train station, stopping
en route at Vietri sul Mare, Cetara, Maiori and Minori. For
Pompeii, take CSTP (☎ 089 48 70 01; www.cstp.it,
in Italian) bus 50 from Piazza Vittorio Veneto. There are
15 daily departures. For the south coast and Paestum,
take the hourly bus 34 from the CSTP stop on Piazza della
Concordia.

CAR // Salerno is on the A3 between Naples and
Reggio di Calabria; the A3 is toll-free from Salerno

south. Take the Salerno exit and follow signs to the
centro (city centre). If you want to hire a car, there's a
Europcar (☎ 089 258 07 75; www.europcar.com;
Via Giacinto Vicinanza) agency not far from the train
station.

PARKING // Salerno has a reasonable number of car
parks. Follow the distinctive blue P sign as you approach
the centre of the city. The most convenient car park for
the *centro storico* is on Piazza Amendola. Near the train
station (and tourist office) other convenient locations
are the large car parks on Piazza della Concordia and the
adjacent Piazza Giuseppe Mazzini. You can expect to pay
around €1.50 an hour for Salerno car parks.

TRAIN // Salerno is a major stop on southbound routes
to Calabria and the Ionian and Adriatic coasts. From the
station in Piazza Vittorio Veneto there are regular trains
to Naples (€6.50, 50 minutes, half-hourly), Rome (Eurostar €33, 2½ hours, hourly) and Reggio di Calabria (€32,
4½ hours, 15 daily).

PAESTUM

Paestum, or Poseidonia as the city
was originally called (in honour of
Poseidon, the Greek god of the sea),
was founded in the 6th century BC
by Greek settlers and fell under
Roman control in 273 BC. Decline
later set in following the demise of
the Roman Empire. Savage raids by
the Saracens and periodic outbreaks
of malaria forced the steadily dwin-
dling population to abandon the city
altogether.

The site's unforgettable temples –
now on Unesco's World Heritage list –
are among the best-preserved monuments of Magna Graecia, the Greek colony that once covered much of southern
Italy. The temples were rediscovered in
the late 18th century, but the site as a
whole wasn't unearthed until as late as
the 1950s.

SALERNO & THE CILENTO

DO INDULGE IN

* **Fresh buffalo mozzarella** Some of the best *mozzarella di bufala* is produced in the Cilento region (p258)

* **Medieval magic** Exploring the historic villages in the Parco Nazionale del Cilento (p211)

* **Stunning Amalfi Coast views** By catching a ferry from Sorrento to Salerno (p207)

* **Best beaches** Kicking back on the Cilento coast's powder-soft sandy beaches (p217)

* **Ricotta and pear tart** The emblematic Cilento dessert, *torta ricotta e pera*, and one of the region's most delicious (p219)

Although most people visit Paestum for the day, there are a surprising number of exceptional accommodation options, and this delightful rural area makes a convenient stopover point for travellers heading for the Cilento region. See the Paestum section of the Accommodation chapter, p286, for recommendations.

ESSENTIAL INFORMATION

EMERGENCIES // Ambulance (☎ 118) Fire (☎ 115) Police (☎ 112 or 113)
TOURIST INFORMATION // Tourist Office (☎ 0828 81 10 16; www.infopaestum.it; Via Magna Crecia 887; ☻ 9am-1.30pm & 2.30-7pm Mon-Sat Jun-Sep, shorter hrs Oct-May)

EXPLORING PAESTUM

♥ **THE RUINS // WANDER THE RUINED TEMPLES THROUGH WILDFLOWERS**
If you are visiting in springtime, the temples (☎ 0828 81 10 23; adult/EU 18-24yr/EU under 18yr & over 65yr €4/2/free; ☻ 8.45am-7.45pm, last entry 7pm) are particularly stunning, surrounded by meadows of colourful wildflowers. Entering from the main entrance on the northern end, the first structure to take your breath away is the 6th-century-BC **Tempio di Cerere** (Temple of Ceres). Originally dedicated to Athena, it served as a Christian church in medieval times.

As you head south, you can pick out the basic outline of the large rectangular forum, the heart of the ancient city. Among the partially standing buildings are the vast domestic housing area and, further south, the amphitheatre; both provide evocative glimpses of daily life here in Roman times.

The **Tempio di Nettuno** (Temple of Neptune), dating from about 450 BC, is the largest and best preserved of the three temples at Paestum; only parts of its inside walls and roof are missing. Almost next door, the so-called **basilica** (in fact, a temple to the goddess Hera) is Paestum's oldest surviving monument. Dating from the middle of the 6th century BC, it's a magnificent sight, with nine columns across and 18 along the sides. Ask someone to take your photo next to a column here, it's a good way to appreciate the scale.

Just east of the site, don't bypass the **museum**, which houses a collection of fascinating, if weathered, *metopes* (bas-relief friezes). This collection includes 33 of the original 36 *metopes* from the **Tempio di Argiva Hera** (Temple of Argive Hera), situated 9km north of Paestum, of which virtually nothing else remains. The star exhibit is the 5th-century-BC fresco *Tomba del Truffatore* (Tomb of the Diver), thought to represent the passage from life to death with its depiction of a diver in midair (don't try this at home).

❦ NONNA SCEPA // A MONUMENTAL DINING EXPERIENCE

There are various restaurants at the site; however, most serve mediocre food at inflated prices. Instead, seek out the superbly prepared, robust dishes at midrange prices at **Nonna Scepa** (☎ 0828 85 10 64; Via Laura 53; meals €30), a friendly restaurant that's rapidly gaining a reputation throughout the region for excellence. Dishes are firmly seasonal and, during the summer, concentrate on fresh seafood like the refreshingly simple grilled fish with lemon. Other popular choices include risotto with zucchini and artichokes, and spaghetti with lobster.

TRANSPORT

BUS // CSTP (☎ 089 48 70 01; www.cstp.it, in Italian) Bus 34 operates to Paestum from Piazza della Concordia in Salerno (€3.10, one hour 20 minutes, 12 daily).

PARCO NAZIONALE DEL CILENTO E VALLO DI DIANO

· · · · · ·

Proving the perfect antidote to the holiday mayhem along the coast, the Parco Nazionale del Cilento e Vallo di Diano (Cilento National Park and the Valley of Diana; hereafter referred to as the Parco Nazionale del Cilento) is a compelling combination of dense woods, flowering meadows, dramatic mountains, and water – lots of it – with streams, rivers and waterfalls. A World Heritage Site, it is the second-largest national park in Italy, covering a staggering 181,048 hectares, including 80 towns and villages.

Inhabited since prehistoric times, the park's isolation has attracted waves of settlers seeking refuge over the ages. First, the Greeks fled here from the ancient Roman towns of Paestum and Velia. Then, early inhabitants of the coastal cities headed inland to escape piracy and pillaging. Benedictine monks subsequently joined the cultural medley, seeking secluded places of worship. Next up were the wealthy feudal lords who set up house (or rather castle) here, from where they could impose their power.

Centuries later, the park was controlled by the feared *briganti* (bandits), which meant it was a no-go area for Grand Tour visitors. This kept the park out of the tourism loop for decades and helps explain why it remains so pristine today.

ESSENTIAL INFORMATION

EMERGENCIES // Alpine Rescue (☎ 118, 338 4351474) Fire (☎ 1515) To report a fire to the Forestry Service.

TOURIST INFORMATION // Paestum Tourist Office (☎ 0828 81 10 16; www.info paestum.it; Via Magna Crecia 887, Paestum; ☽ 9am-1.30pm & 2.30-7pm Mon-Sat Jun-Sep, shorter hrs Oct-May) Has some information on the Parco Nazionale del Cilento. **Sicignano degle Aburni** (☎ 0828 97 37 55; Piazza Plebiscito 13, Sicignano degle Aburni; ☽ 9am-1.30pm & 2.30-5pm Mon-Sat) **Vallo della Luciana** (☎ 0974 71 11 11; http://www.parks.it/parco.nazionale.cilento/Eindex.html; Palazzo Mainenti, Via Polombo 16, Vallo della Luciana; ☽ 9am-1.30pm & 2.30-5pm Mon-Sat) Check out the excellent website.

PARCO NAZIONALE DEL CILENTO (CILENTO NATIONAL PARK)

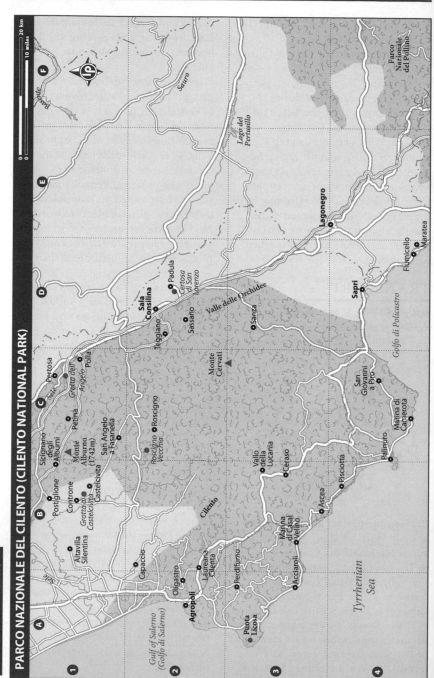

PARCO NAZIONALE DEL CILENTO DRIVING TOUR

Distance: 112km
Duration: three days

Start this drive late morning after an other-worldly visit to the **Grotta di Castelcivita** (p212). Take the SS488 heading north, stopping at **Controne** to grab a pizza at **Il Fagiolo** (p215). Continue northwards on the *strada provinciale* 60, following signs for Postiglione; the road passes soaring cliff faces, ancient drystone walls and lush, arable countryside with wild cherry and fig trees. You need snow chains here in the winter. After 13km, slam on the brakes at **Postiglione**, its medieval town centre crowned by an 11th-century Norman castle. Join the locals for a coffee in one of the bars in Piazza Europa, before continuing on the SS19 towards Auletta. The countryside

here becomes dramatically mountainous, with a wonderful marbled rock face (think rocky road ice cream).

Follow signs eastwards on the SS19 to lovely **Sicignano degli Alburni**. Head for central Piazza Plebiscito, where there's a handy Pro Loco tourist office that can provide you with three printed itineraries for exploring the town, taking in its 14th-century castle, baroque churches and historic convent. Sicignano is also the kick-off point for the two hiking trails that ascend **Monte Alburno** (p214). Stay overnight at the nearby **Sicinius** *agriturismo* (p289), with its excellent restaurant featuring the farm's organic produce. Next day, continue south on *strada provinciale* 35, along which you'll pass the village of **Petina** dramatically straddling a high ridge. Note that this is a fairly rough road; if you prefer more reliable tarmac, head north for the

PARCO NAZIONALE DEL CILENTO DRIVING TOUR

0 — 5 km
0 — 2 miles

Postiglione · Sicignano degli Alburni · Pertosa · Sele · Petina · Grotta dell' Angelo · Polla · Controne · Monte Alburno · Castelcivita · START · END · Grotta di Castelcivita · San Angelo a Fasanella · Teggiano · Sala Consilina · Padula · Certosa di San Lorenzo

SALERNO & THE CILENTO

SS19, which is similarly scenic and continues southeast, passing the turn-off to the fascinating Grotta dell'Angelo (also known as the Grotta di Pertosa; opposite) en route.

The next stop is **Polla**, a strategic town during Roman times and lovely for a stroll, with its riverfront setting, 12th-century castle and brooding dark-stone houses. Pick up picnic fare here and take the SS19 south (the A3 *autovia* is faster but not as scenic), following signs for **Padula**, where you can spend the afternoon exploring the extraordinary **Certosa di San Lorenzo** (opposite). Follow the signs to stunning **Teggiano**, around 15km northwest of here, and bristling with churches and museums, as well as a cathedral and a castle. Stay overnight at **Antichi Feudi** (p289), located just off the picturesque Piazza San Cono and a former palace resurrected into a superb boutique hotel and restaurant.

Bright and early on day three, head north for 7km until you hit the SS166. Follow the signs and make a stop at **San Angelo a Fasanella**, a 13th-century town with a Roman bridge, medieval convents and churches, and an atmospheric *centro storico*. Follow the signs to the Grotta di San Michele, which at the time of research was closed due to a rock fall, but this may have been cleared by the time of your visit. Either way, it's an imposing setting. Continue west some 18km to **Castelcivita**, your starting point.

EXPLORING THE PARCO NAZIONALE DEL CILENTO

To get the best out of the park, you will need a car. For a hire company in nearby Agropoli, see p216. Allow yourself a full day to visit the grottoes and more if you're intending to hike. There are some excellent *agriturismi* here that offer additional activities, including guided hikes, painting courses and horse riding; see the Parco Nazionale del Cilento section of the Accommodation chapter, p288.

🐚 THE GROTTOES // MESMERISING CAVE COMPLEXES

The grottoes are fascinating otherworldly caves that date from prehistoric times. If you're planning to visit, don't forget a jacket, and leave the high heels at home; the paths are wet and slippery. Located 40km southeast of Salerno, the extraordinary **Grotta di Castelcivita** (☎ 0828 77 23 97; Castelcivita; adult/child €8/6.50; ☻ tours 10am, 11.30am, 1.30pm, 3pm & 4.30pm Oct–mid-Mar, 10am, 11am, noon, 1.30pm, 2.30pm, 3.30pm, 4.30pm, 5.30pm & 6.30pm mid-Mar–Aug; ♿ Ⓟ) is well worth a visit and refreshingly noncommercial. Excavations have revealed that the caves were inhabited 42,000 years ago, rating it the oldest settlement in Europe. Although they extend over 4800m, only around half of the cave complex is open to the public. The standard one-hour tour winds through a route surrounded by extraordinary stalagmites and stalactites and a mesmerising play of colours, caused by algae, calcium and iron that tint the naturally sculpted rock shapes. The tour culminates in a cavernous lunar landscape – think California's Death Valley in miniature – called the Caverna di Bertarelli (Bertarelli Cavern). The caves are still inhabited – by bats, and visitors are instructed not to take flash photos for fear of blinding them! There are longer three-hour tours (€20) between May and September when the water deep within the cave complex has dried up. Hard hats and a certain level of fitness and mobility are required.

Compared to the Grotta di Castelcivita, the **Grotta dell'Angelo** (☎ 0975 39 70 37; www.grottedipertosa.it; Pertosa; guided visits adult/child €10/8; ☽ 9am-7pm Mar-Oct, to 4pm Nov-Feb; ℗ ☕), also known as the Grotta di Pertosa, is a youngster, dating back a mere 35 million years to the Neolithic period and only discovered in 1932. Subsequently used by the Greeks and Romans as places of worship, the caves burrow through the mountains for some 2500m with long underground passages and lofty grottoes filled with a mouthful of stalagmites and stalactites. The first part of the tour takes part as a boat (or raft) ride on the river; you disembark just before the waterfall (phew!) and continue on foot for around 800m surrounded by marvellous rock formations and some beautifully luminous crystal accretions. This grotto is more commercial than Castelcivita, with souvenir shops, bars and a €3 parking fee.

🌿 CERTOSA DI SAN LORENZO // FABULOUS MONASTERY IS A BEST-KEPT SECRET

One of the largest monasteries in southern Europe, Carthusian **Certosa di San Lorenzo** (☎ 0975 7 77 45; Padula; adult/child €4/2; ☽ 9am-7.30pm) dates from 1306 and covers 250,000 sq metres. Numerologists can swoon at the following: 320 rooms and halls, 2500m of corridors, galleries and hallways, 300 columns, 500 doors, 550 windows, 13 courtyards, 100 fireplaces, 52 stairways and 41 fountains – in other words, it is *huge!* As you will unlikely have time to cover everywhere here, be sure to visit the highlights, including the vast central courtyard (a venue for summer classical-music concerts), the magnificent wood-panelled library, frescoed chapels and the kitchen with its grandiose fireplace and famous tale: apparently this is where the legendary 1000-egg omelette was made in 1534 for Charles

---

~ WORTH A TRIP ~

The Parco Nazionale del Cilento is a rich natural environment for fauna and flora and has been declared part of Unesco's Biosphere Preservation program. There are a number of extremely rare plant species here, including the primrose of Palinuro (the symbol of the park). Horticulture enthusiasts will likely trip over their pitchforks when they hear that there are also some 265 varieties of wild orchid that flourish annually here (the equivalent of 80% of the total number of wild orchid varieties growing in Europe).

Concentrated in the appropriately named Valle delle Orchidee (Valley of the Orchids), near the picturesque small town of Sassano (9km west of the Certosa di San Lorenzo), this annual dazzle of sumptuous colour encompasses some 70 orchid species and takes place normally from late April to early May. The surrounding countryside is beautiful, so even if you miss the orchids you can still enjoy the drive and may well catch a glimpse of some other form of wildlife: foxes, badgers, wolves, wild boars or a member of the largest otter population in Italy. Take the sign marked *percorso turistico* on the left just as you enter Sassano; you will pass the medieval bridge of Peglio and woods of silver birches before this blooming event unfolds in all its glory in the valley beyond. You can also join an organised tour with the **Gruppo Escursionistico Trekking** (☎ 0975 7 25 86; www.getvallodidiano.it; Via Provinciale 29, Silla di Sassano).

SALERNO & THE CILENTO

V. Unfortunately, the historic frying pan is not on view – just how big was it, one wonders!

Within the monastery you can also peruse the modest collection of the **Museo Archeologico Provinciale della Lucania Occidentale** (☎ 0975 7 71 17; admission free; ☎ 8am-1.15pm & 2-3pm Tue-Sat, 9am-1pm Sun).

❦ HIKING IN THE PARK // SELF-GUIDED AND GUIDED HIKES

The park has 15 well-marked nature trails that vary from relatively easy strolls to serious hiking requiring plenty of stamina and a good set of knees. The countryside in the park is stunning and dramatic, and if you're here in spring you'll experience real flower power: delicate narcissi, wild orchids and tulips hold their own among blowsier summer drifts of brilliant yellow ox-eye daisies and scarlet poppies. Thickets of silver firs, wild chestnuts and beech trees add to the sumptuous landscape, as do the dramatic cliffs, pine-clad mountains – and fauna, including wild boars, badgers and wolves and, for twitchers, the increasingly rare and magnificent golden eagle.

In theory, the tourist offices should be able to supply you with a guide to the trails. In reality, they frequently seem to have run out of copies. Failing this, you can buy the *Parco Nazionale Cilento e Vallo di Diano: Carta Turistica e dei Sentieri* (Tourist and Footpath Map; €7) or the excellent *Monte Stella: Walks & Rambles in Ancient Cilento* published by the Comunita' Montana Alento Monte Stella (€3). Several organisations also arrange guided hikes, including **Gruppo Escursionistico Trekking** (☎ 0975 7 25 86; www.getvallodidiano.it; Via Provinciale 29, Silla di Sassano), **Associazione Trekking Cilento** (☎ 0974 84 33 45; www.trekkingcilento.it, in Italian; Via Cannetiello 6, Agropoli), **Associazione Naturalis-tica Culturale** (☎ 0974 82 38 52; http://noitour.it; Via Ianni 16, Agropoli), **Trekking Campania** (☎ 339 7456795; www.trekkingcampania.it; Via Yuri Gagarin 16, Salerno), and the particularly recommended **Cycling Cilento Adventure** (☎ 328 3652736; www.cyclingcilentoadventure.com), which organises full-day treks departing from Amalfi or Salerno, as well cycling and kayak trips. Prices start at around €10 per person for a half-day hike and vary depending on the route, the duration and the number of people in the group. Check the respective websites for more information.

Most of the *agriturismi* in the park can also organise guided treks. For more information on the latter, see the Accommodation chapter, p288. A popular self-guided hike, where you are rewarded with spectacular views, is climbing Monte Alburno (1742m). There's a choice of two trails, both of which are clearly marked from the centre of the small town of Sicignano degli Alburni and finish at the mountain's peak. Allow approximately four hours for either route.

❦ ROSCIGNO VECCHIA // VISIT A GHOST TOWN

There's something about visiting a ghost town that both fires the imagination and is highly contemplative, especially as the history is virtually always harrowing. In Roscigno Vecchia, located in the heart of the national park 28km west of Teggiano, sudden landslides in the early 20th century caused the population to flee. Excellent testament to rural architecture, most of the original stone houses are still standing today, as well as the church and the central piazza, all ghostly reminders of a formerly thriving community. The residents were eventually permanently moved to Roscigno Nuovo (now simply known as Roscigno).

SALERNO & THE CILENTO

GASTRONOMIC HIGHLIGHTS

There remains a lot of poverty in the small villages that dot the park, but that can mean simple, unadulterated food with hearty meat sauces made from mutton and goat. The flat bread focaccia that you find all over Italy originally came from the Cilento region.

☙ ANTICHI FEUDI €€

☎ 0975 58 73 29; Via San Francesco 2, Teggiano; meals €25, pizzas from €3

This gracious restaurant is located within the sumptuous same-name boutique hotel (see p289) just off Teggiano's elegant main piazza. The menu varies according to what is in season, but typical dishes include juicy chargrilled meat, grilled mussels with olive oil and lemon, and seafood soup. The hotel bar-cafe is good for pizza, including the especially tasty Antichi Feudi with mushrooms, fresh cheese and grilled eggplant (€8).

☙ FRANCO'S €

☎ 0828 97 33 40; Via Mario Pagano 43, Sicignano degli Alburni; meals from €12, pizzas from €3

Ideal for fussy eaters, Franco's has a vast choice, including pizza and gelati (if all else fails). The food is of a steady standard and won't disappoint, with plenty of pizza options, and pastas including *tortelloni con gamberi e zucchini* (tortellini with prawns and zucchini) and a creamily delicious *parmigiana di melanzane* (baked eggplant with tomatoes and Parmesan). Generally crowded with locals, this family-run place is better suited to informal lunches than romantic dinners for two.

☙ IL FAGIOLO €

☎ 338 4523276; Corso Garibaldi 45, Controne; meals from €12, pizzas from €3

Well signposted to the right from the main road going through town, this bright, spacious restaurant has a €10 tourist menu and inexpensive seafood dishes such as the classic *spaghetti alle vongole* (spaghetti with clams) and *risotto di mare* (seafood risotto). You can expect a good grilling as well: meat dishes include steak with pepper sauce and lamb cutlets. The pizzas are crispy based and excellent. There's outdoor seating in the summer.

☙ TAVERNA IL LUPO €

☎ 0975 77 83 76; Via Municipio, Padula; meals from €16

A hospitable, family-run restaurant with a menu of typical Cilento dishes, including vegetarian choices such as vegetable frittatas, *zeppole di fiori di zucca* (baked courgettes) and homemade pasta with onions and white beans. The dessert choice is limited but shouldn't disappoint. Consider a slice of the heavenly, moist *torta di cioccolata* (chocolate cake) before you waddle home.

AGROPOLI & THE CILENTO COAST

· · · · · ·

Located just south of Paestum, Agropoli is a busy summer resort but otherwise a pleasant, tranquil town that makes a good base for exploring the Cilento coastline and park. While the shell is a fairly faceless grid of shop-lined streets, the kernel, the historic city centre, is a fascinating tangle of narrow cobbled streets with ancient churches, venerable residents and a castle with superlative views.

The town has been inhabited since Neolithic times, with subsequent inhabitants including the Greeks, the Romans, the Byzantines and the Saracens. In 915 the town fell into the jurisdiction of the bishops and was subsequently ruled by feudal lords. Agropoli was a target of raids from North Africa in the 16th and 17th centuries, when the population dwindled to just a few hundred. Today the residents number closer to 20,000, making it the largest (and the most vibrant) town along the Cilento coast.

TRANSPORT

BUS // CSTP (☎ 089 48 70 01; www.cstp.it, in Italian) operates regular buses from Salerno and Paestum to several Cilento coastal resorts, including Agropoli, Santa Maria di Castellabate, San Marco di Castellabate and Acciaroli, while **Curcio Viaggi** (☎ 089 25 40 80; www.curcioviaggi.it, in Italian) operates a number of routes that cover the coast and park, including a daily bus from Pertosa to Palinuro that stops at Teggiano, Sassano and Padula. SITA (☎ 089 22 66 04; www.sitabus.it, in Italian) has a daily service from Salerno to Castelcivita and Polla.

CAR // The coastal towns are well signposted and, in general, good for parking. There are plenty of car-rental outfits here, including **Alba Rent Car** (☎ 0974 82 80 99; Via A De Gasperi 82, Agropoli; per day from €45) or similarly priced LT **Trasporti** (☎ 0974 96 13 66; www.ltgroup.it; Via Colombo 11, Santa Maria di Castellabate). The Parco Nazionale del Cilento is similarly easy to navigate by car, provided you have a detailed map. Relying on public transport can be an incredibly frustrating , not to mention time-consuming, business.

TRAIN // Most destinations on the Cilento coast are served by the main rail route from Naples to Reggio di Calabria. Consult **Trenitalia** (www.trenitalia.it) for fares and information. For Palinuro, the nearest train station is Pisciotta, from where there is regular bus service to the resort.

AGROPOLI
ESSENTIAL INFORMATION

EMERGENCIES // Police station (☎ 0974 82 83 69; Via Angrisani 6) Ambulance (☎ 118) Fire (☎ 115)

TOURIST INFORMATION // Tourist Office (☎ 0974 82 74 71; Viale Europa 34; ◷ 9.30am-2pm) Not a lot of information, but it can provide you with a city map.

EXPLORING AGROPOLI

To reach the *centro storico* of Agropoli, head for the Piazza Veneto Victoria, the pedestrian-only part of the modern town where cafes and gelaterie are interspersed with plenty of shopping choice. Head up Corso Garibaldi and take the wide Ennio Balbo Scaloni steps until you reach the fortified medieval *borgo*. Follow the signs to the castle. The town is surrounded by pristine, golden, sandy beaches, including the pretty Baia di Trentova cove just south of town, where you can also find beach bars and sunbed rental.

♥ IL CASTELLO // ENJOY FABULOUS VIEWS FROM THE RAMPARTS

Built by the Byzantines in the 5th century, the castle was further strengthened during the Algevin period, the time of the Vespro war bloodbath. The castle continued to be modified and only part of the original defensive wall remains. It's an enjoyable walk here through the *centro storico* and you can stroll along the ramparts and enjoy magnificent views of the coastline and town below. Not just a tourist sight, the castle is utilised by the locals, with a permanent art gallery showcasing contemporary local artists and a small open-air auditorium where concerts take place during the summer months.

❧ CILENTO SUB DIVING CENTER // FROM SNORKELLING TO WRECK DIVES

Indulge in your favourite watery pursuit at the **Cilento Sub Diving Center** (☎ 338 2374603; www.cilentosub.com; Via San Francesco 30; single dives from €20), where courses include snorkelling for beginners, open-water junior dives (from 12 years) and wreck diving; the latter includes the harrowing (for some) viewing of hulks of ships, tanks and planes that were famously destroyed in the region during WWII. Diving sites include such tantalising areas as the waters off the coast at Paestum, where – who knows? – you may just come across your very own bronze Apollo (see p205)!

GASTRONOMIC HIGHLIGHTS

❧ ANNA €

☎ 0974 82 37 63; Lungomare San Marco 32; meals from €15, pizzas from €3

At the city-centre end of the promenade, across from the sea, this has been a locals' favourite for decades. Family run, with a small B&B upstairs (see p287), Ana offers a €15 tourist menu and unusual dishes such as *spaghetti alla mexicana* (€7), with a spicy chilli-based sauce. More traditional seafood dishes include grilled swordfish. This is also a good place for an energy-stoking sugar start to the day, with more than eight types of *cornetti* to choose from, including white chocolate.

❧ BAR GELATERIA DEL CORSO €

Corso Garibaldi 22-24; ice creams from €2, cakes from €1.50, cocktails from €2.50

The most popular spot in town for slurping an ice cream, sipping a cocktail or salivating over a cream cake. Comfortable wicker chairs are ideally positioned for people watching on this pedestrian shopping street. If ice cream is your weakness, there are some unusual flavours, including *marrón glace* (candied chestnut) and *limone sicilia* (Sicilian lemon), plus yoghurt-based choices such as *frutti di bosco* (fruit of the forest).

❧ U'SGHIZ €

☎ 0974 82 93 31; Piazza Umberto 1; meals €15, pizzas from €3

Enjoying a prime *centro storico* position, the rambling dining rooms in this 17th-century building include the upstairs Sala degli Affreschi, complete with mural of jovial owner Antonio (plus family) rendered in Greek mythological style. The house speciality is seafood, with dishes such as *spaghetti a vongole* and an extensive pizza choice. A quarter carafe of house red wine costs a mere €2 but is better for pickling grandma (sorry, onions); go for one of the marginally more expensive choices instead.

CILENTO COAST

EXPLORING THE CILENTO COAST

While the Cilento stretch of coastline lacks the gloss and sophistication of the Amalfi Coast, it can afford to have a slight air of superiority when it comes to the beaches: a combination of secluded coves and long stretches of golden sand with a welcome lack of overpriced ice creams and sunbeds. Beyond the options outlined below, the westernmost stop along the coastline is **Sapri,** which has two pleasant beaches in the centre of town.

❧ AGROPOLI TO ASCEA // PICTURESQUE VILLAGES AND GREAT BEACHES

Around 14km south of Agropoli is the former fishing village of **Santa Maria di**

Castellabate. Head for the southernmost point, which still has a palatable southern Italian feel with dusky-pink and ochre houses blinkered by traditional green shutters. Santa Maria's golden sandy beach stretches for around 4km, which equals plenty of towel space on the sand, even in midsummer.

Medieval **Castellabate** clings to the side of a mountain 280m above sea level and is one of the most endearing and historic towns on the Cilento coast. Approached from its coastal sidekick Santa Maria de Castellabate, the entrance is marked by the broad belvedere di San Costabile, from where there are sweeping coastal views. Flanking this is the shell of a 12th-century castle, with only the defensive walls still standing, and the adjacent contemporary art gallery. The surrounding labyrinth of narrow pedestrian streets is punctuated by ancient archways, small piazzas and the occasional *palazzo*. The animated heart and soul of town is the numerological mouthful Piazza 10 Ottobre 1123 with its panoramic views of the Valle della Annunziata.

Heading south, the next stop is the pretty little harbour at **San Marco di Castellabate**, overlooked by the handsome, ivy-clad Approdo hotel. This was once an important Greek and Roman port, and tombs and other relics have been discovered that are now on view in the museum at Paestum (p208). The area between Santa Maria di Castellabate and San Marco is popular for diving: contact **Galatea** (☎ 0974 96 67 07, 334 3485643; www.galateateam.it; San Marco di Castellabate marina; single dives from €45). San Marco's blue-flag beach is a continuation of the sandy stretch from Santa Maria di Castellabate (see above).

The coastal road heading south lacks the drama (views *and* traffic) of

its Amalfi counterpart but is still prettily panoramic. It's an area that Ernest Hemingway apparently rated highly, particularly **Acciaroli**, which, despite the disquieting amount of surrounding concrete, has a charming centre. Head for the sea and the peeling facade of the Parrocchia di Acciaroli church with its abstract 1920s stained-glass windows. The surrounding streets and piazzas have been tastefully restored using local stone and traditional architecture, and the cafes, bars and restaurants have a buzzing, fashionable appeal.

A short 10km hop south of here, tiny **Pioppi** has the right to feel smug. It was based on initial observations of this town in the late 1950s that American medical researcher Dr Ancel Keys launched his famous study concerning the health benefits of the Mediterranean diet. Of the residents of Pioppi, Keys famously wrote, 'The people were older and vigorous. They were walking up and down the hillside collecting wild grains, and were out fishing before sun up and going out again in late afternoon and rowing boats.' Join the old men today in their more leisurely pursuit of dozing on the shady benches in lovely Piazza de Millenario. Suitably rested, take a picnic to the pristine, pale pebble beach a few steps away. If you are not yet beached out, head for **Marina de Casal Velino** next, with its small, pretty harbour and family-style stretch of sand, complete with plenty of ice-cream opportunities, plus a playground and pedal boats.

Continuing west, Ascea is home to the Greek ruins of **Velia** (☎ 0974 97 23 96; admission €2; ☺ 9am until 1hr before sunset Mon-Sat), founded by the Greeks in the mid-6th century BC and which subsequently became a popular resort with wealthy Romans. The town is best known as being the home of the philosophers Parmenides and Zeno of Elea, as well as of the famous Eleatic School of Philosophy. You can wander around the evocative ruins today, including parts of the original city walls, with traces of one gate and several towers, as well as the ruins of thermal baths, an Ionic temple, a theatre and parts of the original Greek streets, paved in limestone blocks with the original gutters. After all that archaeological academia, reward yourself with a refreshing dip in the sea; the modern town of Ascea is fronted by 5km of glorious sandy beach.

❦ CILENTO EXPLORER // MOONLIT BOAT TRIPS FOR ROMANTICS

Travelling with your loved one? Then consider a romantic night cruise, searching for the Milky Way, sipping a cocktail and exchanging sweet nothings under the stars. If this doesn't suit (you're travelling solo or with your in-laws) then **Cilento Explorer** (☎ 0974 90 00 50; www. cilentoexplorer.com; Piazza Marconi 79, Marina de Casal Velino) offers a shoal of other watery activities, including boat trips to surrounding grottoes and fishing trips (local fisherman included).

❦ IL CICLOPE // GROOVE IN A NIGHTCLUB CAVE

While the Cilento region may not be well known to your average tourist, it is definitely on the global hit parade when it comes to DJ hotspots. Pete Tong, Tommy Vee, Marco Carola, David Morales…all the big names are elbowing for the chance to spin discs at **Il Ciclope** (☎ 0974 93 03 18; Marina di Camerota), which occupies four limestone caves and is one of the hippest places to strut your stuff this side of Ibiza. Don your glad rags and be the most fashionable cave gal (or guy) since the Flintstones.

GASTRONOMIC HIGHLIGHTS

❦ ARLECCHINO €

☎ 0974 96 18 89; Via Guglielmini, Santa Maria di Castellabate; meals €20, pizzas from €4; 🕑 Mar-Nov

Located across from the beach in the pretty southernmost part of Santa Maria, popular Arlecchino has picture windows overlooking the small sweep of sand. Packed out with families at weekends, and with a smart brick-and-wood interior and a terrace, the restaurant offers primarily seafood-based dishes, including a recommended *sepia alla griglia* (grilled cuttlefish). Finish up with the calorific delight of the local speciality *torta ricotta e pera* (ricotta and pear cake).

❦ IL CAPRICCIO €

☎ 0974 84 52 41; Corso da Spiafriddo, Castellabate; meals €18

Located on the road to Perdifumo, this is a favourite choice of the locals. An unassuming place with an outside terrace, Il Capriccio has a gracious host in owner Enxo. The menu runs the gamut from seafood classics such as *zuppa di cozze* (mussel soup) and *polipetti affogati* (poached octopus) to less fishy options such as *zuppa di ceci* (garbanzo bean soup). The *crostata della nonna* (grandma's cake) is as promising as it sounds: a delicious confection of puff pastry, almonds and seasonal fruit.

❦ LIDO DAL PINCIO €

☎ 0974 96 10 90; Via Domenico Forziati 30, Spiaggia Lungomare Bracate, Santa Maria di Castellabate; meals €15; 🕑 Apr-Nov; Ⓟ

At Lida Dal Pincio, situated at the quieter far-northern end of this approximately 4km beach, you can dine informally on the sprawling terrace, wrapped in a towel with sand between your toes. The menu changes depending on the catch of the day, but

SALERNO & THE CILENTO

you can expect a fishy *frittura* (omelette) choice and simple grilled seafood. Take a look at the adjacent pine trees, bent virtually horizontal with the sea breeze.

♥ PIZZA IN PIAZZA €

☎ 320 0966325; Piazza Vittorio Emanuele, Acciaroli; pizzas from €4; ☼ Apr-Nov

An uppercrust pizza place on this pretty piazza with its magnificent rubber trees and wisteria-draped walls. Sit outside or eat on the go. The pizzas include all the standard choices but are excellent, with crispy edges and garden-fresh ingredients. The *caprese* (€6) comes particularly recommended, with its simple topping of cherry tomatoes, *mozzarella di bufala* and basil leaves.

PALINURO

Despite being hailed as the Cilento coast's main resort, Palinuro remains relatively low-key (and low rise), with a tangible fishing-village feel. Located in a picturesque bay sheltered by a promontory, and with superb beaches, it gets crowded with Italian holidaymakers in August. Note that the majority of hotels and restaurants are seasonal and only open from Easter to October.

EXPLORING PALINURO

Aside from the grottoes, Palinuro is famous for its beaches. For a quiet cove, head east of town to Spiaggia Marmelli, surrounded by lush banks of greenery. The beach is approached via steep steps, and there's a small car park at the top. The town's main beach is Spiaggia Palinuro, which stretches for around 4km north of the centre. Palinuro's postcard-pretty harbour has colourful fishing boats, several bars and a wide swathe of golden sand.

The epicentre of town is the Piazza Virgilio, with its modern octagonal church (which looks transplanted from Salt Lake City), and main street Via Indipendenza, which is good for shopping and light eats.

♥ GROTTA AZZURRA //
BE ENCHANTED BY AN
EXTRAORDINARY BLUE GROTTO

Although it doesn't have the hype of its Capri counterpart, Palinuro's **Grotta Azzurra** is similarly spectacular, with a technicolour play of light and hue. It owes its name to the extraordinary effect produced by the sunlight that filters inside from an underground passage lying at a depth of about 8m. The best time to visit is the afternoon, due to the position of the sun. Several boat companies operate out of kiosks on the harbour front, including **Da Alessandro** (☎ 347 6540931; www.costieradelcilento.it; trips from €8), which will take you to the Blue Grotto as well as four other caves in the area.

GASTRONOMIC HIGHLIGHTS

♥ BAR DA SIENA €

☎ 0974 93 10 19; Via Indipendenza 53; ice creams from €1.50, cocktails from €2.50

Part of the Albergo Santa Caterina, this L-shaped bar serves the best ice cream in town with *semi freddi* (semi cold) and yoghurt-based ices, as well as enticing flavours such as *torroncino al pistachio* (nougat and pistachio) and the possibly less appealing *zuppa inglese* (English trifle). The romantic terrace is a perfect place for a little locked-eyes-over-ice-cream time.

♥ PASTICCERIA EGIDIO €

☎ 0974 93 14 60; Via Santa Maria 15; sfogliatelle €1.50

Run by the reassuringly plump Egidio family, this *pasticceria* has a cake display cabinet backed by the large bakery where breads (including *integrale*) arrive steaming hot for picnic time. The cakes really are as good as they look: *sfogliatelle* filled with fresh ricotta, *frollini* (mini fruit and chocolate tarts), and the all-time favourite, crumbly *ameretti* (macaroons).

❦ RISTORANTE DA ISADORA €

☎ 0974 93 10 43; Via Indipendenza 156; meals €20, pizzas from €3.50; ⊗ Mar-Oct

One of the consistently good restaurants here, with a large terrace and a down-to-earth interior, complete with boisterous Italian families and a TV in the corner. The ample menu includes the highly recommended *pennette alla sicilania* with eggplant and mozzarella, and excellent pizzas and risottos. The house wine is perfectly drinkable, and, if you're in grappa mode, there is an excellent choice.

❦ RISTORANTE MIRAMARE €€

☎ 0974 93 09 70; Corso Pisacane 89; meals from €28

Enjoying a supreme position, with a broad terrace overlooking the sea and a small adjacent cove, this place is part of the same-name hotel. The menu is predominantly seafood based and holds few surprises, although there is the odd nod to the international palate, including roast beef (what, no Yorkshire pud!). Otherwise *spaghetti alla vongole* is a safe bet, as is the camera-clicking coastal view.

BACKGROUND

❧ HISTORY
Whispering sibyls, ruthless royals, and bloody Mafia spats: it just wouldn't be Neapolitan history without a healthy dose of intrigue, drama, and vengeance. (opposite)

❧ BAROQUE NAPLES
Florence may be star of the Renaissance, but Naples is belle of the baroque. From chunky cherub churches to operatic staircases, few cities exceed at excess so well. (p249)

❧ SAINTS, SINNERS & SUPERSTITION
Miraculous doctors, superhero saints and the ever-lurking evil eye. In this part of Italy the Catholic and the cultish make for very intriguing bedfellows. (p239)

❧ THE SUBTERRANEAN CITY
Nowhere is Naples' knack for keeping secrets more vividly illustrated than in its vast and ancient underground labyrinth. (p244)

❧ SOUTHERN STAGE
On the stage or on the street, the Neapolitans are seasoned performers. Get the low down on Campania's irrepressible creativity. (p233)

❧ THE CAMPANIAN TABLE
When a region is home to Italy's two greatest edible exports, your tastebuds know they're onto a good thing. (p255)

HISTORY

· · · · · · ·

With almost 3000 candles on its birthday cake, Naples and its sparkling coastline have seen it all, from pleasure-seeking Romans and Spanish conquests to occupying Nazis. Whoever said history was boring has clearly never known this city.

THE EARLY YEARS

The ancient Greeks were the first major players on the scene, setting up a trading post on Ischia and another settlement at Cumae (Cuma; p83) in the 8th century BC. Their main foothold in Italy, Cumae became the most important city in the Italian peninsula's southwest during the next 200 years; a rich commercial centre whose Sibyl was said to be Apollo's mouthpiece.

According to legend, the traders also established Naples on the island of Megaris, current home of the Castel dell'Ovo (p64), in about 680 BC. Christened Parthenope, its namesake was a suicidal siren. Unable to lure the cunning Ulysses with her songs, she drowned herself, washing up on shore.

Failure would also hit the Tuscany-based Etruscans, who twice invaded Cuma and twice failed. After the second of these clashes, in 474 BC, the Cumaeans founded Neapolis (New Town) where Naples' *centro storico* (historic centre) stands.

Despite the Cumaeans resilience, the Etruscan battles had taken a toll, and in 421 BC the Greeks fell to the Samnites. They, in turn, proved no match for the Romans who took Neapolis in 326 BC. Not long after, in 273 BC, they added Paestum (p207) to their list; a Greek city dating back to the 5th century BC.

TOGAS, TRIUMPH & TERROR

Under the Romans, the Bay of Naples sparkled with lavish villas, thermal spas and cashed-up out-of-towners. Farmland and forests covered Vesuvius' lower slopes, while VIPs indulged by the coast. Notables holidayed in Stabiae (Castellammare di Stabia), Nero's second wife Poppea entertained in upmarket Oplontis (see the boxed text, p107) and Julius Caesar's father-in-law kept a home at Herculaneum (p100). West of Naples, Puteoli (Pozzuoli) became a major international port, docking everything from Alexandrian grain ships to Christ's own PA, St Paul; the latter reputedly stepping on shore in AD 61. Further west, Misenum (Miseno) boasted the ancient world's largest naval fleet.

» 8TH CENTURY B	» 680 BC	» 474 BC
Greeks establish a colony at Cuma in the Campi Flegrei. The area becomes the most important Greek settlement on the Italian mainland and a strategic part of Magna Graecia.	The Cuman Greeks establish Parthenope on the island of Megaris, naming it in honour of a suicidal siren whose song fails to seduce the cunning Ulysses.	The Cumans found Neapolis (New Town) on the site of Naples' *centro storico* (historic centre). The original Greek street plan can still be seen today.

BACKGROUND

DON'T MISS...

ANCIENT WONDERS

★ **Paestum //** A mighty ode to Campania's Greek past (p207)

★ **Acropoli di Cuma //** Home of an ancient agony aunt (p83)

★ **Pompeii & Herculaneum //** Roman streets, shops and frescoed villas (p103 and p100)

★ **Museo Archeologico Nazionale, Naples //** Luscious mosaics, lusty statues and priceless ransacked booty (p54)

★ **Anfiteatro Flavio, Pozzuoli //** An ancient arena for bloody spectaculars (p78)

★ **Oplontis, Torre Annunziata //** Lavish frescoes, perfect porticoes and a giant Roman swimming pool (p107)

Despite the Romans' stronghold on the region, the citizens of Neapolis never completely gave in to their foreign occupiers, refusing (among other things) to relinquish their language. While the Romans may have tolerated the linguistic snub, the Neapolitans' opposition to Rome during the Roman Civil War (88–82 BC) was another story, prompting Cornelius Sulla to take the city and slaughter thousands. Equally catastrophic was the unexpected eruption of Mt Vesuvius in AD 79, which drowned nearby Pompeii and Herculaneum in molten lava, mud and ash. Coming just 17 years after a massive earthquake, it was a devastating blow for the rural Plebs already struggling in the region.

Inside the city walls, Neapolis was booming: General Lucullus built an enviable villa where the Castel dell'Ovo stands and even Virgil moved to town. Offshore, Capri became the centre of Emperor Tiberius' famously debauched operations.

Yet, as Neapolis' welfare was by now tied to that of the Roman Empire, the death of the last Roman emperor, Romulus Augustus, in AD 476, saw the city pass into barbarian hands.

THE NORMANS & THE ANGEVINS

By the beginning of the 11th century, Naples was a prospering duchy. Industry and culture were thriving and Christianity had conquered the masses. Outside the city, however, the situation was more volatile as the Normans began to eye up the Lombard principalities of Salerno, Benevento, Capua and Amalfi.

The Normans had arrived in southern Italy in the 10th century, initially as pilgrims en route from Jerusalem, later as mercenaries attracted by the money to be made fight

» 326 BC	» AD 79	» 536
The Romans conquer Neapolis and the city is absorbed into the Roman Empire. Despite this, locals cling to their Greek heritage and language.	At 10am on 24 August, Mt Vesuvius erupts after centuries of slumber, startling the Neapolitans and burying Pompeii, Herculaneum and other towns on the mountain's slopes.	Byzantine chief general Belisarius and his fighters sneak into the city through its ancient aqueduct and lay siege Conquered, Naples becomes a Byzantine duchy.

ing for the rival principalities and against the Arab Muslims in Sicily. And it was to just one such mercenary, Rainulfo Drengot, that the duke of Naples, Sergio IV, gave the contract to drive the Lombards out of Capua. Capua duly fell in 1062, followed by Amalfi in 1073 and Salerno four years later. By 1130 most of southern Italy, including Sicily, was in Norman hands and it was only a question of time before Naples gave in to the inevitable. It did so in 1139. The Kingdom of the Two Sicilies was thus complete.

The Normans maintained their capital in Sicily, and Palermo began to outshine Naples. And yet the Neapolitans seemed happy with their lot, and when the last of the Norman kings, Tancred, was succeeded by his enemy Henry Hohenstaufen of Swabia in 1194, the mood turned ugly. The Neapolitans despised their new Swabian rulers and were delighted when Charles I of Anjou routed them at the battle of Benevento in February 1265.

Under the French Angevins, Naples' artistic and intellectual credentials grew. Charles built the Castel Nuovo (p61) in 1279, the port was enlarged, and in the early 14th century Robert of Anjou constructed Castel Sant'Elmo. Alas, nasty politicking between family factions marked the last century of Angevin rule. Queen Joan I was suspected of murdering her husband and fled the city between 1348 and 1352, leaving her vengeful Hungarian in-laws to occupy Naples. Some 70-odd years later her namesake, Queen Joan II, could only stop her husband stealing the crown thanks to substantial popular support.

With the royals tangled up in soap-style angst, the time was ripe for the Spanish Aragonese to launch their attack.

AMALFI: THE GOLDEN DAYS

Musing on the fabled town of Amalfi, 19th-century scribe Renato Fucini declared that when the town's inhabitants reach heaven on Judgment Day, it will be just like any other day for them. It must have been a view shared by the Roman patricians shipwrecked on its coast in AD 337. Seduced by the area's beauty, they decided to ditch their long-haul trip to Constantinople and stay put. Despite the fans, Amalfi's golden era would arrive in the 9th century, when centuries of Byzantine rule were ditched for Marine Republic status. Between this time and the ruinous Pisan raids of 1135 and 1137, its ever-expanding fleet brought a little bit of Amalfi to the far reaches of the Mediterranean, from churches named in honour of Sant'Andrea (Amalfi's patron saint), to a 'Little Amalfi' quarter in 10th-century Constantinople, complete with expat shops and schools.

» 1139	» 1265	» 1282
Naples joins the Norman-ruled kingdom of the Two Sicilies after the Norman conquest of Capua, Amalfi and Salerno. The city plays second fiddle to the kingdom's capital, Palermo.	Charles I of Anjou beats Naples' hated Swabian rulers, heralding the city as the capital of the French Anjou dynasty. The port is expanded and Castel Nuovo is built in 1279.	Resentful of the Angevins' demotion of Palermo as capital city, Sicilian rioters kill 2000 French people on Easter Monday in the former capital.

BACKGROUND

ARAGONESE ANGST

Taking control of Naples in 1442, Alfonso of Aragon – dubbed *Il Magnanimo* (The Magnanimous) – did much for Naples, promoting art and science and introducing institutional reforms. What he couldn't do was live down the fact that he'd overthrown the popular Angevins.

In 1485 the city's barons took up arms against Alfonso's successor, Ferdinand I. Within a year, however, the ringleaders had been executed (in the Sala dei Baroni inside Castel Nuovo) and peace restored. In 1495 King Charles VIII of France invaded. Fiercely opposed by the Neapolitan masses, the French monarch was forced out four months later and replaced by Aragonese Ferdinand II.

After Ferdinand II's death in 1496, the mutinous barons crowned Ferdinand's uncle, Frederick, as king. This angered everyone: the Neapolitans, the French and the Spanish had all wanted Ferdinand II's widow Joan to succeed him. The upshot was the joint Franco–Spanish invasion of 1501. Frederick tried to hang on to power, but facing almost total opposition he skulked off, leaving Naples to the Spanish. Thus King Ferdinand of Spain became King Ferdinand III of Naples.

DON PEDRO & THE SPANISH YEARS

As part of the cashed-up Spanish empire, 16th-century Naples prospered. By 1600, it was Europe's largest city, with a population of 300,000. The boom heralded urban expansion, with viceroy Don Pedro de Toledo moving the city walls westward and creating the Quartieri Spagnoli (Spanish Quarters). Hundreds of new churches and monasteries sprung up, giving artistic greats like Caravaggio, Giuseppe de Ribera and Luca Giordano the chance to show off their skills. The most prolific of all Naples' architects was Cosimo Fanzago (1591–1678), whose work on the Certosa di San Martino (p67) is a highlight of Neapolitan baroque.

> *As part of the cashed-up Spanish empire, 16th-century Naples prospered*

Less welcome were the ever-increasing tax hikes, resulting from the economic depression that descended in the early 17th century. When the Spanish introduced a levy on fresh fruit in January 1647, it was one tax too many and on 7 July violence broke out on Piazza del Mercato. Nine days later, the rebellion's illiterate leader – Amalfi fisherman Tommaso Aniello (aka Masaniello) – was murdered in the Chiesa di Santa Maria del

» 1442	» 1503	» 1532–53
Alfonso of Aragon drives out René of Anjou to become Naples' new king and a long period of Spanish control begins.	Two years after a Franco–Spanish invasion of Naples, Spanish general Consalvo di Cordoba enters the city and King Ferdinand of Spain becomes King Ferdinand III of Naples.	Don Pedro de Toledo rules as Spanish viceroy, moving the city walls westwards and constructing the Quartieri Spagnoli.

Carmine (p52). The culprits were extremists from within his own camp: they wanted to drive out the Spanish, their leader was happy with cheaper fruit. Local lore has it that Masaniello lies buried in an unmarked tomb in the church.

The French then tried to cash in by sending the duke of Giusa to take the city; the duke failed, and on 6 April 1648 was captured by the new Spanish viceroy, the Count of Oñate. Order was soon re-established, the rebel leaders executed and life in Naples returned to a semblance of normality.

Putting a spanner in the works was the plague of 1656, which wiped out three-quarters of Naples' population and much of the economy. The horror that infected the city's squalid streets is graphically depicted in the paintings that hang in Room 37 of the Certosa di San Martino (p67).

BOURBON BRILLIANCE & HABSBURG CUNNING

With the death of childless Charles V of Naples (Charles II of Spain) in 1700, Spain's European possessions were up for grabs. Despite Philip, grandson of Charles V's brother-in-law, taking the Spanish throne (and therefore the Neapolitan throne) as King Philip V, Austrian troops nabbed Naples in 1707. Waiting in the wings, however, was King Philip V's Bourbon son Charles, who followed his ambitious mother Elisabetta Farnese's advice to take the city. Between his ascension to the Neapolitan throne in 1734 and Italian unification in 1860, Naples was transformed into Europe's showpiece metropolis. The Palazzo Reale di Capodimonte (p71) hit the skyline, downtown Palazzo Reale (p60) was enlarged and the Teatro San Carlo (p61) became Europe's grandest opera house.

In 1759 Charles returned to Spain to succeed his father as King Charles III. As European law prohibited the simultaneous holding of three crowns (Naples, Sicily and Spain), Naples was left to Charles' eight-year-old son Ferdinand, though in effect, power was left to Charles' conscientious prime minister, Bernardo Tanucci.

When in 1768 the Austrian Maria Carolina arrived in town to marry Ferdinand, Tanucci's days were numbered. Maria was one of 16 children of the Habsburg Empress of Austria (the very person who Tanucci had opposed in the 1740 crisis of Austrian succession). She was beautiful, clever and ruthless; a ready match for Tanucci and an unlikely partner for the famously dim, dialect-speaking Ferdinand.

In accordance with her marriage agreement Maria Carolina joined the Council of State on the birth of her first son in 1777. It was the position she'd been waiting for to oust Tanucci, and into his shoes stepped a French-born English aristocrat, John Acton.

» 1600	» 1656	» 1707
Naples is the biggest city in Europe, boasting a population of more than 300,000. Among its growing number of residents is renegade artist Caravaggio, who arrives in 1606.	A devastating plague hits Naples. Within six months, three-quarters of the city's population is dead and buried in mass graves.	Austrian viceroys rule Naples for 27 years. Tax and university reforms are introduced and coastal roads connecting the city to the slopes of Mt Vesuvius are built.

BACKGROUND

Acton had won Maria over with his anti-Bourbon politics and wish to forge closer links with Austria and Britain. But just as things began to go smoothly with the English, France erupted in revolution.

THE PARTHENOPEAN REPUBLIC

While the Neapolitan court naturally disapproved of the 1789 French Revolution, it would take the beheading of Maria Carolina's sister, Marie Antoinette, to prompt Naples to join the anti-French coalition.

Troops from Naples and revolutionary France clashed in French-occupied Rome in 1798. The Neapolitans claimed the city but within 11 days were scurrying back south with the French in hot pursuit. Panicked, Ferdinand and Maria Carolina headed for Palermo, leaving Naples to its own devices.

Bitterly opposed by most of the population, the French were welcomed by the Neapolitan nobility and bourgeoisie, many of whom had adopted fashionable republican ideas. And it was with the full backing of the French that the Parthenopean Republic was declared on 23 January 1799.

But it wasn't a success. The leaders were an ideologically rather than practically minded lot, and were soon in financial straits. Their efforts to democratise the city failed and the army was a shambles.

Over the water in Palermo, the royal exiles had not been sitting idle. Ferdinand and Maria Carolina dispatched Cardinal Fabrizio Ruffo to Calabria to organise an uprising. On 13 June he entered Naples and all hell broke loose as his men turned the city into a slaughterhouse. With a score to settle, Ferdinand and Maria Carolina returned from Sicily on 8 July and embarked on a systematic extermination of republican sympathisers. More than 200 were executed.

BOURBON DECLINE & NATIONALIST FERVOUR

Despite the Parthenopean Republic's failure, French forces once again marched into Naples in 1806. The royal family once more fled to Sicily and in 1808 Joachim Murat, Napoleon's brother-in-law, became king of Naples. Despite his abolishment of feudalism and kick-starting of local industry, Murat could do no right in the eyes of the royalist masses.

With Murat finally ousted in 1815, Ferdinand returned to claim his throne. But the French revolution had stirred up too many ideas for a return to the age of absolutism

» 1734	» 1737	» 1768
Encouraged by his ambitious mother and backed by his army, Charles takes control from the Austrians and becomes the first Bourbon king of Naples.	The original Teatro San Carlo is built in a swift eight months. Designed by Giovanni Med-rano, it is rebuilt in 1816 after a devastating fire.	Marie Antoinette's sister, Maria Carolina, marries the uncouth Ferdinand IV. Nine years later she enters the Council of State and ousts prime minister and enemy Bernardo Tanucci.

and the ruthless Carbonari society forced Ferdinand to grant the city a constitution in 1820. A year later, however, it was abandoned as Ferdinand called in Austrian troops.

Pressured by rising rebellion across Europe, Ferdinand reintroduced a constitution in 1848, only to dissolve the parliament altogether. He was as blind to the changing times as his equally obstinate son, who succeeded him in 1859.

More popular was nationalist fighter Giuseppe Garibaldi, whose goal was a united Italy. Buoyed by the victory of Piedmontese rebels against the Austrian army, he set sail for Sicily in May 1860 with a volunteer army of 1000 Red Shirts. Although Ferdinand's 25,000-strong Neapolitan army was waiting in Sicily, the Bourbons' repression of liberalism was beginning to cost it goodwill. With an army that had swelled to 5000 men, Garibaldi defeated the half-hearted Bourbon forces, declaring himself dictator in the name of King Vittorio Emanuele II.

In a case of too-little-too-late, Ferdinand's son and successor Francesco II agreed to a constitution in June 1860 but Garibaldi had crossed over to the Italian mainland and was Naples-bound. True to tradition, Francesco fled the city, taking refuge with 4000 loyalists behind the River Volturno, north of Naples. On 7 September Garibaldi marched unopposed into Naples, welcomed as a hero.

A series of last-ditch attacks on the rebels by Bourbon loyalists were defeated at the Battle of Volturno and on 21 October the city voted overwhelmingly to join a united Italy under the Savoy monarchy.

A seasoned royal city, Naples was a serious contender for capital of Italy. But when Rome was wrested from the French in 1870, the newly formed Italian parliament transferred from its temporary home in Florence to the Eternal City. From being the grand capital of a Bourbon kingdom, Naples suddenly became a lowly regional capital – something Naples has never forgotten.

WAR & PEACE

A poorer shadow of its former self, postunification Naples suffered two major blows: mass emigration and a cholera outbreak in 1884. In response to the cholera epidemic, a citywide cleanup was launched. The worst slums near the port were razed, Corso Umberto I was bulldozed through the city centre, and a sparkling new residential quarter appeared on the Vomero.

The Fascists continued the building spree: an airport was built in 1936, railway and metro lines were laid and the Vomero funicular opened for business. No sooner had many of these projects been completed that the strategic port city was hit by the full

» 1799	» 1806	» 1860
he Parthenopean Republic s proclaimed on 23 January. t quickly fails, royal rule is einstalled and more than 200 epublican sympathisers are xecuted.	Joseph Bonaparte occupies the city and declares himself king of Naples. Two years later, Bonaparte is crowned king of Spain.	Garibaldi enters the city to a hero's welcome and Naples votes overwhelmingly to join a united Italy under the Savoy monarchy.

force of WWII. Savage aerial bombing by the Allies left over 20,000 people dead and much of the city in tatters.

Although the Nazis took Naples in 1943, they were quickly forced out by a series of popular uprisings between 26 and 30 September, famously known as the Quattro Giornate di Napoli (Four Days of Naples). Led by locals, especially by young *scugnizzi* (Neapolitan for 'street urchins') and ex-soldiers, the street battles paved the way for the Allied 'liberators' to enter the city on 1 October.

Despite setting up a provisional government in Naples, the Allies were confronted with an anarchic mass of troops, German prisoners of war and bands of Italian fascists all competing with the city's starving population for food. Then in 1944, to make matters worse, Mt Vesuvius erupted.

Overwhelmed, the Allied authorities turned to the underworld for assistance. As long as the Allies agreed to turn a blind eye towards their black-market activities, the Mafia was willing to help. And so the dreaded Camorra (see the boxed text, opposite) began to flourish.

CONTEMPORARY STRUGGLES

The rapacious Camorra made the most of the devastating earthquake that hit the region in 1980, siphoning off billions of lire poured into the devastated region. Striking on 23 November 1980, the 6.83 Richter scale quake left over 2700 dead and thousands more homeless.

In the decade that followed *abusivismo* (illegal construction) flourished, profiteering mobsters partied publicly with the city's football icon Diego Armando Maradona, and public services virtually ceased to exist. The situation was not unique to Naples – corruption and cronyism were rife across Italy.

After humiliating bouts in 2003 and 2006, Naples' street corners were once again submerged in rubbish

It couldn't go on and in 1992 the Mani Pulite (Clean Hands) campaign kicked into gear. What had started as an investigation into bribery at a retirement home in Milan quickly grew into a nationwide crusade against corruption. Industry bosses and politicians were investigated, some imprisoned, and former prime minister Bettino Craxi fled Italy to avoid prosecution.

In Naples, the city voted its approval by electing as mayor former Communist Antonio Bassolino, whose promises to kick-start the city and fight corruption was music to

» 1884	» 1889	» 1934
A mass cholera epidemic strikes the city, prompting the closure of Naples' ancient aqueduct system and the launch of a major urban redevelopment project.	Raffaele Esposito invents pizza margherita in honour of Queen Margherita, who takes her first bite of the Neapolitan staple on a royal visit to the city.	Screen icon Sophia Loren is born, spending her childhood in the old port town of Pozzuoli, west of Naples.

weary Neapolitan ears. In the seven years that followed, a burst of urban regeneration gave Naples a refreshing sense of hope and pride. A-list artists were commissioned to deck out the city's new metro stations, world leaders flew in for the 1994 G7 summit and arts festival Maggio dei Monumenti (p10) spiced up the city's calendar.

Despite winning a second term in 1997, Bassolino couldn't keep up the impressive momentum and in 2000 he was elected president of the Campania region; a move many considered a political fudge to oust him from the day-to-day running of the city.

Into his shoes stepped Rosa Russo Jervolino, a former interior minister and Naples' first female mayor. Elected on a centre-left ticket firstly in 2001, and then for a second term in May 2006, she hasn't had an easy time of it. In April 2002 political chaos ensued after eight policemen were arrested on charges of torturing antiglobalisation protestors arrested at a 2001 government conference.

After humiliating bouts in 2003 and 2006, Naples' street corners were once again submerged in rubbish in 2008 as authorities struggled to sort out the city's refuse contracts. Footage of fed-up residents setting fire to the mounting garbage hit the world's media. While commentators muttered darkly about criminal tactics linked to the lucrative waste-disposal business, residents screamed that they just wanted their streets clean. It was a very Neapolitan drama and one not applauded by the EU, which sued Italy for failing to tackle the ongoing problem.

DRAG, DRUGS & THE CAMORRA

While Mafia arrests are a common occurrence in Naples, the February 2009 arrest of Ugo Gabriele broke the mould like no other. Beefy, ruthless and cunning, the 27-year-old would go down in history as Italy's first cross-dressing mobster. In between managing lucrative prostitution and drug rackets for the city's Scissionisti clan, 'Kitty' (as Gabriele demanded to be addressed) found time to shape his eyebrows, dab on the lipstick and dye his hair a platinum blonde.

Despite the novelty factor, Naples' homegrown Mafia is far from a light read. Vast and sinister, its tentacles have a grip on everything from drug, arms and counterfeit smuggling to construction, transport and waste-disposal contracts. Sadly, the region's high unemployment rates provide fertile ground for Greater Naples' estimated 111 clans. To many of society's most vulnerable, the lure of quick cash is too irresistible, with weekly drug-trade rates ranging from €100 for lookouts to €1000 for those willing to hide the drugs at home. Yet, it's all play money compared to the Camorra's estimated annual turnover, which exceeds a cool €30 million.

1943	» 1980	» 1987
Allied bombing raids wreak havoc on the city, destroying the 14th-century Basilica di Santa Chiara. A year later, Mt Vesuvius erupts.	At 7.34pm on 23 November, a powerful earthquake rocks Campania, causing widespread damage and killing almost 3000 people.	Under Maradona, Napoli wins both the Serie A championship (lo scudetto) and the Coppa Italia. Mass elation sweeps across the city.

Adding insult to injury was the so-called 'Scampia feud' of late 2004 and early 2005; a deadly turf battle fought out by Camorra clans in the tough northern suburbs of Scampia and Secondigliano. In just four months, up to 47 people were gunned down as rival clans fought for control of the city's lucrative drug trade.

Memories of the feud were relived in September 2008, when a Camorra death squad gunned down seven men in the town of Castel Volturno, northwest of Naples. That six of the dead were West African migrants was read as a warning to Nigerian criminal clans muscling in on the local drug market.

Soon after the shooting, Italian defence minister Ignazio La Russa deployed hundreds of soldiers to patrol Naples' city streets in an attempt to quash the wave of Camorra-related crime. To most jaded Neapolitans, it was little more than (another) knee-jerk reaction to a deeply rooted problem; a problem deeply examined in local writer Roberto Saviano's explosive expose *Gomorra*. Bravely documenting the Camorra's growing influence on global commerce and politics, Saviano's 2007 book was adapted for the silver screen in 2008.

Indeed, it's fair to say that 2008 was an annus horribilis for Naples and Jervolino, the year ending with the arrest of four city administrators accused of looting public funds. A fifth accused took his own life. The scandal, not limited to Neapolitan politicians, rocked Italy's political left, who had long enjoyed pointing out the scandals plaguing centre-right prime minister, Silvio Berlusconi.

As Naples enters the second decade of the 21st century, it remains to be seen whether the tumultuous events of the last decade were a momentary hiccup in the city's roller-coaster history or confirmation of a descent back into darker days.

» 1992	» 2004-05	» 2009
The anticorruption campaign known as *Mani Pulite* is launched. The following year, Antonio Bassolino is voted mayor and a major city clean-up begins.	Tension between rival Camorra clans explodes on the streets of suburban Scampia and Secondigliano. In only four months, almost 50 people are gunned down in retribution attacks.	Police in Naples arrest Ugo Gabriele, the world's first-known cross-dressing mob boss. The lipstick-loving *camorrista* operated a drug and prostitution racket.

THE SOUTHERN STAGE

· · · · · · ·

…for all Naples would seem to be out of doors, and tearing to and fro in carriages… Exhibitors of Punch, buffo singers with guitars, reciters of poetry, reciters of stories, a row of cheap exhibitions with clowns and showmen, drums, and trumpets, painted cloths representing the wonders within, and admiring crowds assembled without, assist the whirl and bustle…

Charles Dickens

There is nowhere more theatrical than Naples, a city in which everyday transactions become minor performances and traffic jams give rise to impromptu klaxon concerts. Both literally and metaphorically, locals air their laundry with pride, and the streets and squares are a stage on which to play out life's daily dramas.

Neapolitans know that many of the stereotypes foreigners hold of Italians – noisy, food-loving, passionate and proud – refer to them. And they revel in it. Nowhere else in Italy are the people so conscious of their role in the theatre of everyday life and so addicted to its drama and intensity. Everyone has an opinion to give, a line to deliver or a sigh to perform. Eavesdropping is a popular pastime and knowing everyone else's business is a veritable sport.

Neapolitans joke that if you were to collapse on the street a local would first want to know all the juicy details, and only after that would they think of calling an ambulance. In a city with a population density of 2613 people per square kilometre (nearly 14 times higher than the national average), this penchant for curiosity is understandable. For the most part, life is lived on the street and privacy is a luxury many simply can't afford.

Naples' very setting oozes stage presence, from the amphitheatricality of the bay to the Pinteresque menace of its looming volcano. The very presence of Vesuvius

> *Everyone has an opinion to give, a line to deliver or a sigh to perform*

has played its part in forging the locals' fatalistic streak: with a deadly giant on the doorstep, mortality can take on an intense hue. Walls drip with passionate, spray-painted declarations of love, evoking a sense of urgency, a compulsion to live passionately for the moment, for who knows what might happen next. After seeing Vesuvius in action, Goethe himself proclaimed that the Neapolitans would be different if they weren't stuck between God and Satan.

The city's history reads like the memoirs of a tragi-fabulous diva. Used, abused and adored by powerful emperors, kings and artists alike, the city has survived it all, from gilded eras of wealth and glory to humiliating bouts of poverty, exodus and bloody crime, sometimes simultaneously, and always against one of the world's most inspiring natural backdrops.

All this considered, it's not surprising that the Neapolitans are such masters of pathos, melancholy, irony, and improvisation. Nor is it surprising that Naples has given Italy some of the country's most definitive cultural icons, from the 16th-century commedia

BACKGROUND

dell'arte and the 18th-century operas of Alessandro Scarlatti, to silver-screen legends like Sophia Loren.

THE NEAPOLITAN SCORE

That Italy's first recording studio opened in Naples is testament to the city's musical legacy. In the 1700s, this was the world's opera capital, with industry heavyweights flocking south to perform at the majestic Teatro San Carlo. Locally trained greats like Francesco Durante (1684–1755), Leonardo Vinci (1690–1730) and Tommaso Traetta (1727–79) wowed conservatories across Europe. Naples' greatest composer, Alessandro Scarlatti (1660–1725), trained at the esteemed conservatory at the Chiesa della Pietà dei Turchini on Via Medina, which also gave birth to the renowned music group Pietà de' Turchini (p94).

Creator of circa 100 operatic works, Scarlatti also played a leading role in the development of *opera seria* (serious opera), giving the world the three-part overture and the aria da capo.

Running parallel to the high-brow opera seria was opera buffa (comic opera); the 18th-century's answer to pop music. Inspired by the Neapolitan commedia dell'arte (opposite), the genre began life as light-hearted, farcical interludes – intermezzi – performed between scenes of heavier classical operas. Kick-started by Scarlatti's *Il Trionfe dell'Onore* (The Triumph of Honour) in 1718, the contemporary interludes soon developed into a major, crowd-pleasing genre, with homegrown favourites including Giovanni Battista Pergolesi's *La Serva Padrona* (The Maid Mistress), Niccolò Piccinni's *La Cecchina* and Domenico Cimarosa's *Il Matrimonio Segreto* (The Clandestine Marriage).

The following century saw the rise of the *la canzone napoletana* (Neapolitan song), its roots firmly planted in the annual Festa di Piedigrotta song festival. A vintage 'Idol' of sorts, it saw aspiring musicians present their fresh compositions to a voting public. Some tunes celebrated the city; among them the world-famous 'Funiculì Funiculà', an ode to the funicular that once scaled Mt Vesuvius. Others lamented one's distance from it. Either way, the songs deeply resonated with the locals, especially for the millions who boarded ships in search of a better life abroad. This Neapolitan diaspora would play a major role in turning Neapolitan tunes into the most internationally recognisable form of Italian music. Indeed, when the sheet music to the Italian national anthem was lost at the 1920 Olympic Games in Antwerp, the orchestra broke into 'O Sole Mio' instead… It was the only Italian melody that everyone knew.

The arrival of the American allies in 1943 sparked another one of the Neapolitan's musical predilections: jazz, rhythm and blues. Still a dominant force on the city's live-music scene, it provided yet another influence on the city's homegrown sounds. As music journalist Francesco Calazzo puts it: 'As a port city, Naples has always absorbed foreign influences. Musically, the result is a fusion of styles, from Arab laments and Spanish folk to African percussion and American blues'.

This fusion came to the fore in the late 1970s. A defining moment for Neapolitan music, it saw new-wave pioneers like Eugenio Bennatto, Enzo Avitabile and Pino Daniele revive Neapolitan folk and cross it over with rock, roots and hypnotic African beats. Singing many of his songs in Neapolitan, Daniele's bitter-sweet lyrics about his beloved hometown – epitomised in songs like 'Napul'è' (Naples Is) – struck a particular chord with the public. Some music critics go as far as to tribute the self-taught guitarist with reviving *la canzone napoletana*. While considerably more mainstream these days, Daniele remains one of Italy's most successful musicians, both at home and abroad.

The biting social commentary of Daniele's lyrics found new life in the 1990s with the rise of hip-hop/reggae acts like 99 Posse and Almamegretta. Straight out of Naples' *centri sociali* (left-wing cultural centres) and crime-ridden suburbs, their Neapolitan rapping vented deep bitterness towards corrupt politicians, the Camorra and the social injustices plaguing the city. On their gritty coat tails hang newer hardcore hip-hop acts like Co'Sang (With Blood), a 20-something duo from the drug-infested neighbourhood of Scampia. 'A Vita Bbona (The Good Life), the follow-up to their hard-hitting 2005 debut album, *Chi More Pe'Mme* (Whoever Dies for Me), hit the shelves in 2009.

Also out of Scampia is A67, a rock-crossover group whose hardline anti-Mafia stance saw celebrated writer Roberto Saviano (author of the internationally acclaimed book *Gomorra*) collaborate on their 2008 album *Suburb*.

THEATRICAL LEGACIES

Rivalling Naples' musical prowess is its theatrical tradition, considered one of Italy's oldest. Its most famous contribution to the world stage is the commedia dell'arte, dating back to the 16th century and rooted in the earthy ancient Roman comedy theatre of *Fabula Atellana* (Atellan Farce). Like its ancient inspiration, this highly animated genre featured a set of stock characters in masks acting out a series of semistandard situations. Performances were often used to satirise local situations, and based on a tried-and-tested recipe of adultery, jealousy, old age and love. Understandably, it was a crowd pleaser with the masses, who enjoyed easy access to its curbside stages, manned by troupes of travelling actors.

Not only did commedia dell'arte give birth to a number of legendary characters, including the Harlequin and Punchinello (see the boxed text, p236), it provided fertile ground for the development of popular theatre in Naples and was a tradition in which the great dramatist Raffaele Viviani (1888–1950) was firmly rooted. Viviani's focus on local dialect and the Neapolitan working class won him local success and the enmity of the Mussolini regime.

Despite Viviani's success, the most important figure in modern Neapolitan theatre remains Eduardo de Filippo (1900–84). The son of a famous Neapolitan actor, Eduardo Scarpetta (1853–1925), de Filippo made his stage debut at the age of four and over the next 80 years became a hugely successful actor, impresario and playwright. His body of often bittersweet work, which includes the classics *Il Sindaco del Rione Sanità* (The Mayor of the Sanità Quarter) and *Sabato, Domenica e Lunedì* (Saturday, Sunday and Monday), encapsulated struggles well-known to Neapolitans, from the injustice of being forced to live beyond the law to the fight for dignity in the face of adversity.

BACKGROUND

A PUPPET WITH PUNCH

His aliases are many, from Punchinello or Mr Punch in Britain to Petruska in Russia. In his hometown of Naples, however, he's simply Pulcinella; the best-known character of the commedia dell'arte and one of the city's most ubiquitous souvenirs. In his white costume and black beak-nosed mask, this squeaky voiced clown is equally exuberant and lazy, optimistic and cynical, melancholic and vitreously witty. As a street philosopher, he is antiauthoritarian and is often seen beating the local copper with a stick (hence the term slapstick). At home, however, his wife's the beater and he's the victim. Not surprisingly, many claim that Pulcinella encapsulates the very essence of the Neapolitan spirit. More contentious are Pulcinella's origins. While some trace his creation to a 16th-century actor in the town of Capua, others believe he has been dancing and stirring since the days of togas...or even longer. In fact, his iconic hook-nosed mask appears on frescoed Etruscan tombs in Tarquinia, north of Rome. The mask belongs to Phersu, a vicious Etruscan demon known as the Queen of Hell's servant.

The *furbizia* (cunning) for which Neapolitans are famous is celebrated in de Filippo's play *Filumena Marturano*, in which a clever former prostitute gets her common-law husband to marry her by declaring him to be the father of one of her three *bambini*. Exactly which of the three she won't disclose to ensure that he treats them equally. If you recognise the plot, chances are you've seen the film adaptation, *Matrimonio all'italiana* (Marriage, Italian Style; 1964), starring Naples' homegrown siren Sophia Loren (1934–) and Italian acting legend Marcello Mastroianni (1924–1996).

Roberto de Simone (1933–) is another great Neapolitan playwright, not to mention a renowned composer and musicologist. While lesser known than de Filippo abroad, his theatrical masterpiece *La Gatta Cenerentola* (The Cat Cinderella) enjoyed a successful run in London in 1999. At the time of writing, de Simone had finished reworking the piece, which is based on Giambattista Basile's 16th-century version of the fairy tale.

It is difficult to overestimate the role De Simone has played in the preservation and celebration of Naples' cultural heritage. Artistic director of the Teatro San Carlo in the 1980s and later director of the Naples Conservatory, his extensive research into the city's folkloric tales and tunes has seen him revive rare comic operas and create a cantata for 17th-century Campanian revolutionary, Masaniello, as well as the oratorio *Eleonora*, in honour of the heroine of the Neapolitan revolution of 1799.

De Simone's input aside, Naples' contemporary theatre scene remains fairly hit-and-miss. One of its leading lights is Enzo Moscato (1948–), whose work fuses a vibrant physicality with skilful use of dialect and music. His most famous work is the 1991 multiple-award-winning *Rasoi* (Razors), and the scribe is often found hanging out at the Galleria Toledo (p94), Naples' leading experimental theatre.

A more recent sign of promise is the newly inaugurated Napoli Teatro Festival Italia (p10); a major annual event which sees some of the city's most iconic landmarks host cutting-edge performances from Italy and beyond.

THE SILVER SCREEN

From a buxom Sophia Loren to preppy Hollywood hunks, Naples and the Amalfi Coast have framed countless celluloid stars. Locations read like a red-carpet roll call: 'la Loren' wiggled her booty through Naples' Sanità district in Vittorio de Sica's *Ieri, Oggi, Domani* (Yesterday, Today, Tomorrow; 1963), rival Gina Lollobrigida shook hers on the Amalfi Coast in John Huston's *Beat the Devil* (1953), while Matt Damon and Gwyneth Paltrow toasted and tanned on Ischia and Procida in *The Talented Mr Ripley* (1999).

Naples' homemade offerings have often been intense, introvert and darkly funny, holding a mirror to the city's harsh realities. Feted for his 1948 neorealist masterpiece *Ladri di Biciclette* (Bicycle Thieves), Vittorio de Sica (1901–74) was a master at depicting the bittersweet struggle at the heart of so much Neapolitan humour. His two Neapolitan classics, *L'Oro di Napoli* (The Gold of Naples; 1954) and *Ieri, Oggi, Domani*, delighted audiences throughout the country but nowhere more so than in Naples, his adopted city, where filmgoers thrilled to the sight of Sophia Loren in top form.

Appearing with Loren in both *L'Oro di Napoli* and the slapstick farce *Miseria e Nobilità* (Misery and Nobility; 1954) is the city's other screen deity, Antonio de Curtis (1898–1967), aka Totò. A one-man Neapolitan Abbott and Costello of sorts, Totò depicted the Neapolitan *furbizia* like no other. Born in the working-class Sanità district, he appeared in more than 100 films, typically playing the part of a hustler living on nothing but his quick wits. It was a role that ensured Totò's cult status in a city where the art of *arrangiarsi* (getting by) is a way of life. Even Neapolitan Gen-Xers will relay their favourite Totò scenes, a particularly popular one involving Totò 'assisting' a pompous senator with his luggage, taking each piece and dutifully passing it out the train's window.

In fact, so strong is the cult of Totò that several Totòisms have even found their way into the language, among them '*Siamo uomini o corporali?*' (Are we men or are we corporals).

Inheriting Totò's mantle, Massimo Troisi (1953–94) is best known internationally for his role in *Il Postino* (The Postman). Within Italy, however, he was adored for his unique brand of rambling humour. In his debut film of 1980, *Ricomincio da Tre* (I'm Starting from Three), he humorously tackles the problems faced by Neapolitans who are forced to head north for work. Sadly the message is still relevant 25 years later. Troisi's cameo in the schlock murder mystery *No Grazie, Il Caffè Mi Rende Nervoso* (No Thanks, Coffee Makes Me Nervous; 1982) – arguably one of his funniest – sees a jittery, pyjama-clad Troisi at his rambling best as he hopelessly tries to convince Funiculì Funiculà (an unseen, helium-pitched psychopath set on sabotaging Naples' new jazz festival) that he is only loyal to the city's traditional cultural offerings.

The film itself provided a humorous commentary on the city's struggle to reconcile its traditions with its modern aspirations. Its male lead, Lello Arena (1953–), rose to national fame in the late 1970s as part of the Neapolitan comedy trio La Smorfia, which also included Troisi and Enzo De Caro (1958–).

In more recent times, a new wave of Neapolitan directors, including Antonio Capuano (1945–), Mario Martone (1959–), Pappi Corsicato (1960–) and Antonietta de

BACKGROUND

DON'T MISS...

STERLING PERFORMANCES

★ **Teatro San Carlo, Naples** // Velvet, glamour and thunderous applause (p61)

★ **Around Midnight, Naples** // A veteran of the city's jazz scene (p93)

★ **Centro di Musica Antica Pieta de' Turchini, Naples** // Classical scores and architecture (p94)

★ **Ravello Festival, Ravello** // Summertime tunes in a heavenly garden (p10)

★ **La Mortella, Ischia** // Romantic concerts *en plein air* (p145)

Lillo (1960–), have turned their cameras on the city and its difficulties in films such as Capuano's critically acclaimed *Luna Rossa* (Red Moon) of 2001. While Corsicato's queer-centric classics *Libera* (Free; 1993) and *I Bucchi Neri* (The Black Holes; 1995) evoke the ever-present link between the ancient and modern sides of Naples, de Lillo's finest offering to date, *Il Resto di Niente* (The Remains of Nothing; 2003), focuses on the psychological complexities of Eleonora Pimental de Fonesca; also the inspiration for De Simone's aforementioned oratorio.

Yet no recent film captures Naples' contemporary struggles as intensely or relentlessly as the 2008 release smash *Gomorra* (Gomorrah; 2008). Directed by Rome's Matteo Garrone (1968–) but based on the controversial book by Neapolitan Roberto Saviano, the film intertwines five stories of characters affected by the region's merciless Camorra, from a couple of teenager wannabe gangsters to a haute couture tailor in hiding. A hit across the world, the film earned itself the Grand Prix at the 2008 Cannes Film Festival, as well as the Arii-Zeiss Award at the Munich Film Festival.

SAINTS, SINNERS & SUPERSTITIONS

· · · · · · ·

Far from cliché, to call Naples 'magical' verges on the literal. This is Europe's esoteric metropolis par excellence; a Mediterranean New Orleans with less voodoo and more Catholic guilt. Here, miracles pack-out cathedrals, dreams channel lottery numbers, and horn-shaped charms ward off the dreaded *mal'occhio* (evil eye). Myths and legends litter the streets, from tales of human sacrifice in the Cappella Sansevero to that of a prophetic egg below the Castel dell'Ovo (p64).

FRIENDS IN HIGH PLACES

Headlining the city's supernatural scene are the saints. Veritable celebrities, fireworks explode in their honour, fans flock to kiss their marble feet and newborn *bambini* (children) take on their names. That Gennaro is the most common boy's name in Naples is no coincidence; San Gennaro is the city's patron saint. As in much of southern Italy, Neapolitans celebrate their *giorno omastico* (name day) with as much gusto as they do their actual birthdays. Forgetting a friend's name day is a bigger faux pas than forgetting their birthday because everyone knows (or should know) the most important saints' days.

For the religiously inclined, these haloed helpers play a more significant role in their spiritual life than the big 'G' himself. While the Almighty is seen as stern and distant (just like any old-school Italian papà), the saints enjoy a more familial role as intercessor and confidant. Not everyone is impressed: a sign inside the Santissima Annunziata church reminds the faithful to venerate Christ at the altar before sidling off to the side chapels. Despite the request, many keep marching straight to the saints.

Topping the list of go-betweens is the Virgin Mary, whose status as maternal protector strikes a deep chord in a society where mothers have always fiercely defended the rights of their precious sons. Festival days in honour of the Madonna are known to

VICTORY OF THE SHRINES

It only takes a quick stroll through the *centro storico*, Quartieri Spagnoli or Sanità district to work out that small shrines are a big hit in Naples. A kitschy combo of electric votive candles, Catholic iconography and fresh or plastic flowers, they adorn everything from *palazzo* façades to courtyards and staircases. Most come with an inscription, confirming the shrine as a tribute *per grazie ricevute* (for graces received) or *ex-voto* (in fulfilment of a vow).

The popularity of the shrines can be traced back to the days of Dominican friar Gregorio Maria Rocco (1700–82). Determined to make the city's dark, crime-ridden laneways safer, he convinced the Bourbon monarch to light up the lanes with oil lamps. The lamps were hastily trashed by the city's petty thieves who relied on darkness to trip up their victims with rope. Thankfully, the quick-thinking friar had a better idea. Banking on the city's respect for its saints, he encouraged locals to erect illuminated shrines. The idea worked and the streets did become safer, for even the toughest of petty thieves wouldn't dare upset an adored celestial idol.

BACKGROUND

whip up mass hysteria, best exemplified by the annual Feast of the Madonna dell'Arco. Held on Easter Monday at the Santuario della Madonna dell'Arco, a sanctuary near the village of Sant'Anastasia, it commemorates a miracle in which a statue of the Virgin wept blood in 1450. Thousands flock to the sanctuary, among them hardcore pilgrims called *fujenti* (those who run), best known for running to the sanctuary and collapsing hysterically at the altar.

In Naples, the lead up to the festival is an event in itself. From the week following the Epiphany (6 January) to Easter Monday, hundreds of neighbourhood *congreghe* (instrument-playing congregations) parade through the streets, carrying a statue of the Madonna, collecting offerings for the big day and playing an incongruous medley of tunes (think 'Ave Maria' followed by a 1970s Raffaella Carrà pop hit).

When the blood liquefies the city breathes a sigh of relief

Exactly which saint you consult can depend on what you're after. If it's an addition to the family, chances are you'll head straight to the former home of Santa Maria Francesca delle Cinque Piaghe (p58) to sit on the saint's miraculous chair. It's the closest thing to a free fertility treatment in Naples.

On the opposite side of Via Toledo, in the Chiesa del Gesù Nuovo (p44), entire rooms are dedicated to Dr Giuseppe Moscati, a much-loved local medic canonised in 1987. Here, body-part shaped *ex-voti* smother the walls, each one a testament to the MD's celestial intervention.

For many, the wish list doesn't stop at good health or the pitter-patter of little feet, with common requests ranging from next week's winning lottery numbers to a decent-looking date.

Despite the Madonna's popularity, the city's ultimate holy superhero is San Gennaro. Every year in May, September and December thousands of Neapolitans cram themselves into the Duomo (p49) to pray for a miracle: that the blood of Naples' patron saint, kept here in two phials, will liquefy and save Naples from any potential disaster.

According to scientists, the so-called miracle has a logical explanation. Apparently, it's all to do with thixotrophy, that is the property of certain compounds to liquefy when shaken and then to return to their original form when left to stand. To verify this, however, scientists would have to analyse the blood, something the Church has effectively blocked by refusing permission to open the phial.

And while many locals acknowledge the scientific line, the fact remains that when the blood liquefies the city breathes a sigh of relief. After all, when the miracle failed in 1944 Mt Vesuvius erupted, and when it failed to happen in 1980, a catastrophic earthquake hit the city the same year.

DEATH & THE CITY

Rattled by earthquakes and the odd volcanic eruption, it makes sense that the Neapolitans are a fatalistic lot. Indeed, the city's intense passion for life is only matched by its curious attachment to death. Here, contemporary culture's death-defying delusions are constantly undermined, whether by death notice–plastered walls, shrines dedicated to the dearly departed or edible treats with names like *torrone dei morti* (nougat of the dead), the latter merrily gobbled on All Saints' Day. Carved skulls adorn churches and cloisters, such as those adorning the Chiostro Grande (Great Cloister) inside the Certosa di San Martino (p67); a constant reminder of one's mortal status.

For some, death is just another opportunity to indulge in a little *bella figura* (looking good), their savings blown on grand horse-and-carriage hearses to outdo the neighbours left behind.

Yet, of all the rites and rituals involving death in Naples, none boast the

> ## DON'T MISS...
>
> ### MYSTICAL HOT SPOTS
>
> ★ **Festa di San Gennaro** // Naples' legendary 'Will he or won't he?' miracle (p10)
>
> ★ **Casa e Chiesa di Santa Maria Francesca delle Cinque Piaghe** // A chair with the magic touch (p58)
>
> ★ **Settimana Santa** // Parading Madonnas and marching tunes (p10)
>
> ★ **Madonna del Carmine** // Fervent pilgrims and fireworks (p11)
>
> ★ **Cappella Sansevero** // Pickled servants or esoteric rumours? (p45)

infamy attached to the Cult of the Purgative Souls. Widely practised until the 1970s, it involved adopting a skull at the Cimitero delle Fontanelle (Fontanelle Cemetery; p73), where thousands of plague victims had been unceremoniously dumped and forgotten. Devoid of a proper burial, the bones were thought to belong to souls stuck in purgatory; the so-called *pezzentelle* (little begging souls). Cult devotees believed that with a bit of TLC – usually in the form of gifts and prayers – they could help fast-track their adopted soul's upgrade to heaven. And in a case of 'mutual back scratching', it was also hoped that their grateful supernatural friend would return the favour with a few terrestrial perks, from good health and protection to a healthy dose of good luck. The practice was such a hit that a special tram ran to the cemetery, packed each Monday with flower-laden locals. In 1969 Cardinal Ursi officially banned the cult, branding it fetishistic. And yet, some say this cult is far from dead.

BEWARE THE EVIL EYE

The concept of luck plays a prominent role in the Neapolitan mindset. Curse-deterring amulets are as plentiful as crucifix pendants and the same Neapolitan who makes the sign of the cross when passing a church will make the sign of the horns (by extending their thumb, index finger and little finger and shaking their hand to the ground) to keep the *mal'occhio* (evil eye) at bay.

A common belief throughout Italy, though particularly strong in the country's south, *mal'occhio* refers to misfortune cast upon an individual by a malevolent or envious person. In fact, Neapolitans often refer to this bout bad luck as *jettatura*, a derivative of the Italian verb *gettare* (to throw or cast).

Ready to deflect the bad energy is the city's most iconic amulet-cum-souvenir: the *corno*. Usually red and shaped liked a single curved horn, its evil-busting powers are said to lie in its representation of the bull and its sexual vigour.

BACKGROUND

Another traditional, though increasingly rare, deflector of bad luck is the 'o Scartel-lat. Usually an elderly man, you'll occasionally spot him burning incense through the city's older neighbourhoods, clearing the streets of bad vibes and inviting good fortune. The title itself is Neapolitan for 'hunchback', as the task was once the domain of posture-challenged figures. According to Neapolitan lore, touching a hunchback's hump brings good luck, as does stepping in dog poop and having wine spilt on you accidentally.

According to local lore, one building that could have used a little good luck is the Chiesa del Gesù Nuovo, whose stone-clad façade features mysterious, engraved esoteric symbols. Professors of ancient alchemy argue that the symbols were intended to herald good luck but for some unknown reason were engraved inversely on the building's stones, turning good luck to bad. Indeed, the building's history is a series of inconvenient oustings. The first owner, Antonello Sanseverino, was forced to leave the palace by the Aragon ambassador. The second, Ferrante Sanseverino, was driven out in 1580 by Spanish king Philip II who sold the palace to the Jesuits. In 1767, they were thrown out and Franciscans monks moved in, only to be thrown out themselves in 1821 to allow the Jesuits back in.

SCANDALOUS SOULS

Equally challenged in the good luck department was Maria d'Avalos. The ill-fated wife of Carlo Gesualdo, one of Naples' most famous musicians, the setting of her infamous tale is the Palazzo dei Di Sangro, at Piazza San Domenico Maggiore 9. Here, on the night of 17 October 1590, Gesualdo murdered d'Avalos and her lover, Don Fabrizio Carafa, in a fit of jealous rage. The suspicious Gesualdo had tricked Maria into thinking that he was away on a hunting trip, when in fact he was waiting to catch her with Don Fabrizio *in flagrante delicto*. He did and both Maria and her lover Don Fabrizio paid the ultimate price. Legend has it that the bloodied lovers died in each others' arms.

Gesualdo's jealousy was hardly surprising – so fetching was the younger nobleman that he was known around town as the *l'angelo* (the Angel). Yet the Angel's death wasn't enough for the betrayed husband, who ordered the killing of his own son, suspecting him of being the fruit of his wife's adulterous tryst.

Some say that Maria's ghost still roams Piazza di San Domenico Maggiore streets at night, searching for her slaughtered son and pin-up sweetheart.

The Palazzo dei Di Sangro itself was built for the noble Di Sangro family, whose most famous member, Raimondo di Sangro (1710–71), remains one of Naples' most rumour-ridden characters. Inventor, scientist, soldier and alchemist, the so-called Prince of Sansevero came up with some nifty creations in his time, among them a waterproof cape for personal pal King Charles of Bourbon, a lightweight cannon, and a land-and-water carriage drawn by wooden horses. Credited with introducing freemasonry into the Kingdom of Naples, the prince was subsequently excommunicated by the Catholic Church, a snub later revoked by Pope Benedict XIV on probable account of the Di Sangro family's influence.

But even the papal rethink couldn't quell the salacious stories surrounding the Prince of Sansevero. Depending on who you spoke with, he was culpable of every-

LOTTERY DREAMS

In every visible aspect the Neapolitan lottery is the same as every other lottery – tickets are bought, numbers marked and the winning numbers pulled out of a closely guarded hat. It differs, however, in the way that Neapolitans select their numbers. They dream them, or rather they interpret their dreams with the aid of *La Smorfia*, a kind of dream dictionary.

According to the good book, if you dream of God or Italy and you should pick number one; for a football player choose number 42 (Maradona, a football-playing god – or *nu dio 'e giocatore* in local parlance – is 43). Other symbols include dancing (37), crying (21), fear (90) and a woman's hair (55).

Some leave the interpreting to the lotto-shop expert by whispering their dreams into the shop owner's ears (no-one wants to share a winning combination) and letting them choose the numbers. According to the locals, the city's luckiest *ricevitoria* (lotto shop) is the one at Porta Capuana. Run by the same family for more than 200 years, the current owner's grandmother was considered a dream-theme expert. To this day, people bring their dreams here from as far afield as the US, Spain and Switzerland.

While La Smorfia's origins are obscure, links are often made to the number-word mysticism of the Jewish Kabbalah. The term itself most likely derives from Morpheus, the Greek god of dreams, suggesting that the tradition itself is linked to Naples' ancient Greek origins and to the Hellenic tradition of oneirocriticism (dream interpretation).

thing from castrating young boys to preserve their soprano voices, to knocking off seven cardinals and making furniture with their skin and bones. According to Italian philosopher Benedetto Croce (1866–1952), who wrote about Di Sangro in his book *Storie e Leggende Napoletane* (Neapolitan Stories and Legends), the alchemist held a Faustian fascination for the *centro storico*'s masses. To them, his supposed knack for the dark arts saw him master everything from replicating the miracle of San Gennaro's blood to reducing marble to dust with a simple touch. To this day, rumours surround the two perfect anatomical models in the crypt of the Di Sangro funerary chapel, the Cappella Sansevero (p45). Believed to be the preserved bodies of his defunct domestics, some believe that they were far from dead when the prince got started on the embalming. Tall tale or not, the exact method of their preservation still confounds scientists today.

Equally baffling is the chapel's sculptural highlight, *Il Cristo Velato* (The Veiled Christ). Exactly how Giuseppe Sammartino chiselled Christ's translucent marble veil is still up for debate. According to some, the effect was achieved by covering the statue with a cloth permeated with a solution that then crystallised as calcium carbonate.

Perhaps in order to secure eternal infamy, Di Sangro destroyed his own scientific archive before he died. His descendants, also threatened with excommunication for their relative's dubious hobbies, eradicated the rest of his formulae, findings and writings. And so, like many Neapolitan tales, the legend lives on.

THE SUBTERRANEAN CITY

· · · · · · ·

Mysterious shrines, secret passageways, forgotten burial crypts: it might sound like the set of an *Indiana Jones* film, but we're actually talking about what lurks beneath Naples' loud and greasy streets. Subterranean Naples is one of the world's most thrilling urban wonderlands; a silent, mostly undiscovered sprawl of cathedral-like cisterns, pin-sized conduits, catacombs and ancient ruins.

> *Subterranean Naples is one of the world's most thrilling urban wonderlands*

Speleologists (cave specialists) estimate that about 60% of Neapolitans live and work above this network, known in Italian as the *sottosuolo* (underground). Since the end of WWII, some 700 cavities have been discovered, from original Greek-era grottoes, to Paleo-Christian burial chambers and royal Bourbon escape routes. According to the experts, this is simply a prelude, with another 2 million sq metres of troglodytic treats to unfurl. Somewhat surprisingly (or totally predictable), most Neapolitans never give their underground treasures a passing thought...until a sinkhole swallows up a room and the *sottosuolo* resurfaces in the city's headlines.

Much more passionate are Naples' dedicated caving geeks, who are quick to tell you that their underworld is one of the largest and oldest on earth. Sure, Paris might claim a catacomb or two, but its subterranean offerings don't come close to this giant's 2500-year history.

And what a history it is; from buried martyrs and sneaky foreign invaders, to wife-snatching spirits and drug-making mobsters. Naples' most famous saint, San Gennaro, was interred in the Catacomba di San Gennaro (p72) in the 5th century. A century later, in AD 536, Belisario and his troops caught Naples by surprise by storming the city through its ancient tunnels. According to legend, Alfonso of Aragon used the same trick in 1442, undermining the city walls by using an underground passageway leading into a tailor's shop and straight into town.

Inversely, the 18th-century Bourbons had an escape route built beneath the Palazzo Reale di Capodimonte. A century later, they commissioned a tunnel to connect their central Palazzo Reale (Royal Palace) to their barracks in Chiaia; a perfect crowd-free route for troops or a fleeing royal family. Even the city's underworld has got in on the act. In

DON'T MISS...

UNDERGROUND TREASURES

★ **Chiesa e Scavi di San Lorenzo, Naples** // Time travel back to ancient Neapolis (p48)

★ **Catacomba di San Gennaro, Naples** // Naples' holiest eternal resting place (p72)

★ **Catacomba di San Gaudioso, Naples** // Gruesome burials and 5th-century frescoes (p73)

★ **Rione Terra, Pozzuoli** // Remnants of a Roman port (p79)

★ **Ancient aqueduct, Naples** // Tackle the labyrinth on a speleological tour (opposite)

1992, Naples' dreaded Stolder clan was busted for running a subterranean drug lab, with escape routes heading straight to the clan boss' pad.

FROM ANCIENT AQUEDUCT TO UNDERGROUND TIP

While strategic tunnels and sacred catacombs are important features of Naples' light-deprived otherworld, the city's subterranean backbone is its ancient aqueduct system. Naples' first plumbing masterpiece was built by the ancient Greeks settler, who channelled water from the slopes of Mt Vesuvius into the city's cisterns. The cisterns themselves were created as builders dug out the pliable *tufo* sandstone on which the city stands. At street level, well shafts allowed citizens to lower their buckets and quench their thirst.

Not to be outdone, the Romans wowed the Plebs (abbreviated term for 'plebeians', common Roman citizens) with their new, improved 70km aqueduct, transporting water from the River Serino near Avellino to Naples, Pozzuoli and Baia, where it filled the enormous Piscina Mirabilis (p83).

The next update came in 1629, with the opening of the Spanish-commissioned 'Carmignano' aqueduct. Expanded in 1770, it finally met its Waterloo in the 1880s, when cholera outbreaks heralded the building of a more modern, pressurised version.

Dried up and defunct, the ancient cisterns went from glorious feats of ancient engineering to handy in-house rubbish tips. As rubbish clogged the well shafts, access into the *sottosuolo* became ever more difficult and within a few generations, the subterranean system that had nourished the city was left bloated and forgotten.

MYTH OF THE LITTLE MONK

It's only natural that a world as old, dark, and mysterious as Naples' *sottosuolo* should breed a few fantastical urban myths. The best-known and most-loved is that of the *municello* (little monk), a Neapolitan leprechaun of sorts known for being both naughty and nice. Said to live in the wine cellar, sightings of the hooded sprite were regularly reported in the 18th and 19th centuries. Some spoke of him as a kindred soul, a bearer of gifts and good fortune. To others, the *municello* spelt trouble – sneaking into homes to misplace objects, steal precious jewels and seduce the odd lonely housewife.

While a handful of Neapolitans still the curse the hooded imp whenever the car keys go missing, most now believe that the cheeky *municello* was actually the city's long-gone *pozzari* (aqueduct cleaners). Descending daily down the wells, the small-statured *pozzari* fought off the damp, cool conditions with a heavy, hooded mantel. Naturally, most would pop back up for a breath of fresh air, sometimes finding themselves in people's very homes. For some, the temptation of scouring through drawers in search of valuables was all too tempting. For others, it was a way of making new acquaintances, or a way of bringing a little company to the odd neglected housewife. Whatever the intentions, it quickly becomes clear just how the tale of the 'minimonk' began.

THE WWII REVIVAL

It would take the wail of air-raid sirens to reunite the city's sunlit and subterranean sides once more. With Allied air attacks looming, Mussolini ordered that the ancient cisterns be turned into civilian shelters. The lakes of rubbish were compacted and covered, old passageways were enlarged, toilets were built and new staircases erected. As bombs showered the city above, tens of thousands took refuge in the dark, damp shelters below.

The fear, frustration and anger of those who took shelter, lives on today in the historic graffiti that still covers the walls, from hand-drawn caricatures of Hitler and 'Il Duce' to poignant messages like *'Mamma, non piangere'* (Mum, don't cry). For the many whose homes were destroyed, these subterranean hideouts became semipermanent dwellings. Entire families cohabited cisterns, partitioning their makeshift abodes with bedsheets and furnishing them with the odd ramshackle bed.

Alas, once rebuilding on the ground began, the aqueducts were once again relegated the role of subterranean dumpsters, with everything from wartime rubble to scooters and Fiats thrown down the shafts. And in a case of history repeating itself, the historic labyrinth and its millennia-old secrets faded from the city's collective memory.

SPELEOLOGICAL SAVIOURS & REDISCOVERED SECRETS

Thankfully, all is not lost, as a passionate league of professional and volunteer speleologists continues to rediscover, document and render accessible long-lost sites and secrets. Leading the effort is Naples' two speleological associations: NUg (Napoli Underground Group) and CSM (Centro Speleologico Meridionale). Heading the latter is Clemente Esposito. Nicknamed *Papa del sottosuolo* (Pope of the Underground), the veteran cave crusader's dedication is encapsulated in his Museo del Sottosuolo Napoletano (Museum of the Neapolitan Underground); a work-in-progress ode to speleologists and the treasures they find. Hidden away behind an unmarked door on Piazza Cavour, its series of restored underground cisterns re-creates real-life sites inaccessible to the public, from a phallocentric shrine to the Greco-Roman god of fertility, Priapus, to a luridly hued Hellenic-era hypogeum. Precious debris that once filled the voids is now displayed, from rare majolica tiles to domestic WWII-era objects.

NUg (p36), which offers tours of the museum, has gained impressive international interest, from the likes of National Geographic, BBC and academics, not to mention from lay adventure buffs seeking a radically different tour of Naples. The group's lively, information-packed website – a testament to NUg's intensive research of the city's ancient aqueducts and caves – has played a significant role in this ever-growing exposure. Undoubtedly, it has also boosted the popularity of NUg's tours, which take in unexplored nooks few locals will ever see. On these tailor-made journeys, surprise discoveries are far from rare, whether it's another secret wartime hideout, an early Christian engraving or an even older Greek urn.

Better known to most tourists are Naples' two cultural *sottosuolo* associations: LAES (www.lanapolisotterranea.it) and Napoli Sotterranea (p49). Less research driven and more tourism-focused, both offer easy tourist walks through parts of the city's ancient aqueducts. While LAES is best known for its tours of the WWII shelters below Via Chiaia, Napoli Sotterranea takes a steady stream of visitors below the *centro storico* for a look at remnants of a Roman theatre frequented by mad-capped Emperor Nero, as well as to a cistern returned to its original, wonderfully water-filled splendour.

INTERVIEW: FULVIO SALVI & LUCA CUTTITTA

Dubbed everything from 'the parallel city' to 'the negative city', Neapolitan speleologists Fulvio and Luca prefer to call Naples' subterranean world '*la macchina del tempo*' (the time machine). As Fulvio explains, 'In 30 to 40 metres you're transported from the 21st century to 2000 BC. Some of the axe pick marks on the *tufo* stone predate Christ himself.'

While Fulvio's speleological tendencies developed while studying geology at university, Luca's passion was sparked while working for a land-surveying firm: 'Within my first year on the job, I was sent underground to survey cavities for the city council. I'll never forget the thrill of being able to touch things that most people don't even know exist.'

For these caving aficionados, the constant possibility of new discoveries is addictive: 'We can descend into the same cistern 30 times and still find new objects, like oil lamps used by the Greek and Roman excavators.'

One of their most memorable discoveries to date was made after stumbling across an unusual looking staircase behind an old chicken coop in an old *palazzo* in the district of Arinella.

As Fulvio recalls, 'I headed down the stairs and through a hole in the wall. Reaching the bottom, I switched on my torch and was quickly dumbstruck to find carved columns and frescoes of the ancient Egyptian deities Isis, Osiris and Seth on the walls. We believe we've found part of the Secretorum Naturae Accademia, the laboratory used by scholar, alchemist and playwright Giambattista della Porta (c 1535–1615) after the Inquisition ordered an end to his experiments. We're currently trying to track down the *palazzo*'s new owner to gain access to the site again. A Neapolitan journalist has asked to see it. He plans to write about it and hopefully procure funding for its restoration.'

Despite the high level of personal interest and passion, speleological associations like NUg play a vital role in preserving Naples' collective heritage: 'There are between 10 to 15 NUg members, each with a specific role to play on our expeditions, from photographer or filmmaker to medical support. We're like a well-oiled machine whose role is to sew up the little tears in our city's history. It's a bit like a puzzle and each new passageway or cistern we find is a piece of that puzzle that we're trying to put together. It's too enormous for us to finish in our lifetimes, but at least we will have contributed to what are important scientific, historical and archaeological discoveries.'

President and Vice-President of NUg respectively, speleologists Fulvio Salvi and Luca Cuttitta prefer dark cisterns to southern sunshine any day.

MIXED BLESSINGS

And yet, not even the infectious enthusiasm of Naples' speleologists is enough to secure the protection and preservation of the city's *sottosuolo*. The golden era of the 1990s, which saw the city council provide generous funding of speleological research, has since been supplanted by standard Italian bureaucracy and political bickering. As a result, many precious sites uncovered by the city's speleologists remain indefinitely abandoned, with little money to salvage and restore them. As NUg's Fulvio Salvi laments: 'The problem with Naples is that it's almost too rich in historical treasure. It creates a certain amount of indifference to such marvels because they are almost a dime a dozen here'.

A more positive outcome involved NUg's discovery of a long, ring-shaped corridor beneath the Quartieri Spagnoli. Part of the ancient Largo Baracche district, the unearthing called for its transformation into a much-needed community centre – a wish that fell on deaf ears at City Hall. Destined to become a squat, its saving grace was a gung-ho group of young community activists called SABU. Giving the space a mighty scrub, the group opened it as a nonprofit art lab and gallery in 2005, headed by 24-year-old archaeology students Giuseppe Ruffo and Pietro Tatafiore. As Giuseppe explains, 'The gallery is an open space where emerging artists can exhibit their work, amongst them young graduates from Naples' Accademia delle Belle Arti. Unfortunately, such spaces are lacking in Naples.'

Largo Baracche's role as a cultural centre for underprivileged local youth has been equally important. In 2008, SABU collaborated with French photographer Nicholas Pascarel, supplying kids from the Quartieri Spagnoli with digital cameras and asking them to capture glimpses of their present lives and hopes for their future. The thousands of snaps were subsequently collected, selected and exhibited in a major exhibition; an event remembered fondly by Giuseppe: 'There were up to 400 people at the opening. It goes to show just how important it is that these kids have an alternative, a space in which to see things differently, to think and express themselves constructively.'

Above ground, the gallery's graffiti-pimped piazza has also found new purpose, hosting everything from alfresco cinema sessions to a fashion show. The 2007 catwalk show, which showcased the work of fashion graduates from Milan, caused particular excitement. Says Giuseppe: 'Most of the people in the neighbourhood had never seen a fashion show in their lives. The great thing was being able to simultaneously support a budding designer and help raise the Quartieri Spagnoli's public profile'.

BAROQUE NAPLES

· · · · · · ·

Innately extravagant, effusive and loud, Naples found its soul mate in the baroque of the 17th and 18th centuries. Finally, the city had found an aesthetic to suit its exhibitionist streak; a style that celebrated the bold, the gold and the over-the-top.

Neapolitan baroque rose out of heady times. Under 17th-century Spanish rule, the city became Europe's biggest. Swelling crowds and counter-Reformation fervour sparked a building boom, with taller-than-ever *palazzi* mixing it with glittering showcase churches. Ready to lavish the city's new landmarks was a brash, arrogant and fiery league of artists and architects, who brushed aside artistic tradition and rewrote the rule books.

THE CARAVAGGIO EFFECT

The main influence on 17th-century Neapolitan art was Caravaggio (1573–1610). A controversial character, he escaped to Naples in 1606 after killing a man in Rome, and although he only stayed for a year his impact was huge. Caravaggio's dramatic depiction of light and shade, his supreme draughtsmanship and his naturalist style had an electrifying effect on the city's younger artists. Take a look at his *Flagellazione* (Flagellation) in the Palazzo Reale di Capodimonte (p71), *Le Sette Opere di Misericordia* (Seven Acts of Mercy) in the Pio Monte della Misericordia (p45) or *Il Martirio di Santa Ursula* (The Martyrdom of St Ursula) in the Galleria di Palazzo Zevallos Stigliano (p58) and you'll understand why.

> "the city had found an aesthetic to suit its exhibitionist streak"

One of Caravaggio's greatest fans was artist Giuseppe (or Jusepe) de Ribera (1591–1652), an aggressive, bullying Spaniard who arrived in Naples in 1616 after a seven-year stint in Rome. Once settled in Naples, his career took off, thanks largely to his marrying the daughter of Giovanni Battista Azzolini, an important art dealer. According to legend, Azzolini sold his son-in-law's talent to the Spanish viceroy by displaying Ribera's depiction of The Martydom of St Bartholomew (now in Madrid's Prado) on the family balcony. It was the break Ribera had been waiting for and the commissions began to flow in.

Ribera's combination of shadow, colour and gloomy naturalism proved hugely popular with Naples' wealthy patrons, turning the dark character into the leading light of the city's mid-17th-century art scene. Yet success did nothing to diminish Ribera's vicious streak. Along with the Greek artist Belisiano Crenzio and local painter Giambattista Caracciolo, Lo Spagnoletto (The Little Spaniard, as Ribera was known) formed a cabal to stamp out any potential competition. Merciless in the extreme, they shied away from nothing to get their way. Ribera reputedly won a commission for the Cappella del Tesoro in the Duomo by poisoning his rival Domenichino (1581–1641) and wounding the assistant of a second competitor, Guido Reni (1575–1642). Much to the relief of other nerve-racked artists, the cabal eventually broke up when Caracciolo died in 1642.

While the Palazzo Reale di Capodimonte is home to several of Ribera's works, among them St Jerome and the Angel of Judgement and Apollo and Marsyas, his *capo lavoro* (masterpiece), the Pietà, calls the Certosa di San Martino (p67) home.

BRUSH-CLUTCHING GREATS

While Caravaggio and Ribera influenced the city's new-school baroque artists, the sumptuous frescoes of Giovanni Lanfranco (1582–1647) would play a more explicit role in the city's shift towards a baroque aesthetic. After successful stints in Rome, where he famously frescoed the dome of the Chiesa di Sant'Andrea della Valle, Lanfranco headed south in 1634 to liven up the cupola of the Chiesa del Gesù Nuovo. While only the *Four Evangelists* survive in the since-reconstructed dome, his vainglorious creations in the Duomo's Cappella di San Gennaro and in the Certosa di San Martino lay testament to his theatrical vision and illusionary skills.

Another pioneer of the Neapolitan baroque was Calabrian-born artist Mattia Preti (1613–99). Dubbed Il Cavaliere Calabrese (The Calabrian Knight), his relatively brief Neapolitan sojourn (from 1653 to 1660) had a significant influence on the city's next-gen artists. Preti's forte was his skilful use of incandescent light, as well as his ability to infuse thunderous, apocalyptic scenes with a deep, affecting humanity. Famed for his ceiling canvases in the Chiesa di San Pietro a Maiella (p44), his mastery of colour, light and shade is equally clear in paintings like *The Feast of Absalom*, whose clever portico setting was intentionally chosen to show off the master's deftness in the field. Considered one of his finest Neapolitan works, you'll find it in the Palazzo Reale di Capodimonte.

Even more influential than Preti was Naples native Luca Giordano (1632–1705), affectionately nicknamed Luca fa presto (Luca does it quickly) for his dexterous way with a brush. A fledging apprentice to Ribera, Giordano found great inspiration in Preti's brushstrokes, not to mention the pomp of Venetian artist Paolo Veronese and the flounce of Rome-based artist and architect Pietro da Cortona.

By the second half of the 17th century, Giordano would become the single most important artist in Naples, perfecting his airy baroque style and gracing the city's walls and domes with his freshly hued frescoes and paintings. Among the privileged buildings is the Chiesa dei Girolamini and the Duomo (p49), the latter flaunting Giordano's skills (and those of his students) in the space between the windows and the arches in the nave. The ceiling painting in the adjacent Basilica di Santa Restituta is also attributed to the homegrown great.

Further east in the *centro storico*, the Chiesa del Gesù Nuovo (p44) boasts several Giordano creations, including vault and wall frescoes in the Cappella della Visitazione and canvases in the Cappella di San Francesco Saverio. The latter chapel is also home to vault frescoes by Giordano's protégé, painter Paolo de Matteis (1662–1728). Of all the works in Giordano's impressive catalogue, however, it's his Triumph of Judith, a ceiling fresco in the treasury of the church of the Certosa di San Martino, which takes the cake.

A contemporary of Giordano, Francesco Solimena (1657–1747) was also influenced by Ribera, although his use of shadow and solid form showed a clearer link with Caravaggio. Like Giordano, Solimena would become an icon of Neapolitan baroque, and his lavish compositions represented an accumulation of more than half a century of experimentation and trends, spanning Lanfranco to Preti and Giordano himself. Lavish colour and grandiose attitude defines his works, among them the operatic fresco *Expulsion of Eliodoro from the Temple* in the Chiesa del Gesù Nuovo, as well as those in the sacristies of the Chiesa di San Paolo Maggiore (p49) and the Chiesa di San Domenico Maggiore.

While Giordano and Solimena receive top billing, the cast of painters who transformed Naples into the New York of the time is long and varied. Indeed, when Giordano was still a *bambino*, fencer-cum-painter Aniello Falcone (1600–65) was already establishing a reputation for his epic battle scenes A student of Ribera, the Napoli native would leave a significant mark on the city's interiors, from the vault frescoes and gilded stuccoes in the Chiesa del Gesù Nuovo's sacristy to his cupola frescoes in the Cappella Firrao di Sant'Agata in the Chiesa di San Paolo Maggiore.

Falcone's student, Salvatore Rosa (1615–73), would also launch a sterling career spanning printmaking, poetry and painting. Another fan of terrified stallions and tumbling soldiers, Rosa's biggest hits would be his hauntingly beautiful landscapes paintings. Peppered with shepherds, bandits and ruins and latently romantic, they were particularly popular with Brits, fuelling their Mediterranean fantasies.

> ## DON'T MISS...
>
> ### BAROQUE ICONS
>
> ★ **Certosa di San Martino** // A jewel-box church from baroque's crème de la crème (p67)
>
> ★ **Chiesa di San Gregorio Armeno** // Ecclesial Versace dripping in gilt and glitz (p47)
>
> ★ **Palazzo dello Spagnuolo** // It's a staircase, Jim, but not as we know it (p74)
>
> ★ **Duomo** // Lanfranco's swirling dome fresco is halfway to heaven (p49)
>
> ★ **Palazzo Reale (Reggia di Caserta)** // Vanvitelli's glorious epilogue to baroque excess (p60)
>
> ★ **Cappella Sansevero** // Effervescent frescoes meet sculptured brilliance (p16)

MASONRY, MARBLE & THE BUILT BAROQUE

Like the Neapolitans themselves, the city's baroque architecture is idiosyncratic and independently minded. Architects working in Naples at the time often ignored the trends sweeping through Rome and northern Italy. Pilasters may have been all the rage in late 17th-century Roman churches, but in Naples, architects like Dionisio Lazzari (1617–89) and Giovanni Battista Nauclerio (1666–1739) went against the grain, reasserting the value of the column and effectively paving the way for Luigi Vanvitelli's columnar architecture and the neoclassicism which would sweep Europe in the mid-18th century.

In domestic Neapolitan architecture, a *palazzo*'s *piano nobile* (principal floor) was often set on the 2nd floor (not the 1st as was common), encouraging the creation of the epic porte-cocheres (coach porticos) that distinguish so many Neapolitan buildings.

Equally grandiose were the city's open staircases, which reached perfection in the hands of Naples-born architect Ferdinando Sanfelice (1675–1748). His double-ramped creations in Palazzo dello Spagnuolo and Palazzo Sanfelice (p74) exemplify his ability to transform humble home staircases into operatic statements.

Another star on the building scene was Antonio Domenico Vaccaro (1678–1745). Originally trained as a painter under Francesco Solimena, his architectural legacy would include the redesign of the cloisters at the Basilica di Santa Chiara (p44), the decoration of three chapels of the church inside the Certosa di San Martino, as well as the design of the soaring *guglia* (obelisk) on Piazza San Domenico Maggiore (p47).

With the help of his father, Lorenzo (himself a renowned sculptor), Vaccaro had also contributed a bronze monument decicated to Philip V of Spain, which topped the Guglia dell'Immacolata on Piazza del Gesù Nuovo. Alas, the work would later be toppled by Charles III and replaced with a much less controversial, and still-standing Madonna.

For many of Naples' baroque architects, the saying 'It's what inside that counts' had a particularly strong resonance. Due in part to the city's notorious high density and lack of showcasing piazzas, many invested less time on adorning hard-to-see façades and more on lavishing interiors. The exteriors of churches like the Chiesa del Gesù Vecchio on Via Giovanni Paladino or the Chiesa di San Gregorio Armeno (p47) gives little indication of the detailed opulence waiting inside, from cheeky cherubs and gilded ceilings to polychromatic marble walls and floors.

The saying 'It's what inside that counts' had a particularly strong resonance

In fact, the indulgent deployment of coloured, inlaid marbles is one of the true highlights of Neapolitan baroque design. Used to adorn tombs in the second half of the 16th century, the inlaid look really took off at the beginning of the 17th century, with everything from altars and floors to entire chapels clad in mix-and-match marble concoctions.

The undisputed meister of the form was Cosimo Fanzago. Revered sculptor, decorator and architect, he would cut the stone into the most whimsical of forms, producing luscious, technicolour spectacles. From early works like the *Tomb of Mario Carafa* in the Santissima Annunziata (p51) and a marble epitaph to Cardinal Ottavio Acquaviva in the Cappella del Monte di Pietà (p45), the fiery Fanzago got his big break in 1623 with a commission to complete and decorate the Chiostro Grande (Great Cloister) in the Certosa di San Martino. To Giovanni Antonio Dosio's original design he added the statues above the portico, the ornate corner portals and the white balustrade around the monks' cemetery.

Impressed, the resident Carthusian monks offered him further work on the Certosa church, a job he continued on and off for 33 years, and one reeked with legal dramas (see the boxed text, opposite). Despite the animosity, Fanzago gave his robe-clad clients one of Italy's greatest baroque creations, designing the church's façade and lavishing its interior with polychrome Sicilian marble. The result would be a mesmerising kaleidoscope of colours and patterns, and the perfectly accompaniment to works of

THE NOT-SO-BRILLIANT LIFE OF COSIMO FANZAGO

Like many stars of the Neapolitan baroque, Cosimo Fanzago (1591–1678) was not actually Neapolitan by birth. Born in small town Clusone in northern Italy, the budding sculptor-decorator-architect ventured to Naples at the eager age of 17 and quickly earned a reputation for his imaginative way with marble. Alas, it wasn't the only reputation he incurred. According to legal documents, Fanzago was not impartial to the odd violent outburst, attacking his mason Nicola Botti in 1628 and reputedly knocking him off completely two years later. His alleged involvement in the 1647 Masaniello revolt (p226) saw him flee to Rome for a decade to avoid the death sentence on his head.

Yet Fanzago's ultimate downfall would come from his notorious workplace practices, which included missing deadlines, disregarding clients' wishes, and using works created for one client for competing clients' projects. Responsible for giving him his enviable commissions at the Certosa di San Martino, the Carthusian monks would ultimately learn to loathe the man revamping their hilltop home, suing the artist in a long, arduous legal battle that ultimately affected Fanzago's health and the number of his commissions. By the time of his death in 1678, the greatest baroque master Naples had ever seen cut a poor, neglected figure.

other artistic greats, among them painters Giuseppe Ribera, Massimo Stanzione and Francesco Solimena.

Indeed, Fanzago took the art of marble inlay to a whole new level of complexity and sophistication, as also seen in the Cappella di Sant'Antonio di Padova and the Cappella Cacace, both inside the Chiesa di San Lorenzo Maggiore (p48). The latter chapel is considered to be his most lavish expression of the form.

Fanzago's altar designs were equally influential on the era's creative ingénues. Exemplified by his beautiful high altar in the Chiesa di San Domenico Maggiore, his pieces inspired the work of other sculptors, including Bartolomeo and Pietro Ghetti's altar in the Chiesa di San Pietro a Maiella (p44), Bartolomeo Ghetti and siblings Giuseppe and Bartolomeo Gallo's version in the Chiesa del Gesù Nuovo (p44), and Giuseppe Mozzetti's exquisite choir in the Chiesa di Santa Maria del Carmine (p52).

Another marble maestro was Giuseppe Sanmartino (1720–93). Arguably the finest sculptor of his time, his ability to breathe life into his creations won him a legion of fans, amongst them the city's Bourbon rulers and the bizarre alchemist prince, Raimondo di Sangro. And it's in the Di Sangro family chapel, the Cappella Sansevero (p45), that you'll find Sanmartino's astounding *Cristo Velato* (Veiled Christ), completed in 1753. Considered the apogee of his technical brilliance, it's quite possibly the greatest sculpture of 18th-century Europe. Even the great neoclassical sculptor Antonio Canova wished it was his own.

Canova may have wished the same of the Reggia di Caserta. Officially known as Caserta's Palazzo Reale (p46), the epic royal residence was one of several grand-scale legacies of the Bourbon years. Designed by late-Baroque architect Luigi Vanvitelli (1700–73), son of Dutch landscape artist Gaspar van Wittel (1653–1736), the Reggia not only outsized Versailles, but it would go down in history as the greatest example of Italian baroque.

Ironically, while it does feature many of the genre's theatrical telltale hallmarks, from acres of inlaid marble to allegorical statues set into wall niches, its late-baroque style echoed a classicising style more indebted to contemporary French and Spanish models and less to the exuberant playfulness of the homegrown brand. According to the Bourbon blue bloods, the over-the-top Neapolitan brand of baroque was *plutôt vulgaire* (rather vulgar). And as the curtain began to draw on Naples' baroque heyday, a more restrained neoclassicism was waiting in the wings.

THE CAMPANIAN TABLE

· · · · · · ·

A leading star of Italian regional cooking, Campanian cuisine alone merits a trip to the region. This is a land where culinary traditions are sacred and top-notch ingredients are the staple of daily noshing. The region's larder is an intensely flavoursome experience, reflecting the locals' own infamous seductiveness. Everything seems to taste that little bit better here – the tomatoes are sweeter, the mozzarella silkier and the *caffè* richer and stronger. Some put it down to the rich volcanic soil, others to the Campanian sun and the local water. Complementing these natural perks is the advantage of well-honed traditions, passed down through the generations and still faithfully followed. While LA and London fuss about with fusion, Neapolitan cooks remember what their mammas taught them: keep it simple, seasonal and fresh.

A HISTORICAL MELTING POT

Campania's culinary line-up is an exotic culmination of foreign influence and local resourcefulness. In its 3000-year history, Naples has played countless roles, from Roman holiday resort and medieval cultural hot spot to glittering European capital. As the foreign rulers have come and gone, they've left their mark – on the art and architecture, on the local dialect and on the food. The ancient Greeks turned up with the olive trees, grapevines and durum wheat. Centuries later, the Byzantines and Arab traders from nearby Sicily brought in the pine nuts, almonds, raisins and honey that they used to stuff their vegetables. They also brought what was to become the mainstay of the Neapolitan diet and, in time, Italy's most famous food – pasta.

The region's larder is an intensely flavoursome experience

Although it was first introduced in the 12th century, pasta really took off in the 17th century when it established itself as the poor man's food of choice. Requiring only a few simple ingredients – just flour and water at its most basic – pasta proved a life saver as the city's population exploded in the 17th century. The nobility, however, continued to shun pasta until Gennaro Spadaccini invented the four-pronged fork in the early 18th century.

During Naples' Bourbon period (1734–1860), two parallel gastronomic cultures developed: that of the opulent Spanish monarchy; and that of the streets, the *cucina povera* (cuisine of the poor). As much as the former was elaborate and rich, the latter was simple and healthy.

The food of the poor, the so-called *mangiafoglie* (leaf eaters), was largely based on pasta and vegetables grown on the fertile volcanic plains around Naples. Aubergines (eggplants), artichokes, courgettes (zucchini), tomatoes and peppers were among the staples, while milk from sheep, cows and goats was used to make cheese. Flat breads imported from Greek and Arab lands, the forebear of the pizza, were also popular. Meat and fish were expensive and reserved for special occasions.

DON'T MISS...

CAMPANIAN KITCHEN ESSENTIALS

★ **Graniano pasta** // Naturally dried, 100% durum-wheat perfection

★ **Colline Salernitane olive oil** // So distinctly good it's DOP labelled

★ **Mozzarella di bufala** // Possibly the world's finest buffalo milk cheese

★ **San Marzano tomatoes** // Sweet plum tomatoes perfect for *sughi* (sauces)

★ **Colatura di alici** // Cetara's famous anchovy essence

★ **Taralli** // Crunchy, almond-studded snacks for lazy cooks

★ **Procida lemons** // The island's celebrated citrus giants

Meanwhile, in the court kitchens, the top French cooks of the day were working to feed the insatiable appetites of the Bourbon monarchy. The headstrong queen Maria Carolina, wife of King Ferdinand I, was so impressed by her sister Marie Antoinette's court in Versailles that she asked to borrow some chefs. These Gallic imports obviously took to the Neapolitan air, creating among other things highly elaborate *timballi di pasta* (pasta pies), the *gattò di patate* (potato tart) and the iconic *babà*, a mushroom-shaped sponge cake soaked in rum and sugar.

More contentious are the origins of Naples' most famous pastry: the flaky, seashell-shaped *sfogliatella*. Filled with cinnamon-infused ricotta and candied fruit, it was created, some say, by French chefs for the king of Poland in the 18th century, others that it was invented by 18th-century nuns in Conca dei Marini, a small village on the Amalfi Coast. Nowadays it comes in three forms: soft and doughy, deep-fried, and the justifiably popular crispy 'frolla' version.

CAMPANIAN CULINARY ICONS

Despite the Bourbons' lavish legacy, Campania's no-nonsense attitude to food – keep it simple, keep it local and keep it coming – remains deeply rooted in the traditions of the poor. This is especially true in its predilection for pasta and pizza, both mainstays of *cucina povera* and the foundation on which Naples' gastronomic reputation stands.

The latter, a derivation of the flat breads of ancient Greece and Egypt, was already a common street snack by the time the city's 16th-century Spanish occupiers introduced the tomato to Italy. The New World topping cemented the pizza's popularity and in 1738 Naples' first pizzeria opened its doors on Port'Alba (p41), where it still stands. Soon after, the city's *pizzaioli* (pizza makers) began to enjoy minor celebrity status.

To this day, the city's most famous dough-kneader remains Raffaelle Esposito, inventor of the classic pizza margherita. As the city's top *pizzaiolo*, Esposito was summoned to fire up a treat for a peckish king Umberto I and his wife Queen Margherita on a royal visit in 1889. Determined to impress the Italian royals, Esposito based his creation of tomato, mozzarella and basil on the red, white and green flag of the newly unified Italy. The resulting topping met with the queen's approval and was subsequently named in her honour.

More than a century later, pizza purists claim that you really can't top Esposito's classic combo when made by a true Neapolitan *pizzaiolo*. Not everyone is in accordance and Italians are often split between those who favour the thin-crust Roman variant, and those who go for the thicker Neapolitan version. Whatever your choice, the fact remains that the pizza they make in Naples is nothing short of superb.

Pizza's bedfellow, pasta, arrived in Naples via Sicily where it had first been introduced by Arab merchants. The dry, windy Campanian climate was later found to be ideal for drying pasta, and production took off in a big way, especially after the 1840 opening of Italy's first pasta plant in Torre Annunziata. The staple itself is divided into *pasta fresca* (fresh pasta), devoured within a few days of purchase, and *pasta secca* (dried pasta), perfect for long-term storage. Specialist shops producing fresh pasta are rare in Naples, which is more famous for its *pasta secca*, the most obvious examples of which are spaghetti, maccheroni, penne (smallish tubes cut at an angle) and rigatoni (similar to penne but with ridges on them). Made from *grano duro* (durum wheat) flour and water, it's often served (al dente, of course) with vegetable-based *sughi* (sauces), which are generally less rich than the traditional *pasta fresca* varieties.

The queen of the region's artisanal pastas comes from the small town of Gragnano, some 30km southeast of Naples. A pasta-producing hub since the 17th century, its main street was specifically built along the sun's axis so that the pasta put out to dry by the town's *pastifici* (pasta factories) would reap a full day's sunshine.

Poverty and sunshine also helped develop Campania's prowess with vegetables. Dishes like *zucchine fritte* (panfried courgettes), *parmigiana di melanzane* (fried aubergines layered with hard-boiled eggs, mozzarella, onion, tomato sauce and basil) and *peperoni sotto aceto* (marinated peppers) are common features of both antipasto buffets and the domestic kitchen table.

Some of the country's finest produce is grown in the mineral-rich volcanic soil of Mt Vesuvius and its surrounding plain, including tender *carciofi* (artichokes) and *cachi* (persimmons), as well as Campania's unique green *friarielli* – a bitter broccoli-like vegetable often served warm with diced pork sausages. In June, slow-food fans should look out for *albicocche vesuviana* (Vesuvian apricots), known locally as *crisommole* and given IGP (Indicazione Geografica Protetta; Protected Denomination of Origin) status.

DOC (Denominazione di Origine; Certified Designation of Origin) status is granted to another lauded local, the *pomodoro* San Marzano (San Marzano plum tomato). Grown near the small Vesuvian town of the same name, it's Italy's most famous and cultivated tomato, best known for its low acidity and intense, sweet flavour. Its sauce, *conserva di pomodoro*, is made from super-ripe tomatoes, cut and left to dry in the sun for at least two days to concentrate the flavour. This is the sauce that adorns so many of Naples' signature pasta dishes, including the colourfully named *spaghetti alla putanesca* (whore's spaghetti), whose sauce is a lip-smacking blend of tomatoes, black olives, capers, anchovies and (in some cases) a dash of red chilli.

A richer tomato-based classic with aristocratic origins is the Neapolitan *ragù*, whose name stems from the French ragout. A tomato and meat sauce, it is left to simmer for about six hours before being served with maccheroni. Another local favourite is *pasta al forno* (baked pasta), a mouth-watering, gut-filling combination of maccheroni, tomato sauce, mozzarella and, depending on the recipe, hard-boiled egg, meatballs and sausage. A gastronomic 'event' of sorts, it's often cooked for Sunday lunch and special occasions.

REGIONAL SPECIALITIES

Campania's regional specialities are testament to the locals' obsession for produce with a postcode. Beyond the STG (Specialità Tradizionale Garantita; Guaranteed Traditional Speciality) protected pizza margherita, surprisingly light *fritture* (fried snacks) and fragrant pastries, Naples' bounty of staples include *pizza di scarole* (escarole pie), 'Napoli' salami, wild fennel sausages, and *sanguinaccio* (a cream of candied fruits and chocolate made during Carnevale).

West of Naples, in the Campi Flegrei, Pozzuoli's lively fish market (p80) attests to the town's reputation for superlative seafood. Another Campi Flegrei local is the IGP-status Annurca apple, ripened on a bed of straw to produce the fruit's distinctive stripy red hue.

Seafood revelations are also the norm on the island of Procida, where local concoctions include *volamarina* (moonfish) tripe with tomato and chilli and anchovy-stuffed squid. And while neighbouring Ischia is equally seafood-savvy, the island's agricultural history shines through in classics like *coniglio all'ischitana* (see the boxed text, p149), made using locally bred rabbits.

> *In Naples superlative meals usually come without the hype*

To the southeast of Naples, the Sorrentine peninsula also heaves with local specialities, from the ubiquitous *gnocchi alla sorrentina* to refreshing *limoncello* sorbet. Feast on *burrino incamiciato* (*fior di latte* mozzarella cheese wickedly filled with butter) and pizza-by-the-metre in Vico Equinese, or ricotta-stuffed cannelloni in Sorrento, whose famous walnuts are used to make nocino liqueur. Almonds and chocolate are the key ingredients in the sugar-dusted *torta caprese* (Caprese cake) which alongside seafood dishes like linguine pasta in scorpion-fish sauce, and the refreshing *insalata caprese* (a salad made of mozzarella, tomato, basil and olive oil) call the isle of Capri home.

Predictably, fish features strongly on Amalfi Coast menus, from cod and monkfish, to *coccio* (rockfish) and grey mullet. You'll also find two essential larder staples down here – *colatura di alici* (an intense anchovy essence) in Cetara and Colline Salernitane DOP olive oil in Salerno.

Nearby, the Cilento region expresses its earthy tendencies in hearty peasant grub like *cuccia* (a soup of chickpeas, lentils, beans, chickling, maize and wheat) and *pastorelle* (fried puff pastry filled with chestnut custard).

Its most famous edible gem, however, is the rightfully revered *mozzarella di bufala* (buffalo-milk mozzarella), made in the area around Paestum. Campania's other famous mozzarella-making region lies to the north of Naples, in the plains around Caserta. Served fresh in trattorie (informal restaurants) and restaurants across Campania, its high fat content and buffalo milk protein give it the distinctive, pungent flavour so often absent in the versions sold abroad.

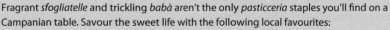

CULTURE, CUSTOMS & A PASSION FOR CAFFÈ

In Naples, superlative meals usually come without the hype. That many trattorias and restaurants appear stuck in a fluoro-lit, retro time warp only attests to the region's emphasis on what's on the plate, not on the walls. Indeed, much of the best food is served in places that don't even have a menu; places where the waiter simply speeds through the day's specials, themselves dictated by whatever looked best at the morning market.

Loud, crowded and exhilarating, the markets themselves are a technicolour testament to the role fresh produce plays in the daily life of locals. Watching the hard-to-please hagglers bullying vendors into giving them precisely what they want at stalwarts like Mercato di Porta Nolana (p52) and La Pignasecca (p57) is to understand that quality really matters here. And it's these people, the *nonne* (grandmothers) and *casalinghe* (housewives), who keep the region's culinary traditions alive.

One of the most enduring of these traditions is the Sunday lunch, when time stands still as parents, grandparents, siblings, partners and friends gather round the table to banter, laugh and gossip over dish after dish of heavenly, home-cooked classics, from *pasta al ragù* (pasta with tomato sauce) and meaty *costata alla pizzaiola* (veal cutlet served in a tomato and oregano sauce) to the ubiquitous tray of *dolci* (sweets) fresh from the *pasticceria* (pastry shop).

While weekday lunching may not be as elaborate, its traditional status as the day's main meal is yet to be toppled. Most locals don't lunch until about 1.30pm, with dinner left to a very Spanish 9.30pm or later. As is the case in the rest of Italy, breakfast usually consists of little more than a powerful espresso, sometimes accompanied by a *cornetto* (Italian croissant) or *sfogliatella*.

The early morning coffee will be one of several consumed throughout the day – an integral yet surprisingly brief ritual where the lingering, seated latte sessions you may be accustomed to are substituted for a quick, unceremonious swill standing at the local bar. But don't be fooled – the speed with which it's consumed does not diminish the importance of its quality. And while the most common variation is *un caffè* (a potent espresso served in a hot cup and already sugared), popular variations include *un caffè macchiato* (an espresso with a drop of milk), and a cappuccino (generally served luke-

THE DOLCE VITA

Fragrant *sfogliatelle* and trickling *babà* aren't the only *pasticceria* staples you'll find on a Campanian table. Savour the sweet life with the following local favourites:

Cassatina The Neapolitan version of the Sicilian cassata, this minicake is made with *pan di Spagna* (sponge), ricotta and candied fruit, and covered in glazed sugar.

Pastiera Traditionally baked at Easter (but available year-round), this latticed tart is made of shortcrust pastry and filled with ricotta, cream, candied fruit and cereals flavoured with orange-blossom water.

Torta di Ricotta e Pera A ricotta-and-pear torte that's light, tangy and dangerously moreish.

Delizia al Limone A light, tangy lemon cake made with *limoncello*.

Paste Reali Cleverly crafted miniatures of fruit and vegetables, these sweets are made of almond paste and sugar (marzipan) and gobbled up at Christmas.

Raffioli A yuletide biscuit made with sponge and marzipan, and sprinkled with icing sugar.

BACKGROUND

warm rather than hot). For a more wa-
tered-down coffee (shame on you!) ask
for a *caffè lungo* or a *caffè americano*. In
summer, a cappuccino *freddo* (cold cappuccino) is a refreshing alternative and
perfect for lazy piazza-lounging session.

THE CAMPANIAN VINE REVIVAL

Revered by the ancients and snubbed
by modern critics, Campanian wine is
once again hot property, with a new
generation of wine-makers creating some
brilliant drops. Producers such as Feudi
di San Gregorio, Mastroberardino, Terre-
dora di Paolo and Mustilli have returned
to their roots, cultivating ancient grape
varieties like the red Aglianico (thought
to be the oldest cultivated grape in Italy)
and the whites Falanghino, Fiano and Greco (all growing long before Mt Vesuvius
erupted in AD 79). Indeed, Feudi di San Gregorio created waves with the release of
their delectable red Serpico.

Campania's three main wine-producing zones are centred around Avellino, Benevento and Caserta. And it's in the high hills east of Avellino that the region's best red
is produced. Taurasi, a full-bodied Aglianico wine, sometimes known as the Barolo
of the south, is one of southern Italy's finest labels and one of only three in the region
to carry Italy's top quality rating, DOCG (Denominazione di Origine Controllata e
Garantita; Controlled & Guaranteed Denomination of Origin). The other two wines to
share this honour are Fiano di Avellino and Greco di Tufo, both whites and both from
the Avellino area.

Other vino-producing areas include the Campi Flegrei (home to DOC-labelled
Piedirosso and Falanghina vines), Ischia (whose wines were the first to receive DOC-
status) and the Cilento region, home to the DOC Cilento bianco (Cilento white) and
to the Aglianico Paestum. Mt Vesuvius' most famous drop is the Lacryma Christi
(Tears of Christ), a blend of locally grown Falanghina, Piedirosso and Coda di Volpe
grapes.

And while vines also lace the Amalfi Coast, the real speciality here are the fruit
and herbal liqueurs, with flavours spanning mandarin, myrtle and wild fennel, to the
ubiquitous *limoncello*; a simple yet potent concoction of lemon peel, water, sugar and
alcohol traditionally served in a frozen glass after dinner. *Limoncello* fans take note:
the greener the tinge, the better quality the drop.

PICK A PLONK

To help you navigate Campania's ever-
growing wine list, here are some of the
region's top wines:

Taurasi A DOCG since 1991, this dry, intense red
goes well with boiled and barbecued meat.

Fiano di Avellino A dry, fresh DOCG white
wine, this is one of Campania's historic wines. Ideal
with seafood.

Greco di Tufo Another long-standing favourite,
this DOCG white comes in both dry and sparkling
versions.

Falerno del Massico Its red and white versions
originate from the volcanic slopes of Mt Massico in
the north of the region.

Aglianico del Taburno Good all-round red,
white and rosé from near Benevento.

FOOD & DRINK GLOSSARY

· · · · · · ·

FOOD

PLACES TO EAT & DRINK

enoteca e·no·*te*·ka wine bar
friggitoria free·jee·to·*ree*·a fried-food kiosk
osteria os·te·*ree*·a informal restaurant
pasticceria pas·tee·che·*ree*·a patisserie/pastry shop
ristorante ree·sto·*ran*·te restaurant
trattoria tra·to·*ree*·a informal restaurant

AT THE TABLE

cameriere/a ka·mer·*ye*·re/a waiter (m/f)
carta dei vini *kar*·ta dey *vee*·nee wine list
cena *che*·na dinner
coltello kol·*te*·lo knife
conto *kon*·to bill/cheque
cucchiaio koo·*kya*·yo spoon
forchetta for·*ke*·ta fork
pranzo *pran*·zo lunch
prima colazione *pree*·ma ko·la·*zyo*·ne breakfast
spuntini spun·*tee*·nee snacks
tovagliolo to·va·*lyo*·lo napkin/serviette
vegetaliano/a ve·je·ta·*lya*·no/a vegan (m/f)
vegetariano/a ve·je·ta·*rya*·no/a vegetarian (m/f)

STAPLES

aceto a·*che*·to vinegar
aglio *a*·lyo garlic
burro *boo*·ro butter
fior di latte fyor dee *la*·te cow-milk mozzarella
formaggio for·*ma*·jo cheese
insalata een·sa·*la*·ta salad
latte *la*·te milk
limone lee·*mo*·ne lemon
miele *mye*·le honey
mozzarella di bufala mo·tsa·*re*·la dee *boo*·fa·la
buffalo-milk mozzarella
olio *o*·lyo oil
oliva o·*lee*·va olive
pane *pa*·ne bread

panna *pa*·na cream
pepe *pe*·pe pepper
peperoncino pe·pe·ron·*chee*·no chilli
pizza margherita *pee*·tsa mar·ge·*ree*·ta pizza topped
with tomato, mozzarella and basil
pizza marinara *pee*·tsa ma·ree·*na*·ra pizza topped
with tomato, garlic, oregano and olive oil and seafood
riso *ree*·zo rice
rucola *roo*·ko·la rocket
sale *sa*·le salt
uovo/uova *wo*·vo/*wo*·va egg/eggs
zucchero *tsoo*·ke·ro sugar

PESCE E FRUTTI DI MARE (FISH & SEAFOOD)

acciughe a·*choo*·ge anchovies
aragosta a·ra·*go*·sta lobster
calamari ka·la·*ma*·ree squid
carpaccio kar·*pa*·cho thin slices of raw fish (or meat)
cozze *ko*·tse mussels
frutti di mare *froo*·tee dee *ma*·re seafood
gamberoni gam·be·*ro*·nee prawns
granchio *gran*·kyo crab
merluzzo mer·*loo*·tso cod
ostriche *os*·tree·ke oysters
pesce spada *pe*·she *spa*·da swordfish
polpi *pol*·pee octopus
sarde *sar*·de sardines
seppia *se*·pya cuttlefish
sgombro *sgom*·bro mackerel
tonno *to*·no tuna
vongole *von*·go·le clams

CARNE (MEAT)

agnello a·*nye*·lo lamb
bistecca bee·*ste*·ka steak
capretto ka·*pre*·to kid (goat)
coniglio ko·*nee*·lyo rabbit
fegato *fe*·ga·to liver
manzo *man*·dzo beef

pollo *po*·lo chicken
prosciutto cotto pro·*shoo*·to *ko*·to cooked ham
prosciutto crudo pro·*shoo*·to *kroo*·do cured ham
salsiccia sal·*see*·cha sausage
trippa *tree*·pa tripe
vitello vee·*te*·lo veal

COOKING METHODS

arrosto/a a·*ro*·sto/a roasted
bollito/a bo·*lee*·to/ta boiled
cotto/a *ko*·to/a cooked
crudo/a *kroo*·do/a raw
fritto/a *free*·to/a fried
alla griglia a la *gree*·lya grilled (broiled)

FRUTTA (FRUIT)

arancia a·*ran*·cha orange
ciliegia chee·lee·e·ja cherry
fragole *fra*·go·le strawberries
mela *me*·la apple
melone me·*lo*·ne cantaloupe; musk melon; rockmelon
pera *pe*·ra pear
pesca *pe*·ska peach
uva *oo*·va grapes

VERDURA (VEGETABLES)

asparagi as·*pa*·ra·jee asparagus
carciofi kar·*cho*·fee artichokes
carota ka·*ro*·ta carrot
cavolo *ka*·vo·lo cabbage
cipolle chee·*po*·le onions
fagiolini fa·jo·*lee*·nee green beans
finocchio fee·*no*·kyo fennel
friarielli free·a·*rye*·lee Neapolitan *broccoletti*
(broccoli-like vegetable)
funghi *foon*·gee mushrooms
melanzane me·lan·*dza*·ne aubergine/eggplant
patate pa·*ta*·te potatoes
peperoni pe·pe·*ro*·nee capsicums; peppers
piselli pee·*ze*·lee peas
pomodori po·mo·*do*·ree tomatoes
spinaci spee·*na*·chee spinach
tartufo tar·*too*·fo truffle

DOLCI (DESSERTS)

babà ba·*ba* rum-soaked sponge cake
pasta *pas*·ta pastry
semifreddo se·mee·*fre*·do semifrozen gelato-based
dessert
sfogliatella frolla sfo·lya·*te*·le *fro*·la short-crust
pastry filled with cinnamon-infused ricotta
sfogliatella riccia sfo·lya·*te*·le *ree*·cha puff-pastry
pastry filled with cinnamon-infused ricotta
torta *tor*·ta cake
zeppole *tse*·po·le doughnuts/fritters

GELATO FLAVOURS

amarena a·ma·*re*·na wild cherry
bacio *ba*·cho chocolate and hazelnuts
cioccolata cho·ko·*la*·ta chocolate
cono *ko*·no cone
coppa *ko*·pa cup
crema *kre*·ma cream
frutta di bosco *froo*·ta dee *bos*·ko fruit of the forest
(wild berries)
nocciola no·*cho*·la hazelnut
vaniglia va·*nee*·lya vanilla
zuppa inglese *tsoo*·pa een·*gle*·ze 'English soup', trifle

DRINKS

acqua *a*·kwa water
amaretto a·ma·*re*·to almond-flavoured liqueur
amaro a·*ma*·ro a dark liqueur prepared from herbs
birra *bee*·ra beer
caffè ka·*fe* coffee
espresso es·*pre*·so short black coffee
tè te tea
vino rosso *vee*·no *ro*·so red wine
vino bianco *vee*·no *byan*·ko white wine

ACCOMMODATION

FINDING ACCOMMODATION

There is no shortage of accommodation in Naples and the surrounding region, although the latter and, in particular, the Amalfi Coast and Bay of Naples' islands of Ischia, Capri and Procida, tend towards the high end of the market and are generally seasonal.

In the crumbling historic city of Naples, you can sleep under frescoes in a 16th-century palazzo, kick back in a converted candle-lit convent or dream sweetly in an architect's style-savvy pad. From five-star hotels to a cheerful *pensione*, Naples isn't short on sleeping options. Particularly hot right now are the city's B&Bs – far from dowdy and constraining, many newer B&Bs are run by young professionals who'll happily give you your room key and let you come and go as you please.

Finding somewhere to stay on the high-profile islands of Capri, Ischia and Procida and Amalfi Coast resorts can be more problematic in high season due to the sheer number of visitors, and it is strongly advisable to book ahead as

far as possible. *Agriturismi* (farm stay accommodation) are increasingly opening up inland from the Costiera Amalfiatana and, still more in the Cilento region, particularly in and around the national park. This can be an option to seriously consider if you prefer to holiday away from camera-wielding tourists and stay in a rural environment, with the possibility of activities such as trekking and mountain bike riding readily accessible. See the boxed text, p266, for *agriturismi* websites. Otherwise, the range of accommodation in these areas is similar to Naples, in that it runs the gamut between sumptuous *palazzi* to

BOOK YOUR STAY ONLINE

For more accommodation reviews and recommendations by Lonely Planet authors, check out the online booking service at www.lonelyplanet.com/hotels. You'll find the true, insider lowdown on the best places to stay. Reviews are thorough and independent. Best of all, you can book online.

(generally pricey) B&Bs, with a sprinkling of budget *pensioni* and camp sites.

The respective tourist offices can provide you with a list of accommodation in the area, including B&Bs and camp sites, as well as (ideally) point them out on a map.

PRICES & BOOKING

Accommodation prices vary according to season in Naples and the surrounding region. Peak seasons overall are April to mid-June, Christmas and New Year. Where applicable, we have included the low and high season prices in the listings. The majority of hotels on the Amalfi Coast and the islands of Capri, Ischia and Procida are strictly seasonal and close from October to Easter. Prices here are also generally high with few options to euro economise. Visitors on a budget can try the less well-known resorts east of Sorrento and the Cilento coast.

Increasingly, when you book your hotel you will need to provide a credit-card number as a deposit. Cheaper places may request that you organise a bank transfer to cover the first night's stay. If you are arriving late in the evening, be sure to inform reception ahead of time, in case staff are tempted to give up your room to a walk in. Check-out time is surprising early in Italy compared to elsewhere in Europe and can be 10am, although 11am is more standard.

PRICE GUIDE

The following is a guide to the pricing system used in this chapter. Unless otherwise stated, prices quoted are for a double room with private bathroom

€	up to €100
€€	€100 to €200
€€€	€200 plus

NAPLES

CENTRO STORICO & MERCATO

A high-voltage shot of historical sights, buzzing squares and street life, the *centro storico* (historic centre) is Naples' heart and soul and a convenient spot to slumber. Options span secret B&Bs, designer dens and converted baroque *palazzi*.

Closer to the train station, Mercato is awash with budget hotels; the option we've listed was clean and reliable at the time of writing (Hotel Zara), but be warned that the area is bedlam by day and dodgy by night.

❦ B&B DONNAREGINA   €
Map pp42-3; ☎ 393 9518804, 339 7819225; Via Settembrini 80; d/tr/q incl breakfast €65/93/120; Ⓜ Cavour; ⊠ ▯ ⊚

Part gallery, part family home, this place is a heaving treasure trove of art, books and anecdotes. Four spacious bedrooms boast individual designs, original artwork, bathroom and satellite TV. The garrulous artist-owner cooks breakfast, which is served at a huge old wooden table. Pride of place is given to his organic pancetta.

❦ BELLA CAPRI HOSTEL & HOTEL €
Map pp42-3; ☎ 081 552 94 94; www.bellacapri.it; Via G Melisurgo 4; dm €16-18, s €50-70, d €55-80, s with shared bathroom €40-50, d with shared bathroom €45-60, incl breakfast; ▯ R2 to Via Agostino Depretis; ⊠ ▯ ⊚

This central, friendly spot offers hotel and hostel options on two separate floors. Hotel rooms are a little dowdy but clean and comfy. The much funkier hostel boasts bright citrus tones, a kitchen, more beds than bunks and a bathroom in each dorm. Laundry service costs €4 and there's no curfew. Bring €0.05 for the lift.

ACCOMMODATION

♥ BELLE ARTI RESORT €€

Map pp42-3; ☎ 081 557 10 62; www.belleartire sort. com; Via Santa Maria di Constantinopoli 27; s €65-99, d €80-160; Ⓜ Dante; 🞩 🖳

More boutique than B&B, this urbane hideaway combines contemporary cool with vintage touches. Four of the impeccable rooms (some as big as small suites) boast ceiling frescoes while all feature marble bathrooms and funky painted bedheads. Languid red drapes in the corridor accentuate the airy, glammed-up vibe.

♥ CARAVAGGIO HOTEL €€

Map pp42-3; ☎ 081 211 00 66; www.caravaggio hotel.it; Piazza Riario Sforza 157; s €80-140, d €120-190, ste €150-240; 🚌 CS to Via Duomo; 🞩 🖳 🛜

Bold abstract paintings face stone arches, yellow sofas line 300-year-old brick walls and original wood-beamed ceilings cap the comfortable, four-star bedrooms at this hotel. A few rooms boast a Jacuzzi, there's a stylish communal lounge and the breakfast buffet features regional produce.

♥ COSTANTINOPOLI 104 €€

Map pp42-3; ☎ 081 557 10 35; www.constantino poli104.com; Via Santa Maria di Constantinopoli 104; s/d incl breakfast €170/220; Ⓜ Museo; Ⓟ 🞩 🖳 🛜 🚗

Chic and tranquil, Costantinopoli 104 is set in a neoclassical villa in the city's bohemian heartland. Although showing a bit of wear in places, rooms remain understatedly elegant, comfortable and spotlessly clean – those on the 1st floor open onto a sun terrace, while ground-floor rooms face the small, palm-fringed pool. Antique furniture and Liberty-era, stained-glass windows add a dash of vintage glam.

♥ DECUMANI HOTEL DE CHARME €€

Map pp42-3; ☎ 081 551 81 88; www.decumani.it; Via San Giovanni Maggiore Pignatelli 15; s €90-105, d €105-130, deluxe d €130-150; 🚌 R2 to Via Mezzocannone; Ⓟ 🞩 🖳 🛜

Don't be fooled by the scruffy staircase and lift; this new boutique hotel is fresh, elegant and located in the former palazzo of Cardinal Sisto Riario Sforza; the last bishop of the Bourbon Kingdom. The simple, stylish rooms feature high ceilings, parquet floors, 19th-century furniture and modern bathrooms with roomy showers and rustic wooden benchtops. Deluxe rooms boast a Jacuzzi. The piece de resistance, however, is a breathtaking baroque hall, used to host cultural soirees.

♥ DILETTO A NAPOLI €

Map pp42-3; ☎ 081 033 09 77, 338 9264453; www. dilettoanapoli.it; Vicolo Sedil Capuano 16; s €35-55, d €50-75, tr €65-90, q €80-105, incl breakfast; 🚌 CS to Via Duomo; Ⓟ 🞩 🛜

In a 15th-century *palazzo*, this savvy B&B features four rooms with vintage *cotto* floor tiles, organza curtains, local artisan lamps and handmade furniture designed by its architect owners. Bathrooms are equally stylish, while the urbane communal lounge comes with a kitchenette and dining table for convivial noshing and lounging.

♥ DIMORA DEI GIGANTI €

Map pp42-3; ☎ 081 033 09 77, 338 9264453; www. dimoradeigiganti.it; Vico Giganti 55; s €40-60, d €55-80, tr €70-95, q €85-110, incl breakfast; 🚌 CS to Via Duomo; Ⓟ 🞩 🛜

Owned by the super-helpful couple behind B&B Diletto a Napoli (above), this urbane B&B offers four colour-coordinated bedrooms with specially commissioned sculptural lamps, ethnic-inspired furnishings and designer bathrooms. There's a modern kitchen, cosy lounge and a charming majolica-tiled terrace.

✪ HOSTEL OF THE SUN €

Map pp42-3; ☎ 081 420 63 93; www.hostelnapoli. com; Via G Melisurgo 15; dm €16-20, s €45-50, d €60-70, tr €80-90, with shared bathroom s €40-45, d €50-55, tr €69-75, incl breakfast; ☒ R2 to Via Depretis; ☒ ☐

Handy for the ferry terminal, this welcoming private hostel is a backpacker favourite thanks to its charismatic young staff. Recently renovated, it now features a bigger, funkier communal kitchen and communal area, and a Skype phone for cheap calls. There's free internet for guests and a laundry service for stays of more than four days. Bring €0.05 for the lift.

✪ HOTEL PIGNATELLI €

Map pp42-3; ☎ 081 658 49 50; www.hotelpignatel linapoli.com, in Italian; Via San Giovanni Maggiore Pignatelli 16; s/d incl breakfast €45/80; ☒ R2 to Via Mezzocannone; ☐

Cheap yet chic, Hotel Pignatelli sits pretty in a restored 15th-century house. Rooms are decorated in a rustic Renaissance style, with wrought-iron beds and bronze wall lamps; some rooms also have original wood-beamed ceilings. At the time of research, construction was underway on five new rooms, with plans for a panoramic rooftop terrace. Best of all, staff are warm and genuinely hospitable.

✪ HOTEL ZARA €

Map pp42-3; ☎ 081 28 71 25; www.hotelzara.it; 2nd fl, Via Firenze 81; s €39-45, d €46-62, tr €60-80, with shared bathroom s €30-35, d €40-50; Ⓜ Garibaldi; ☒ ☐

An easy walk from the main train station, this spotless hotel is a world away from the grungy street below. Rooms are spartan but clean, with functional modern furniture, TV and double-glazed windows. There's a book exchange and breakfast is an optional €4. Don't forget €0.05 to use the lift.

✪ PORT ALBA RELAIS €€

Map pp42-3; ☎ 081 564 51 71; www.portal barelais.com; Via Port'Alba 33; s €65-99, d €80-160, incl breakfast; Ⓜ Dante; ☒ ☐

On a vintage street lined with bookshops, the foyer at this sassy B&B features soaring bookshelves lined with literature, objet d'art and vintage paraphernalia (including a 1745 edition of Dante's *The Divine Comedy*). The six rooms ooze Armani-inspired chic, from muted tones and stainless-steel detailing to mosaiced showers; room 216 comes with a Jacuzzi. While windows look out onto the lively Piazza Dante, double-glazing does a good job of keeping the noise at bay.

ONLINE RESOURCES

★ **Rent a Bed** (www.rentabed.com) has an extensive selection of B&Bs and apartments covering Naples, the bay islands and the Amalfi Coast

★ **Farm Stays** (www.agriturismo.com, www. en.agriturismo.it, www.agriturismo.it) offers a wide range of *agriturismi* options with descriptions, reservation details and general information

★ **Sorrento Tourism** (www.sorrentotourism. com) Includes accommodation info on the Sorrentine peninsula

★ **Porta Napoli** (www.hotel.portanapoli. com) has a comprehensive list of rental apartments, B&Bs and hotels in Naples, Bay of Naples, Amalfi Coast and the Cilento region

ACCOMMODATION

☻ ROMEO HOTEL €€€

Map pp42-3; ☎ 081 017 50 08; www.romeohotel.
it; Via Cristoforo Colombo 45; classic r €165-330,
deluxe r €225-450, ste €1500-2000, incl breakfast;
▨ ▢ ⊚

A quick walk from the ferries, Naples'
hottest new hotel is a design buff's
dream. Designed by Paul Tange (son of
Japanese starchitect Kenzo Tange), it's
a striking combo of Artesia stone and
ivory interiors, A-list art and furniture,
metro-glam sushi bar and rooftop restaurant, and jaw-dropping spa centre.
'Classic' category rooms are small but
luxe and supremely comfortable, with
personal DeLonghi espresso machine
and seriously sexy bathrooms. Up a
notch, 'Deluxe' rooms offer the same
perks but with added space and bay
views.

TOLEDO & QUARTIERI SPAGNOLI

Via Toledo is Naples' main retail strip
and a favourite spot for strolling. Directly to the west, the earthy Quartieri
Spagnoli (whose reputation for crime
is somewhat exaggerated) offers an atmospheric mix of razor-thin laneways,
lively trattorie and cosy slumber spots
spanning homey hotels to a cosy rooftop
B&B.

☻ ALBERGO NAPOLIT'AMO €

Map p55; ☎ 081 497 71 10; www.napolitamo.it; Via
San Tommaso d'Aquino 15; s €55-70, d €69-89, incl
breakfast; ▣ R2 to Via Medina; ▨ ▢

An easy 600m from the ferry terminals,
this friendly, laid-back three-star hotel
is a zesty mix of lime green, yellows and
blues. The newer 5th-floor wing has the
best rooms, and all boast proper shower
cubicles. There's a view of the Castel
dell'Ovo from the breakfast room. Bring
€0.10 for the lift.

☻ HOTEL IL CONVENTO €€

Map p55; ☎ 081 40 39 77; www.hotelilcon
vento.com; Via Speranzella 137A; s €55-110,
d €65-160, incl breakfast; ▣ R2 to Piazza Trieste e
Trento; ▨ ▢

Taking its name from the neighbouring
convent, this lovely hotel is a soothing
blend of antique Tuscan furniture, erudite book shelves and candle-lit stairs.
Rooms are cosy and elegant, combin-
ing creamy tones and dark woods with
patches of 16th-century brickwork. For
€80 to €180 you get a room with a private roof garden. The hotel is wheelchair
accessible.

☻ HOTEL TOLEDO €€

Map p55; ☎ 081 40 68 71; www.hotel
toledo.com; Via Montecalvario 15; s/d/ste
incl breakfast €85/130/180; ▣ CS to Via Toledo;
Ⓟ ▨ ▢

Snugly situated in an old three-storey
building, Hotel Toledo offers comfy,
smallish rooms with terracotta tiles and
mod cons; the rooms are a little on the
dark side, however. Suites come with
a stovetop, and breakfast is served on
the rooftop terrace when the weather
warms up.

☻ LA LOCANDA DELL'ARTE & VICTORIA HOUSE €

Map p55; ☎ 081 564 46 40; www.bbnapoli.org;
Via Enrico Pessina 66; s/d incl breakfast €50/70;
Ⓜ Dante; Ⓟ ▨ ▢

An easy stroll from bohemian Piazza
Bellini and the *centro storico*, these
two homey B&B options are run by the
same owners in a building overlooking
artistic Via Bellini. Rooms come with
all the requisite comforts, although
those in La Locanda are more modern
than the larger Victoria rooms. Breakfast is served in the trendy downstairs
cafe-restaurant.

ACCOMMODATION

🍃 NAPOLIT'AMO €

Map p55; ☎ 081 552 36 26; www.napolitamo.it; Via Toledo 148; s €55-65, €79-99, incl breakfast; 🚌 R2 to Via Toledo; ✖ 🖳

Escape the common hordes and live like nobility in the 16th-century Palazzo Tocco di Montemiletto. Admittedly a little tired in places, there are still enough gilded mirrors and lofty ceilings to satisfy the snob within. Service is courteous and, best of all, its Via Toledo address makes it handy for airport buses and retail therapy.

🍃 SUI TETTI DI NAPOLI €

Map p55; ☎ 081 033 09 77, 338 9264453; www.suiitettidinapoli.net; Vico Figuerelle a Montecalvario 6; s €35-65, d €45-80, tr €60-95, incl breakfast; 🚌 CS to Via Toledo; ✖ 🛜

A block away from Via Toledo, this well-priced B&B is more like four apartments atop a thigh-toning stairwell. While two apartments share a terrace, the rooftop option boasts its own, complete with mesmerising views. All apartments include a kitchenette (the cheapest two share a kitchen), simple-yet-funky furnishings, private bathroom and a homey vibe.

SANTA LUCIA & CHIAIA

With lavish seaside hotels and sparkling island vistas, Santa Lucia is where presidents and pop stars say goodnight. However, there are still affordable options, some with stunning bay vistas. As a general rule, rooms with water views cost a little more.

A-list Chiaia is *the* place for designer shopping and bar-hopping, so accommodation is chic rather than cheap, though a funky B&B is keeping it real.

🍃 B&B CAPPELLA VECCHIA 11 €

Map pp62-3; ☎ 081 240 51 17; www.cappella vecchia11.it; Vico Santa Maria a Cappella Vecchia 11;
s €50-70, €75-100, incl breakfast; 🚌 C25 to Piazza dei Martiri; ✖ 🖳 🛜

Run by a superhelpful young couple, this B&B is a first-rate choice. Six simple, comfy rooms feature funky bathrooms and different Neapolitan themes, from *mal'occhio* (evil eye) to *peperoncino* (chilli) There's a spacious communal area for breakfast, and free internet available 24/7. Check the website for monthly packages.

🍃 B&B I 34 TURCHI €

Map pp62-3; ☎ 081 764 71 36; www.i34turchi.it; Via Marino Turchi 34; s €70, d €80-100, tr €120-140, q €130-170, incl breakfast; 🚌 C25 to Via Partenope

This urbane, gay-friendly B&B offers guests their own self-contained, two-level apartment, with a small double room and a sofa bed in the living area. Divided from the family home, you get your own key to come and go as you please, although you'll probably end up reclined on the rooftop terrace. Bring €0.20 for the lift.

🍃 CHIAJA HOTEL DE CHARME €€

Map pp62-3; ☎ 081 41 55 55; www.hotelchiaia.it; Via Chiaia 216; s €95-105, d €99-145, superior d €145-165, incl breakfast; 🚌 CS to Piazza Trieste e Trento; ✖ 🖳 🛜

Posh yet personable, this renovated marquis' residence is a soothing blend of pale-lemon walls, gilt-framed portraits, restored original furnishings and elegantly draped curtains. Each room is unique, and those facing boutique-flanked Via Chiaia come with a bubbling Jacuzzi. The breakfast buffet showcases Campanian produce, and it's worth checking the website for the occasional special offer.

🍃 GRAND HOTEL VESUVIO €€€

Map pp62-3; ☎ 081 764 00 44; www.vesuvio.it; Via Partenope 45; s €230-370, d €290-450, incl breakfast 🚌 C25 to Via Partenope; 🅿 ✖ 🖳 🛜

Known for bedding legends – past guests include Rita Hayworth and Humphrey Bogart – this five-star heavyweight is a decadent wonderland of dripping chandeliers, period antiques and opulent rooms. Count your lucky stars while drinking a martini at the rooftop restaurant.

☙ HOTEL EXCELSIOR €€€

Map pp62-3; ☎ 081 764 01 11; www.excelsior.it; Via Partenope 48; s/d €270/330; 🚍 C25 to Via Partenope; 🗙 🖳 🛜

Facing yacht-packed Borgo Marinaro, the Excelsior sets the scene for your own *Pretty Woman* moment – think marble columns, dark limousines and apartment-sized *fin de siècle* rooms. Jaw-dropping water views provide a suitable love-scene backdrop.

☙ PARTENO €€

Map pp62 3; ☎ 081 245 20 95; www.parteno.it; Via Partenope 1; s €80-100, d €100-125, incl breakfast; 🚍 C25 to Via Partenope; 🗙 🖳 🛜

Six chic rooms, each named after a flower, are exquisitely decorated with period furniture, vintage Neapolitan prints and silk bedding. The azalea room (€130 to €165) steals the show with its silver-screen view of sea, sky and Capri. Hi-tech touches include satellite TV and free land-line calls to Europe, USA and Canada. Call ahead for good-value, last-minute offers.

VOMERO, CAPODIMONTE & LA SANITÀ

Middle-class Vomero feels a world apart from the seething sprawl below. It's not exactly bursting with sights, but the views are divine, the streets are leafy and that heady Neapolitan chaos is just a funicular ride away.

Slumberwise, expect old-school glamour at new-school prices, with a touch of cheap chic further down the hill.

☙ CERASIELLO €

Map pp68-9; ☎ 081 033 09 77, 338 9264453; www.cerasiello.it; Via Supportico Lopez 20; s €40-60, d €55-80, tr €70-95, q €85-110; 🗙 🛜

Technically in the Sanità district, but a short walk from the *centro storico*, is this gorgeous B&B with four en-suite rooms, an enchanting communal terrace (with barbecue) and an ethno-chic look melding Neapolitan art with North African furnishings. The stylish communal kitchen offers a fabulous view of the Certosa di San Martino, a view shared by all rooms (or their bathroom) except *Fuoco* (Fire), which looks out at a beautiful church cupola. Bring €0.10 for the lift.

☙ GRAND HOTEL PARKER'S €€€

Map pp68-9; ☎ 081 761 24 74; www.grandhotelparkers.com; Corso Vittorio Emanuele I 35; s €200-290, d €250-360, incl breakfast; 🚍 C28 to Via Tasso; 🅿 🗙 🖳 🛜

Darling of the Grand Tour set, this stately old pile once hosted the likes of Virginia Woolf and Robert Louis Stevenson. Today, Prada-clad guests lounge on Louis XVI armchairs, take *aperitivo* (apéritifs) on the sea-view terrace and nibble by candlelight at the George restaurant. The luxe in-house spa retreat is one of the city's best.

☙ HOTEL SAN FRANCESCO AL MONTE €€€

Map pp68-9; ☎ 081 423 91 11; www.hotelsanfrancesco.it; Corso Vittorio Emanuele I 328; s €160-190, d €170-225, incl breakfast; Funicular Centrale to Corso Vittorio Emanuele I; 🗙 🖳 🛜 📺

Housed in a 16th-century monastery, this hotel is magnificent. The monks' cells are stylish rooms, the ancient

ACCOMMODATION

cloisters house an open-air bar, and the barrel-vaulted corridors are cool and atmospheric. To top it all off there's a swimming pool on the 7th floor.

❦ LA CASA DI LEO €

Map pp68-9; ☎ 081 544 78 43; Via Girolamo Santacroce 5A; s/d with shared bathroom incl breakfast €50/70; Ⓜ Salvator Rosa

Bold colours, art books and the odd abstract painting define this erudite pad, home of a heritage architect. Two airy bedrooms offer simple, stylish decor and leafy courtyard views. The shared bathroom is spacious, the kitchen is yours to use, and there's a metro stop down the street.

❦ LA CONTRORA €

Map pp68-9; ☎ 081 549 40 14; www.lacontrora.com; Piazzetta Trinità alla Cesarea 231; dm €15-24, s €28-30, d €30-32, incl breakfast; Ⓜ Salvator Rosa; 🕸 🖳

Stainless-steel lamps, a sleek bar, blonde-wood bunks, spearmint bathrooms, and a communal kitchen that's very Jamie Oliver: this award-winning hostel melds economy and style. Snooze in a courtyard hammock or surf the net for €1 per 30 minutes.

MERGELLINA & POSILLIPO

With Liberty *palazzi*, anchored yachts and a buzzing seafront scene, Mergellina is well connected to the city centre and handy for an early-morning hydrofoil out to the bay islands.

❦ HOTEL AUSONIA €€

Map p75; ☎ 081 68 22 78; www.hotelausonia napoli.com; Via Francesco Caracciolo 11; s/d/tr incl breakfast €80/100/120; 🚌 140 to Via Francesco Caracciolo; 🕸 🖳

This modest and friendly hotel sits opposite the Mergellina marina, a fact not played down in the decor – think portholes, barometers and bedheads in the shape of ships' steering wheels. Corny? A little, but the rooms are clean and comfy, and the few facing the sea won't cost you extra.

❦ HOTEL PARADISO €€

Map p75; ☎ 081 247 51 11; www.hotelparadiso napoli.it; Via Catullo 11; s €90-130, d €100-230, incl breakfast; Funicular Mergellina to S Gioacchino; 🕸 🛜

Located some way above the city centre, your efforts in getting up here are rewarded with jaw-dropping views over the Bay of Naples to Mt Vesuvius. Most of the well-furnished rooms come with a balcony, and staff are courteous and efficient. Expect to pay slightly less for a room without a view.

THE ISLANDS

CAPRI

This island is all about lemon trees, pavement cafes, sultry summer evenings and wearing the largest pair of shades you can get your hands on. In other words, accommodation is strictly seasonal, which means bed space is tight and, in general, costly.

❦ ALBERGO LORELEY // ANACAPRI €€

Map p124; ☎ 081 837 14 40; www.loreley.it; Via Giuseppe Orlandi 16; s €60-90, d €95-130, tr €105-150, incl breakfast; 🕙 Apr-Oct

A welcoming, old-school hotel, the Loreley is surrounded by mature gardens and, despite being located just off the main road into Anacapri, is surprisingly quiet. Rooms are spacious and decorated in styles ranging from granny chintz to Mediterranean classic – cool tiled floors and heavy antique furniture.

✿ BELVEDERE E TRE RE // MARINA GRANDE €€

Map p117; ☎ 081 837 03 45; www.belvedere
-tre-re.com; Via Marina Grande 264; s/d incl breakfast
€100/120; ☷ Apr-Nov; ▣

A five-minute walk from the port with superb boat-spotting views, this hotel dates from 1900 and has had a past: the 'tre re' in the name refers to the three kings (no biblical reference intended) who stayed here in its Grand Tour heyday. A fairly modest two-star today, rooms have been recently modernised and have private covered balconies. There's a sun-bronzing terrace on the top floor.

✿ CAPRI PALACE // ANACAPRI €€€

Map p124; ☎ 081 978 01 11; www.capripalace.com;
Via Capodimonte 2b; s/d/ste incl breakfast from
€195/295/620; ☷ Apr-Oct; ▣ ▣

A VIP favourite (Harrison Ford, Liz Hurley and Naomi Campbell have all languished here), the super-slick Capri Palace is the hotel of the moment. Its stylish Mediterranean interior is enlivened with eye-catching contemporary art and its guest rooms are never less than lavish – some even have their own terraced garden and private pool. For stressed guests, the health spa is said to be the island's best. Note that there's a three-night minimum stay in high season.

✿ GRAND HOTEL QUISISANA // CAPRI TOWN €€€

Map p121; ☎ 081 837 07 88; www.quisi.com; Via
Camerelle 2; r/ste incl breakfast from €300/620;
☷ mid-Mar–1st week Nov; ▣ ▣

One of only three hotels here to boast a five-star L (luxury) rating, the Quisisana is Capri's most prestigious address and, fittingly, a few espadrille steps from the Piazzetta. A hotel since the 19th century, it's a bastion of unapologetic opulence, with two swimming pools, a fitness centre

and spa, subtropical gardens, restaurants and bars. Rooms are suitably palatial with cool colour schemes and classy furniture.

✿ HOTEL BELLAVISTA // ANACAPRI €€

Map p124; ☎ 081 837 14 63; www.bellavistacapri.
com; Via Giuseppe Orlandi 10; s €90-160, d €130-240;
☷ Apr-Oct; ▣ ▣

A grand dame among hotels here – more than 100 years old, the rooms are large and have 1960s-style tile floors with enormous flower motifs which you will love (or loathe). On the plus side, it's conveniently positioned near the entrance to Anacapri, boasts a tennis court, a restaurant with truly beautiful views and discounted access to a nearby swimming pool.

✿ HOTEL BUSSOLA DI HERMES // ANACAPRI €€

Off Map p124; ☎ 081 838 20 10; www.bussol
ahermes.com; Traversa La Vigna 14; s €50-120,
d €70-140; ☷ year-round; ▣ ▣

New owner Cristiano has put some zap into this hotel, which has been thoughtfully revamped and moved up several elegant notches from its previous incarnation as a hostel-cum-hotel. The sun-filled rooms have luxurious drapes and a cheery blue-and-white colour scheme, while the public spaces have a whiff of Pompeii with columns, statues and vaulted ceilings. To get here take the bus up to Piazza Vittoria and call for the hotel shuttle service.

✿ HOTEL CARMENCITA // ANACAPRI €€

Map p124; ☎ 081 837 13 60; www.hotelcarmencita
-capri.com; Via de Tommaso 4; s €69-95, d €110-145;
☷ mid-Mar–mid-Nov; ▣ ▣ ▣

Near the town bus station, the Carmencita is run by a chatty couple who extend a warm welcome. They'll even come and pick you up from the ferry terminal at

ACCOMMODATION

ACCOMMODATION

Marina Grande if you phone ahead with your arrival details. The atmosphere is homey and old fashioned in the public areas, while the rooms are bright – think floral bedspreads and majolica ceramic tiling – big and comfortable. Small terraces overlook the pool and small garden a hallway of family knick-knacks. Rooms have high ceilings and a spare-room feel with old-fashioned wardrobes and beds and balconies (ask for a sea view). There are lovely gardens with fruit trees but a decidedly unlovely dining room, which is more like an institutional canteen.

❦ HOTEL ESPERIA // CAPRI TOWN €€

Map p121; ☎ 081 837 02 62; www.esperiacapri. eu; Via Sopramonte 41; r incl breakfast €130-180; ☺ Apr-Oct; ❋

The peeling facade, handsome columns and giant urns lend an air of faded elegance to this 19th-century former wealthy private home. A short uphill walk from the centre of town, the rooms are large and airy with modern furniture and a floral theme. The best (and most expensive) have good-sized terraces with sea views.

❦ HOTEL GATTO BIANCO // CAPRI TOWN €€

Map p121; ☎ 081 837 51 43; www.gattobianco-capri. com; Via Vittoria Emanuele 32; s €100-170, d €150-230, incl breakfast; ☺ Apr-Nov; ❋ ▭

This gracious hotel dates from 1953 with leafy courtyards and terraces and a white Persian cat – presumably from a long lineage. The light-filled rooms are decorated in traditional style with stunning blue-and-yellow majolica tiling, a tasteful colour scheme and views of Mt Cesina. The hotel is classily placed for your mid-morning coffee, a few minutes' walk from La Piazzetta,

❦ HOTEL ITALIA // MARINA GRANDE €€

Map p117; ☎ 081 837 06 02; www.pensioneitalia capri.com; Via Marina Grande 204; r incl breakfast €90-135; ☺ Apr-Nov

This third-generation hotel has a homey feel with a *nonna* (grandma) around and

❦ HOTEL LA TOSCA // CAPRI TOWN €

Map p121; ☎ 081 837 09 89; www.latoscahotel.com; Via Dalmazio Birago 5; s €45-80, d €65-125; ☺ Apr-Oct; ❋

Away from the glitz of the centre, this charming one-star *pensione* is hidden down a quiet back lane overlooking the Certosa di San Giacomo and the mountains. The rooms are plain, but comfortable, with pine furniture, striped fabrics and large bathrooms. Several have private terraces. The owner, a genial, hospitable guy, extends a warm welcome.

❦ HOTEL SENARIA // ANACAPRI €€

Map p124; ☎ 081 837 32 22; www.senaria.it; Via Follicara 6; r with breakfast €130-160; ☺ Apr-Nov; ❋

It's quite a trek to this delightful family run hotel in Anacapri's original town centre, but worth the effort. Housed in a discreet whitewashed villa, rooms are decorated in a sparse, but elegant, Mediterranean style with terracotta tiles and cooling cream tones, plus the tasteful watercolours of local artist Giovanni Tessitore. It's a very quiet spot and except for Sunday-morning church bells you're unlikely to be disturbed by anything other than the breeze.

❦ HOTEL VILLA EVA// ANACAPRI €€

Map p124; ☎ 081 837 15 49; www.villaeva.com; Via La Fabbrica 8; r €100-120; ☺ Mar-Oct; ▭ ▨

A veritable rural retreat, Villa Eva is hidden among fruit and olive trees, which are strung with hammocks. The rooms have lashings of white linen – and character, including tiled fireplaces and domed ceilings. Ideal for families, facilities include a swimming pool, snack bar and treetop views down to the sea. The only drawback is that it's tricky to get to (take the Grotta Azzurra bus from Anacapri and ask the driver where to get off, or cough up €24 for a port-side pick-up).

❦ HOTEL VILLA KRUPP // CAPRI TOWN €€

Map p121; ☎ 081 837 03 62; www.villakrupp.it; Viale Matteotti 12, Parco Augusto; s €110, d €140-170, incl breakfast; Apr-Oct; Ⓟ ⊠

Housed in the former residence of Russian author, Maxim Gorky, this historic hotel oozes old-school charm, with floral tiling, fading antiques and heavy bedsteads. It also commands some fabulous views over the Giardini di Augusto and beyond to the Isole Faraglioni. If your room doesn't have the view (and not all do), simply adjourn to the delightful terrace outside reception.

❦ HOTEL VILLA SARAH // CAPRI TOWN €€

Off Map p121; ☎ 081 837 06 89; www.villasarah.it; Via Tiberio 3A; s €90-140, d €140-210, incl breakfast; Easter-Oct; ⊠ ⊠

On the road up to Villa Jovis – a 10-minute walk from the centre of Capri Town – Villa Sarah retains a rustic appeal that so many of the island's hotels have long lost. Surrounded by its own fruit-producing gardens, it has 19 airy rooms, all decorated sunny Med-blue and white with private terraces. The healthy breakfast includes organic produce.

❦ PENSIONE GUARRACINO // CAPRI TOWN €€

Map p117; ☎ /fax 081 837 71 40; Via Mulo 13; s €70-85, d €90-115; ⊙ year-round; ⊠

'Value for money' is a relative term when used in connection with Capri and accommodation but if you'll find it anywhere, you'll find it here, at this small, family run *pensione*. A short walk from the centre of Capri Town and within easy striking distance of Marina Piccola, it has 13 sparkling white rooms, each decked out with a comfy bed, decent shower and independent air-con.

❦ RELAIS MARESCA // MARINA GRANDE €€

Map p117; ☎ 081 837 96 19; www.relaismaresca.it; Via Marina Grande 284; r incl breakfast €130-220; ⊙ Mar-Dec; ⊠

A delightful four-star, this is the top choice in Marina Grande. The look is classic Capri, with acres of gleaming ceramic in turquoise, blue and yellow, and stylish furniture. There is a range of rooms (and corresponding prices); the best have balconies and sea views. There's a truly lovely flower-filled 4th-floor terrace. Minimum two-day stay in at weekends in July and August.

ISCHIA

Like its classy little sister, most hotels close in winter here and prices drop considerably at those that stay open. In addition to the hotels listed here, there are the spa hotels, most of which only take half- or full-board bookings. The tourist office can supply you with a list. The largest island of the trio here, an overnight stay here makes good sense.

❦ ALBERGO IL MONASTERO // ISCHIA PONTE €€

Map pp140-1; ☎ 081 99 24 35; www.albergoilmonastero.it; Castello Aragonese, Rocca del Castello; s €70-85, d €100-120, incl breakfast; ⊙ Easter-Oct; ⊠

The former monks' cells still have a certain appealing sobriety about them with

ACCOMMODATION

dark wood furniture, crisp white walls, vintage terracotta tiles, and no TV (no worries – the views are sufficiently prime time). Elsewhere there is a pleasing sense of space and style with vaulted ceilings, chic plush sofas, a sprinkle of antiques and bold contemporary art by the late owner and artist Gabriele Mattera.

♥ ALBERGO MACRÌ // ISCHIA PORTO €

Map pp140-1; ☎/fax 081 99 26 03; Via Iasolino 96, Ischia Porto; s €38-46, d €65-78; year-round; P ⊠

Down a blind alley near the main port, this place is run by a smiley lady and has a friendly low-key vibe. While the pine and bamboo furnishings won't snag any design awards, rooms are clean, bright and comfy. All 1st-floor rooms have terraces and the small downstairs bar serves a mean espresso.

♥ CAMPING MIRAGE // BARONA D'ISCHIA €

Map pp140-1; ☎ 081 99 05 51; www campingmirage .it; Via Maronti 37, Spiaggia dei Maronti, Barano d'Ischia; camp sites per person €12; year-round; P

On one of Ischia's best beaches within walking distance of Sant'Angelo, this shady camping ground offers 50 places, showers, laundry facilities, a bar and a restaurant serving lip-smacking plates of pasta.

♥ HOTEL CASA CELESTINO // SANT'ANGELO €€

Map pp140-1; ☎ 081 99 92 13; www.casacelestino. it; Via Chiaia di Rose 20, Sant'Angelo; s €120-135, d €130-140, incl breakfast; Jan-Oct; ⊠ ▣

Hugging the headland, this chic little number is a soothing blend of creamy furnishings, whitewashed walls, contemporary art and bold paintwork. The uncluttered bedrooms boast majolica-tiled

floors, modern bathrooms and enviable balconies overlooking the sea. There's a good, unfussy restaurant across the way.

♥ HOTEL LA MARTICANA // ISCHIA PORTO €€

Map pp140-1; ☎ 081 333 44 31; www.lamarticana.it; Via Quercia 48-50, Ischia Porto; r incl breakfast €72-135; year-round; P ⊠

A short suitcase trundle from the ferry, this small hotel has a friendly homey feel and there's a well-established garden with grapevines, tomato plants and a barbecue (available for guests). Rooms are small, but well equipped with fridge, TV and hairdryer. The breakfast buffet is more generous than most.

♥ HOTEL LA SIRENELLA // LACCO AMENO €€

Map pp140-1; ☎ 081 99 47 43; www.lasirenella.net; Corso Angelo Rizzoli 41, Lacco Ameno; s/d incl breakfast €70/140; Apr-Oct; ⊠

This is a family-owned beachside hotel where you can practically roll out of bed onto the sand. Rooms are bright and colourful with seafront terraces. Sparkling tiled bathrooms and a breezy fun-in-the-sun vibe add to the appeal, as does the downstairs restaurant with its excellent pizzas.

♥ HOTEL SEMIRAMIS // FORIO €€

Map pp140-1; ☎ 081 90 75 11; www.hotelsemira misischia.it; Spiaggia di Citara, Forio; r incl breakfast €100-140; Apr-Oct; P ⊠ ▣

A few minutes' walk from the Poseidon spa complex, this bright hotel, run by friendly Giovanni and his German wife, has a tropical oasis feel with its central pool surrounded by lofty palms. Rooms are large and beautifully tiled in the traditional yellow-and-turquoise pattern. The garden is glorious with fig trees, vineyards and distant sea views.

♥ MEZZATORRE RESORT & SPA // FORIO €€€

Map pp140-1; ☎ 081 98 61 11; www.mezzatorre.it; Via Mezzatorre 23, Lacco Ameno; s €220-320, d €270-395, ste €500-700, incl breakfast; ⊗ mid-Apr–Oct; P ⊠ ☐ ⊠

Perched on a bluff above the sea, this luxurious resort is surrounded by a 2.8-hectare pine wood. An in-house spa centre and tennis courts crank up the spoil factor. The sitting rooms and some guest rooms are located in a 15th-century defensive tower. Rooms are decorated in earthy colours, some have private garden and Jacuzzi. Check out the infinity pool above the beach for the ultimate film-star setting. If funds are short, just have a long, slow drink in the adjacent bar.

♥ UMBERTO A MARE // FORIO €€

Map pp140-1; ☎ 081 99 71 71; www.umbertoamare. it; Via Soccorso 2, Forio; s €75-110, d €110-170, incl breakfast; ⊗ Apr-Oct; ⊠

Easy to find, right next to Forio's emblematic mission-style church, these 12 quiet rooms ooze understated chic with cool ceramic tiles, modern bathrooms and traditional green shutters. Head out to a sunbed on the terracotta terrace with its holiday-brochure-style sea views. You won't have to stray far to eat well, the hotel is tucked under one of Ischia's finest restaurants.

PROCIDA

The island returns to the locals after the day trippers have gone and takes on a palatable and tranquil Med-island feel. Fittingly, accommodation tends to be of the small-scale variety – think converted farmhouses and family run hotels. A good choice of self-contained bungalows and apartments can work out quite cheap if you're in a group. Many places close over the winter and book out in August – so check ahead during these periods.

♥ CASA GIOVANNI DA PROCIDA // PROCIDA €

Map p153; ☎ 081 896 03 58; www.casagiovannida procida.it; Via Giovanni da Procida 3; s €50-80, d €65-100, incl breakfast; ⊗ closed Feb; P ⊠

This chic converted farmhouse B&B features split-level, minimalist rooms with low-rise beds and contemporary furniture. Bathrooms are small but slick, with bronze and aqua tiling, cool cube basins, huge showerheads and the odd vaulted ceiling. In the lush garden, chilled-out guests read and eat peaches under the magnolia tree.

♥ CASA SUL MARE // MARINA CORRICELLA €€

Map p153; ☎ 081 896 87 99; www.lacasasulmare.it; Salita Castello 13; s €70-100, d €90-120, incl breakfast; ⊗ Apr-Oct; ⊠

A fabulous place with the kind of evocative views that helped make *The Talented Mr Ripley* such a memorable film. Overlooking the picturesque marina, the rooms are elegant with exquisite tiled floors, wrought-iron bedsteads and a warm Mediterranean colour scheme. There's a boat service to the nearest beaches, the service is great and the morning cappuccino, courtesy of Franco, may well be the best you've ever had.

♥ HOTEL CRESCENZO // PROCIDA €€

Map p153; ☎ 081 896 72 55; www.hotelcrescenzo.it; Via Marina di Chiaiolella 33; r incl breakfast €70-120; ⊗ year-round; ⊠

Just 10 smallish rooms; choose between a bay view or balcony with sea view. The decor is a suitably nautical blue and white with sparkling clean bathrooms. This hotel is fronted by a restaurant, generally bursting with an affable local crowd and where you can enjoy breakfast after a long lie in as it is, unusually, served until noon. Check the website for good deals on longer stays.

♥ HOTEL LA CORRICELLA // MARINA CORRICELLA €€

Map p153; ☎ 081 896 75 75; www.hotelcorricella.it; Via Marina Corricella 88; s €70-100, d €90-120, incl breakfast; ☺ Apr-Oct

One bookend to Marina Corricella, it's hard to miss this peach-and-yellow candycane colour scheme. Low-fuss rooms feature modular-style furniture with fan and TV. The large shared terrace boasts top-notch harbour views, the restaurant serves decent seafood and a boat service reaches the nearby beach.

♥ HOTEL RIVIERA // MARINA DI CHIAIOLELLA €

Map p153; ☎ 081 896 71 97; www.hotelrivierapro cida.it; Via Giovanni da Procida 36, Marina di Chiaiolella; s/d incl breakfast €35/70; ☺ Apr-Oct; ⓟ ⊠

This hotel is quite a hike up the hill from the marina, but you will be amply rewarded with birdsong and rural peace and quiet. The rooms are modern and fairly characterless, but they're clean and comfortable and, all in all, this place is a bargain.

♥ LA ROSA DEI VENTI // PROCIDA €

Map p153; ☎ /fax 081 896 83 85; www.vacanzeapro cida.it; Via Vincenzo Rinaldi 34; per week s €320-490, d €390-690, tr €450-750; ☺ Mar-Oct; ⓟ ⊡

Perched on a tranquil cliff top, these 18 self-contained bungalows feature private cooking facilities, patios and clean, nofrills interiors. There's a private rocky beach and vineyard, and matriarch Titta cooks up a weekly Procidian feast, eaten under a lemon-clad pergola. Sailing excursions may be arranged.

♥ LE GRAND BLEU GUESTHOUSE // PROCIDA €€

Map p153; ☎ 081 896 95 94; www.isoladiprocida.it; Via Flavio Gioia 37; apt per week €250-950; ☺ closed mid-Dec–Jan; ⊠ ⊡

Within strolling distance of Chiaia beach, these central apartments have had a recent fresh lick of paint and are looking good. They feature bright functional furniture, funky bathrooms, stovetops, internet access and a cool rooftop terrace with wood-fired oven, barbecue and views of Ischia. Wheelchair access.

THE AMALFI COAST

SORRENTO

Accommodation is thick on the ground in this town, although if you're arriving in high summer (July and August) you'll still need to book ahead. Most of the big city-centre hotels are geared towards package tourism and prices are correspondingly high. There are, however, some excellent choices, particularly on Via Capo, the coastal road west of the centre. This area is within walking distance of the city centre but if you're carrying luggage it's easier to catch a SITA bus for Sant'Agata or Massa Lubrense.

♥ CASA ASTARITA €

Map p164; ☎ 081 877 49 06; www.casastarita.com; Corso Italia 67, Sorrento; r incl breakfast €80-100; ⊠ ⊡

A pocket-size gem, this B&B is housed in a 16th-century building in the city centre. All six rooms combine original structural elements, like niches and vaulted ceilings, with the modern comforts of flat screen TV, fridge and excellent water pressure. Brightly painted doors, tasteful art work and antiques complete the eclectic look. Rooms surround a central

ACCOMMODATION

parlour where breakfast is served on a large country-farm style oak table.

♥ GRAND HOTEL EXCELSIOR VITTORIA €€€

Map p164; ☎ 081 807 10 44; www.exvitt.it; Piazza Tasso 34; s/d/ste incl breakfast €340/390/690; ⊙ year-round; (P) (X) (≋)

A hotel for more than 170 years, the grand old dame of Sorrento oozes belle-epoque elegance. Huge potted palms adorn gilded public rooms awash with sunlight and antique furniture. Guest rooms vary in size and style, ranging from tasteful simplicity to extravagant, frescoed opulence. All, however, have views, either of the hotel's lush, gardens dripping with crimson bougainvillea or over the sea to Mt Vesuvius. Past guests have included Pavarotti, Wagner, Goethe, Sophia Loren and British royalty.

♥ HOTEL ASTORIA €

Map p164; ☎ 081 807 40 30; www.hotelastoria sorrento.com; Via Santa Maria delle Grazie 24, Sorrento; s €60-80, €80-100, incl breakfast; (X)

This recently renovated classic has the advantage of being located in the heart of the *centro storico* and the disadvantage of no parking. Overall, it's an excellent choice. The interior sparkles with colourful glossy tiles and blue and buttercup-yellow paintwork. The large enclosed back terrace is a delight with seats set under orange and lemon trees and colourful tiled murals lining the back wall.

♥ HOTEL CAPRI €€

Map p164; ☎ 081 878 12 51; www.albergocapri.it; Corso Italia 212; r incl breakfast €90-120; ⊙ Mar-Nov; (X) (≋)

A decent three-star near the train station, the Capri has comfortable, modern

ACCOMMODATION

TOP FIVE

AGRITURISMI

★ **Agriturismo La Tore** (p280)
★ **Agriturismo Serafina** (p282)
★ **Agriturismo i Moresani** (p288)
★ **Agriturismo Sicinius** (p289)
★ **Agroturismo Fattoria Terranova** (p280)

rooms decorated with lemon-and-blue majolica tiles and functional furniture. They're not large, but they come with satellite TV and sound-proofing, something not to be sniffed at given the hotel's roadside location. Apparently the guests mainly hail from the UK and Ireland – hence the bottles of Guinness in the bar.

♥ HOTEL DESIRÉ €

Off Map p164; ☎ 081 878 15 63; www.desireeho telsorrento.com; Via Capo 31b; s/d incl breakfast €60/90; ⊙ Mar-Dec; (P) (X)

One of a cluster of hotels along Via Capo, the Desiré is a top budget choice. It's not so much the simple, sunny rooms (although they're fine) or the facilities (a TV lounge and panoramic roof terrace) as the relaxed atmosphere, friendly owner and beautiful views. The lift down to the rocky beach below is a further plus, even if you still have to pay for the umbrellas and deck chairs.

♥ HOTEL ELIOS €

Off Map p164; ☎ 081 878 18 12; Via Capo 33; s/d €40/70; ⊙ Easter-Nov

Offering views that many city-centre hotels would charge the earth for, the Elios is a great little *pensione*. Run by a charming old dear, it boasts no frills (unless you count the views), just impeccable old-fashioned hospitality, light, airy rooms and penny-wise prices. If your room doesn't have a balcony, and few do, enjoy the views from the downstairs terrace.

☙ HOTEL RIVAGE €
Map p164; ☎ 081 878 18 73; www.hotelrivage.com; Via Capo 11; s €70-90, d €70-110; ☺ Mar-Oct; Ⓟ ▢

A low-rise modern hotel just beyond the shops on the western edge of town, you can sunlounge on the roof terrace and there's a reasonable bar and restaurant. The rooms are bland hotel style but have good-size terraces. This place has a slight tour-group feel but is well located and priced.

☙ MIGNON €€
Map p164; ☎ 081 807 38 24; www.sorrentohotel mignon.com; Via Sersale 9; s €60-85, d €80-100, incl breakfast; ☺ Apr-Oct & Christmas; ▨

The interior designer here had a serious fit of the blues. From the striking dark-blue-and-white floor tiles, to the pale-blue walls and bed covers, this is the predominant colour throughout. Contemporary artwork and black-and-white historic photos of Sorrento complete the decor theme. The rooms are spacious and there is a rooftop solarium for catching the rays.

☙ LA TONNARELLA €€
Off Map p164; ☎ 081 878 11 53; www.latonnarella. it; Via Capo 31; d €150-190, ste €270-280, incl breakfast; ☺ Apr-Oct & Christmas; Ⓟ ▨ ▢

A splendid choice – but not for minimalists, La Tonnarella is a dazzling canvas of blue-and-yellow majolica tiles, antiques, chandeliers and statues. Rooms, most of which have their own balcony or small terrace, continue the sumptuous classical theme with traditional furniture and discreet mod cons. The hotel also has its own private beach,

accessible by lift, and a highly regarded terrace restaurant.

☙ NEFFOLA RESIDENCE €€
Off Map p164; ☎ 081 878 13 44; www.neffolaresi dence.com; Via Capo 21; prices on request only; ▨

Ideal for self-caterers and families, there are 10 self-contained flats in this stone farmhouse, surrounded by cherry, olive and citrus trees. Sleeping from two to four people, they all have their own kitchen area and bathroom and most have private balconies. If not, there's a communal sun terrace with views over the surrounding tree tops and, beyond that, to the sea. Guests have free access to the swimming pool at the adjacent Nube d'Argento camp site.

☙ NUBE D'ARGENTO €
Off Map p164; ☎ 081 878 13 44; www.nubedargento. com; Via Capo 21; camp sites per person €11, 2-person bungalows €50-85, 4-person bungalows €65-115; ☺ Mar-Dec; ▢ ▨

This inviting camping ground is an easy 1km drive west of the Sorrento town centre. Pitches and wooden chalet-style bungalows are spread out beneath a canopy of olive trees – a source of much-needed summer shade – and the facilities are excellent. Youngsters in particular will enjoy the open-air swimming pool, table-tennis table, slides and swings.

☙ PENSIONE LINDA €
Map p164; ☎/fax 081 878 29 16; Via degli Aranci 125; s/d €50/75; ☺ year-round

Located within an anonymous concrete block, Pensione Linda is a homey welcoming place, run by a mother, daughter and golden retriever trio. The rooms could do with an update and fresh coat of paint but have all the necessary ingredients, plus balconies, and a couple are larger with sofas and desks. There's no air-con but fans are provided in summer.

☙ SANTA FORTUNATA €

☎ 081 807 35 74; www.santafortunata.com; Via Capo 39; camp sites per person €11, 2-person bungalows €60-75, 4-person bungalows €90-120; ⏰ Mar-Oct; ▢ ▣

A large and well-equipped camping ground with a range of sleeping options. Other than camp sites, there are 35 wooden bungalows and 25 mobile homes dotted around the verdant site. Note that credit cards are not accepted.

☙ SEVEN HOSTEL // SANT'AGNELLO €€

Off Map p164; ☎ /fax 081 878 67 58; www.seven hostel.com; Via lommella Grande 99, Sant'Agnello; dm from €26, s/d €60/80; ⏰ year-round; ▢ ▣

The ethos of the young owners here is to offer the best hostel in the world, as well as the first *ostello di design*. They are on the right path with the evocative raw material of an 8th-century former convent setting surrounded by olive and lemon trees. There are veritable five-star touches, like the grand terrace with its comfortable deep-seated wicker chairs and sofas, plus a lounge bar with live music and jam sessions. The rooms are a delight.

☙ VILLA ELISA €

Map p164; ☎ 081 878 27 92; www.villaelisasorrento.com; Piazza Sant'Antonino 19; d €70-80, tr €80-90, ste €90-120; ⏰ year-round; ▣

Rooms here come with cooking facilities and overlook over a central courtyard. Up a steep staircase, the self-contained suite has a pint-sized living room, bathroom, bedroom and kitchen, but the washing machine's a definite plus. Mario will cook for you if you ask nicely and also gives tours (with his daughter) of the region.

MASSA LUBRENSE

Mainly frequented by Italian tourists in the know, pretty Massa Lubrense makes a good base and offers a quieter location than some of its higher-profile Amalfi neighbours.

☙ AGRITURISMO AGRIMAR €

☎ 081 808 96 82; www.agri-mar.it; Via Maggio 9; B&B per person €35; ⏰ Easter–mid-Oct; ℗

Surrounded by olive and citrus groves, this back-to-basics *agriturismo* is ideal for those who want to escape telephones and TVs. There are walking trails nearby, including a pathway leading to the sea. Nestled among the trees are six spotless chalets, big enough for a double bed, tiny bathroom and not a lot else. Hammocks have been thoughtfully hung about the place and deck chairs laid out on a platform overlooking the sea. Dinner is available on request.

☙ HOTEL RISTORANTE PRIMAVERA €

☎ 081 878 91 25; www.laprimavera.biz; Via IV Novembre 3G; s/d incl breakfast €75/100; ⏰ year-round; ▣

A welcoming family-run two-star with spacious airy rooms decorated in the Mediterranean standard of ceramic tiling, light wood and industrial quantities of white paint; several have terraces. The bathtubs (in most, not all, rooms) are an unexpected treat. The bright terrace-restaurant serves typical local fare. Expect to pay around €30 for a full dinner.

SANT'AGATA SUI DUE GOLFI

In a superb position overlooking the two gulfs of Salerno and Naples, Sant'Agata is fast gaining a reputation for its *agriturismi* (as well as restaurants). Book ahead if you are planning to visit in high season.

ACCOMMODATION

♥ AGRITURISMO FATTORIA TERRANOVA €

☎ 081 533 02 34; www.fattoriaterranova.it; Via Pontone 10; d incl breakfast €80; ☺ Mar-Dec; Ⓟ ⊠

Stone floors, dried flowers hanging from heavy wooden beams and large wine barrels artfully positioned – this great *agriturismo* is the epitome of rural chic. The accommodation is in small apartments spread over the extensively cultivated grounds. They're fairly simple, but the setting is delightful and the swimming pool is a welcome luxury. See p171 for details of the farm shop in Sorrento.

♥ AGRITURISMO LA TORE €

☎ 081 808 06 37; www.letore.com; Via Pontone 43; s/d incl breakfast €55/110, half-board per person €60; ☺ Easter-end Oct; Ⓟ

A working organic farm amid 14 hectares of olive groves, producing olive oil, sundried tomatoes (and paste) and marmalade (among other products), La Tore is a wonderful place to stay. Decidedly off the beaten track, it offers seven barnlike rooms with a lovely rustic farmhouse hidden among fruit trees. Terracotta tiles and heavy wooden furniture add to the rural appeal. Children between two and six years of age are offered a 50% discount (30% discount for seven- to 10-year-olds) if they sleep in their parents' room. During the winter, there is a self-contained apartment available.

MARINA DEL CANTONE

A delightful low-key place, you should have little problem finding accommodation here, aside from in August when the tidal wave of holidaying Italians swamp the hotels in this holiday hotspot of the Sorrentine peninsula.

♥ PENSIONE LA CERTOSA €

☎ 081 808 12 09; www.hotelcertosa.com; Marina del Cantone; r incl breakfast €85-95, half-/full board per person €75/85; ☺ year-round; ⊠

This rambling seafront hotel has a good terrace restaurant (meals around €30) and unspectacular modern rooms. The low wooden ceilings and concrete box–balconies are a curious feature but the rooms are whistle clean and so close to the beach that you can virtually step directly onto the pebbles below. Half-board is compulsory in August.

♥ VILLAGGIO RESIDENCE NETTUNO €

☎ 081 808 10 51; www.villaggionettuno.it; Via A Vespucci 39; camp sites per person €13, apt €110-215; ☺ Mar-Nov

Marina's camping ground – in the terraced olive groves by the entrance to the village – offers an array of accommodation options (camp sites, apartments for two to six people, mobile homes for two to four people) priced according to a complex seasonal scale. It's a friendly, environmentally sound place with excellent facilities and a comprehensive list of activities.

POSITANO

Positano is a glorious place to stay, but be aware that prices are, overall, high. Like everywhere on the Amalfi Coast it gets very busy in summer, so book ahead, particularly at weekends and in July and August. Ask at the tourist office about rooms or apartments in private houses.

♥ ALBERGO CALIFORNIA €€

Map p179; ☎ 089 87 53 82; www.hotelcalifornia positano.com; Via Cristoforo Colombo; r incl breakfast €130-160; Ⓟ ⊠

This Hotel California is a long way from the West Coast (and the elderly owners don't look like Eagles fans). Housed in a magnificent 18th-century palace with a facade washed in well-aged pinks and yellows, the rooms in the older part of the house are magnificent with ceilings painted with original friezes. The new rooms are spacious and luxuriously decorated. Breakfast is served in a lovely front terrace.

❦ CASA CELESTE €
Map p179; ☎ 089 87 53 63; Via Fornillo 10; s €42, d €80-90, incl breakfast; year-round

First of all, a warning: Celeste's home-made *limoncello* (which she will ply you with at any opportunity) has more vodka in it than most. In her 80s, she's a gem, and also makes all the breakfast preserves and cakes. Son Marco is behind the tasteful restoration of the 17th-century rooms (when he is not running his beach bar), which are attractively furnished with bright tile work and dark wood furniture. Go for room five with its atmospheric vaulted ceiling.

❦ FLORIDA RESIDENCE €
Map p179; ☎ 089 87 58 01; www.floridaresidence.net; Viale Pasitea 171; d €85-105; Apr-Oct;

There are two rarities here: free parking and boiled eggs for breakfast! This friendly place won't disappoint with the rooms either, they are well equipped with fridge and hairdryer and several have tubs, as well as showers. There is plenty of communal kickback space, including a rooftop solarium and garden, complete with gazebo. The owner only speaks Italian.

❦ HOTEL PALAZZO MURAT €€€
Map p179; ☎ 089 87 51 77; www.palazzomurat.it; Via dei Mulini 23; s €120-250, d €150-375, incl breakfast; May–mid-Jan;

Hidden behind an ancient wall from the surge of tourists who pass this pe-

destrian thoroughfare daily, the Palazzo Murat is a magnificent hotel. Housed within the 18th-century *palazzo* that the one-time King of Naples used as his summer residence, the lush gardens contain banana trees, bottlebrush, Japanese maple and pine trees. Rooms, five in the original part of the building (more expensive), 25 in the newer section, are decorated with sumptuous antiques, original oil paintings and plenty of glossy marble.

❦ HOTEL PUPETTO €€
Map p179; ☎ 089 87 50 87; www.hotelpupetto.it; Via Fornillo 37; s €90-100, d €130-170, incl breakfast; Apr–mid-Nov;

Overlooking Spiaggia del Fornillo, this is as close to the beach as you can get without sleeping on a sunlounger. A bustling, cheerful place, the hotel forms part of a large, rambling beach complex, with a popular terraced restaurant (meals around €25), a nautical-themed bar and, upstairs, the airy guest rooms. Recently renovated, they have sea-green or terracotta tiles and some lovely sea views.

❦ PENSIONE MARIA LUISA €
Map p179; ☎ 089 87 50 23; www.pensionemarialuisa.com; Via Fornillo 42; s €50, d €70-80; year-round;

The best budget choice in town, the Maria Luisa is run by lovely Carlo, a larger then life character who will go out of his way to assist and advise. The rooms and bathrooms have recently been updated with shiny new blue tiles and fittings; those with private terraces are well worth the extra €10 for the view of the bay and visits from the affectionate resident ginger Tom. The sunny communal area (with fridges, coffee machine, books and views) is a major plus.

☘ SAN PIETRO €€€

Off Map p179; ☎ 089 87 54 55; www.ilsanpietro.it;
Via Laurito 2; r incl breakfast from €420; ⊙ Apr-Oct;
Ⓟ ⊠ ⊠

For such a talked-about hotel, the San
Pietro is remarkably discreet. Built into
a rocky headland 2km east of Positano,
it's almost entirely below road level – if
driving, look for an ivy-clad chapel and
a red British telephone box by the side
of the road. Once safely ensconced, you
probably won't want to leave. All of
the individually decorated rooms have
spectacular sea views, a private terrace and Jacuzzi; there's a tennis court,
semicircular swimming pool, Michelin-
starred restaurant and, a whopping 88m
below reception, a private beach (accessible by lift).

☘ VILLA FLAVIO GIOIA €€

Map p179; ☎ 089 87 51 72; www.villaflaviogioia.it;
Piazza Flavio Gioia 2; r €129-179; ▣

Located within confessional distance of
the church, this is one of the few places
in town that stays open all year, the
studio apartments here are elegantly
furnished with glossy earth colours
and sparkling marble. There are small
kitchenettes, dining areas and balconies
with ecclesiastical and sea views. There
are also larger apartments available. In
August a minimum of one week's stay
is required.

☘ VILLA FRANCO €€€

Map p179; ☎ 089 87 56 55; www.villafrancahotel.
it; Viale Pasitea 318; r incl breakfast €190-340;
⊙ Apr–mid-Oct; Ⓟ ⊠

This immaculate boutique hotel has
a sparkling blue-and-white Mediterranean feel while the rooftop pool has
some of the best views in town. The
rooms are small but bright and have
classical-themed tiled frescoes. Down-

stairs, there's a small bar, plus a gym
with hi-tech machinery (as if you didn't
get enough exercise in this town) and
a Turkish bath. A new annexe opened
recently with nine more rooms with
similar decor.

☘ VILLA NETTUNO €

Map p179; ☎ 089 87 54 01; www.villanettunopositano
.it; Viale Pasitea 208; s/d €70/85; ⊙ year-round

Hidden behind a barrage of perfumed
foliage, Villa Nettuno oozes charm.
Go for one of the original rooms in the
300-year-old part of the building with
frescoed wardrobes, heavy rustic decor
and communal terrace. Rooms in the
renovated part of the villa obviously
lack the same character. That said, you
probably won't be thinking of the furniture as you lie in your bed while gazing
out to sea.

POSITANO TO AMALFI

One of the most stunning stretches of
road on the coast, accommodation here
is mostly centred around Praiano.

☘ AGRITURISMO SERAFINA // FURORE €

☎ 089 83 03 47; www.agriturismoserafina.it; Via
Picola 3, Loc Vigne; s/d incl breakfast €30/60, half-
board €45/90; ⊙ year-round; ⊠

It's difficult to get more off the beaten
track than this superb *agriturismo*. But
make it up here and you'll find one of
the best deals on the coast. Accommodation is in seven spruce, air-conditioned
rooms in the main farmhouse, each with
its own small balcony and views over the
lush green terraces below. The food is
quite special, virtually everything made
with the farm's own produce (which
includes salami, pancetta, wine, olive oil,
fruit and veg).

☙ HOTEL CONTINENTALE & LA TRANQUILITA // PRAIANO €

☎ 089 87 40 84; www.continental.praiano.it; Via Roma 21; camp sites €30, s €40-60, d €60-85, apt per week €850-1250, mini-apt per week €400-800; ⊙ r Apr-Oct, apt year-round

On the main road just to the east of Pra- iano, this gay-friendly hotel offers the full gamut of accommodation. There are cool, white rooms with sea views and several apartments (sleeping up to four people); plus space for 15 tents on a series of grassy terraces, from where a private staircase leads down to a rocky platform on the sea.

AMALFI

Despite its reputation as a day-trip desti- nation, Amalfi has plenty of accommoda- tion. It's not especially cheap, though, and most hotels are in the midrange to upper price brackets. Always try to book ahead, as the summer months are very busy and many places close over winter. Note that if you're coming by car, consider a hotel with a car park, as finding on-street park- ing could lead to an attack of the vapours.

☙ ALBERGO SANT'ANDREA €

Map p187; ☎ 089 87 11 45; Via Santolo Camera; s/d €70/80; ⊙ Mar-Oct; ⊠

Enjoy the atmosphere of busy Piazza del Duomo from the comfort of your own room. This modest two-star has basic rooms with brightly coloured tiles that range from purple to baby blue and burgundy – with coordinating fabrics. Although it doesn't equal the most soothing of surroundings, the view of the cathedral across the piazza should be sufficiently appeasing.

☙ HOTEL AMALFI €€

Map p187; ☎ 089 87 24 40; www.starnet.it/hamalfi; Vico dei Pastai 3; s €60-120, d €80-160, incl break- fast; Ⓟ ⊠

TOP FIVE

B&BS

- ★ **B&B Donnaregina**, Naples (p264)
- ★ **Dimora dei Giganti**, Naples (p265)
- ★ **Casariello**, Naples (p269)
- ★ **Casale Giancesare**, Paestum (p286)
- ★ **Casa Astarita**, Sorrento (p276)

ACCOMMODATION

Located in the backstreets just off Amal- fi's main pedestrian thoroughfare, this family run three-star is elegant and cen- tral. Rooms, some of which have their own balconies, sport pale-yellow walls, majolica-tiled flooring and a deft strip of stencilling. The glossily tiled bathrooms have a choice of tub or shower. Upstairs, the roof garden is a relaxing place to idle over a drink.

☙ HOTEL CENTRALE €€

Map p187; ☎ 089 87 26 08; www.hotelcentraleamal fi.it; Largo Piccolomini 1; s €60-120, d €70-140, tr €90-170, q €100-180, incl breakfast; ⊙ year-round; Ⓟ ⊠ ⌨

For the money, this is one of the best- value hotels in Amalfi. The entrance is on a tiny little piazza in the *centro storico* but many rooms actually overlook Piazza del Duomo (room 24 is a good choice). The bright-green-and-blue tile work gives the place a vibrant fresh look and the views from the rooftop terrace are magnificent.

☙ HOTEL LA CONCHIGLIA €

Off Map p187; ☎ /fax 089 87 18 56; Lungomare dei Cavalieri; d €100, half-board per person €80; ⊙ Easter-Oct; Ⓟ

One of the few budget options in Amalfi, this unpretentious place is a five-minute walk west of the centre on the seafront beyond the marina. It's not

ACCOMMODATION

in a particularly scenic spot but the airy rooms are comfortable enough, with their cool white walls and old-fashioned furniture. The parking is a definite plus in a town where space is a much sought-after commodity.

❦ HOTEL LIDOMARE €

Map p187; ☎ 089 87 13 32; www.lidomare.it; Largo Duchi Piccolomini 9; s/d incl breakfast €50/110; ⊙ year-round; ✗ ☐

Family run, complete with grandma on a Zimmer frame, this old-fashioned hotel has real character. The spacious rooms have an air of gentility, with their appealingly haphazard decor, vintage tiles and fine antiques. Surprisingly, some, such as room 31, even have Jacuzzi bathtubs; others, room 42 among them, have sea views. Breakfast is laid out, unusually, on top of a grand piano! It's all part of the very special character here.

❦ HOTEL LUNA CONVENTO €€€

Off Map p187; ☎ 089 87 10 02; www.lunahotel.it; Via Pantaleone Comite 33; s €220-280, d €240-300, incl breakfast; ⊙ year-round; ℗ ✗ ☒

This former convent was founded by St Francis in 1222 and has been a hotel for some 170 years. Rooms in the original building are in the former monks' cells, but there's nothing pokey about the bright tiles, balconies and seamless sea views. The newer wing is equally beguiling, with religious frescoes over the bed (to stop any misbehaving). The cloistered courtyard is magnificent.

❦ HOTEL SANTA CATERINA €€€

Off Map p187; ☎ 089 87 10 12; www.hotelsantacaterina.it; Strada Amalfitana 9; d €250-700, ste from €500; ⊙ Mar-Oct; ℗ ✗ ☒ ☎

An Amalfi landmark, the Santa Caterina is one of Italy's most famous hotels. Everything about the place oozes luxury,

from the discreet service to the fabulous gardens, the private beach to the opulent rooms. And if that weren't enough, the views are among the best on the coast. For honeymooners, the Romeo and Juliet suite is the one to go for, a private chalet in the colourful grounds, it's a snip at anywhere between €650 and €1300 per night.

❦ RESIDENZA DEL DUCA €

Map p187; ☎ 089 873 63 65; www.residencedelduca.it; Via Mastalo 11 Duca 3; s €40-60, d €80-100, incl breakfast; ⊙ Mar-Oct; ✗

A family run small hotel with just six rooms, daughter Daniella speaks excellent English. Call ahead if you are carrying heavy luggage as it's a seriously puff-you-out-climb to reach here and a luggage service is included in the price. The rooms are prettily furnished with antiques, majolica tiles and the odd chintzy decorative cherub. They are light and sunny; room two is a particular winner with its French windows and stunning views.

RAVELLO

Ravello is an upmarket town and the accommodation reflects this, both in style and price. There are some superb top-end hotels, several lovely midrange places and a fine *agriturismo* nearby. Book well ahead for summer – especially if you're planning to visit during the music festival (p10).

❦ AFFITACAMERE IL ROSETO €

Map p193; ☎ 089 858 64 92; Via Trinità 37; www.ilroseto.it; d €80; ⊙ year-round

If you're after a no-frills, clean room within easy walking distance of everything, come here. There are only two rooms, both of which have been decorated in medical white, with white walls, white sheets and white floors. But what they lack in charm they make up for in value, and, if you want colour, you can always sit outside under the lemon trees. No coincidence, perhaps, that the owners also run the Profumi della Costiera shop (p195).

☙ AGRITURISMO MONTE BUSARA €

☎ 089 85 74 67; www.montebrusara.com; Via Monte Brusara 32; per person incl breakfast €35, half-board €50

An authentic working farm, this mountainside *agriturismo* is the real McCoy. Located a tough half-hour walk of about 1.5km from Ravello centre (a car is not essential but it's highly recommended), it's ideal for families with kids – they can feed the pony while you sit back and admire the views – or for those who simply want to escape the crowds. The three rooms are comfy but basic, the food is fabulous and the owner is a charming, garrulous host.

☙ ALBERGO RISTORANTE GARDEN €€

Map p193; ☎ 089 85 72 26; www.hotelgardenravello. it; Via Boccaccio 4; r €110; ☙ mid-Mar–late Oct

Take a look at the photos behind reception and you can see current owners Ana and Marco playing with the Jackie Kennedy brood many years ago. Although no longer the celebrity magnet that it once was, this family run three-star is still a good bet. The smallish rooms leave little impression (clean with nondescript decor) but the views are superb and fridges are a welcome touch. Apparently Gore Vidal was a regular at the terrace restaurant here (meals from around €25).

☙ HOTEL CARUSO €€€

Map p193; ☎ 089 85 88 01; www.hotelcaruso.com; Piazza San Giovanni del Toro 2; s €446, d €608-743, incl breakfast; ☙ mid-Mar–Nov; ☙ ☙ ☙

There can be no better place to swim than the Caruso's sensational infinity pool. Seemingly set on the edge of a precipice, its blue waters merge with sea and sky to magical effect. Inside the sublimely restored 11th-century *palazzo* is no less impressive, with Moorish arches doubling as window frames, 15th-century vaulted ceilings and high-class ceramics. Rooms are suitably mod-conned with a TV/DVD system that slides sexily out of a wooden cabinet at the foot of the bed.

☙ HOTEL TORO €€

Map p193; ☎ /fax 089 85 72 11; www.hoteltoro.it; Via Wagner 3; r incl breakfast €85-118; ☙ Easter-Nov; ☙

A hotel since the late 19th century, the Dutch artist Escher stayed in room six here and was possibly inspired by the dizzily patterned tiles. The rooms are decked out in traditional Amalfi Coast style with terracotta or light marble tiles, soothing cream furnishings and tasteful landscape paintings; several rooms have fridges. Outside, the grassy, walled garden is a delightful place to sip your sun downer.

☙ HOTEL VILLA AMORE €

Map p193; ☎ /fax 089 85 71 35; Via dei Fusco 5; s €50-60, d €75-100, incl breakfast; ☙ year-round; ☙

A welcoming family run *pensione*, this is the best budget choice in town. Tucked away down a quiet lane, it has modest, homey rooms and sparkling bathrooms. Some, like room three, have their own balcony; others have bathtubs – a few have both. The restaurant is a further plus with a terrace with (still more) fabulous views: the food's good, the views are memorable and the prices are right (around €20 for a meal).

ACCOMMODATION

ACCOMMODATION

♥ PALAZZO SASSO €€€

Map p193; ☎ 089 81 81 81; www.palazzosasso.com; Via San Giovanni del Toro 28; d incl breakfast €330, with sea view €650; ☽ Mar-Oct; ⊠ ▣ ⊠

One of three luxury hotels on Ravello's millionaire row, Palazzo Sasso has been a hotel since 1880, providing refuge for many 20th-century luminaries – General Eisenhower planned the Allied attack on Monte Cassino here while later Roberto Rossellini and Ingrid Bergman giggled over dinner in the hotel restaurant. A stunning pale-pink 12th-century palace, its decor couples tasteful antiques with Moorish colours and modern sculpture. The 20m swimming pool commands great views and its Michelin-starred restaurant, Rossellinis, is one of the best in town. A small spa opened here in 2009.

SALERNO & THE CILENTO

SALERNO

The little accommodation that Salerno offers is fairly uninspiring, although, conveniently, there are several reasonable hotels near the train station. Prices tend to be considerably lower than on the Amalfi Coast.

♥ HOTEL MONTESTELLA €

Map p204; ☎ 089 22 51 22; www.hotelmontestella. it; Corso Vittorio Emanuele 156; s/d/tr incl breakfast €75/100/110; ⊠

Within walking distance of just about anywhere worth going to, the Montestella is on Salerno's main pedestrian thoroughfare, halfway between the *centro storico* and train station. And it's this, combined with the competitive prices, that is the hotel's forte. The 45 guest rooms are perfectly adequate – clean with air-con, TV, and a dubious orange-and-brown colour combo – but are hardly memorable.

♥ HOTEL PLAZA €

Map p204; ☎ 089 22 44 77; www.plazasalerno. it; Piazza Vittorio Veneto 42; s/d/tr incl breakfast €65/100/115; ⊠ ▢

A two-minute chug from the train station, the Plaza is convenient, comfortable and fairly charmless, especially the dowdy public areas. But it's not an unfriendly place and the good-sized rooms, with their brown carpet and gleaming bathrooms, are actually pretty good value for money. Those around the back have terraces overlooking the city and, beyond, the mountains.

PAESTUM

Given the fact that most people visit Paestum on a day visit, there is a surprising number of hotels here. Aside from the inevitable modern three-star hotels geared towards coach tours, there are some excellent options.

♥ CASALE GIANCESARE €

☎ 0828 72 80 61; www.casale-giancesare.it; Via Giancesare 8; s €45-60, d €65-90, incl breakfast; ℗ ⊠ ▢ ⊠

A 19th-century former farmhouse, this charming stone-clad B&B is run by delightful Anna who will happily ply you with her homemade wine and *limoncello*. Located 2.5km from Paestum and surrounded by vineyards and olive and mulberry trees, the views are stunning, particularly from the swimming pool. Anna works at the tourist office in Agropoli, so is a handy fount of knowledge on the area.

♥ HOTEL CALYPSO €€

☎ 0828 81 10 31; Via Mantegna 63; www.calypso hotel.com; s €50-75, d €100-150, incl breakfast; ℗ ⊠ ▢

A top choice for artistically or alternatively inclined folk, with a macrobiotic restaurant (member of the Slow Food Movement) and tastefully decorated rooms with private balconies and local art and handicrafts. Owner Roberto is a world traveller who can also advise on the local area. Concerts are regularly staged here during the summer, ranging from folk to classical.

AGROPOLI & THE CILENTO COAST

A popular destination for Italian tourists in the summer months, Agropoli and the main coastal resorts have a good range of accommodation, mainly centred on the respective seafronts.

☙ ALBERGO IL CASTELLO // CASTELLABATE €
☎ 0974 96 71 69; www.hotelcastello.co.uk; Via Amendola; r incl breakfast €80-110; ☒ ℗
This ivy-clad old-fashioned hotel is housed in an early 19th-century building with large rooms still with the original floor tiles, plus exposed stone walls and spacious private terraces. The courtyard is a delight with its lemon trees and abundance of plants; the perfect place to enjoy a sun downer at the end of an energetic day.

☙ ANNA // AGROPOLI €
☎ 0974 82 37 63; www.bbanna.it; Via S Marco 28-30; s €35-50, d €50-70, incl breakfast; ℗ ☒
A great location, across from the town's sweeping sandy beach, this trim budget choice is best known locally for its downstairs restaurant (p217), as you will appreciate while salivating over your home-made morning *cornetti* (Italian-type croissant). The rooms are bright and cheerful with white walls, smart striped fabrics and balconies; specify a sea view if possible. Sunbeds and bicycles can be hired for a minimal price.

☙ LA LANTERNA // AGROPOLI €
☎ 089 79 02 51; Via della Lanterna 8; 2-/4-person cabin €40/60, dm incl breakfast €14; ℗ ▢
Ivo and Tiziana are great hosts at this friendly place, around 1km from the centre of town. The homey cabin accommodation is great value, set in the gardens with large terraces, sea views and plenty of storage space. The dorms are straightforward and clean with lockers, while the breakfast of rolls with cream cheese or jams and home-made cake is better than most. Internet costs €1 per hour.

☙ IL CEPPO // AGROPOLI €
☎ 0974 84 30 44; www.hotelristoranteilceppo.com; Via Madonna del Carmine 31; s €50-75, d €80-90, incl breakfast; ℗ ☒
Across from the renowned restaurant of the same name this small, modern hotel has a bright, fresh look with wicker furniture and pale-pink paintwork in the rooms. The bathrooms are minimalist and modern. Located around 4km due southeast from the centre of town, it should only be considered if you are travelling by car.

☙ LA CONCHIGLIA // PALINURO €€
☎ 0974 93 10 18; www.hotellaconchiglia; Via Indipendenza 52; r incl breakfast €80-110; ℗ ☒ ▢
Superb hotel on the main street, with walls washed in ochre, plus terracotta tiles and tasteful artwork. A large terrace overlooks the sea with comfy pine chairs and a handy adjacent bar. The satellite TV here is a rare treat in these parts, and a major plus if you are suffering from CNN withdrawal.

☙ PENSIONE ANNA// PALINURA €€
☎ 0974 93 10 59; Piazza Virgilio 22; s €25-65, d €50-130, incl breakfast; ℗ ☒
The perks of this family run place include the position, right on the town's vibrant

ACCOMMODATION

ACCOMMODATION

main square, and the delightful old-fashioned front terrace with its plants, vines and congenial granddad, who has his own seat in the corner. The rooms are simply furnished but clean with jaunty red shutters. Prices are very reasonable, aside from the silly season (August).

☙ RAGGIO DI SOLE // CASTELLABATE €

☎ 0974 96 73 56; www.agriturismoraggiodisole.it, in Italian; Via Terrate; r incl breakfast €80; Apr-Nov; ⊠ Ⓟ

Situated on the outskirts of town coming from Santa Maria di Castellabate, this welcoming *agriturismo* is just one mountain peak away from the town, so the views are superb, with the sea and the island of Capri beyond. The main house is surrounded by trees, including lofty eucalyptus, citrus and olive trees, while below there is a small farmyard with goats, geese, ducks and at least one donkey. A totally reformed 200-year-old farmhouse, the rooms are plain and modern with balconies. Meals are available.

☙ U'SGHIZ // AGROPOLI €

☎ 0974 82 93 31; Piazza Umberto 8; s €45-50, d €45-80, incl breakfast; ⊠

In the heart of the *centro storico*, with an excellent restaurant (see p217), Antonio (or Antoine – he lived many years in Quebec) has lovingly restored this 1600 building and opened in 2009 with a choice of just three atmospheric rooms. Furnished with antiques, they have soothing colour schemes of pale green, peach and cream. Fridges are an agreeable extra.

☙ VILLA SIRIO // SANTA MARIA DI CASTELLABATE €€

☎ 0974 96 01 62; www.villasirio.it; Via Lungamare de Simone 15; s €85-130, d €120-200, incl breakfast; ⊠ Apr-Nov; Ⓟ ⊠

Dating from 1912, this family owned hotel has a classic and elegant facade with its ochre paintwork and traditional green shutters. The rooms are brightly furnished with a yellow, blue and turquoise colour scheme plus shiny marble-clad bathrooms complete with Jacuzzi bathtubs. The small balconies have forfeited the plastic for tasteful marble tables and have seamless sea views with Capri in the distance.

PARCO NAZIONALE DEL CILENTO

Unsurprisingly, the dramatic and lush scenery in the park makes it an excellent place to stay in an *agriturimso* – and there is plenty of choice. Aside from the listings here, check the *agriturismi* websites (p266) at the beginning of this chapter.

☙ AGRITURISMO ANTICO CASOLARE // CASTELCIVITA €

☎ 339 4572986; www.anticocasolare.com; Contrada Suvero 6; s/d incl breakfast €35/60; ⊠ Mar-Oct; Ⓟ ⊠

On the edge of the park, just 6km inland from the coast, come here for fabulous views and a no-frills rural stay in an 18th-century farmhouse, still in the same Ricciardella family. A large outside terrace is hung with corn cobs, tomatoes and an original oven for baking bread. The rooms are pleasant with wrought-iron or dark wood furnishings and small tiled bathrooms. Various activities, including trekking and horse riding, can be organised.

☙ AGRITURISMO I MORESANI // CASAL VELINO €

☎ 0974 90 20 86; www.imoresani.com; Loc Moresani; r incl breakfast €45-80; ⊠ Mar-Oct ⊠

If you are seeking utter tranquillity, head here. The setting is bucolic with rolling hills in every direction, interspersed with grape vines, grazing pastures and olive trees. Family run, the 18-hectare farm produces its own *caprino* goat's cheese. The restaurant uses primarily homegrown products and has an outside terrace, which fronts onto vineyards. The rooms have cream-and earth-coloured decor and surround a pretty private garden. Horse riding, cooking and painting courses are regularly held; check the website and contact the friendly owners for a schedule.

❦ AGRITURISMO LA LOGGIA DEGLI ALBURNI // SICIGNANO DEGLI ALBURNI €

☎ 334 3204398; Sicignano e'Alburni; s/d incl breakfast €30/40; P ⊠

More of a country hotel than a true *agriturismo*, but the setting is sublime, high up in a grove of chestnut trees overlooking the magnificent castle (follow the signs from the village). The rooms are large, modern and comfortable. The dining room, complete with colourful hunting mural, serves good traditional fare like home-made *tagliolini* pasta in a ragù sauce (meals €25). Popular with walkers.

❦ AGRITURISMO TERRA NOSTRA // CORLETO MONFORTE €

☎ 333 8069231; www.agriturismoterranostra.it; Contrada Galdo; s/d incl breakfast €20/40; ⊙ Mar-Oct; P ⊠ ▣

Owned by the Salamonte family who lived in England for several years (hence the gnomes in the garden), this folksy place enjoys a lovely pastoral setting, right outside this delightful medieval village. Goats, sheep, ducks and dogs are just part of the menagerie. The rooms are simply furnished with dark wood furniture, dazzling white walls and terracotta tile floors. The large restaurant dishes up excellent local dishes and has an open fireplace during the winter months.

❦ ANTICHI FEUDI // TEGGIANO €

☎ 0975 58 73 29; www.antichifeudi.com; Via San Francesco 2; r incl breakfast €45-80; ⊠

Located just off the picturesque main Piazza San Cono, this former palace is distinguished by its sumptuous burnt sienna coloured exterior. An atmospheric and remarkably inexpensive boutique hotel, the rooms are all different, but share a sumptuous attention to detail with decorative painted wardrobes, canopy beds and even the occasional chandelier. The public spaces include a small courtyard with its original well and an excellent restaurant (see p215).

❦ CASALE SAN MARTINO // LAUREANA CILENTO €

☎ 0974 83 22 13; www.casalesanmartino.eu; Contrada Vignali 5; r incl breakfast €65-85; ⊙ Mar-Oct; P ⊠

Opened in 2009, this exquisite B&B has stunning panoramic views of Agropoli and the coast to the west and rolling countryside to the east. Sleep under the beams in the tastefully decorated bedrooms with their stone walls, earth colours and five-star quality bathrooms with mosaic marble tiles. The young family menagerie includes goats and ducks and, if you time your visit right, breakfast will include fresh figs from the garden.

❦ SICINIUS // SICIGNANO DEGLI ALBURNI €

☎ 330 869287; www.sicinius.com; Contrada Piedi La Serra 22; r incl breakfast €65; ⊙ Apr-Oct P ⊠

A solar-energised 12-hectare farm that is committed to cultivating organic crops,

ACCOMMODATION

including olives, and offers massages and aromatherapy treatments, and has a small health shop on the premises. The rooms are simple, with superb views of Mt Alburni, and there are mountain bikes available for guests, as well as an excellent restaurant.

🍴 ZIO CRISTOFORO // CASAL VELINO €€

☎ 0974 90 75 52; www.agriturismoziocristoforo.com; Via Chiuse 24; s €80-120, d €90-140, incl breakfast; 🛇 🅿

If *agriturismi* had stars, this one would have five. That said, it is more like a boutique hotel than a farmstay. No one seems to be trudging around in muddy boots here, although there *is* a surrounding farm and the animals raised do feature in the popular restaurant menu. The rooms are rustic, yet elegant, with wrought-iron bedheads, terracotta tiles and a soothing green-and-white colour scheme. Cooking classes are available during the winter months (€150 for three days).

DIRECTORY

BUSINESS HOURS

Shops in Naples generally open from 9.30am to 1.30pm and 4.30pm to 8.30pm Monday to Saturday, with many closed on Monday morning in winter and on Saturday afternoon in summer. In Naples most supermarkets have continuous opening hours from 9am to 8.30pm Monday to Saturday. Some even open from 9am to 1pm on Sunday.

Banks open from 8.30am to 1.30pm and 2.45pm to 3.45pm Monday to Friday. They are closed at weekends, but it is always possible to find a *cambio* (exchange office) open in Naples and major tourist areas.

Major post offices are open from 8.30am to 6pm Monday to Friday; smaller branches close at 1.30pm Monday to Friday, and at 12.30pm on the last business day of each month. All post offices are open from 8.30am to 1pm on Saturday.

Farmacie (pharmacies) are open from 9am to 1pm and 4pm to 7.30pm Monday to Friday. Most open on Saturday mornings and close on Sundays, although a few remain open on a rotation basis. A few are open 24 hours. All closed pharmacies are obliged to display a list of the nearest one that is open.

Bars and cafes generally open from 7.30am to 8pm, although some stay open until the small hours, typically 1am or 2am.

Restaurants typically open from noon to 3pm and 7.30pm to 11pm (later in summer). Restaurants and bars are required to close for one day each week, although in busy tourist areas this rule is not always observed.

Opening hours for museums, galleries and archaeological sites vary enormously, although many are closed on Mondays or Tuesdays. Increasingly, the major national museums and galleries remain open until 10pm during the summer.

Note that trading hours on the Amalfi Coast and even outer suburban Naples will vary from central Naples.

CUSTOMS REGULATIONS

Goods imported and exported within the EU incur no additional taxes, provided

DIRECTORY

duty has been paid somewhere within the EU and the goods are for personal consumption.

Duty-free sales within the EU no longer exist. Visitors coming into Italy from non-EU countries can import the following duty free: spirits (1L), wine (2L), perfume (50mL), eau de toilette (250mL), 200 cigarettes and other goods up to a total of €175.50; anything over this limit must be declared on arrival and the appropriate duty paid. You can also bring up to €10,000 in cash into Italy.

Upon leaving the EU, non-EU citizens can reclaim any Imposta di Valore Aggiunto (IVA) value-added tax on purchases equal to or over €155. The refund only applies to purchases from affiliated retail outlets that display a 'Tax Free for Tourists' sign. You have to complete a form at the point of sale, then get it stamped by Italian customs as you leave. For more information pick up a pamphlet about the scheme from participating stores.

PRACTICALITIES

* Italy uses the metric system for weights and measures.
* Plugs have two or three round pins, so bring an international adapter.
* The electric current is 220V, 50Hz and two-pin adapter plugs can be bought at electrical shops.
* Naples' major daily newspaper is *Il Mattino*, although the national *La Repubblica* also has a Neapolitan section.
* Foreign newspapers are available, generally one or two days late, at the larger city kiosks and, more commonly, at nearby tourist resorts. The same applies to English- or foreign-language magazines.

DANGERS & ANNOYANCES

Naples has a certain (and often exaggerated) reputation for being unsafe. While you're highly unlikely to be caught in mafia crossfire, it pays to guard your valuables closely on the streets as pickpockets and scooter snatchers are active in the main tourist areas.

Travellers should be careful about walking alone in the streets at night, particularly in the Mercato, La Sanità and Quartieri Spagnoli districts, and around Piazza Garibaldi.

Away from Naples there are no great issues, although in Pompeii you should watch out for touts posing as legitimate guides.

POLLUTION

Noise and air pollution are problems in Naples. Periodic pollution alerts warn the elderly, children and people who suffer respiratory problems to stay indoors. Keep yourself informed through the tourist office or your hotel.

SCAMS

Avoid buying mobile phones and other discounted electrical goods from vendors on Piazza Garibaldi and at street markets. It's not unusual to get home and discover that you've bought a box with a brick in it.

At Stazione Centrale in Naples, ignore touts offering taxis; use only registered white taxis with a running meter. Many of these touts will drive you to your destination then demand an extortionist fare (two American travellers were ordered to pay a jaw-dropping €50 for the 3km journey from the train station to a central city hostel). For official taxi fare rates, see p311.

Many cons play on people's insecurity with foreign bank notes. Short-changing is a common trick. One popular dodge goes as follows: you pay for a €4 *panino* (sandwich) with a €20 note. The cashier then distractedly gives you a €1 coin and a €5 note before turning away. The trick here is to wait and chances are that the €10 note you're waiting for will appear without a word being said.

Note swapping is another thing to be aware of. This con involves you paying for a taxi fare or a train ticket with a €20 note. The taxi driver or ticket seller then deftly palms your note and produces a €10 note claiming that you paid with this and not the €20 you thought you had given. In your confusion you're not quite sure what you did and so accept their word.

THEFT

Pickpockets are most active in dense crowds, especially in busy train stations and on public transport. A common ploy is for one person to distract you while another whips through your pockets. Beware of gangs of dishevelled-looking kids waving newspapers and demanding attention. In the blink of an eye, a wallet or camera can go missing. Remember also that some of the best pickpockets are well dressed.

When going out, spread your valuables, cash and cards around your body or in different bags. A moneybelt with your essentials (passport, cash, credit cards, airline tickets) is usually a good idea; however, to avoid delving into it in public, carry a wallet with enough cash for the day. Don't flaunt watches, cameras and other expensive goods. Cameras and shoulder bags are an open invitation for snatch thieves, many of whom work from motorcycles or scooters. Wear

cameras and bags across the body and keep under your arm. Also be very careful at cafes and bars – always loop your bag's strap around your leg while seated.

Parked cars, particularly those with foreign number plates and/or rental-agency stickers, are prime targets for petty criminals. While driving in cities, beware of thieves at traffic lights – keep doors locked and windows rolled up high. A favourite ploy of snatchers is for a first scooter rider to brush past your car, knocking the side-mirror out of position; then, as you reach out to readjust it, an accomplice on a second scooter races past snatching your watch as he goes.

Car theft is a problem in Naples, so it pays to leave your car in a supervised car park. If you leave your car on the street, you'll often be approached by an unofficial (illegal) parking attendant asking for money. Clearly you don't have to pay them but if you refuse you run the risk of returning to a damaged car.

In case of theft or loss, always report the incident to the police within 24 hours, and ask for a statement otherwise your travel-insurance company won't pay out.

TRAFFIC

Neapolitan traffic requires some getting used to. Drivers are not keen to stop for pedestrians, even at pedestrian crossings, and are more likely to swerve. Locals simply step off the footpath and walk through the (swerving) traffic with determination. It is a practice that seems to work, but if you feel uncertain, wait and cross with a local.

In many cities, roads that appear to be for one-way traffic have lanes for buses travelling in the opposite direction – always look both ways before stepping onto the road.

DIRECTORY

DISCOUNT CARDS

At many state museums and archaeological sites EU citizens under 18 and over 65 enter free, and those aged between 18 and 25 get a 50% discount. To claim these discounts you'll need a passport or an ID card.

When sightseeing consider a *biglietto cumulativo* (cumulative ticket), a ticket allowing admission to a number of associated sights for less than the combined cost of separate admission fees (see below).

The **International Student Identity Card** (ISIC), issued by the **International Student Travel Confederation** (ISTC; www.isic.org), is no longer sufficient at many tourist sites as prices are based on age, so a passport, driving licence or **Euro<26** (www.euro26.org) card is preferable. An ISIC card will still, however, prove useful for cheap flights and theatre and cinema discounts. A similar card is also available to teachers (the ITIC; International Teacher Identity Card).

Student cards are issued by student unions, hostelling organisations and some youth travel agencies. In Naples try CTS (Map pp42-3; ☎ 081 552 79 60; www.cts.it, in Italian; Via Mezzocannone 25).

EMBASSIES & CONSULATES

For foreign embassies and consulates not listed here, look under 'Ambasciate' or 'Consolati' in the telephone directory. Alternatively, tourist offices generally have a list. The following are in Naples:
France (Map pp68-9; ☎ 081 59 80 711; Via Francesco Crispi 86, 80122)
Germany (Map pp68-9; ☎ 081 248 85 11; Via Francesco Crispi 69, 80121)
Netherlands (Map pp42-3; ☎ 081 551 30 03; Via Agostino Depretis 114, 80133)
UK (Map pp62-3; ☎ 081 423 89 11; Via dei Mille 40, 80121)
USA (Map p75; ☎ 081 583 81 11; Piazza della Repubblica 2, 80122)

FOOD & DRINK

WHERE TO EAT & DRINK

Eateries are divided into several categories. At the most basic level a *tavola calda* serves preprepared pasta, meat and vegetable dishes canteen-style. The quality is usually fine, although dishes tend to be heavy on the olive oil. A pizzeria obviously specialises in pizza, but might also offer a range of antipasti and pasta. On the whole

CUMULATIVE TICKETS

Coming in various forms, the **Campania Artecard** (☎ 800 600 601; www.campaniartecard.it) is a cumulative ticket that covers museum admission and transport, as well as discounted entry to cultural events including performances at Teatro San Carlo (p61) and the Centro di Musica Antica Pietà de' Turchini (p94). The three-day Naples and Campi Flegrei ticket (adult €16, 18-25yr €10) gives free admission to three participating sites, a 50% discount on others and free transport in Naples and the Campi Flegrei. Other ticket options range from €12 to €30 and cover sites as far afield as Pompeii and Paestum. The tickets can be bought at train stations, hotels, newsagencies, participating museums, on the internet or through the call centre.

If you're intending to visit Pompeii and Herculaneum, you'll save by buying the combined **ticket** (adult €20, EU 18-25yr €10, EU under 18yr & over 65yr free), which also covers Oplontis, Stabiae and Boscoreale.

pizzerias are more informal than restaurants and the turnaround is quick and they're not a place to linger. Even more informal, *friggitorie* specialise in takeaway local tempura and other Neapolitan street food staples, including *crocchè* (fried potato balls filled with mozzarella).

For a glass of wine your best bet is an *enoteca*, a wine bar that usually offers a choice of delicatessen-type snacks or a couple of hot dishes. Similarly cafes will often have a menu of light meals and *panino*.

For a sit-down meal of pasta and meat or fish you'll want a trattoria or a *ristorante* (restaurant). The difference between the two is now fairly blurred, although as a general rule you'll pay more at a *ristorante*. Traditionally, trattorie were simple, family-run places that offered a basic menu of local dishes at affordable prices. Thankfully many still do. For gastronomic innovation and sassy presentation head for a *ristorante*.

Neapolitans aren't big drinkers, although there are plenty of bars and cafes. These range from slick designer locales to hole-in-the-wall drinking dens. For an ice cream *gelaterie* abound, while the sweet-toothed will find their nirvana in the well-stocked *pasticcerie*.

Restaurants and *trattorias* usually open for lunch from noon to 3pm and in the evening from about 7.30pm to 11pm. Many cafes are open all day from early to late, while the fashionable drinking bars often open around 6pm for aperitifs and don't close until the early hours.

VEGETARIANS & VEGANS

Although vegetarianism is not specifically catered to in the region, the abundance of high-quality vegetables means that many pasta dishes, pizzas and antipasti feature veg in some form or other. Salads are common and tasty, though you'll need to watch out for the odd anchovy or slice of ham. Also check that your tomato sauce hasn't been cooked with meat in it. Ask for *senza carne o pesce* (without meat or fish).

Vegans are in for a tough time. Cheese is widespread – to avoid it request *senza formaggio* (without cheese) – and *pasta fresca* (fresh pasta) is made with eggs.

GAY & LESBIAN TRAVELLERS

Homosexuality is legal in Italy and well tolerated in Naples; however, try to avoid overt displays of affection, particularly in smaller towns on the Amalfi Coast. The legal age of consent is 16.

Naples' largest gay organisation is **Arcigay Napoli** (Map pp42-3; ☎ 081 552 88 15; www.arcigaynapoli.org; Vico San Geronimo alle Monarche 19; ⏰ 5.30-11pm Thu-Sun), which organises special events and can provide information on the city's gay scene. You can also pick up a copy of the free magazines *Clubbing* and *Pegasus*, which have club and event listings.

Spartacus International (www.spartacus world.com) publishes the *Spartacus International Gay Guide* (US$32.99; UK£19.99), a male-only directory of gay venues worldwide. Alternatively, log onto **GuidaGay.it** (www.gay.it/guida, in Italian) or **GayFriendlyItaly.com** (www.gayfriendlyitaly. com) for addresses of gay bars and hotels.

Some gay venues (including saunas) insist you have a **tessera Arcigay** (Arcigay membership card; Italians €15, foreigners €7), available from those venues that require it.

HEALTH

Italy's public health system is legally bound to provide emergency care to everyone. EU nationals are entitled to reduced cost, sometimes free, medical care with a European Health Insurance Card (EHIC), available from your home health authority; non-EU citizens should take out health insurance (see right).

For emergency treatment, go straight to the *pronto soccorso* (casualty) section of an *ospedale* (public hospital), where it's also possible to receive emergency dental treatment. For less serious ailments call the local *guardia medica* (duty doctor); ask at your hotel or nearest tourist office for the number. Pharmacists will fill prescriptions and can provide basic medical advice.

Ambulance (☎ 118)

Ospedale Loreto-Mare (Loreto-Mare Hospital; Map pp42-3; ☎ 081 20 10 33; Via Amerigo Vespucci 26)

HOLIDAYS

Most Italians take their annual holiday in August. This means that many businesses and shops close down for at least a part of the month, particularly around Ferragosto (Feast of the Assumption) on 15 August.

Italian schools close for three months in the summer, from mid-June to mid-September, for three weeks over Christmas and for a week at Easter. See (p10) for a calendar of the region's special events and festivals.

Public holidays include the following:

Capodanno (New Year's Day) 1 January
Epifania (Epiphany) 6 January
Pasquetta (Easter Monday) March/April
Giorno della Liberazione (Liberation Day) 25 April
Festa del Lavoro (Labour Day) 1 May
Festa della Repubblica (Republic Day) 2 June
Ferragosto (Feast of the Assumption) 15 August
Festa di Ognisanti (All Saints' Day) 1 November
Festa della Immacolata Concezione (Feast of the Immaculate Conception) 8 December
Natale (Christmas Day) 25 December

Festa di Santo Stefano (Boxing Day) 26 December

INSURANCE

MEDICAL INSURANCE

If you're an EU citizen (or from Switzerland, Iceland or Norway), a European Health Insurance Card (EHIC) covers you for most medical care in public hospitals free of charge, but not for emergency repatriation home or nonemergencies. The card is available from health centres and (in the UK) from post offices. Citizens from other countries should find out if there is a reciprocal arrangement for free medical care between their country and Italy (Australia, for instance, has such an agreement; carry your Medicare card).

If you do need health insurance, make sure you get a policy that covers you for the worst case scenario, such as an accident requiring an emergency flight home. Find out in advance if your insurance plan will make payments directly to providers or reimburse you later for overseas health expenditures.

TRAVEL INSURANCE

A travel-insurance policy to cover theft, loss and medical problems is strongly recommended. It may also cover you for cancellation or delays to your travel arrangements. Paying for your ticket with a credit card can often provide limited travel accident insurance and you may be able to reclaim the payment if the operator doesn't deliver. Ask your credit-card company what it will cover.

INTERNET ACCESS

Public wi-fi hot spots are fairly thin on the ground, although an ever-increasing number of hotels, B&Bs and hostels offer them. Many hostels and several hotels provide a computer for internet access.

If you're bringing your own kit (laptop or PDA), you shouldn't have too many problems hooking up in your room, or at least in the lobby or other communal areas. Many midrange and top-end hotels now have dataports for customer use and those that don't will usually let you plug your modem into the phone line. You might need a power transformer (to convert from 110V to 220V if your notebook isn't set up for dual voltage), an RJ-11 telephone jack that works with your modem and a plug adaptor.

If you need an Internet Service Provider (ISP) with local dial-up numbers, try **AOL** (www.aol.com), **AT&T** (www.att.com) and **CompuServe** (www.compuserve.com).

LEGAL MATTERS

The most likely reason for a brush with the law is if you have to report a theft. If you do have something stolen and you want to claim it on insurance you must make a statement to the police; insurance companies won't pay up without official proof of a crime.

The Italian police is divided into three main bodies; the *polizia* who wear navy-blue jackets; the *carabinieri* (technically military police but they cover the same duties as the *polizia*) in a black uniform with a red stripe; and the grey-clad *guardia di finanza* (fiscal police), who are responsible for fighting tax evasion and drug smuggling. If you run into trouble you're most likely to end up dealing with the *polizia* or *carabinieri*. If, however, you land a parking ticket, you'll need to speak to the *vigili urbani* (traffic wardens).

In general, the consulate section of your embassy should be able to provide you with lists of lawyers, interpreters and translators in Naples. See the front of each destination chapter for police and other emergency numbers.

DRINK & DRUGS

Italian law sees no distinction between hard and soft drugs, effectively putting cannabis on the same legal footing as cocaine, heroin and ecstasy. If caught with what the police deem to be a deal-able quantity (5g of cannabis or more), you risk fines of up to €260,000 or prison sentences of between six and 20 years.

Regarding alcohol, the legal limit for a driver's blood-alcohol reading is 0.05% and random breath tests do occur.

MAPS

The maps throughout this book, combined with tourist-office maps, are generally adequate for navigating the region's main centres. Tourist offices can also provide walking maps, although if you're intent on serious hiking you should consider a specialist map. One of the best is the CAI's (Club Alpino Italiano) *Monti Lattari, Penisola Sorrentina, Costiera Amalfitana: Carta dei Sentieri* (€9.50).

The best road maps and city plans are published by de Agostini, Touring Club Italiano (TCI) and Michelin, and are available at bookshops throughout the area.

MONEY

Italy's currency is the euro. The euro is divided into 100 cents. Coin denominations are one, two, five, 10, 20 and 50 cents, €1 and €2; the notes are €5, €10, €20, €50, €100, €200 and €500.

Exchange rates are given on the inside front flap of this book. For the latest rates check out www.xe.com.

DIRECTORY

The best way to manage your money is to use your debit/credit cards while keeping a fistful of travellers cheques as backup.

CHANGING MONEY

You can change money in banks, at post offices or in a *cambio* (exchange office). Banks are generally the most reliable and tend to offer the best rates. *Cambio* offices usually, but not always, offer worse rates or charge higher commissions. Hotels are almost always the worst places to change money.

CREDIT & DEBIT CARDS

Credit and debit cards can be used in ATMs (which are widespread and known locally as *bancomat*) displaying the appropriate sign. Visa and MasterCard are widely recognised, as are Cirrus and Maestro; Amex is accepted but is less common. If you don't have a PIN, some (but not all) banks will advance cash over the counter. Credit cards can also be used in many supermarkets, hotels and restaurants, although *pensioni,* smaller trattorias and pizzerias still tend to accept cash only.

When you withdraw money from an ATM, the amounts are converted and dispensed in local currency; however, there will be fees involved. Typically, you'll be charged a withdrawal fee (usually 2% for a minimum withdrawal of €2 or more) as well as a conversion charge; if you're using a credit card, you'll also be hit with interest on the cash withdrawn.

If an ATM rejects your card, don't despair. Try a few more ATMs displaying your card's logo before assuming the problem lies with your card.

If your credit card is lost, stolen or swallowed by an ATM, telephone toll-free to have an immediate stop put on it. For Visa call ☎ 800 81 90 14; MasterCard ☎ 800 87 08 66; and for Amex ☎ 800 87 43 33.

RECEIPTS

Under Italian law you're supposed to ask for and retain receipts for absolutely everything that you pay for. Although it rarely happens, you could, in theory, be asked by the *guardia di finanza* (fiscal police) to produce a receipt immediately after you leave a shop. If you don't have one, you risk a fine.

TIPPING

You are not expected to tip on top of restaurant service charges, although if you feel the service merits it feel free to leave a small amount, perhaps €1 per person. If there is no service charge, you should consider leaving a 10% to 12% tip, but this is by no means obligatory. In bars, Italians often place a €0.10 or €0.20 coin on the bar when ordering coffee. Tipping taxi drivers is not common practice, but you are expected to tip the porter at top-end hotels (€3 to €5).

TRAVELLERS CHEQUES

Increasingly overlooked by card-wielding travellers, travellers cheques are a dying breed. They should not, however, be written off entirely as they're an excellent form of backup, especially as you can claim a refund if they're stolen (providing you've kept a separate record of their numbers).

Amex, Visa and Travelex cheques are the easiest to cash, particularly if in US dollars, British pounds or euros. Increasingly banks are charging hefty commissions, though, even on cheques denominated in euros. Whatever currency they are in, travellers cheques can be difficult to change in smaller towns. Always take your passport as identification when cashing travellers cheques.

For lost or stolen cheques call: Amex ☎ 800 91 49 12; MasterCard ☎ 800 87 08 66; Travelex ☎ 800 87 20 50; or Visa ☎ 800 87 41 55.

POST

Italy's postal system, **Poste** (☎ 803 160; www.poste.it), has improved a lot in recent years but is hardly a model of efficiency. Delivery is guaranteed to Europe within three days and to the rest of the world within four to eight days.

Francobolli (stamps) are available at post offices and authorised tobacconists (look for the official *tabacchi* sign: a big 'T', usually white on black). Urgent mail can be sent by *postacelere* (also known as CAI Post), the Italian post office's courier service. You'll find Naples' **main post office** (Map p55; ☎ 081 551 20 69) on Piazza Matteotti.

TELEPHONE

DOMESTIC CALLS

Telephone rates in Italy are among the highest in Europe, particularly for long-distance calls. A local call from a public phone costs €0.10 every minute and 10 seconds. For a long-distance call within Italy you pay €0.10 when the call is answered and then €0.57 every 57 seconds. These peak rates apply from 8am to 6.30pm Monday to Friday and until 1pm on Saturday. The cheapest time to call, for all domestic and international calls, is from midnight to 8am and any time on Sundays.

Naples' area code is 081. All telephone area codes begin with ☎ 0 and consist of up to four digits. Area codes, including the

first zero, are an integral part of all Italian phone numbers and should be used even when calling locally. Mobile-phone numbers begin with a three-digit prefix such as ☎ 330, ☎ 339; toll-free (free-phone) numbers are known as *numeri verdi* and usually start with ☎ 800; national call rate numbers start with ☎ 848 or ☎ 199.

For directory inquiries dial ☎ 89 24 12 or ☎ 1254 (or online at http://1254.alice.it).

INTERNATIONAL CALLS

Direct international calls can easily be made from public telephones by using a phonecard. Dial ☎ 00 to get out of Italy, then the relevant country and area codes, followed by the telephone number. A three-minute call to a landline in most European countries is around €0.85, to Australasia €2.85. From a public phone it costs more. You are better off using your country's direct-dialling services (such as AT&T in the US and Telstra in Australia) paid for at home-country rates. Get the access numbers before leaving home. Alternatively, try making calls using an international calling card *(scheda telefonica internazionale)*, often on sale at newspaper stands.

To make a reverse-charge (collect) international call, dial ☎ 170. All operators speak English. Alternatively, use the direct dialling (Country Direct) service provided by your home-country phone company (such as AT&T in the USA and Telstra in Australia). You simply dial the relevant access number and request a reverse-charges call via the operator in your country. Numbers for this service include the following:

Australia (Telstra)	☎ 800 172 610
Canada	☎ 800 172 213
New Zealand	☎ 800 172 641
USA (AT&T)	☎ 800 172 444

DIRECTORY

International phone numbers can be requested at ☎ 1254 (or online at http://1254.alice.it). To call Italy from abroad, dial ☎ 39 and then the area code, including the first zero.

MOBILE PHONES

Italian mobile phones operate on the GSM 900/1800 network, which is compatible with the rest of Europe and Australia but not with the North American GSM 1900 or the Japanese system (although some GSM 1900/900 phones do work here).

If you have a GSM, dual- or tri-band mobile phone that you can unlock (check with your service provider), it can cost as little as €10 to activate a *prepagato* (prepaid) SIM card in Italy. **TIM** (Telecom Italia Mobile; www.tim.it), **Wind** (www.wind.it) and **Vodafone** (www.vodafone.it) all offer SIM cards and all have retail outlets in Naples and Salerno. You'll need your passport to open an account. To recharge a card, simply pop into the nearest outlet or buy a charge card *(ricarica)* from a tobacconist. Per-minute call rates are typically €0.25 to Italian fixed phones and €0.50 to Europe and the US.

PHONECARDS

You'll find Telecom Italia silver payphones on the streets, in train stations, in some stores and in Telecom offices. Most payphones accept only *carte/schede telefoniche* (telephone cards), although some still accept credit cards and coins.

Phonecards (in denominations of €3 and €5) are available at post offices, tobacconists and newsstands. You must break the top left-hand corner off the card before you can use it.

There are cut-price call centres throughout Naples. These are run by various companies and the rates are lower than Telecom payphones for international calls. You simply place your call from a private booth inside the centre and pay for it when you've finished.

TIME

Italy is one hour ahead of GMT. Daylight saving time, when clocks are moved forward one hour, starts on the last Sunday in March. Clocks are put back an hour on the last Sunday in October. Italy operates on a 24-hour clock.

TOILETS

Public toilets are rare in Naples. Most people use the facilities in bars and cafes, although you might need to buy a coffee first. Public toilets are readily available at museums, and there are public toilets at the main bus and train stations.

On the Amalfi Coast, several public toilets have attendants, who'll expect a small tip – €0.50 should do.

There are free toilets at Pompeii and Herculaneum.

TOURIST INFORMATION

You'll find tourist offices throughout the region. Some are more helpful than others, but all can supply accommodation lists, maps, transport details and information on the major sights.

Generally, they are open from 8.30am or 9am to 12.30pm or 1pm, and from 3pm to 7pm Monday to Saturday. These hours are usually extended in summer, when some offices open on Sunday.

English, and sometimes French or German, is spoken at tourist offices in the major tourist areas and printed information is generally provided in a variety of languages.

In Naples, Campania's **main tourist office** (Map pp62-3; ☎ 081 410 72 11; Piazza dei Martiri 58; ☼ 9am-2pm Mon-Fri) is in Chiaia.

More useful, however, are the tourist information offices at the following locations, all of which stock the essential tourist brochure *Qui Napoli:*

Piazza del Gesù Nuovo (Map pp42-3; ☎ 081 552 33 28; ☼ 9am-7pm Mon-Sat, 9am-2pm Sun)

Stazione Centrale (Map pp42-3; ☎ 081 26 87 79; ☼ 9am-7pm Mon-Sat)

Stazione Mergellina (Map p75; ☎ 081 761 21 02; ☼ varies)

Via San Carlo 7 (Map pp62-3; ☎ 081 40 23 94; ☼ 9.30am-1.30pm & 2.30-6pm Mon-Sat, 9am-1.30pm Sun)

Visitors to Naples can also call the helpful **tourist information hotline** (☎ 081 007 90 20, 800 22 33 66; ☎ 8.30am-7.30pm) for information on everything from museum opening times to train and ferry timetables.

For local tourist offices outside the city see the relevant town sections in The Islands, The Amalfi Coast and Salerno & the Cilento chapters.

TRAVELLERS WITH DISABILITIES

Naples is not an easy city for travellers with disabilities. Cobbled streets, blocked pavements and tiny lifts make life difficult for the wheelchair-bound, while the anarchic traffic can be very disorientating for partially sighted travellers or those with hearing difficulties. Elsewhere, the uneven surfaces at Pompeii virtually rule out wheelchairs and the steep slopes of many Amalfi Coast towns pose a considerable obstacle.

The excellent website www.turismo accessibile.it gives a rundown on the disabled facilities at Naples' museums and hotels and on its transport services.

For those travelling by train, the **customer services office** (☎ 081 567 29 91; ☼ 7am-9pm) at Naples' Stazione Centrale (Map pp42–3) can arrange for wheelchair-bound passengers to be helped to their trains. To use this service you'll need to phone 24 hours prior to your departure and present yourself at the office 45 minutes before your train leaves. Similarly, personnel from **Metrò del Mare** (Map pp42-3; ☎ 199 60 07 00; www.metro delmare.com) will escort wheelchair-bound passengers on and off ferries.

Some city buses, including R2 and R3, are set up with access ramps and space for a wheelchair.

The following organisations might be of assistance:

Accessible Italy (☎ 378 94 11 11; www.acessible italy.com) A San Marino–based company that specialises in holiday services for the disabled.

Consorzio Cooperative Integrate (COIN; ☎ 06 712 90 11; www.coinsociale.it) Based in Rome, COIN is the best reference point for disabled travellers in Italy, with contact points throughout the country.

VISAS & PERMITS

EU citizens do not need a visa to enter Italy and, with a *permesso di soggiorno* (permit to stay), can stay as long as they like. Nationals of some other countries, including Australia, Canada, Israel, Japan, New Zealand, Switzerland and the USA, do not need visas for stays of up to 90 days in Italy, or in any Schengen country.

Italy is one of the 15 signatories of the Schengen Convention, an agreement whereby participating countries abolished customs checks at common borders. The standard tourist visa for a Schengen country is valid for 90 days. The Schengen countries are Austria, Belgium, Denmark, Finland, France, Germany, Greece, Iceland, Italy, Luxembourg, the Netherlands, Norway, Portugal, Spain and Sweden. As a rule, a Schengen visa issued by one country is valid for travel in other Schengen countries, although it's always worth checking as individual countries may impose additional restrictions on certain nationalities. You must apply for a Schengen visa in your country of residence and you can not apply for more than two in any 12-month period. They are not renewable inside Italy.

Technically all foreign visitors to Italy are supposed to register with the local police within eight days of arrival; however, if you're staying in a hotel or hostel, you don't need to bother as the hotel will do this for you – this is why they always take your passport details.

Up-to-date visa information is available on www.lonelyplanet.com – follow links through to the Italy destination guide.

WOMEN TRAVELLERS

The most common source of discomfort for women travellers is harassment. Local men are rarely shy about staring at women and this can be disconcerting, especially if the staring is accompanied by the occasional *'ciao bella'*. The best response is to ignore unwanted approaches. If that doesn't work, politely tell them that you are waiting for your *marito* (husband) or *fidanzato* (boyfriend) and, if necessary, walk away. Avoid becoming aggressive as this may result in an unpleasant confrontation. If all else fails, approach the nearest member of the police.

Wandering hands can also be a problem, particularly on crowded public transport. If you feel someone touching you, make a fuss; molesters are no more admired in southern Italy than anywhere else, so a loud and pointed *'Che schifo!'* ('How disgusting!') should work.

In Naples, women travelling alone should be highly vigilant in the Quartieri Spagnoli, La Sanità and Mercato districts, and the Piazza Garibaldi area at night. Women should also avoid hitchhiking alone.

TRANSPORT

ARRIVAL & DEPARTURE

AIR

AIRPORTS

Capodichino airport (NAP; ☎ 081 789 62 59; www.gesac.it), 7km northeast of the city centre, is southern Italy's main airport, linking Naples with most Italian and several major European cities, as well as New York.

To get there by public transport you can either take the regular **ANM** (☎ 800 63 95 25) bus 3S (€1.10, 45 minutes, every 15 minutes) from Piazza Garibaldi, or the **Alibus** (Map pp42-3); ☎ 081 53 11 705) airport shuttle (€3, 45 minutes, every 30 minutes) from Piazza del Municipio or Piazza Garibaldi.

Official taxi fares to the airport are as follows: €21 from a seafront hotel or from Mergellina hydrofoil terminal; €18 from Piazza del Municipio; and €14.50 from Stazione Centrale.

Curreri (☎ 081 801 54 20; www.curreriviaggi. it) runs six services a day between the airport and Sorrento. The cost of the 1¼-hour journey is €9 and tickets are available on board.

BUS

Travelling by bus from London to Naples takes 35 hours with two stops in Paris and Milan and costs €100. For more information check the **Eurolines** (www.eurolines.com) website.

CAR & MOTORCYCLE

If you are planning to drive to Naples, bear in mind the cost of toll roads and the fact that fuel prices in Italy are among the highest in Europe. If you are

THINGS CHANGE...

The information in this chapter is particularly vulnerable to change. Check directly with the airline or a travel agent to make sure you understand how a fare (and ticket you may buy) works and be aware of the security requirements for international travel. Shop carefully. The details given in this chapter should be regarded as pointers and are not a substitute for your own careful, up-to-date research.

CLIMATE CHANGE & TRAVEL

Climate change is a serious threat to the ecosystems that humans rely upon, and air travel is the fastest-growing contributor to the problem. Lonely Planet regards travel, overall, as a global benefit, but believes we all have a responsibility to limit our personal impact on global warming.

FLYING & CLIMATE CHANGE

Pretty much every form of motor travel generates CO_2 (the main cause of human-induced climate change) but planes are far and away the worst offenders, not just because of the sheer distances they allow us to travel, but because they release greenhouse gases high into the atmosphere. The statistics are frightening: two people taking a return flight between Europe and the US will contribute as much to climate change as an average household's gas and electricity consumption over a whole year.

CARBON OFFSET SCHEMES

Climatecare.org and other websites use 'carbon calculators' that allow jetsetters to offset the greenhouse gases they are responsible for with contributions to energy-saving projects and other climate-friendly initiatives in the developing world – including projects in India, Honduras, Kazakhstan and Uganda.

Lonely Planet, together with Rough Guides and other concerned partners in the travel industry, supports the carbon offset scheme run by climatecare.org. Lonely Planet offsets all of its staff and author travel.

For more information check out our website: lonelyplanet.com.

driving from London to Naples, the distance is around 1750km (not counting channel crossings), which will probably take you at least a couple of days. Most importantly, however, if you are spending time in Naples, it is unlikely you will feel tempted to drive and you will also have to pay for secure parking. Although a definite bonus for visiting more remote areas of Campania, like west of Sorrento and the Parco Nazionale del Cilento, given the cost of driving here, renting a car is perhaps a wiser option.

TRAIN

The national rail company, **Trenitalia** (☎ 89 20 21; www.trenitalia.com) has a comprehensive network throughout the country, and also operates long-distance trains throughout Europe. For example, you can catch a train from Naples to London, Paris and Madrid. Check schedules and prices via the excellent English-language website.

Naples is the rail hub for the south of Italy. For information, call ☎ 89 20 21. The city is served by *regionale* (regional), *diretto* (direct), Intercity and the superfast Eurostar trains. They arrive and depart from **Stazione Centrale** (Map pp42-3; ☎ 081 554 31 88) or **Stazione Garibaldi** (Map pp42-3; on the lower level). There are up to 30 trains daily to and from Rome.

GETTING AROUND

BICYCLE

Cycling is a dangerous option in Naples – a city where all road rules are seemingly ignored. Not only is there a real fear of knocking over an elderly nun or mother pushing a pram (nobody takes any heed of pedestrian crossings here), but most drivers speed, chat on their mobile phones and ignore traffic lights. Also, bicycle and motorcycle theft is rife.

HIRE

Bicycle hire is costly in Naples (from €20 per day), so if you are staying for some time and are deadset on taking to the saddle, it may be cheaper to actually buy one. Taking your bicycle to the Amalfi Coast is also a fraught option: think blind corners and sheer, precipitous drops.

BOAT

Naples, the bay islands and Amalfi Coast are served by a comprehensive ferry network. With its main base in Naples, the **Metro del Mare** (www.metrodelmare.com) was established in 2002 as a ferry extension of the urban public transport. The routes connect the northern ports of Bacoli and Pozzuoli to Naples, and from there goes to Sorrento, Positano and Amalfi. From Easter to October Amalfi, Positano, Salerno, Capri, Naples and Sorrento are connected by ferry or hydrofoil with three boats a day between Naples and Positano. Overall it is the cheapest way to get around by sea.

In addition to this public transport service, there are numerous commercial ferries and hydrofoils that run year-round. Note, however, that ferry services are pared back considerably in the winter, especially along the Amalfi Coast. Adverse sea conditions may also affect sailing schedules.

Most of the shorter trips leave from Naples' Molo Beverello harbour (in front of Castel Nuovo), while longer-distance ferries for Palermo, Cagliari, Milazzo, the Aeolian Islands (Isole Eolie) and Tunisia

ONLINE TICKETS

Cheap Flights (www.cheapflights.com)
Ebookers.com (www.ebookers.com)
Expedia (www.expedia.com)
Kayak (www.kayak.com)
Last minute (www.lastminute.com)
Orbitz (www.orbitz.com)
Priceline (www.priceline.com)
Travelocity (www.travelocity.com)

leave from the **Stazione Marittima** (Map pp42–3). Tickets for shorter journeys can be bought at the ticket booths on Molo Beverello and at Mergellina. For longer journeys try the offices of the ferry companies or at a travel agent. The monthly publication *Qui Napoli* lists timetables for Bay of Naples services.

Following is a list of ferry and hydrofoil routes and the destinations they service. The fares, unless otherwise stated, are for a one-way high-season, deck-class single.

Alilauro (Map pp42-3; ☎ 081 497 22 67; www.alilauro.it; Stazione Marittima, Naples) Operates hydrofoils from Naples to Sorrento (€9, seven daily), Ischia (€16, 10 daily) and Forio (€15.50, five daily); also ferries between Capri and Ischia (€15.50, one daily) and Amalfi (€13.50, two daily).

Caremar (Map pp62-3; ☎ 081 551 38 82; www.caremar.it; Molo Beverello, Naples) Runs services from Naples to Capri (ferry/hydrofoil €9.60/11, five daily), Ischia (€9.10/16, 13 daily) and Procida (€7/8.60, 12 daily); also between Sorrento and Capri (€7.50, four daily).

Linee Marittime Partenopee (LMP; Map pp42-3; ☎ 081 704 19 11; www.consorziolmp.it; Via Guglielmo Melisurgo 4, Naples) Runs hydrofoils from Sorrento to Capri (€13.50, 23 daily) and frequent daily hydrofoils/ferries from Capri to Positano (€16.50/14.50), Amalfi (€17/15) and Salerno (€16/17.50).

Medmar (Map pp42-3; ☎ 081 551 33 52; www.medmargroup; Stazione Marittima, Naples) Operates services from Naples to Ischia (€9.60, seven daily) and a daily service to Procida (€4.50).

TRANSPORT

Metrò del Mare (Map pp62-3; ☎ 199 44 66 44; www.metrodelmare.com) Runs summer-only services between Naples and Sorrento (€6.50, three daily), Positano (€14, four daily), Amalfi (€15, six daily) and Salerno (€16, two daily) as well as between the main Amalfi Coast towns.

Navigazione Libera del Golfo (NLG; Map pp62-3; ☎ 081 552 07 63; www.navlib.it, in Italian; Molo Beverello, Naples) From Naples NLG runs hydrofoils to and from Capri (€17, four daily) year-round.

Siremar (Map pp42-3; ☎ 081 017 19 98; www.sire mar.it; Stazione Marittima, Naples) Operates boats to the Aeolian Islands and Milazzo (seat €62, six times weekly in summer, dropping by 50% in the low season).

SNAV (Map pp42-3; ☎ 091 428 55 55; www.snav. it; Stazione Marittima, Naples) Runs hydrofoils to Capri (€16, seven daily), Procida (€13.60, four daily) and Ischia (€16, four daily); also ferries to Palermo (€30, one daily). In summer there are daily services to the Aeolian Islands (€60 to Lipari).

Tirrenia (Map pp42-3; ☎ 081 720 11 11; www. tirrenia.it; Stazione Marittima, Molo Angioino, Naples) From Naples runs a weekly boat to and from Cagliari (deck class €35) and Palermo (deck class €44). The service increases to twice weekly in summer. From Palermo and Cagliari there are connections to Tunisia, directly or via Trapani (Sicily).

TraVelMar (☎ /fax 089 87 29 50; Largo Scario 5, Amalfi) Operates from Salerno to Amalfi (ferry/hydrofoil €6.50/7, seven daily) and Positano (ferry/hydrofoil €8.50/9, seven daily); from Amalfi to Positano (ferry/hydrofoil €8/9.50, seven daily) and Sorrento (€10, four daily); and from Positano to Sorrento (€8.50, three daily).

BUS

In Naples, buses are operated by the city transport company **ANM** (☎ 800 63 95 25; www.anm.it, in Italian). There's no central bus station but most busses pass through Piazza Garibaldi, the city's chaotic transport hub. To locate your bus stop you'll probably need to ask at the ANM information kiosk (Map pp42–3) in the centre of the square.

One effortless way of getting orientated with the city is hopping on the **Citysightseeing Napoli** (☎ 081 551 72 79; www.napoli.city-sightseeing.it) bus, which costs €22 for a 24-hour ticket. There are three routes: the Art Tour, which covers the Archaeological Museum and Capodimonte, as well as the *centro storico* and Castel Nuovo. Route B follows the *lungomare* and the scenic Posillipo road, while Route C heads for Vomero and includes a visit to Villa Floridiana. A multilingual commentary is included.

Useful urban bus services:

3S From Piazza Garibaldi to the airport.

24 From Piazza del Municipio up to Piazza Dante and on to Capodimonte.

140 Santa Lucia to Posillipo via Mergellina.

152 From Piazza Garibaldi, along Corso Garibaldi, Via Nuova Marina and Via Colombo, to Molo Beverello, Via Santa Lucia, Piazza Vittoria and Via Partenope.

201 From Stazione Centrale to the Museo Archeologico Nazionale, down to Piazza del Municipio and then back to Piazza Garibaldi, via Piazza Dante.

404D A night bus operating from 11.20pm to 4am (hourly departures) from Stazione Centrale to Piazza del Municipio, on to Mergellina and Vomero, and then back down to Stazione Centrale.

C9 From Piazza Vittoria, along Riviera di Chiaia to Piazza Sannazzaro, Viale Augusto and Via Diocleziano, to Bagnoli and Via Coroglio.

C25 Piazza Amedeo to Piazza Bovio via Castel dell'Ovo and Piazza del Municipio.

C28 From Piazza Vittoria up Via dei Mille and on to Piazza Vanvitelli in Vomero.

E1 From Piazza del Gesù, along Via Constantinopoli, to Museo Archeologico Nazionale, Via Tribunali, Via Duomo, Piazza Nicola Amore, Corso Umberto I and Via Mezzocannone.

R1 From Piazza Medaglie D'Oro to Piazza Carità, Piazza Dante and Piazza Bovio.

R2 From Stazione Centrale, along Corso Umberto I, to Piazza Bovio, Piazza del Municipio and Piazza Trento e Trieste.

R3 From Mergellina along the Riviera di Chiaia to Piazza del Municipio, Piazza Bovio, Piazza Dante and Piazza Carità.

R4 From Capodimonte down past Via Dante to Piazza Municipio and back again.

TICKETS PLEASE

Tickets for public transport in Naples and the surrounding Campania region are managed by the **Unico Campania consortium** (www.unicocampania.it). There are various plans, depending on where you are planning to travel. The Unico Costiera ticket covers SITA bus trips and Circumvesuviana trains and is available for durations of 45 minutes (€2), 90 minutes (€3), 24 hours (€6) or 72 hours (€15). Aside from the SITA buses, the 24- and 72-hour tickets also allow you to hop on the City Sightseeing tourist bus which travels between Amalfi and Ravello and Amalfi and Maiori. The Unico Napoli 90-minute ticket costs €1.10 and the 24-hour ticket costs €3.10 (reduced to €2.60 at weekends). Other deals include the Unico 3T, a 72-hour ticket for €20, which covers rail travel throughout Campania, including the Alibus and transport on the islands of Ischia and Procida; Unico Ischia costing €1.20 for 90 minutes and €1.20 for 24 hours of bus travel on Ischia and a similar deal offered with Unico Capri, which covers bus travel on Capri. All Unico Campania tickets are sold at stations, ANM booths and tobacconists.

A comfortable way to travel along the Amalfi Coast and Sorrento Peninsula is by bus. Regional bus services are operated by a number of companies, the most useful of which is **SITA** (☎ 199 73 07 49; www.sitabus.it, in Italian), which runs buses from Naples to Pompeii (40 minutes, half-hourly), Sorrento (one hour 20 minutes, twice daily), Positano (two hours, twice daily), Amalfi (two hours, six daily) and Salerno (every 25 minutes, one hour 10 minutes). It also connects Salerno with Amalfi (one hour 10 minutes, half-hourly) and links towns along the Amalfi Coast. See the boxed text, above, about the convenient Unico Campania payment scheme. Casting wider, it runs from Salerno to Bari via Naples (€22.50, 4½ hours, twice daily) and operates a service to Germany, including Frankfurt (€105), Düsseldorf (€118) and Hamburg (€124). You can buy SITA tickets and catch buses either from Stazione Marittima or from Via G Ferrari, near Stazione Centrale; you can also buy tickets at **Bar Clizia** (Corso Arnaldo Lucci 173).

Most national buses depart from Piazza Garibaldi. Check destinations carefully or ask at the information kiosk in the centre of the piazza. **Marino** (☎ 080 311 23 35) has buses to Bari (€22, three hours), **Miccolis** (☎ 081 20 03 80) runs to Taranto (€17.50, four hours), Brindisi (€25.20, five hours) and Lecce (€28.50, 5½ hours), while **CLP** (☎ 081 531 17 07) serves Foggia (€11, two hours), Perugia (€29.45, 3½ hours) and Assisi (€32, 4½ hours).

Don't forget that you must clip your ticket in the yellow/orange machine that you will see in front of you as you climb the steps. Occasionally an agent will board the bus and ask to check the ticket and if the ticket is not clipped, you will have to pay a fine.

CAR & MOTORCYCLE

There can be no greater test of courage than driving in Naples. As a means of locomotion, however, it's of limited value. The weight of the anarchic traffic means that cars rarely travel faster than walking pace and parking is an absolute nightmare. A scooter is quicker and easier to park but is even more nerve-wracking to ride. Car/bike theft is also a major problem.

TRANSPORT

If you're determined to drive there are some simple guidelines to consider: get used to tailgaters; worry about what's in front of you not behind; watch out for scooters; give way to pedestrians no matter where they appear from; approach all junctions and traffic lights with extreme caution; and keep cool.

Officially much of the city centre is closed to nonresident traffic for much of the day. Daily restrictions are in place in the *centro storico*, in the area around Piazza del Municipio and Via Toledo, and in the Chiaia district around Piazza dei Martiri. Hours vary but are typically from 8am to 6.30pm, possibly later. On many Sunday mornings all vehicles are banned. For more-detailed information, check the website www.comunie.napoli. it (in Italian)

Away from the city, a car becomes more practical. However, be aware that driving along the Amalfi Coast can be quite a hair-raising experience as buses career around impossibly tight hairpin bends and locals brazenly overtake any-thing in their path. On the bay islands – Capri, Ischia and Procida – hiring a scooter is an excellent way of getting around.

Naples is on the north–south Autostrada del Sole, the A1 (north to Rome and Milan) and the A3 (south to Salerno and Reggio di Calabria). The A30 skirts Naples to the northeast, while the A16 heads across to Bari.

When approaching the city, the motorways meet the Tangenziale di Napoli, a major ring road around the city. The ring road hugs the city's northern fringe, meeting the A1 for Rome and the A2 to Capodichino airport in the east, and continuing towards Campi Flegrei and Pozzuoli in the west.

AUTOMOBILE ASSOCIATIONS

Italy's automobile association, the **Automobile Club d'Italia** (ACI; ☎ 081 725 38 11; www.aci.it; Piazzale Tecchio 49/D), is the best source of motoring information. It also operates a 24-hour **recovery service** (☎ 80 31 16).

DISTANCE CHART (KM)

Note: Distances between destinations are approximate

	Caserta	Naples	Ercolano	Pompeii	Sorrento	Capri	Positano	Ravello	Amalfi	Salerno	Paestum	Agropoli	Ascea	Palinuro
Naples	30													
Ercolano	10	08												
Pompeii	47	24	16											
Sorrento	66	43	35	22										
Capri	64	34	53	40	18									
Positano	73	49	41	28	13	31								
Ravello	69	68	78	45	32	50	16							
Amalfi	90	64	55	40	25	43	10	03						
Salerno	68	50	39	24	50	68	38	21	18					
Paestum	106	88	79	63	90	108	74	63	58	27				
Agropoli	119	97	90	71	102	120	82	75	70	45	17			
Ascea	157	136	125	111	143	161	120	110	105	79	47	32		
Palinuro	182	163	154	140	170	188	151	138	136	112	69	62	15	
Sapri	212	197	186	173	200	218	182	169	168	120	90	77	51	29

TRANSPORT

BRINGING YOUR OWN VEHICLE

If you are determined to bring your own car to Naples, ensure that all the paperwork is in order and that you carry a hazard triangle and a reflective jacket in your car – and don't forget that Italians drive on the right-hand side! Arriving in Naples you should be prepared for heavy traffic jams, particularly at commuter times and at lunchtime. Familiarise yourself with important road signs like *uscita* (exit) and *raccordo* (ring road surrounding a city).

DRIVING LICENCE & DOCUMENTATION

An EU driving licence is valid for driving in Italy. However, if you've got an old-style green UK licence or a licence issued by a non-EU country you'll need an International Driving Permit (IDP). Valid for 12 months, these are inexpensive (about US$21 or UK£5.50) and are easily available from your national automobile association – take along a passport photo and your driving licence. When driving you should always carry the IDP with your home licence, as it's not valid on its own.

FUEL & SPARE PARTS

Petrol stations are located along the main highways where they are open 24 hours. In smaller towns, the opening hours are generally 7am to 7pm Monday to Saturday with a lunchtime break. At the time of writing the cost of *benzina senza piombo* (unleaded petrol) and *gasoil* (diesel) was €1.275 and €1.125 per litre.

An increasing number of petrol stations are self-service, which can be a harrowing experience to the uninitiated. It's actually simpler than it seems: you need to key in the number of the pump, the amount you require and then insert the necessary bill (only acceptable in denominations of €5, €10, €20 and €50).

If you run into mechanical problems, the nearest petrol station should be able to advise a reliable mechanic, although few have workshops on site and they are, overall, very poor at stocking car parts (although very good at stocking *panini*). If you are driving a hire car and run into any serious problems, your hire-car company will probably have an emergency tow service with a toll-free call. You will need to report which road you are on, which direction you are heading, the make of car and your license plate number *(targa)*.

HIRE

The major car-hire firms are all represented in Naples.

Avis (Map pp42-3; ☎ 081 28 40 41; www.avis autonoleggio.it; Corso Novara 5 & Capodichino airport)
Europcar (☎ 081 780 56 43; www.europcar.it; Capodichino airport)
Hertz (Map pp42-3; ☎ 081 20 62 28; www.hertz. it; Via Giuseppe Ricciardi 5, Capodichino airport & in Mergellina)
Maggiore (Map pp42-3; ☎ 081 28 78 58; www. maggiore.it; Stazione Centrale & Capodichino airport)
Rent Sprint (Map pp62-3; ☎ 081 764 13 33; Via Santa Lucia 36) Scooter hire only.

Elsewhere you'll find any number of hire agencies in Sorrento and the Amalfi Coast (see the relevant chapters for details).

An economy car will cost about €60 per day; for a scooter expect to pay about €35. If possible, try to arrange your rental in advance, as you'll get much better rates. Similarly, airport agencies tend to charge more than city-centre branches.

To hire a car you'll need to be over 21 (25 for some larger cars) and have a credit card. When hiring always make sure you understand what's covered in the rental agreement (unlimited mileage, petrol, insurance etc). Extra insurance for theft and collision damage is very expensive, at least €30 a day. Without this you will have to pay an excess of around €1700 for theft and €1000 for damage. Disconcertingly, some of the car-hire agencies elsewhere in Italy (more specifically at Rome airport) will not provide insurance coverage for theft or collision if you are planning to travel to Naples!

If you are involved in an accident, remember that an official police report must be included in the claim and that, in general, they should be submitted within 10 days of the incident.

PARKING

Parking in Naples is no fun. Blue lines by the side of the road denote pay-and-display parking – buy tickets at the meters or from tobacconists – with rates ranging from €1.50 to €2 per hour. Elsewhere street parking is often overseen by illegal attendants who will expect a €1 to €2 fee for their protection of your car. It's usually easier to bite the bullet and pay them than attempt a moral stance. To the west of the city centre there's a 24-hour car park at Via Brin (€1.30 for the first four hours, and €7.20 for 24 hours). It is also the safer option as thieves often target hired or foreign registered cars. Fines for parking violations are steep and you are not safe in a hire car as the car hire company will use your credit card to settle any fines incurred.

Elsewhere in the region, parking can be similarly problematic, especially at the main resorts on the Amalfi Coast and, even more especially, in August. See the Transport section in the specific chapters for more detailed information.

ROAD RULES

Contrary to appearances there are road rules in Italy. The main ones are as follows:

★ Drive on the right and overtake on the left.

★ Wear seat belts in the front and, if fitted, in the back.

★ Wear a helmet on all two-wheeled transport.

★ Carry a warning triangle and a fluorescent safety vest to be worn in the event of an emergency.

★ The blood alcohol limit is 0.05%.

★ Using hand-held mobile phones while driving is illegal.

★ Headlights are required to be on while driving on all roads outside municipalities.

★ Watch for the *zona di silenzio* (no hooting) sign in built up areas.

★ And now for the good news…

★ The police have the power to levy on-the-spot fines.

TOLL ROADS

Toll roads are increasing all over Italy but, overall, are reasonable, especially when compared to France or parts of Spain (ie the toll from Rome to Naples costs €11). The procedure is fairly standard. Pick up a card from the automatic machine and pay a cashier at the exit. Telepass, an electronic toll collection system, can only be used for drivers holding an Italian credit card or bank account. For more information, check the website www.telepass.it.

TRANSPORT

SPEED LIMITS

Speed limits are 130km/h on autostrade, 110km/h on nonurban dual highways and 50km/h in built-up areas.

FUNICULAR

Three of Naples' four funicular railways connect the centre with Vomero:
Funicular Centrale (⏱ 6.30am-10pm Mon & Tue, 6.30am-12.30am Wed-Sun) Ascends from Via Toledo to Piazza Fuga.
Funicular di Chiaia (⏱ 6.30am-10pm Wed & Thu, 6.30am-12.30am Fri-Tue) Travels from Via del Parco Margherita to Via Domenico Cimarosa.
Funicular di Montesanto (⏱ 7am-10pm) From Piazza Montesanto to Via Raffaele Morghen.
The fourth, **Funicular di Mergellina** (⏱ 7am-10pm), connects the waterfront at Via Mergellina with Via Manzoni. Unico Napoli tickets are valid onboard.

METRO

Naples' **Metropolitana** (☎ 800 56 88 66; www.metro.na.it) is, in fact, mostly above ground.
Line 1 (⏱ 6am-10.20pm) Runs north from Piazza Dante stopping at Museo (for Piazza Cavour and Line 2), Materdei, Salvator Rosa, Cilea, Piazza Vanvitelli, Piazza Medaglie D'Oro and seven stops beyond.
Line 2 (⏱ 5.30am-11pm) Runs from Gianturco, just east of Stazione Centrale, with stops at Piazza Garibaldi

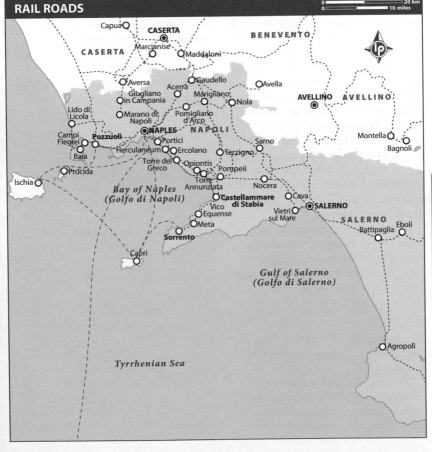

RAIL ROADS

TRANSPORT

(for Stazione Centrale), Piazza Cavour, Montesanto, Piazza Amedeo, Mergellina, Piazza Leopardi, Campi Flegrei, Cavaleggeri d'Aosta, Bagnoli and Pozzuoli.

Metro journeys are covered by Unico Napoli tickets (see the boxed text, p307).

TAXI

Official taxis are white, metered and bear the Naples symbol, the Pulcinella (with his distinctive white cone-shaped hat and long hooked nose) on their front doors. They generally ignore kerbside arm-wavers. There are taxi stands at most of the city's main piazzas or you can call one of the five taxi cooperatives: **Napoli** (☎ 081 556 44 44), **Consortaxi** (☎ 081 20 20 20), **Cotana** (☎ 081 570 70 70), **Free** (☎ 081 551 51 51) and **Partenope** (☎ 081 556 02 02).

The minimum fare for a ride is €4.75, of which €3.10 is the starting fare. There's also a baffling range of additional charges: €0.95 for a radio taxi call, €2.10 extra on Sundays and holidays, €2.40 more between 10pm and 7am, €2.95 for an airport run and €0.60 per piece of luggage in the boot (trunk). Guide dogs for the blind and wheelchairs are carried free of charge. See p303 for details of set fares to and from the airport.

Taxi drivers may tell you that the meter's kaput. However, you can (and should) insist that they switch it on.

For official set rates on popular routes to/from the airport, see p97.

TRAIN

International trains departing from Naples include services to London, Paris and Madrid.

The Ferrovia Cumana and the **Circumflegrea** (☎ 800 00 16 16; www.sepsa.it), based at Stazione Cumana di Montesanto (Map p55) on Piazza Montesanto,

500m southwest of Piazza Dante, operate services to Pozzuoli (€1.10, every 25 minutes) and Cuma (€1.10, six per day).

The **Circumvesuviana** (Map pp42-3; ☎ 081 772 24 44; www.vesuviana.it; Corso Giuseppe Garibaldi), southwest of Stazione Centrale (follow the signs from the main concourse in Stazione Centrale), operates trains to Sorrento (€3.30, 70 minutes) via Ercolano (€1.80, 20 minutes), Pompeii (€2.40, 40 minutes) and other towns along the coast. There are about 40 trains daily running between 5am and 10.30pm, with reduced services on Sunday.

TRAMS

The following trams may be useful:
Tram 1 Operates from east of Stazione Centrale, through Piazza Garibaldi, the city centre and along the waterfront to Piazza Vittoria.
Tram 29 Travels from Piazza Garibaldi to the city centre along Corso Giuseppe Garibaldi.

TRANSPORT

LANGUAGE

Italian is a Romance language related to French, Spanish, Portuguese and Romanian. The Romance languages belong to the Indo-European group of languages, which includes English, so you might spot some similarities between English and Italian. In addition, as English has borrowed many words from Romance languages, you will recognise many Italian words.

Modern literary Italian began to develop in the 13th and 14th centuries, predominantly through the works of Dante, Petrarch and Boccaccio, who wrote chiefly in the Florentine dialect. The language drew on its Latin heritage and many dialects to develop into the standard Italian of today. Although many dialects are spoken in everyday conversation, standard Italian is the national language of schools, media and literature, and is understood throughout the country.

GRAMMAR

Italian has polite versus informal forms for 'you'. Many older Italians still expect to be addressed by the third person polite for 'you', that is, *Lei* instead of *tu*.

Also, it is not considered polite to use the greeting *ciao* when addressing strangers, unless they use it first; it's better to say *buongiorno* (or *buona sera*, as the case may be) and *arrivederci* (or the more polite form, *arrivederla*). We have used the polite address for most of the phrases in this guide. Use of the informal address is indicated by 'inf'.

Italian has masculine and feminine forms of nouns and accompanying adjectives (masculine and feminine words often end in 'o' and 'a' respectively). Where both forms are given in this guide, they are indicated by 'm' and 'f'.

If you'd like a more comprehensive guide to the language, pick up a copy of Lonely Planet's *Italian Phrasebook*.

PRONUNCIATION

Italian pronunciation isn't very difficult to master once you learn a few easy rules. Although some vowels and the stress on double letters require careful practice by English speakers, it's easy enough to make yourself understood.

VOWELS

Vowel are pronounced shorter in un-stressed syllables; longer, in stressed, open syllables:

a	as in 'art', eg *caro* (d*car*); sometimes short, eg *amico* (friend)
e	short, as in 'let', eg *mettere* (to put); long, as in 'there', eg *mela* (apple)
i	short, as in 'it', eg *inizio* (start); long, as in 'marine', eg *vino* (wine)
o	short, as in 'dot', eg *donna* (woman); long, as in 'port', eg *ora* (hour)
u	as the 'oo' in 'book', eg *puro* (pure)

CONSONANTS

The pronunciation of most Italian consonants is similar to that of their English counterparts. Pronunciation of some consonants depends on certain rules:

c	as the 'k' in 'kit' before a, o, u and h; as the 'ch' in 'choose' before e and i
g	as the 'g' in 'get' before a, o, u and h; as the 'j' in 'jet' before e and i
gli	as the 'lli' in 'million'
gn	as the 'ny' in 'canyon'
h	always silent (ie not pronounced)
r	a rolled 'r' sound
sc	as 'sk' before a, o, u and h; as the 'sh' in 'sheep' before e and i
z	at the beginning of a word, as the 'dz' in 'adze'; elsewhere, as the 'ts' in 'its'

Note that when ci, gi and sci are followed by a, o or u, the 'i' is not pronounced unless the accent falls on the 'i'. Thus, the name 'Giovanni' is pronounced joh·*vahn*·nee.

A double consonant is pronounced as a longer, more forceful sound than a single consonant. This can directly affect the meaning of a word, eg *sono* (I am), *sonno* (sleep).

WORD STRESS

Stress is indicated in our pronunciation guide by italics. Word stress generally falls on the second-last syllable, as in *spaghetti* (spa·*ge*·tee), but when a word has an accent, the stress falls on that syllable, as in *città* (chee·*ta*), meaning 'city'.

ACCOMMODATION

I'm looking for a …	*Cerco …*	cher·ko …
guest house	*una pensione*	oo·na pen·*syo*·ne
hotel	*un albergo*	oon al·*ber*·go
youth hostel	*un ostello per la gioventù*	oon os·*te*·lo per la jo·ven·*too*

Where is a cheap hotel?

Dov'è un albergo	do·*ve* oon al·*ber*·go
a buon prezzo?	a bwon *pre*·tso

What's the address?

Qual'è l'indirizzo?	kwa·*le* leen·dee·*ree*·tso

Could you write the address, please?

Può scrivere l'indirizzo,	pwo skree·ve·re leen·dee·*ree*·tso
per favore?	per fa·*vo*·re

Do you have any rooms available?

Avete camere libere?	a·ve·te ka·me·re lee·be·re

May I see it?

Posso vederla?	*po*·so ve·*der*·la

I'd like (a) …	*Vorrei …*	vo·ray …
bed	*un letto*	oon *le*·to
single room	*una camera singola*	oo·na ka·me·ra seen·go·la
double room	*una camera matrimoniale*	oo·na ka·me·ra ma·tree·mo·*nya*·le
room with two beds	*una camera doppia*	oo·na ka·me·ra *do*·pya
room with a bathroom	*una camera con bagno*	oo·na ka·me·ra kon *ba*·nyo
to share a dorm	*un letto in dormitorio*	oon *le*·to een dor·mee·*to*·ryo

MAKING A RESERVATION

Use these expressions in letters, faxes and emails:

To ...	A ...
From ...	Da ...
Date	Data
I'd like to book ...	Vorrei prenotare ...
in the name of ...	a nome di ...
for the night(s) of ...	per (la notte/le notti) di ...
credit card (...)	(...) carta di credito
number	numero della
expiry date	data di scadenza della
Please confirm	Prego confermare
availability and price.	disponibilità e prezzo.

How much is it ...?	Quanto costa ...?	kwan·to ko·sta ...
per night	per la notte	per la no·te
per person	per persona	per per·so·na

Where is the bathroom?
Dov'è il bagno?   do·ve eel ba·nyo
I'm/We're leaving today.
Parto/Partiamo oggi.   par·to/par·tya·mo o·jee

CONVERSATION & ESSENTIALS

Hello.	Buongiorno./	bwon·jor·no/
	Ciao. (inf)	chow
Goodbye.	Arrivederci./	a·ree·ve·der·chee/
	Ciao. (inf)	chow
Yes.	Sì.	see
No.	No.	no
Please.	Per favore./	per fa·vo·re/
	Per piacere.	per pya·chay·re
Thank you.	Grazie.	gra·tsye
You're welcome.	Prego.	pre·go
Excuse me.	Mi scusi.	mee skoo·zee
I'm sorry.	Mi scusi./	mee skoo·zee/
	Mi perdoni.	mee per·do·nee
Just a minute.	Un momento.	oon mo·men·to

What's your name?		
	Come si chiama?	ko·me see kya·ma
	Come ti chiami? (inf)	ko·me tee kya·mee
My name is ...		
	Mi chiamo ...	mee kya·mo ...
Where are you from?		
	Da dove viene?	da do·ve vye·ne
	Di dove sei? (inf)	dee do·ve se·ee
I'm from ...		
	Vengo da ...	ven·go da ...
I (don't) like ...		
	(Non) Mi piace ...	(non) mee pya·che ...

DIRECTIONS

Where is ...?		
	Dov'è ...?	do·ve ...
Go straight ahead.		
	Si va sempre diritto.	see va sem·pre dee·ree·to
	Vai sempre diritto. (inf)	va·ee sem·pre dee·ree·to
Turn left.		
	Giri a sinistra.	jee·ree a see·nee·stra
Turn right.		
	Giri a destra.	jee·ree a de·stra
at the next corner		
	al prossimo angolo	al pro·see·mo an·go·lo
at the traffic lights		
	al semaforo	al se·ma·fo·ro

behind	dietro	dye·tro
in front of	davanti	da·van·tee
far (from)	lontano (da)	lon·ta·no (da)
near (to)	vicino (di)	vee·chee·no (dee)
opposite	di fronte a	dee fron·te a
beach	la spiaggia	la spya·ja
bridge	il ponte	eel pon·te
castle	il castello	eel kas·te·lo
cathedral	il duomo	eel dwo·mo
island	l'isola	lee·so·la
(main) square	la piazza	la pya·tsa
	(principale)	(preen·chee·pa·le)
market	il mercato	eel mer·ka·to
old city	il centro	eel chen·tro
	storico	sto·ree·ko
palace	il palazzo	eel pa·la·tso
ruins	le rovine	le ro·vee·ne
sea	il mare	eel ma·re
tower	la torre	la to·re

SIGNS

Aperto	Open
Camere Libere	Rooms Available
Chiuso	Closed
Completo	Full/No Vacancies
Gabinetti/Bagni	Toilets
Uomini	Men
Donne	Women
Informazione	Information
Ingresso/Entrata	Entrance
Proibito/Vietato	Prohibited
Polizia/Carabinieri	Police
Questura	Police Station
Uscita	Exit

EATING OUT

I'd like ..., please.
Vorrei ..., per favore.   vo·ray ... per fa·vo·re
That was delicious!
Era squisito!   e·ra skwee·zee·to
I don't eat (fish).
Non mangio (pesce).   non man·jo (pe·she)
Please bring the bill.
Mi porta il conto,   mee por·ta eel kon·to
per favore?   per fa·vo·re

I'm allergic to ...	Sono allergico/a ... (m/f)	so·no a·ler·jee·ko/a ...
dairy produce	ai latticini	ai la·tee·chee·nee
eggs	alle uova	a·le wo·va
nuts	alle noci	a·le no·chee
seafood	ai frutti di mare	ai froo·tee dee ma·re

HEALTH

I'm ill.	Mi sento male.	mee sen·to ma·le
It hurts here.	Mi fa male qui.	mee fa ma·le kwee
antiseptic	antisettico	an·tee·se·tee·ko
aspirin	aspirina	as·pee·ree·na
condoms	preservativi	pre·zer·va·tee·vee
contraceptive	contraccetivo	kon·tra·che·tee·vo
diarrhoea	diarrea	dee·a·re·a
medicine	medicina	me·dee·chee·na
sunblock cream	crema solare	kre·ma so·la·re
tampons	tamponi	tam·po·nee

I'm ...	Sono ...	so·no ...
asthmatic	asmatico/a (m/f)	az·ma·tee·ko/a
diabetic	diabetico/a (m/f)	dee·a·be·tee·ko/a
epileptic	epilettico/a (m/f)	e·pee·le·tee·ko/a

I'm allergic ...	Sono allergico/a (m/f)...	so·no a·ler·jee·ko/a ...
to antibiotics	agli antibiotici	a·lyee an·tee·bee·o·tee·chee
to aspirin	all'aspirina	a·la·spe·ree·na
to penicillin	alla penicillina	a·la pe·nee·see·lee·na

LANGUAGE DIFFICULTIES

Do you speak English?
Parla inglese?   par·la een·gle·ze
Does anyone here speak English?
C'è qualcuno che   che kwal·koo·no ke
parla inglese?   par·la een·gle·ze
How do you say ... in Italian?
Come si dice ... in   ko·me see dee·che ... een
italiano?   ee·ta·lya·no
What does ... mean?
Che vuol dire ...?   ke vwol dee·re ...
I understand.
Capisco.   ka·pee·sko
I don't understand.
Non capisco.   non ka·pee·sko
Please write it down.
Può scriverlo, per favore?   pwo skree·ver·lo per fa·vo·re
Can you show me (on the map)?
Può mostrarmelo   pwo mos·trar·me·lo
(sulla pianta)?   (soo·la pyan·ta)

NUMBERS

0	zero	dze·ro
1	uno	oo·no
2	due	doo·e
3	tre	tre
4	quattro	kwa·tro
5	cinque	cheen·kwe
6	sei	say
7	sette	se·te
8	otto	o·to
9	nove	no·ve

10	dieci	dye-chee
11	undici	oon-dee-chee
12	dodici	do-dee-chee
13	tredici	tre-dee-chee
14	quattordici	kwa-tor-dee-chee
15	quindici	kween-dee-chee
16	sedici	se-dee-chee
17	diciassette	dee-cha-se-te
18	diciotto	dee-cho-to
19	diciannove	dee-cha-no-ve
20	venti	ven-tee
21	ventuno	ven-too-no
22	ventidue	ven-tee-doo-e
30	trenta	tren-ta
40	quaranta	kwa-ran-ta
50	cinquanta	cheen-kwan-ta
60	sessanta	se-san-ta
70	settanta	se-tan-ta
80	ottanta	o-tan-ta
90	novanta	no-van-ta
100	cento	chen-to
1000	mille	mee-le
2000	due mila	doo-e mee-la

PAPERWORK

name	nome	no-me
nationality	nazionalità	na-tsyo-na-lee-ta
date/place of birth	data/luogo di nascita	da-ta/lwo-go dee na-shee-ta
sex (gender)	sesso	se-so
passport	passaporto	pa-sa-por-to
visa	visto	vee-sto

QUESTION WORDS

Who?	Chi?	kee
What?	Che?	ke
When?	Quando?	kwan-do
Where?	Dove?	do-ve
How?	Come?	ko-me

SHOPPING & SERVICES

I'd like to buy ...
   Vorrei comprare ...   vo-ray kom-pra-re ...
How much is it?
   Quanto costa?   kwan-to ko-sta

EMERGENCIES

Help!
   Aiuto!   a-yoo-to
There's been an accident!
   C'è stato un   che sta-to oon
   incidente!   een-chee-den-te
I'm lost.
   Mi sono perso/a. (m/f)   mee so-no per-so/a
Go away!
   Lasciami in pace!   la-sha-mi een pa-che
   Vai via! (inf)   va-ee vee-a

Call ...!	Chiami ...!	kee-ya-mee ...
a doctor	un dottore/	oon do-to-re/
	un medico	oon me-dee-ko
the police	la polizia	la po-lee-tsee-ya

I don't like it.
   Non mi piace.   non mee pya-che
May I look at it?
   Posso dare   po-so da-re
   un'occhiata?   oo-no-kya-ta
I'm just looking.
   Sto solo guardando.   sto so-lo gwar-dan-do
It's cheap.
   Non è caro/cara. (m/f)   non e ka-ro/a
It's too expensive.
   È troppo caro/a. (m/f)   e tro-po ka-ro/a

I want to	Voglio	vo-lyo
change ...	cambiare ...	kam-bya-re ...
money	del denaro	del de-na-ro
travellers	assegni di	a-se-nyee dee
cheques	viaggio	vee-a-jo

I'll take it.
   Lo/La compro. (m/f)   lo/la kom-pro
Do you accept credit cards?
   Accettate carte   a-che-ta-te kar-te
   di credito?   dee kre-dee-to

more	più	pyoo
less	meno	me-no
smaller	più piccolo/a (m/f)	pyoo pee-ko-lo/a
bigger	più grande	pyoo gran-de

LANGUAGE

ROAD SIGNS

Dare la Precedenza	Give Way
Deviazione	Detour
Divieto di Accesso	No Entry
Divieto di Sorpasso	No Overtaking
Divieto di Sosta	No Parking
Entrata	Entrance
Passo Carrabile/Carraio	Keep Clear
Pedaggio	Toll
Pericolo	Danger
Rallentare	Slow Down
Senso Unico	One Way
Uscita	Exit

I'm looking for …	Cerco …	cher·ko …
a bank	un banco	oon ban·ko
the church	la chiesa	la kye·za
the city centre	il centro	eel chen·tro
the … embassy	l'ambasciata di …	lam·ba·sha·ta dee …
the market	il mercato	eel mer·ka·to
the museum	il museo	eel moo·ze·o
the post office	la posta	la po·sta
a public toilet	un gabinetto	oon ga·bee·ne·to
the telephone centre	il centro telefonico	eel chen·tro te·le·fo·nee·ko
the tourist office	l'ufficio di turismo	loo·fee·cho dee too·reez·mo

TIME & DATES

What time is it?	Che ore sono?	ke o·re so·no
It's (eight o'clock).	Sono (le otto).	so·no (le o·to)
in the morning	di mattina	dee ma·tee·na
in the afternoon	di pomeriggio	dee po·me·ree·jo
in the evening	di sera	dee se·ra
When?	Quando?	kwan·do
today	oggi	o·jee
tomorrow	domani	do·ma·nee
yesterday	ieri	ye·ree
Monday	lunedì	loo·ne·dee
Tuesday	martedì	mar·te·dee
Wednesday	mercoledì	mer·ko·le·dee
Thursday	giovedì	jo·ve·dee
Friday	venerdì	ve·ner·dee

Saturday	sabato	sa·ba·to
Sunday	domenica	do·me·nee·ka
January	gennaio	je·na·yo
February	febbraio	fe·bra·yo
March	marzo	mar·tso
April	aprile	a·pree·le
May	maggio	ma·jo
June	giugno	joo·nyo
July	luglio	loo·lyo
August	agosto	a·gos·to
September	settembre	se·tem·bre
October	ottobre	o·to·bre
November	novembre	no·vem·bre
December	dicembre	dee·chem·bre

TRANSPORT

PUBLIC TRANSPORT

What time does … leave/ arrive?	A che ora parte/ arriva …?	a ke o·ra par·te/ a·ree·va …
the boat	la nave	la na·ve
the (city) bus	l'autobus	low·to·boos
the (intercity) bus	il pullman	eel pool·man
the plane	l'aereo	la·e·re·o
the train	il treno	eel tre·no
I'd like a … ticket.	Vorrei un biglietto …	vo·ray oon bee·lye·to …
one-way	di sola andata	dee so·la an·da·ta
return	di andata e ritorno	dee an·da·ta e ree·toor·no
1st class	di prima classe	dee pree·ma kla·se
2nd class	di seconda classe	dee se·kon·da kla·se

I want to go to …	
Voglio andare a …	vo·lyo an·da·re a …
The train has been cancelled/delayed.	
Il treno è soppresso/ in ritardo.	eel tre·no e so·pre·so/ een ree·tar·do

the first	il primo	eel pree·mo
the last	l'ultimo	lool·tee·mo
platform (2)	binario (due)	bee·na·ryo (doo·e)
ticket office	biglietteria	bee·lye·te·ree·a
timetable	orario	o·ra·ryo
train station	stazione	sta·tsyo·ne

LANGUAGE

PRIVATE TRANSPORT

I'd like to hire a/an ...	Vorrei noleggiare ...	vo·ray no·le·ja·re ...
car	una macchina	oo·na ma·kee·na
4WD	un fuoristrada	oon fwo·ree·stra·da
motorbike	una moto	oo·na mo·to
bicycle	una bici(cletta)	oo·na bee·chee·(kle·ta)

Is this the road to ...?

Questa strada porta a ...? — kwe·sta stra·da por·ta a ...

Where's a service station?

Dov'è una stazione di servizio? — do·ve oo·na sta·tsyo·ne dee ser·vee·tsyo

Please fill it up.

Il pieno, per favore. — eel pye·no per fa·vo·re

I'd like (30) litres.

Vorrei (trenta) litri. — vo·ray (tren·ta) lee·tree

diesel	gasolio/diesel	ga·zo·lyo/dee·zel
petrol/gasoline	benzina	ben·dzee·na

(How long) Can I park here?

(Per quanto tempo) Posso parcheggiare qui? — (per kwan·to tem·po) po·so par·ke·ja·re kwee

Where do I pay?

Dove si paga? — do·ve see pa·ga

I need a mechanic.

Ho bisogno di un meccanico. — o bee·zo·nyo dee oon me·ka·nee·ko

The car/motorbike has broken down (at ...).

La macchina/moto si è guastata (a ...). — la ma·kee·na/mo·to see e gwas·ta·ta (a ...)

The car/motorbike won't start.

La macchina/moto non parte. — la ma·kee·na/mo·to non par·te

I have a flat tyre.

Ho una gomma bucata. — o oo·na go·ma boo·ka·ta

I've run out of petrol.

Ho esaurito la benzina. — o e·zo·ree·to la ben·dzee·na

I've had an accident.

Ho avuto un incidente. — o a·voo·to oon een·chee·den·te

TRAVEL WITH CHILDREN

Is there a/an ...?	C'è ...?	che ...
I need a/an ...	Ho bisogno di ...	o bee·zo·nyo dee ...
baby change room	un bagno con fasciatoio	oon ba·nyo kon fa·sha·to·yo
car baby seat	un seggiolino per bambini	oon se·jo·lee·no per bam·bee·nee
child-minding service	un servizio di babysitter	oon ser·vee·tsyo dee be·bee·see·ter
children's menu	un menù per bambini	oon me·noo per bam·bee·nee
(disposable) nappies/diapers	pannolini (usa e getta)	pa·no·lee·nee (oo·sa e je·ta)
formula (milk)	latte in polvere	la·te in pol·ve·re
(English-speaking) babysitter	un/una babysitter (che parli inglese) (m/f)	oon/oo·na be·bee·see·ter (ke par·lee een·gle·ze)
highchair	un seggiolone	oon se·jo·lo·ne

Do you mind if I breastfeed here?

Le dispiace se allatto (il bimbo/la bimba) qui? (m/f) — le dees·pya·che se a·la·to (eel beem·bo/la beem·ba) kwee

Are children allowed?

I bambini sono ammessi? — ee bam·bee·nee so·no a·me·see

Also available from Lonely Planet:
Italian phrasebook

LANGUAGE

GLOSSARY

Albergo (alberghi) – hotel (hotels)
alimentari – grocery shop
allergia – allergy
archeologica – archaeology
autostrada (autostrade) – motorway, highway (motorways, highways)

bagno – bathroom, also toilet
bambola (bambole) – doll (dolls)
bancomat – Automated teller machine (ATM)
bassi – one-room, ground-floor apartments mostly found in the traditionally poorer areas of Naples
benzina – petrol
biblioteca (biblioteche) – library (libraries)
biglietto – ticket
biglietto giornaliero – daily ticket

caffettiera – Italian coffee perculator
calcio – football (soccer)
camera – room
cambio – currency-exchange bureau
campanile – bell tower
canzone (canzoni) – song (songs)
cappella – chapel

carabinieri – police with military and civil duties
carta d'identità – identity card
carta telefonica – phonecard
casa – house, home
casareccio – home style
castello – castle
catacomba – underground tomb complex
centro – city centre
centro storico – historic centre, old city
chiesa (chiese) – church (churches)
chiostro – cloister
cimitero – cemetery
colle/collina – hill
colonna – column
commissariato – local police station
comune – equivalent to a municipality or county; town or city council; historically, a commune (self-governing town or city)
concerto – concert
corno – horn; horn-shaped amulet
corso – main street
cripta – crypt
cupola – dome

Dio (Dei) – God (Gods)

faraglione (faraglioni) – rock tower; rock pinnacle (rock towers; rock pinnacles)
farmacia – pharmacy
ferrovia – train station
festa – feast day; holiday
fiume – river
fontana – fountain
forno – bakery
forte/fortezza – fort
forum (fora) – (Latin) public square (public squares)
francobollo (francobolli) – stamp (stamps)

gabinetto – toilet, WC
gasolio – diesel
gelateria – ice-cream parlour
giardino (giardini) – garden (gardens)
golfo – gulf
gratis – free (no cost)
guglia – obelisk

isola – island

lago – lake
largo – small square
lavanderia – laundrette
Liberty – Italian Art Nouveau
libreria – bookshop
lido – beach
lungomare – seafront, esplanade

maestro – teacher
mare – sea
medicina (medicine) – medicine (medicines)
mercato – market
monte – mountain
mura – city wall
museo – museum

nazionale – national
nuovo/a – new (m/f)

orto botanico – botanical gardens
ospedale – hospital
ostello – hostel

palazzo (palazzi) – mansion, palace, large building of any type (including an apartment block)
panetteria – bakery
panino (panini) – sandwich (sandwiches)
parcheggio – carpark
parco – park
passeggiata – a stroll
pasticceria – cake shop
pastificio – pasta-making factory
pensione – small hotel or guesthouse, often offering board
pescheria – fish shop
piazza (piazze) – square (squares)
piazzale – large open square
pinacoteca – art gallery
piscina – pool
polizia – police
ponte – bridge
porta – city gate
porto – port
presepe (presepi) – nativity scene (nativity scenes)
professore (professori) – professor (professors)

questura – police station

reale – royal
ruota – wheel

sala – room in a museum or a gallery
salumeria – delicatessen
santuario – sanctuary
scavi – archaeological ruins
scheda telefonica – phonecard

GLOSSARY

sedia a rotelle – wheelchair
seggiolone – child's highchair
sentiero – path; trail; track
servizio – service charge in restaurants
sole – sun
sottosuolo – underground
spiaggia – beach
statua – statue
stazione – station
strada – street; road

tabaccheria – tobacconist's shop
teatro – theatre
tempio – temple
terme – baths
torre – tower
treno – train

via – street, road
vecchio – old
vicolo – alley, alleyway

BEHIND THE SCENES

THIS BOOK

This is the 3rd edition of *Naples & the Amalfi Coast*. Duncan Garwood and Cristian Bonetto wrote the previous edition. The guidebook was commissioned in Lonely Planet's London office, and produced in Melbourne by the following:

Commissioning Editor Paula Hardy
Coordinating Editor Justin Flynn
Coordinating Cartographer Xavier Di Toro
Coordinating Layout Designer Yvonne Bischofberger
Managing Editors Imogen Bannister, Laura Stansfeld
Managing Cartographers Adrian Persoglia, Herman So
Managing Layout Designer Laura Jane

Assisting Editors Sarah Bailey, Jackey Coyle, Kristin Odijk
Assisting Cartographers Tadhgh Knaggs, Alex Leung
Cover Research Marika Mercer, lonely planetimages.com
Internal Image Research Aude Vauconsant, lonelyplanetimages.com
Language Content Robyn Loughnane
Project Manager Rachel Imeson
Thanks to Mark Adams, Lucy Birchley, Sally Darmody, Janine Eberle, Owen Eszeki, Mark Germanchis, Michelle Glynn, Penelope Goodes, Imogen Hall, Lauren Hunt, Paul Iacono, Nic Lehman, John Mazzocchi, Lucy Monie, Wayne Murphy, Darren O'Connell, Trent Paton, Julie Sheridan, Cara Smith, Glenn van der Knijff

THE LONELY PLANET STORY

Fresh from an epic journey across Europe, Asia and Australia in 1972, Tony and Maureen Wheeler sat at their kitchen table stapling together notes. The first Lonely Planet guidebook, *Across Asia on the Cheap,* was born.

Travellers snapped up the guides. Inspired by their success, the Wheelers began publishing books to Southeast Asia, India and beyond. Demand was prodigious, and the Wheelers expanded the business rapidly to keep up. Over the years, Lonely Planet extended its coverage to every country and into the virtual world via lonelyplanet.com and the Thorn Tree message board.

As Lonely Planet became a globally loved brand, Tony and Maureen received several offers for the company. But it wasn't until 2007 that they found a partner whom they trusted to remain true to the company's principles of travelling widely, treading lightly and giving sustainably. In October of that year, BBC Worldwide acquired a 75% share in the company, pledging to uphold Lonely Planet's commitment to independent travel, trustworthy advice and editorial independence.

Today, Lonely Planet has offices in Melbourne, London and Oakland, with over 500 staff members and 300 authors. Tony and Maureen are still actively involved with Lonely Planet. They're travelling more often than ever, and they're devoting their spare time to charitable projects. And the company is still driven by the philosophy of *Across Asia on the Cheap*: 'All you've got to do is decide to go and the hardest part is over. So go!'

THANKS

CRISTIAN BONETTO
For their incredible generosity, warmth and insight, *grazie infinite* to my very own San Lucano, his partner in crime Silvana, Valentina Vellusi and Francesco Calazzo. A huge thank you to Santiago Faraone Mennella, Fulvio Salvi, Luca Cuttitta, Sally O'Brien and Denis Balibouse, Penelope Green, Antonio Romano, Carmine Romano, Daniela Ibello, Mario Spada, Daniele Sanzone, Nello Nocera, and Renato and Gianni for their support and friendship, as well as to the many locals who let slip a secret or four.

SEND US YOUR FEEDBACK

We love to hear from travellers – your comments keep us on our toes and help make our books better. Our well-travelled team reads every word on what you loved or loathed about this book. Although we cannot reply individually to postal submissions, we always guarantee that your feedback goes straight to the appropriate authors, in time for the next edition. Each person who sends us information is thanked in the next edition – and the most useful submissions are rewarded with a free book.

To send us your updates – and find out about Lonely Planet events, newsletters and travel news – visit our award-winning website: **lonelyplanet.com/contact**.

Note: We may edit, reproduce and incorporate your comments in Lonely Planet products such as guidebooks, websites and digital products, so let us know if you don't want your comments reproduced or your name acknowledged. For a copy of our privacy policy visit lonelyplanet.com/privacy.

A giant thanks to Paula Hardy, Josephine Quintero, Herman So and the carto team, Justin Flynn and Sarah Bailey for their hard work and encouragement, to my family for putting up with me, and to Vale for the songs and memories.

JOSEPHINE QUINTERO
Firstly, many thanks to Robin Chapman for his sense of humour, map-reading skills and for sharing his expertise on hunting down the ultimate slice of pizza perfect, along with the best wines. Also a mega thank you to my Italy-based cousin, Sandi, for her hospitality and insider tips. Thanks also to the staff of the tourist offices, particularly those lovely ladies in Salerno, who went out of their way to dig out information on Paestum. Finally, mega thanks to Paula Hardy and Cristian Bonetto for their troop-rallying emails and terrific support during research.

OUR READERS

Many thanks to the travellers who used the last edition and wrote to us with helpful hints, useful advice and interesting anecdotes:
Carol Cherpeau, Peter De Bruijn, Mariken Smit, Elena Dominguez-Mejias, Alison Edmondson, Catherine Haylock, Edward Hendriks, Nich Hogben, Kim Jones, Wendy Lotter, Marcelo Marazzi, David Millar, Mike Moseley, David Norman, Debbie Purcell, Jennifer Stark, Laura Strect, Mie Thomsen, David Townsend, Marilyn Watts.

ACKNOWLEDGMENTS

All images are the copyright of the photographers unless otherwise indicated. Many of the images in this guide are available for licensing from Lonely Planet Images: lonelyplanetimages.com.

INDEX

INDEX

INDEX

INDEX

MAP LEGEND

Note Not all symbols displayed below appear in this guide.

ROUTES

- Tollway
- Freeway
- Primary Road
- Secondary Road
- Tertiary Road
- Lane
- Unsealed Road
- Under Construction
- Tunnel
- Pedestrian Mall
- Steps
- Walking Track
- Walking Path
- Walking Tour
- Walking Tour Detour
- Pedestrian Overpass

TRANSPORT

- Ferry Route & Terminal
- Metro Line & Station
- Monorail & Stop
- Bus Route & Stop
- Train Line & Station
- Underground Rail Line
- Tram Line & Stop
- Cable Car, Funicular

AREA FEATURES

- Airport
- Beach
- Building
- Campus
- Cemetery, Christian
- Cemetery, Other
- Land
- Mall, Plaza
- Market
- Park
- Sportsground
- Urban

HYDROGRAPHY

- River, Creek
- Canal
- Water
- Swamp
- Lake (Dry)

BOUNDARIES

- International
- State, Provincial
- Suburb
- City Wall
- Cliff

SYMBOLS IN THE KEY

Essential Information
- Tourist Office
- Police Station

Exploring
- Beach
- Buddhist
- Castle, Fort
- Christian
- Diving, Snorkelling
- Garden
- Hindu
- Islamic
- Jewish
- Monument
- Museum, Gallery
- Place of Interest
- Snow Skiing
- Swimming Pool
- Ruin
- Tomb
- Winery, Vineyard
- Zoo, Bird Sanctuary

Gastronomic Highlights
- Eating
- Cafe

Nightlife
- Drinking
- Entertainment

Recommended Shops
- Shopping

Accommodation
- Sleeping
- Camping

Transport
- Airport, Airfield
- Cycling, Bicycle Path
- Border Crossing
- Bus Station
- Ferry
- General Transport
- Train Station
- Taxi Rank

Parking
- Parking

OTHER MAP SYMBOLS

Information
- Bank, ATM
- Embassy, Consulate
- Hospital, Medical
- Internet Facilities
- Post Office
- Telephone

Geographic
- Cave
- Lighthouse
- Lookout
- Mountain, Volcano
- National Park
- Picnic Area

LONELY PLANET OFFICES

AUSTRALIA
Head Office
Locked Bag 1, Footscray, Victoria 3011
☎ 03 8379 8000, fax 03 8379 8111
talk2us@lonelyplanet.com.au

USA
150 Linden St, Oakland, CA 94607
☎ 510 250 6400, toll free 800 275 8555
fax 510 893 8572
info@lonelyplanet.com

UK
2nd fl, 186 City Road, London EC1V 2NT
☎ 020 7106 2100, fax 020 7106 2101
go@lonelyplanet.co.uk

Published by Lonely Planet Publications Pty Ltd
ABN 36 005 607 983
© Lonely Planet 2010
© photographers as indicated 2010
Cover photograph Ocean views from a vantage point near Ravello, David C Tomlinson/Getty Images. **Internal title-page photograph** Sweeping ocean vistas from the 13th-century Villa Rufolo, Ravello, Glenn Beanland/Lonely Planet Images.

Many of the images in this guide are available for licensing from Lonely Planet Images: lonelyplanetimages.com.

All rights reserved. No part of this publication may be copied, stored in a retrieval system, or transmitted in any form by any means, electronic, mechanical, recording or otherwise, except brief extracts for the purpose of review, and no part of this publication may be sold or hired, without the written permission of the publisher.

Printed by Toppan Security Printing Pte. Ltd. Singapore

Lonely Planet and the Lonely Planet logo are trademarks of Lonely Planet and are registered in the US Patent and Trademark Office and in other countries.

Lonely Planet does not allow its name or logo to be appropriated by commercial establishments, such as retailers, restaurants or hotels. Please let us know of any misuses: lonelyplanet.com/ip.

Mixed Sources
Product group from well-managed forests and other controlled sources
www.fsc.org Cert no. SGS-COC-005002
© 1996 Forest Stewardship Council
FSC

Although the authors and Lonely Planet have taken all reasonable care in preparing this book, we make no warranty about the accuracy or completeness of its content and, to the maximum extent permitted, disclaim all liability arising from its use.